THE CULTURE OF HISTORY

The Culture of History

English Uses of the Past 1800–1953

BILLIE MELMAN

OXFORD
UNIVERSITY PRESS

This book has been printed digitally and produced in a standard specification in order to ensure its continuing availability

OXFORD
UNIVERSITY PRESS

Great Clarendon Street, Oxford OX2 6DP

Oxford University Press is a department of the University of Oxford. It furthers the University's objective of excellence in research, scholarship, and education by publishing worldwide in

Oxford New York

Auckland Cape Town Dar es Salaam Hong Kong Karachi Kuala Lumpur Madrid Melbourne Mexico City Nairobi New Delhi Shanghai Taipei Toronto

With offices in

Argentina Austria Brazil Chile Czech Republic France Greece Guatemala Hungary Italy Japan South Korea Poland Portugal Singapore Switzerland Thailand Turkey Ukraine Vietnam

Oxford is a registered trade mark of Oxford University Press in the UK and in certain other countries

Published in the United States by Oxford University Press Inc., New York

Reprinted 2010

ISBN 978-0-19-929688-0

For my son Yotam D. Melman
for shared pasts, and to his future,
with love

Acknowledgements

My journey to and in this book was circuitous. I had intended to write a monograph on professional historians between the two World Wars. But I was diverted from my intended route by popular literary, visual, and aural histories, and drawn backwards and forwards in time. Paradoxically, the broadening of the subject and stretching of the time-span focused questions about history and culture I have been asking myself and debating over with colleagues and students during the last two decades. I ended up writing a book touching on both.

Along this track I received huge help from colleagues who lent me their advice, offered their wisdom, and uncommonly generously helped with information. My greatest debt is to Pat Thane and Martha Vicinus, who both persevered through garbled drafts of the book. David Trotter listened patiently over the years to changes in the book's plan and commented on Chapter 8. Colleagues discussed with me segments of the book at its different incarnations, listened uncomplainingly, gently but firmly restrained high-flying ideas, helped decide about painful sections, and imparted data on numerous details. I have accumulated debts of gratitude to Rosemary Ashton, Hedva Ben-Israel, Gisela Bock, Stefan Collini, Becky Conekin, Margot Finn, Matthew Hilton, David S. Katz, Ute Kornmeier, Tom Laqueur, Alison Light, Joseph Mali, Peter Mandler, Avner Offer, Ariel Rubinstein, Jennifer Shaw, Reba Soffer, Gareth Stedman-Jones, Daniel Ussishkin, James Vernon, and Shulamit Volkov. Jonathan Rose and Robert Patten generously shared with me their encyclopedic knowledge of working-class autodidacts and middle-class illustrators respectively, and John Sutherland continued to answer in good faith queries about Victorian publishers and authors, editions and archives, and with touching frankness discussed with me his own grandmother's book-thieving and reading habits. Natalie Zemon Davis encouraged me to embark on the study of film and history in culture. For personal memoirs of the Coronation and insight on the monarchy and the New Elizabethans I am grateful to Anna Davin, Janet Nelson, Jennifer Shaw, Michael Wolfers, and Bernard Wasserstein, historians become memorialists. One of my ventures into the field of elite, minoritarian culture, in the form of the last chapter on opera and history, would have been impossible without the generous help of specialists, historians of music, musicians, and composers. I am extremely grateful to Yehezkel Braun, Christopher Grogan, Nicholas Clark, and the late Alexander Volkov. It was his perceptive musician's remarks on English operas and festivals that started off my interest in post-war opera, its producers and consumers.

Kate Bradley, Hemi Sheinblat, Orly Shevi, and Daniel Ussishkin have accumulated hours of xeroxing, and Moshe Elhanati generously lent his knowledge of digital technologies and shared with me some of his knowledge of working-class exhibitions. But they have been much more than brilliant graduates, wonderful assistants, and expert photocopiers: their insistent questions, and those of a few generations of their colleagues, made for a better book. I thank them individually and collectively. Kate deserves special thanks for bringing to my attention Maurice Birley's multi-volume manuscript of 'Illustrations of British History', in the care of Toynbee Hall, where she is Archivist and Librarian. And she tops the list of archivists and librarians who kept their equanimity during my forays to the archives and long periods of professional correspondence. I am indebted to them all: Janet Moat at the British Film Institute (BFI) Special Collections and the staff at the BFI reading-room and Stills Department; Alexia Bleathman, Archivist at the Victoria and Albert Museum (Archive of Art and Design); Dr Nicholas Clark, Curator for Readers Services at the Britten–Pears Library, Aldeburgh; Dr Christopher Grogan, Librarian at the Britten–Pears Library, for his resourcefulness and generosity; Undine Concannon, former archivist at Madame Tussaud's and her successors, Susanna Lamb and Rosy Cantor; Stephen Freeth, Keeper of Manuscripts at the Guildhall Library Manuscript Collection; Beverly Hunt and Sarah Ogilvie at Oxford University Press Archives; Martin Kileen at Special Collections, Birmingham University Library; Dr Geoffrey Parnell, Keeper of Tower History, Royal Armouries, HM Tower of London; the librarian and photographic services at the Royal Armouries, Leeds; and the staff of the Tate Library and Archive Collection at the Hyman Kreitman Research Centre, Tate Modern, London.

I benefited from discussing ideas and materials in the book at workshops and seminars, most rewardingly at the University of California at Berkeley, and during a series of workshops on consumption, bringing together historians of many fields at the Freie Universität, Berlin, the University of Sussex, and Tel Aviv University. If nothing else, the workshops demonstrated the need for historians of different fields and of colleagues practising other disciplines to tolerate each other's language and talk across interpretative gaps. Unexpectedly and sadly, the workshops ended abruptly on 9/11 2001. One ambition of this book is to carry on this unfinished dialogue on the uses of culture and of history.

At Oxford University Press I am indebted to my editors, past and present, Ruth Parr, Anne Gelling, and Rupert Cousens, for their unwavering faith in my project, their support, and their generosity. The devoted Eva Nyika watched over the production of the book. I thank her and Zoe Washford. Bonnie Blackburn, my copy-editor and indexer, the most scrupulous reader and a fine musicologist, has shown patience and a keen interest in my text. I am most grateful to her.

My mother and first history teacher, Glila Rosenzweig, was one of my first readers. Reading to her the entire manuscript was a delight of the kind familiar to some of the individuals described in this book, and a pleasurable bonding experience. If I have not lost direction during this long journey, this is because of the support and love I have so amply received from my fellow travellers, Yossi, Yotam, and Daria. The book is my gift to them all and a special offering to Yotam, who is to embark on his own voyage through life.

B.M.

September 2005

Contents

PART V. NEW ELIZABETHANS? POST-WAR CULTURE AND FAILED HISTORIES

List of Illustrations

Abbreviations

AHR	*American Historical Review*
BBFC	British Board of Film Censors
BFI	British Film Institute
CEMA	Council for the Encouragement of Music and the Arts
EEN	*East End News*
ELO	*East London Observer*
HA	Historical Association
HWJ	*History Workshop Journal*
ILN	*Illustrated London News*
LCC	London County Council
LMA	London Metropolitan Archives
MO	Mass Observation
MTA	Archive, Madame Tussaud's London
PRO	Public Record Office
SDUK	Society for the Diffusion of Useful Knowledge
THI	*Tower Hamlets Independent*

Introduction

PROLOGUE: MAURICE BIRLEY'S 'ILLUSTRATIONS OF BRITISH HISTORY'

Maurice Birley was rescued from the rubbish heap of history. Literally. Sometime in the summer of 2003, John T. Price, an antiquarian book dealer and collector, travelled to north Wiltshire to a sale of fans in a house previously owned by a deceased London dealer in antiques. In an adjacent old barn he came upon one lot of books piled on the floor, including a number of particularly dusty and mildewy volumes which seemed of little interest. After he had successfully bid for the lot and unearthed an additional volume from a nearby shed, Price discovered that he had become the owner of fifteen volumes of a manuscript entitled 'Illustrations of British History', by one Maurice Birley. Having found out that Birley had served as warden of Toynbee Hall in Whitechapel, London, between 1911 and 1914, Price appropriately made a first offer of the collection to the Hall, which accepted it. In a manner of speaking, Birley returned 'home' and was salvaged from destruction and oblivion.[1]

The fifteen buckram-bound volumes surviving out of a total of twenty-seven seem out of pace with the age in which they were written, after the First World War and before Birley's death at the age of 80 in 1951. The laborious writing by hand, the spidery handwriting, and an abundance of 'illustrations', cut out from other books and documents and pasted into the text, appear to belong to an antiquarian tradition and a slow tempo of life, allowing leisure and an amateur work in history. These appear to make the volumes a quaint and atypical vestige, surviving into the period of history's academization and professionalization and the rise of modern, mass-produced forms of telling about the past (notably the historical film). Birley's work came to a halt two years before the introduction of television as a mediator between the past and British audiences, and just a few months before the Festival of Britain's celebration of a people's history fit for a vision of modernity. Yet Birley was entirely of his age and class. Born in 1870 and educated at Uppingham and New College, Oxford, where he read history, he reached Toynbee Hall in November 1904 and stayed for a decade. Founded in 1884 as an all-male residential colony in the midst of London's 'darkest' territory, the Hall became the flagship of the university settlement movement. It was the site of experimentation with reform, cross-class relations, and with ideas

[1] Correspondence with John T. Price, 3 Aug. 2004.

on aesthetics and masculinity.[2] And it launched the 'settlers' into careers in academia, the civil service, and politics. Birley was one of its lesser-known members, modestly working in the shadow of men of stellar talent and drive, including the future historians, reformers, and statesmen R. H. Tawney, William Beveridge, T. H. Harvey, and Clement Attlee. He resigned his wardenship in 1914 and, notwithstanding his age, volunteered for active service, returning after the Great War to the East End of London and spending the rest of his working life as a social worker in Limehouse. History was his other life and his passion.[3]

His volumes are important neither for their ample and meandering contents, covering the era between 'the Anglo Saxons, the Romans in Britain, Hadrian Wall', featured in the first volume, and 'the early years of George V, the Great War of 1914 to 1919, English Sculpture from the Nineteenth Century and Spanish painting', featured in the twenty-seventh and last extant volume, nor for their structure—linear but rambling and taking many diversions according to Birley's fancy and interest.[4] These volumes are significant for the use Birley made of the past and the place the latter played in his everyday life. If ever there was a 'use of history', this was Birley's. He aimed 'to give an account' (to himself mostly) 'of some of the more personal and domestic events in the history of England'. The revealing reference to a 'history of England' seems to belie the apparently inclusive British history the volumes purport to illustrate. Like so many of his contemporaries Birley often used 'English' and 'British' as synonyms. To render his account, he generously helped himself to textbooks, the great Whig texts, the works of the early twentieth-century public historians (with generous helpings from G. M. Trevelyan), and some extras, including the works of early professionals from Lord Acton to Frederick Pollock and F. W. Maitland, and expert work on subjects which really fascinated him, like the history of design and objects (from furniture and tableware to women's dress and toys), the arts, and styles of life across classes. As he was producing the 'Illustrations', Birley consumed others' histories, especially visual ones. His appetite for the appropriate illustrations which his text accompanies was gargantuan and he consumed in the original sense of this term. He savaged books, vandalized guidebooks, devoured catalogues of exhibitions and sales, and looted newspapers and atlases, cutting out and pasting his bounty onto the manuscript so successfully that at first glance they seem to be imprinted in the text. (See Figs. 1 and 2.)

Birley's collage of history, his patchwork of the works of greater historians, and his collector's mania for texts and pictorial presentations of objects point at some continuities between his poaching habits and older uses of the past. The

[2] Seth Koven, *Slumming: Sexual and Social Politics in Victorian London* (Princeton, 2004), 231–76.

[3] 'Maurice Birley', obituary, *The Times*, 8 Jan. 1951. 'Toynbee Hall Residents 1884–*c.*1940', database compiled by Katherine Bradley, Barnett Research Centre, 2005; J. A. R. Pimlott, *Toynbee Hall: Fifty Years of Social Progress, 1884–1934* (London, 1935), 134–5, 283. Maurice Birley, 'Illustrations of British History', Maurice Birley, Part of Barnett Research Centre, Toynbee Hall, Special Collections, BRC/MBI/IBH, vols. 1, 3, 4, 5, 6, 8, 9, 12, 14, 16, 18, 19, 22, 24, 26.

[4] BRC/MBI/IBH, vol. 1, p. 1; vol. 26.

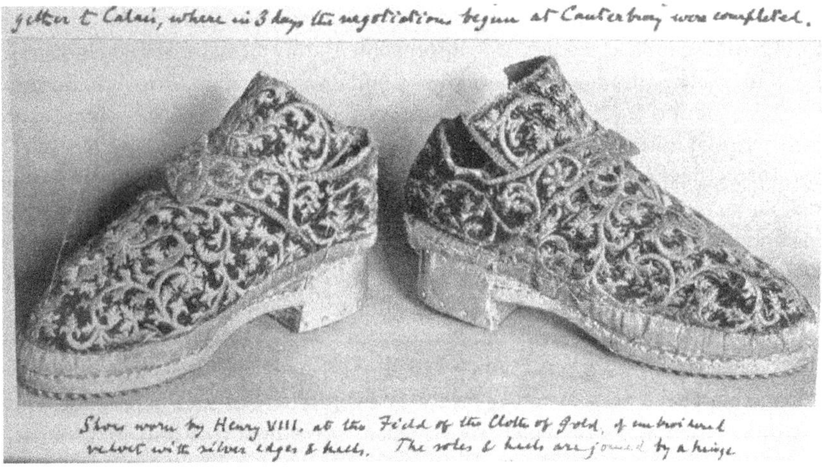

Fig. 1. 'Shoes worn by Henry VIII at the Field of the Cloth of Gold', pasted Maurice Birley's manuscript 'Illustrations of British History'. Birley consumed others' histories to produce his own and indulge his lifelong passion

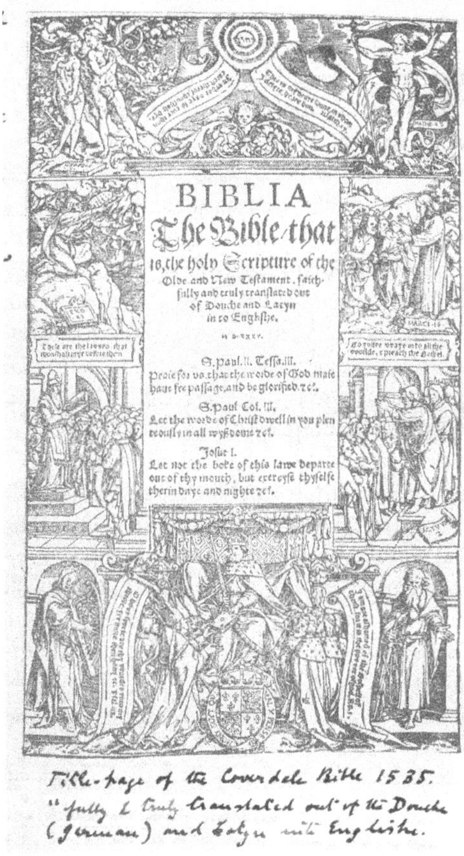

Fig. 2. 'Title page of the Coverdale Bible'. Maurice Birley, 'Illustrations of British History'. The pasting of the illustration into Birley's 'illustrations' creates the illusion of a manuscript within a manuscript, and of a collage of histories, apparently produced in a 'traditional' and non-industrial way

'Illustrations' demonstrate an allegiance to the illustrated Victorian histories and 'cyclopedias' aimed at readers' self-improvement, but they also reveal changes in access to history through the mass media and especially mass-distributed newspapers, which he readily ransacked and recycled into materials for a handmade manuscript. These relationships between continuities and changes in uses of the past during the first half of the twentieth century, and the story of Birley and his passion, may serve as an illustration of a culture of history which emerged in England about the time of the French Revolution (to which Birley devoted an entire volume) and took its initial shape during the decades of wars following it, and which survived well into the decade after the Second World War.

My book is about this culture, which I shall now briefly define as the productions of segments of the past, or rather pasts, the multiplicity of their representations, and the myriad ways in which the English—as individuals and in groups—looked at this past (sometimes in the most literal sense of 'looking') and made use of it, or did not, both in a social and material world and in their imaginary. I explain later my choice and usages of 'England' and 'English'. Suffice it to say here that I employ the former narrowly in a geographic sense, and broaden definitions of the latter and of 'Englishness'.[5] I take stock of the way in which access to history was formed and defined by different, albeit related, constructs, such as the state, the rapidly capitalized local and global apparatuses of cultural production (like transnational publishing, advertising, and the distribution of mass-produced artefacts such as books and films) and their markets, class, and gender. I seek to recoup how this access was negotiated and contested, gained, lost, and regained by individuals operating within and in relation to these constructs and their constrictions on choice and consumption. The individuals include antiquarians of all sorts (including Birley's) and historians, novelists, and publishers, cartoonists and illustrators, painters and their collectors, social reformers trading with history to influence local politics, and educationalists, playwrights and actors, film directors, producers and film stars, musicians and composers. 'Individuals' also comprises readers possessing various degrees of literal and oral literacy, spectators, including visitors to historical monuments and museums, theatre and, later, film-goers and radio listeners, and the many users (and makers) of ordinary everyday objects with history for their theme: from impracticable gadgets displayed in working-men's exhibitions during the 1860s, to postcards, from games to matchboxes and cigarette packets featuring royals and battles. The book thus follows the circulation of history between its images and the forms and social lives and meanings given to these images through procedures and practices of usage and, when possible, through the imagination and fantasy. It is about both the representational aspect of history and its materiality within culture, seeking to explore its dynamics during the period of its long, contested, irregular, and perturbed democratization.

[5] 'Introduction', p. 17; p. 23, conclusion.

A NOTE ON THE HISTORIOGRAPHY

Of course, to say that nineteenth-century and early twentieth-century English culture was soaked in history, that pasts—in the plural (Stefan Collini's term)—became ubiquitous precisely during the era and experiences which we have come to define as 'modernity', has now become commonplace.[6] The turn to history, and the ubiquity and riches, from the early nineteenth century, of what Stephen Bann has described as a 'generosity of representations', are hardly under-researched subjects.[7] Over the last decades uses of the past have received ample attention from intellectual historians like John Burrow and Collini, students of history as an academic discipline like Reba Soffer, from art historians and historians of architecture and design (including Mark Girouard, Simon Thurley, and Bann himself), cultural historians like Peter Mandler, students of collective 'theatres of memory' (like Raphael Samuel), and a growing contingent of non-historians, including scholars affiliated with literary criticism (Kate Flint and Alison Light), cultural studies, and the field of visual culture (most notably Tony Bennett), and music historians.[8] The expanding coverage of uses of the past has registered shifts within the discipline of history and its relationship to other fields and broader agendas. From monographs of historians and selected historical and literary-historical texts, we have moved to accounts considering the gender and class of historians before the academization and professionalization of history, thence to studies of non-literary representations like urban spectacles (studied by Burrow and Richard Altick), pageants, centenaries, and millenaries (considered by Paul Readman), illustrated histories (examined by Rosemary Mitchell), historical painting (considered by Bann), sites, buildings, and monuments (mapped

6 Stefan Collini, *English Pasts: Essays in History and Culture* (Oxford, 1999).

7 Stephen Bann, *The Clothing of Clio: A Study of the Representation of History in Nineteenth-Century Britain and France* (Cambridge, 1984), 5.

8 John W. Burrow, *A Liberal Descent: Victorian Historians and the English Past* (Cambridge, 1981); Collini, *English Pasts*; Collini, Richard Whatmore, and Brian Young (eds.), *History, Religion and Culture: British Intellectual History, 1750–1950* (Cambridge, 2000). On history as an academic discipline see Reba Soffer, *Discipline and Power: The University, History and the Making of an English Elite 1870–1930* (Stanford, Calif., 1994). For popular illustrated histories and uses of history such as tourism see Rosemary Mitchell, *Picturing the Past: English History in Text and Image, 1830–1870* (Oxford, 2000); Peter Mandler, *The Fall and Rise of the Stately Home* (New Haven, 1997); and Raphael Samuel, *Theatres of Memory*, i: *Past and Present in Contemporary Culture* (London, 1994) and ii: *Island Stories: Unravelling Britain* (London, 1999). For art, architecture, and design see Roy Strong, *And When Did You Last See Your Father? The Victorian Painter and British History* (London, 1978); Mark Girouard, *Life in the English Country House: A Social and Architectural History* (New Haven, 1978); and Becky E. Conekin, *'The Autobiography of a Nation': The 1951 Festival of Britain* (Manchester, 2003). For film see Marcia Landy, *British Genres: Cinema and Society 1930–60* (Princeton, 1991) and *Cinematic Uses of the Past* (Minneapolis, 1996), and Sue Harper, *Picturing the Past: The Rise and Fall of the British Costume Film* (London, 1994). The most fruitful discussion of history and visual techniques is to be found in Tony Bennett, *The Birth of the Museum: History, Theory, Politics* (London, 1995; repr. 1999) and Kate Flint, *The Victorians and the Visual Imagination* (Cambridge, 2000).

by Girouard, Mandler, and Lynda Nead), landscapes and preservation (David Matless), architecture and design (Becky Conekin), film (Marcia Landy, Sarah Street, and Sue Harper), and music (Meirion Hughes and Robert Stradling).[9] Although the majority of studies cover comparatively short spans and sometimes even moments of change in attitudes to and sentiments about the past, such as the era between the 1820s and the 1860s, that between the 1870s and 1930s or 1951, rather than long stretches of modernity, they are not sectional and segmental but trace homologies in the sense of history across genres and forms of representations belonging to families of genres.

Running through much of this vast and multidisciplinary corpus of studies is an almost unanimous consensus, based on a few commonly shared assumptions about 'naturally' English attitudes to and sentiments about the past, as well as about the role or roles of history within culture (defined in different ways), society, and politics. It may be useful briefly, and inevitably roughly, to outline the contours of this consensus, not only as a service to the general reader but also in order to locate my own adherences to and divergence from the historiography. One set of assumptions concerns the content, or substance, of discussion and representations of the past and the emotions or mentalities aligned with, and often deduced from, these representations, and revolves around two strands of thought. One strand stresses that the past was described and imagined as a comfortable and secure place, that British history was envisioned as more orderly, more harmonious, and more stable than other national histories.

[9] On history and historians see G. P. Gooch, *History and Historians in the Nineteenth Century* (1913; repr. Boston, 1959); F. M. Powicke, *Modern Historians and the Study of History* (London, 1955); J. P. Kenyon, *The History Men: The Historical Profession in Britain since the Renaissance* (London, 1983); Philippa Levine, *The Amateur and the Professional: Antiquarians, Historians and Archaeologists in Victorian England, 1838–1886* (Cambridge, 1986); Harvey J. Kaye, *The British Marxist Historians: Introductory Analysis* (Cambridge, 1984); Alon Kadish, *Historians, Economists and Economic History* (London, 1989); and Peter Novick, *That Noble Dream: The 'Objectivity Question' and the American Historical Profession* (Cambridge, 1993). On history, gender, and class see Bonnie G. Smith, *The Gender of History: Men, Women and Historical Practice* (Cambridge, Mass., 1998); Maxine Berg, 'The First Women Economic Historians', *Economic History Review*, 45 (1992), 308–29; Billie Melman, 'Gender, History and Memory: The Invention of Women's Past in the Nineteenth and Early Twentieth Centuries', *History and Memory*, 5 (1993), 5–41 and 'Changing the Subject', in Ina Zweiniger-Bargielowska (ed.), *Women in Twentieth-Century Britain* (London, 2001), 16–35. On literature and history see Avrom Fleishman, *The English Historical Novel: Walter Scott to Virginia Woolf* (Baltimore, 1971); Andrew Sanders, *The Victorian Historical Novel 1840–1880* (London, 1978); J. C. Simmons, *The Novelist as Historian: Essays on the Victorian Historical Novel* (The Hague and Paris, 1973); and Billie Melman, 'Claiming the Nation's Past: The Invention of an Anglo-Saxon Tradition', *Journal of Contemporary History*, 26, nos. 3–4, Special Issue: *The Impact of Western Nationalisms*, ed. Jehuda Reinharz with George L. Mosse (1991), 575–97. On history as spectacle and show see Richard Altick, *The Shows of London* (Cambridge, Mass., 1978) and John W. Burrow, 'Images of Time: From Carlylean Vulcanism to Sedimentary Gradualism', in Collini, Whatmore, and Young (eds.), *History, Religion and Culture*, 198–224. On pageants see Paul Readman, 'The Place of the Past in English Culture, c.1890–1914', *Past and Present*, 186 (Feb. 2005), 147–201. On music see Meirion Hughes and Robert Stradling, *The English Musical Renaissance 1860–1940: Construction and Deconstruction* (London, 1993).

Moreover, this history was imagined and interpreted with confidence—confidence, as Burrow has noted, in both possessing the past and understanding and deciphering continuities between it and the present. Such confidence drew on and was buttressed by interest in specifically English judicial and representative institutions, in an unwritten constitution, and in personal and national liberties and prosperity, and was shared across political and social divisions.[10] There have of course been studies of shades of the notion of the comfortable Whig interpretations—most notably of Catholic historiography, the Saxonist historians, women historians, popular ethnologies stressing plebeian rather than learned images of the past, and of dissenting histories such as Marxist histories after the Second World War, but these shades and dissensions, runs the argument, did not counter the idea and images of security in and of history.[11]

Another strand of thought and scholarship is the assumption that Britons, especially the English, envisaged their past largely as Country, that their longest-living and most resilient images of it were ruralist, occasionally pastoralist, and, at times, organicist. For a particularly *longue durée*, from the end of the eighteenth century and the beginning of the nineteenth (if not earlier) until well into the twentieth, the very period associated with modernization and including the capitalization of agriculture, the First and Second Industrial Revolutions, massive urbanization, and rapid colonial expansion, thence decline from power, England was envisaged as a pasture, a 'green and pleasant land', a gentle place, as 'Deep England' and sometimes as a 'South' country, as old and changeless.[12] Indeed the more urbanized Britain became, the more imperial and global its rule, the more rural, inward-looking, and localized the image of its cherished past.[13] Segments of this ruralist version such as the decline and rise of the country house, the symbolic village, preservation, pastoralist music (during the English musical renaissance between the 1870s and 1940), not to mention 'country writing', from William Morris's *Merrie England* to Robert Blatchford's,

[10] Burrow, *A Liberal Descent*; Reba Soffer, 'The Conservative Historical Imagination in the Twentieth Century', *Albion*, 27, no. 4 (Winter 1995), 1–17, esp. 2–5, and 'British Conservative Historiography and the Second World War', in Benedikt Stuchtey and Peter Wende (eds.), *British and German Historiography 1750–1950* (Oxford, 2000), 373–99.

[11] For Catholic interpretations of the past see Mitchell, *Picturing the Past*, 170–202 and Reba Soffer, 'The Historian, Catholicism, Global History, and National Singularity', *Storia della storiografia*, 35 (1999), 113–27. For the public historians' variants of the Whig interpretation see P. B. M. Blass, *Continuity and Anachronism: Parliamentary and Constitutional Development in Anti-Whig Reaction between 1890–1939* (The Hague and Boston, Mass., 1978) and Victor Feske, *From Belloc to Churchill: Private Scholars, Public Culture, and the Crisis of British Liberalism, 1900–1939* (Chapel Hill, NC, 1996).

[12] On Country and city, and strands of ruralism see Raymond Williams, *The Country and the City* (London, 1973); Martin J. Wiener, *English Culture and the Decline of the Industrial Spirit 1850–1980* (Cambridge, 1981, repr. Harmondsworth, 1985); Alun Howkins, 'The Discovery of Rural England', in Robert Colls and Philip Dodd (eds.), *Englishness: Politics and Culture 1880–1920* (Beckenham, 1987), 62–89. On garden and 'deep country' images see Colls, *Identity of England* (Oxford, 2002), 203–75.

[13] The inward-looking, 'Heimat' character of images of the past has been stressed by Readman, 'The Place of the Past'.

from the Romantic to the Georgian poets, conservative and radical ruralism, have been related to modernity, occasionally regarded as backward-looking, and sometimes associated with broader conservatism in culture, society, and the economy. Though the images of a pre-modern and rural 'real' England have usually been taken to be reactive and to reverse modernity, they have also been imaginatively and usefully detached from mere nostalgia (by Mandler and Conekin) and welded with notions of the modern and of the future.[14]

Even more ubiquitous than the set of assumptions about the substance of history, its dominant narrative and representations, is a cluster of suppositions about its roles and uses in relation to power and authority, which in certain influential renditions sometimes are firmly aligned with theories of culture, as well as with a body of approaches to it, cutting across disciplines. Central to this cluster is the premiss that history is a means or an instrument for indirect control. Versions of the past were cultural impositions, rarely coercive and usually seductive and aimed at national or social consolidation (particularly during periods of national emergencies), or at the consolidation of a politics, or the liberal state in one of its variants (or, in one recent rendition, of a 'rule of freedom' within the nineteenth-century Liberal city), or at sustaining specific forms of capitalism from an individualist to a welfare capitalism, aligned in Britain with a variety of democracy. Put succinctly, history was constructed for 'something else'. The interpretation of the past as 'history for' is indicative of the widespread tendency to look at culture in general as something that is a clue to something else: a Liberal ideology and world-view, or rule, the 'imagined' national 'community', or the consolidation of the interests of the middle class.[15]

One particularly influential recent usage of the indirect-control approach has had to do with the impact of Michel Foucault's work, especially his *Discipline and Punish*, on the majority of studies of nineteenth-century urban spectacles and the new regime of exhibition, display, and spectatorship which developed in civic spaces and venues (such as museums), in which many of the new popular forms of visual history evolved. Following Foucault, students of urban visual culture have argued that its expansion and the exposure of its sites and venues to crowds, together with the expansion of forms of literary culture, served effectively to diffuse self-governing, so essential to the new forms of rule instituted from the early nineteenth century on. The new culture went in tandem with a new regime of punishment epitomized in the penitentiary and new methods of

[14] Mandler, *The Fall and Rise of the Country Home*; Conekin, *The Autobiography of a Nation*, 80–116; and David Matless, *Landscape and Englishness* (London, 1998), 9–25. On organicist interpretations see pp. 136–73.

[15] Bennett, *The Birth of the Museum*; David Boswell and Jessica Evans (eds.), *Representing the Nation: A Reader. Histories, Heritage and Museums* (London, 1999). On history's role in and for the preservation of forms of capitalism see Wiener and, from a different point of view, Tom Nairn, *The Break-up of Britain: Crisis and Neo-nationalism* (London, 1977). On history as the builder of imagined communities see Mitchell, *Picturing the Past*. On histories for a Liberal rule see Patrick Joyce, *The Rule of Freedom: Liberalism and the Modern City* (London, 2003), 144–83.

crowd-policing and monitoring in cities.[16] The democratized historical museum and the new prison were complementary parts of one whole described as 'the archipelago of incarceration', where bodies became transparent and subject to an omnipresent power. History inculcated in exhibitions, museums, and national monuments distanced the present from an unruly past and increasingly associated modern city dwellers with a new system of rule based on self-governing.[17]

In another influential variant of the indirect-control interpretations, drawing on the work of Antonio Gramsci, dominant versions of history and forms of historical consciousness and knowledge are seen to be the result of negotiations about the past within a cultural hegemony. The Gramscian version has substituted older approaches to culture as the reflection of social production and class division, in offering historians the dynamic and apparently flexible mechanism of 'negotiation' over and about hegemony. And it has gained hold in studies of the film as the modern disseminator of versions of the past by Jeffrey Richards, Sue Harper, and Marcia Landy.[18] This interpretation, however, reduces historical consciousness and feelings about the past to manifestations of (and instruments to and for) the ruling classes, or elites. Indeed stemming from these two and other variants of the analysis of history as mainly an aid to, or instrument of and for, rule, cohesion, or mobilization is the assumption that history's uses, especially in their popular forms, are conservative, sometimes with a capital C, supporting a certain rule, group, or system and often mobilized by it.[19] Attempts to challenge control and hegemony narratives have not directly engaged with these analyses of power and culture, but addressed assumptions about manipulation made empirically, by examining popular, cross-class demand for history. These attempts have been very few and tentative. While criticizing simplistic, top-down interpretations of the role of the past in British society, they have paradoxically buttressed the approach to history and culture as a key to 'something else', thus remaining within the consensus about the role and characteristics of English images of the past.[20]

16 Michel Foucault, *Discipline and Punish: The Birth of the Prison*, trans. Alan Sheriden (London, 1977). The most perceptive use of Foucault is to be found in Bennett, *The Birth of the Museum*, 1, 22–5, 95 and Flint, *The Victorians and the Visual Imagination*, 7–8.

17 Bennett, *The Birth of the Museum*, 63–4.

18 For useful remarks on Gramsci's influence see John Storey, *Cultural Consumption and Everyday Life* (London, 1999), 149–73 and J. M. Golby and A. W. Purdue, *The Civilisation of the Crowd: Popular Culture in England 1750–1900* (Stroud, repr. 1999). The Gramscian interpretation is applied in Jeffrey Richards, *The Age of the Dream Palace: Cinema and Society in Britain 1930–39* (London, 1984); Harper, *Picturing the Past*, 3–5; and Landy, *British Genres*, 5–10. Useful references to publications influenced by Gramsci's approach are to be found in Francis Mulhern, *Culture/MetaCulture* (London, 2000), 103–6.

19 For the assumption about conservatism see Alison Light, *Forever England: Femininity, Literature and Conservatism between the Wars* (London, 1991); Nairn, *The Break-up of Britain*; and Wiener, *English Culture*.

20 For example Readman, 'The Place of the Past'. The characteristics of the past he describes are almost identical to those in more traditional interpretations and evolve around a sense of continuity within the nation. See pp. 197–201.

To a practising cultural historian both sets of assumptions are disturbing: the first because it presents a homogeneous vision of the past which is taken as the dominant and sometimes only version of history; the second for its disregard, or bypassing, of the agency of individuals in culture and their interventions in the production of versions of history, and for the insufficient attention paid to the dynamics and mechanisms of the production of the past and the apparatuses which circulated histories in society. Accompanying these are additional reservations about the inherent conservatism of popular histories and indeed British popular culture and a broader concern about the section of culture into 'high' and 'low', elite and minority representations of the past, and majority or mass attitudes to it. Forms deemed generically working-class like the film have been studied separately from those seen to have been generically minoritarian and accessible to elites like straightforward history, or historical opera. These are sometimes thought better left to specialists who are not historians and quite irrelevant to widespread and majority views and sentiments.[21]

A CULTURAL HISTORIAN'S ARGUMENT

I do not wish to debunk the assumptions about the content of dominant histories, or to dissent from them. To ignore, or belittle, the importance and centrality of Country in the construction of English history and of Englishness, or that of the sense of and hankering after a secure and comfortable past, would be wholly misguided and misleading. Nor do I wish to deny the role of power exercised by elites, political parties, or groups and the state on ideas about the past and some of its uses: this would be naive. I propose a corrective to the historiography which may help give a rounder and more balanced picture of the ways in which the English imagined, produced, and consumed histories. Such an interpretative corrective is also intended as a study in culture, based on the premiss that the latter reveals itself and its actual workings through its notions about the past, the ways in which it gains access to it, and the practices it employs to appropriate it.

My argument is simple and, I hope, not simple-minded. From about 1800 there developed an English popular culture of history, and I mean English in the geographically narrow sense of the word. This culture was of course related to class and national identity and to the changing Liberal state, and due attention is paid to them here, but mostly the book is alert for historical themes and images and their resonances beyond the tripartite repertoire related to these structures. Put differently, I aim at a close look at the layers and percolations of practices, uses, and the meanings given by individuals to the past more than at an inventory of structures of manipulation and control. This is because we need to

[21] Ross McKibbin, *Classes and Cultures: England, 1918–1951* (Oxford, 2000), p. vi. On this separation see also Collini, *English Pasts*, 1–37.

pay more attention to the actual dynamics of culture at work, the forms and procedures which made it 'tick' and made versions of history meaningful and workable for individuals within the constrictions of society, the economy, and the state. The culture of history mapped in this book was strongly urban and metropolitan. It had the city as its real and imaginary locus, both in the sense that numerous new historical forms and genres evolved in cities and particularly in London, and in that it related to and imagined change, or the lack of it, in cities and in relation to urbanization. In this version of the past, which successfully competed with the confident (characteristically but not exclusively Whig) narrative about the past, history was neither a confident place nor particularly comfortable or cosy. It was a place of danger, disorder, and degrees of violence. The urban interpretation remained powerful until after the Second World War, interacting with rather than substituting for ruralism and pastoralism. Throughout the better part of the nineteenth century it evolved around a new sense and definition of horror, which I explore in the first half of the book and which configured the past and the past's appeal as horror, in what Charles Dickens, referring to that ultimate abode of horror, Madame Tussaud's famous chamber, described as 'the attraction of repulsion'.[22] History, I argue, was imagined and experienced as urban and uncosy in two other senses. First, it lived in a dense grid of growing new urban forms and genres, including literary genres, spectacles like the panoramas and dioramas thriving between the 1790s and 1860s, the latter forms developing from the 1890s and 1900s into films. Second, access to and senses of the past were acquired and conventionalized through new and distinct technologies of looking and a vast repertoire of practical ways of looking at the representations or at historical objects—ranging from monuments to everyday utensils and things. We may not overstate the centrality of the visual aspect of history and its social dimension throughout the nineteenth and early twentieth centuries. The more literate, more exposed to words and education English society became, the more exposed it was to visual histories. Birley's obsession with the visual exemplifies this trend and the centrality of the visual not merely for the partly or uncomfortably literate, but also for the highly literate consumer of history. To paraphrase Jean-Louis Comolli's observation about *fin de siècle* Europe and extend it to the nineteenth century, men and women in the modern city were living 'in a frenzy of the visual'.[23]

[22] Cited in Murray Baumgarten, 'Fictions of the City', in John O. Jordan (ed.), *The Cambridge Companion to Charles Dickens* (Cambridge, 2001), 106–18 at 107.

[23] Jean-Louis Comolli, 'Machines of the Visible', in Theresa de Lauretis and Stephen Heath (eds.), *The Cinematic Apparatus* (Basingstoke, 1980), 121–41. On the visual aspects of 19th-c. culture see Flint, *The Victorians*, 1–37. For a broader context of attitudes to vision and visuality see Martin Jay, *Downcast Eyes: The Denigration of Vision in Twentieth-Century French Thought* (Berkeley, 1993), and for a critique on the privileging of the visual in cultural studies and art history see Jonathan Crary, *Suspensions of Perception: Attention, Spectacle, and Modern Culture* (Cambridge, Mass., 2001).

Culture is defined in a broad and inclusive sense as a complex dynamic whole accommodating forms of knowledge—often practical ones—artefacts and beliefs, customs, habits, and practices acquired by individuals within their everyday, lived-in environment and society.[24] And I apply the adjective 'popular' not as a substitute for 'working-class' or 'low' or 'majority culture', or to exclude forms of reflexive writing and creation. I include artefacts conventionally seen as 'high' and 'minoritarian' (opera, experimental biography) and 'plebeian' and 'low' (wax shows, the popular theatre, and films). Indeed one argument the book makes is that a section of the culture of history into the articulate and reflexive on the one hand and the popular on the other may rehearse binary divisions of culture which pit the mass-produced artefact against 'minority' or elite productions and the conventional against the exceptional.[25] Popular here denotes a cross-class exchange between and through different yet interacting genres. For example, during the first two-thirds of the nineteenth century, emphasis on the disorderly and violent aspects of history appeared in both plebeian forms of literature and entertainment and in the new types of fiction, such as the urban historical novel, the popular tourist guide, and what may be described as the earliest 'hands on' historical museums in monuments such as the Tower of London. During the first part of the twentieth century, complex images of the historical monarchy and empire as the sites of both security and arbitrary power, of confidence and fragility, resounded in both experimental historical biography and forms of music, and in mass-produced films emanating from a global multinational cinema and film-advertising industries. And in quite a few instances, as will be demonstrated, ideas and representations travelled 'upwards', from mass-produced forms to 'high' ones.

BOUNDARIES AND EXCLUSIONS

Chronologically my study is confined between 1802 and 1953. I begin with the launching of Madame Tussaud's collection of thirty full-size wax figures,

[24] For working definitions useful to historians see Lynn Hunt (ed.), *The New Cultural History* (Berkeley, 1989) and the literature discussed there, and Hunt and Victoria E. Bonnel, *Beyond the Cultural Turn: New Directions in the Study of Society and Culture* (Berkeley, 1999). See also William H. Sewell Jr., 'The Concept(s) of Culture', in Gabrielle M. Spiegel (ed.), *Practicing History: New Directions in Historical Writing after the Linguistic Turn* (New York, 2005), 76–97. On the breadth and variety of definitions see Mulhern, *Culture/MetaCulture*. The present book is *not* on how culture speaks of itself (his topic), but rather on how it works. For a useful critique of Mulhern which also touches on definitions see Stefan Collini, 'Culture Talk', *New Left Review*, 7 (Jan.–Feb. 2001), Mulhern's response, 'Beyond Metaculture', ibid. 16 (July–Aug. 2002), and Collini's repartee, 'Defending Cultural Criticism', ibid. 18 (Nov.–Dec. 2002).

[25] See McKibbin, *Classes and Cultures*, Preface, and for uses of 'populist' Peter Mandler, '"In the Olden Time": Romantic History and English National Identity, 1820–50', in Lawrence Brockliss and David Eastwood (eds.), *A Union of Multiple Identities: The British Isles c.1750–1850* (Manchester, 1997), 78–92.

brought over from Paris during the brief interval in revolutionary warfare made possible by the Peace of Amiens and temporarily installed at the Lyceum, Leicester Square, London, and eventually becoming the first museum of the Revolution.[26] The collection was established at the tail of an unprecedented proliferation, from about the time of the Revolution itself, of spectacles and shows with history among their subjects which offered new repertoires of possibilities for marketing and displaying the past, possibilities that evolved around new technologies of looking which generated some modern forms of the consumption of history through spectatorship. The new technologies and the new array of procedures of looking organized themselves around two main forms of seeing: the panorama, or all-encompassing view, established in the Regency panoramas and dioramas and in multiple historical texts and genre painting, and the pedestrian, hampered look at street level, or—so central to the plebeian culture investigated at the beginning of the book and for sixty or seventy years taking over the panorama—the look from what may be described as below-street level: the dungeon or cellar view of history.[27] As shown in Part I, the dungeon and gallows competed with the panorama and became not merely a metaphor and theme of myriad descriptions of the past, but a means for its imagining which dominated approaches to history, because the images of the dungeon were relatable to the urban environment, its physical aspects and politics.

1802 marks more than the inauguration of a new urban culture; it points to the centrality and resonances of the French Revolution in the English modern imagining and feeling of and for history, to the Revolution's significance for the very shaping of historical forms, and its wider meaning for English culture and politics. It was vital to the feel and usages of the past not only in the sense that it shaped a national identity and modern British selves—this has recently been established by a number of historians—but in that the Revolution became a framework for making sense of, creating meanings for, and using the past and, through it, responding to processes of modernity.[28] The Revolution released and

[26] The latest history of the museum is Pamela Pilbeam, *Madame Tussaud and the History of Waxworks* (London, 2002). Recent histories emanating from the museum itself include Pauline Chapman, *The French Revolution as Seen by Madame Tussaud, Witness Extraordinary* (London, 1989) and *Madame Tussaud in England: Careeer Woman Extraordinary* (London, 1992).

[27] On panoramas and the panoramic look see Richard Altick, *The Shows of London*, 128–62; Ralph Hyde, *Panoramania! The Art and Entertainment of the 'All-Embracing' View* (London, 1988); and Stephan Oettermann, *The Panorama: History of a Mass Medium*, trans. Deborah Lucas Schneider (New York, 1997). On the look at street level see Lynda Nead, *Victorian Babylon: People, Streets and Images in Nineteenth-Century London* (London and New Haven, 2000), 74–9; and Deborah Epstein Nord, *Walking the Victorian Streets: Women, Representation, and the City* (Ithaca, NY, 1995), 1–19, 49–81.

[28] A shortlist of studies on the impacts of the Revolution should include Linda Colley, *Britons: Forging the Nation 1707–1837* (New Haven, 1992); Clive Emsley, *British Society and the French Wars 1793–1815* (London, 1979; repr. 1996); Dror Wahrman, *Imagining the Middle Class: The Political Representation of Class in Britain c.1780–1840* (Cambridge, 1995), 21–31 and *The Making of the Modern Self: Identity and Culture in Eighteenth-Century England* (New Haven, 2004), 218–65 and 312–22. The best survey on the Revolution's impact on British historiography

reinforced older plebeian urban sensationalism and experiences, which were now recycled, changed, and related to contemporary experience. The privileged status of the Revolution would remain a staple of the new culture of history, long after the event itself would lose its political immediacy. And this status survived the sense and feel of urban danger associated with it until the 1870s.

I chose to end in 1953. Not because the Coronation and the frenzy of revivals of the Elizabethans surrounding it marked an end to the role of history in culture and society. Far from it: debate over history and historical heritages, historical curricula and access to and ownership of the past remained vociferous after that date and still remain so. Indeed the entry of a new welfare state into culture and its declared position as culture provider, articulated throughout the Second World War and the fifties, widened informed and popular debate on these topics, as well as on the relationship between history and politics. And starting from the early 1960s there occurred bouts of preservations of old monuments and buildings, the 'living history' movements, and frenzies of 'retro' styles of many sorts.[29] However, the post-war period and especially the period between the two festivals, of 'Britain' in 1951 and the Coronation in 1953, which mark the culmination of historical revival and spectacle for mass consumption, also exemplifies discontinuities and breaks from established patterns, most notably the decline of film and the appearance and rise of television as the main mediator between the past and audiences. Another break is the crystallization of a new role for the state in culture. In a broader sense 1953 and the furore which broke out in it over resurrections of the past also mark a broader change in the definition and uses of democracy within culture, addressed in the second part of the book.[30]

The scope of the subject and my interest in the actual dynamics of culture during a long stretch of time led to my combining the long course, that *longue durée* which allows us the panoramic view (if one may borrow the early nineteenth-century term) of change and non-change in practices and meanings, with a close look at specific periods and moments of quick and sometimes dramatic change. Such moments occurred in the 1830s and 1840s, around the 1870s and 1880s, and during the 1930s. Obviously such a strategy necessitates, indeed imposes, exclusions which must be plainly stated, having to do with the geography of my study which to some readers would seem narrow and, more important, with the periods, historical forms, images, and versions of the past which other readers may accuse me of leaving out.

remains Hedva Ben-Israel, *English Historians and the French Revolution* (Cambridge, 1968, reissued in 2002).

[29] See David Lowenthal, *The Heritage Crusade and the Spoils of Modern History* (Cambridge, 1997); Samuel, *Theatres of Memory*, i. 83–119, 169–205, 259–74.

[30] On the Festival and the period between it and the Coronation consult Conekin, *'The Autobiography of a Nation'*. On continuities and change during the post-war era see Conekin, Frank Mort, and Chris Waters (eds.), *Moments of Modernity: Reconstructing Britain 1945–1964* (London, 1999). On political and economic change and continuity see George L. Bernstein, *The Myth of Decline: The Rise of Britain since 1945* (London, 2004).

No study of the vast popular culture of history—and, for that matter, no history—may be inclusive. And a study which seeks to pay equal and close attention to production and representation, to structures and individuals over the long term, demands selection. No less significant, selection and exclusion have been part and parcel of the growing and workings of history within cultures and societies. As Stefan Collini has usefully reminded us, the British and, one might add, any historically minded and 'remembering' society have never been attached to one past deemed 'national', a single hallowed period which they elevated to the embodiment of history.[31] Different historical periods and moments were more or less successfully 'invented', constructed, and resurrected, then used inadvertently or to address agendas of historians, politicians, and ordinary people. During the nineteenth and twentieth centuries some periods—the Civil War for example—did not resonate well in cross-class repertoires. Others, notably the Middle Ages, had had enduring and variegated impacts upon different publics throughout the nineteenth century. Yet others, like the Georgian period, were discovered, rehabilitated, and put up front in the showroom of history only between the 1900s and 1930s, as shown in detail in Chapter 8. We may best describe the flow and ebb of histories, the taste for them, and the changing fashions whose percolation and resonances changed in accordance with expectations, needs, and available apparatuses of cultural productions, as competing pasts. The 1800s witnessed the spread and availability of the spectacles belonging to the family of panoramas. The period between the 1820s and 1840 saw the quick development in printing, lithography production, copyright law, and publishing and distribution.[32] The 1880s experienced the rise of mass journalism, the birth of a truly popular press, and the further expansion of the market for historical fiction, and the media revolution repeated itself with the burgeoning of the film industry after the First World War.

The notion of competing pasts may prove useful because it is flexible enough to contain the dominance of certain periods over others in collective memory and usages without excluding other periods. From at least the beginning of the nineteenth century through to the present, Roman Britain, the Anglo-Saxons, 1066, the Civil War, and the Jacobite rebellion had generated antiquarian interest, streams of historical novels, bouts of archaeological curiosity, and various forms of connoisseur and popular tourism.[33] Arguably the resonance of these different periods was surpassed by fascination with the Gothic Middle Ages,

[31] Collini, *English Pasts*, 9–11.

[32] For changes in technologies with a special stress on changes in copyright laws and their implications for reading see William St Clair's encyclopedic *The Reading Nation in the Romantic Period* (Cambridge, 2004).

[33] On the Romans in Victorian Britain see Levine, *The Amateur and the Professional.* On the Anglo-Saxons and 1066 see Melman, 'Claiming the Nation's Past'. For the Stuarts see Timothy Lang, *The Victorians and the Stuart Heritage: Interpretation of a Discordant Past* (Cambridge, 1995). On the era of the Settlement and Augustan period see Mark Girouard, *Sweetness and Light: The Queen Anne Movement 1860–1900* (Oxford, 1977).

which from the 1820s had shaped political visions as varied as Young England high Toryism and shades of socialism which challenged capitalist consumption and industrialization, mostly in the works and action of John Ruskin, William Morris, and the Arts and Crafts Movement, and moulded tastes and styles in the arts and design. The reinvention of medieval chivalry had, as Girouard and Paul Fussell have demonstrated, effectively impinged upon concepts and repertoires of public and private morality, ideas of 'character', respectability, and masculinity.[34] I exclude all of these resurrections not only because they have been amply covered but because these pasts did not have resonances across all social classes and groups and because their appeal had waned before they could become material forms of mass consumption and iconic symbols of the past.

I have chosen to focus on the Tudor era, occasionally described by the Victorians as the 'Olden Time', and the eighteenth century, especially the decades of Revolution, the latter decades naturalized and transformed into a key event in English history and consciousness.[35] The special and privileged status of both periods has been noted above. Additionally, both these periods became the locus of narratives, memories, and uses that constituted alternatives to the narratives of confidence. Both had been initially comprehended, imagined, and represented as times of crisis and danger. Indeed the longevity of the appeal of both ensued from the mixture of attraction, awe, and repulsion which the 'dangerous' and horrible generated. Both these slices of the past also served as urban histories for their times, representing urban experiences still recognizable in material traces which survived waves of demolition and improvement in the modern city, especially in London, the definitive mega-city and site of forms of modernity which were both local and connected to a world empire and global processes, especially from the 1870s. Both thus could be placed within the orbit of modernity. And both periods, when seen as times of contestation of political power and authority, were connectable to the growing urban mass democracy.

The caveats referred to earlier also apply to geographic exclusions. I am all too well aware that my focus on England and London may court criticism of my privileging English and metropolitan uses of history over local and territorial ones and of altogether excluding the Scottish, Welsh, and Irish interpretations of the past. I do not doubt that the Revolution, especially in its republican–democratic phase, and the Elizabethan state and empire, figured in Scottish histories or Irish ones in ways fundamentally different from their English configurations.[36] My

[34] Girouard, *The Return to Camelot: Chivalry and the English Gentleman* (New Haven, 1981); Alice Chandler, *A Dream of Order: The Medieval Ideal in Nineteenth-Century English Literature* (London, 1970); Paul Fussell, *The Great War and Modern Memory* (Oxford, 1975).

[35] On 'the Olden Time' see Mandler, '"In the Olden Time": Romantic History and English National Identity'.

[36] See e.g. Edwin Jones, *The English Nation: The Great Myth* (Stroud, repr. 2000); P. Morgan, 'Early Victorian Wales and its Crisis of Identity', in Brockliss and Eastwood (eds.), *A Union of Multiple Identities*, 93–107; and George Rosie, *Curious Scotland: Tales from a Hidden History* (London, 2004).

interest in the powerful geographic centre has to do with the special place of London in English cultural and political life and in the politics and culture of empire. A 'world city' growing from a population of a little below the 1,000,000 mark in 1801 to 8,000,000 after the First World War, and until 1927 the world's biggest city, London was the centre of culture markets, drawing talent and capital, both national and foreign.[37] Madame Tussaud's own migration to the city and final settling in it in 1838 is the first of many examples examined here of the metropolis's drawing power. London also became the centre of the main industries of history, from publishing and spectacle to film. And the combination of urban history and that of empire in its culture of history also serves to expand our notion of history as a discretely national phenomenon.

MODALITIES AND CHANGES IN THE CULTURE OF HISTORY: AN OUTLINE

To recoup the emergence, circulation, and resonances of history across culture and their relations to both forms and processes of modernization, and to individuals' moving in culture, we may look at the making of popular histories as combined processes of production and consumption.[38] I use production throughout as, first, the actual manufacture of histories seen as artefacts in the material sense of this term. Serialized historical fiction or fiction in book form, travel guides, monuments, and films were the end-line of applied industrial technologies and kinds of entrepreneurship which, to use Elizabeth L. Eisenstein's phrase, became agents of change.[39] Production is also used here to describe the making of representations and is essentially about the workings of texts—written, visual, and, in Chapter 9, aural, and of objects, as ensembles of contesting images and narratives about the past. This kind of production via representation has been somewhat marginalized in historians' work on popular culture. This dual

[37] A select primary list of publications on the development of London as metropolis and national centre should include Leonard Schwarz, 'London 1700–1840', in *The Cambridge Urban History of Britain*, ii: *1540–1840*, ed. Peter Clark (Cambridge, 2000), 641–71; Martin Daunton, 'Introduction' and Richard Dennis, 'Modern London', in *The Cambridge Urban History of Britain*, iii: *1840–1950*, ed. Martin Daunton (Cambridge, 2001), 1–59, 95–133; Roy Porter, *London: A Social History* (Harmondsworth, 2000), 197–394; and Nead, *Victorian Babylon*.

[38] There is a vast historiography on the consumption of culture. Particularly useful are Storey, *Cultural Consumption and Everyday Life*, and Ann Bermingham and John Brewer (eds.), *The Consumption of Culture, 1600–1800: Image, Object, Text* (London, 1995). I have found the following particularly inspiring: Craig Clunas, 'Modernity Global and Local: Consumption and the Rise of the West', *American Historical Review*, 104 (1999), 1497–1511; Arjun Appadurai (ed.), *The Social Life of Things: Commodities in Cultural Perspective* (Cambridge, 1988); Grant McCracken, *Culture and Consumption: New Approaches to the Symbolic Character of Consumer Goods and Activities* (Indianapolis, Ind., 1988); and Victoria De Grazia, *The Sex of Things: Gender and Consumption in Historical Perspective* (Berkeley, 1996).

[39] Elizabeth L. Eisenstein, *The Printing Press as an Agent of Change: Communications and Culture Transformation in Early Modern Europe* (Cambridge, 1980). See also St Clair, *The Reading Nation*.

look at the two facets of culture production seeks to correct the swing from a history of production to the study of consumption and from producers to their clients. In histories about cultural consumption this has been quite apparent in the move away from *auteurs* and texts towards readers and spectators, viewers and listeners.

Clearly production is only one part of the story told here and its interpretation. For this book is also about how individuals moved between productions of the past and appropriated or dispensed with them, the actual environment in which this movement took place, and how it impinged on their relating to histories. To grasp this set of dynamics between histories and people, yet stay attuned to 'big change', we may draw on Michel de Certeau's characterization of the ways in which consumers move across the landscape of cultural production.[40] Their field of operation and the places where they meet culture is the everyday and the familiar, where children, women, and men make do with available pasts. Their engagement with stories they read, monuments they see, or films they watch goes beyond the moment of economic exchange which results in purchasing a historical package in the form of a book, a print, or an admittance ticket to a monument, a museum, or a film. Not only de Certeau but a number of sociologists, ethnographers, and anthropologists of culture have long realized that consumers are active beings and that their activity amounts to a 'secondary production' or even a co-production of culture.[41] Their activity is dispersed and insinuates itself through using the products others make. He likens this activity to 'poaching', both texts and sights.[42] Birley's quick hand with scissors illuminates this kind of practice. Like poachers, consumers temporarily inhabit the real and imaginary places they occupy or make them habitable. Or, in de Certeau's succinct and elegant rendition: consumers/poachers of a culture are like renters and lodgers, or have the wisdom of insinuating their countless differences into the place they inhabit, even when there are obvious hierarchies between them and owners/producers. No less useful for this book, the landscape de Certeau describes is that of the modern big city, where individuals move in and out of places and respond to the modern urban experience. And the book relates the emergence and development of the culture of history to cities and to modes and practices of individuals circulating in them and looking at them. His kind of approach is useful because it can accommodate both constrictions and impersonal changes—to do with class, gender, capital and state, and individual agency. This practical approach (which he titles 'a practical theory of culture') also diffuses dichotomies between structures and agents and between Culture with a capital C, or the sum of creations which make it, and the individuals

[40] Michel de Certeau, *The Practice of Everyday Life*, trans. Steven Rendall (Berkeley, 1988) and Storey, *Cultural Consumption*, 108–28.

[41] In addition to the work of Appadurai I have benefited from McCracken, *Culture and Consumption*.

[42] De Certeau, *The Practice of Everyday Life*, 165–77.

whose workings make it. The approach's rather general terms and de Certeau's own allegiances to ethnology, the social sciences, and literature may be unappealing to some practising historians and bracket him as belonging to 'cultural studies'. But in the words of Michèle Lamont, he does offer a framework of sorts for looking at how the 'weak'—that is the ordinary and even marginal in all classes—make use of the 'strong', the national state in its varied forms, elites, cross-national, and global apparatuses for the distribution of leisure and entertainment. The attention to practices in culture also makes a place for autonomies in relation to the constraints within which people operate. And they may help the practising historian grasp how people make meanings and do with histories.[43]

Consider the following examples. Around the middle of the nineteenth century, young men and boys belonging to London's floating population and its casual labour force and occasionally inhabiting the casual wards in East End workhouses were far removed from power. They had limited access to literary histories and even illustrated ones; they were also beyond the reach of most reformers and organizations imparting useful historical knowledge to improve the labouring poor. But they were the kind of appropriators of the past whom de Certeau and other anthropologists and social historians of the city describe. In 1849 and 1850 some of these boys demonstrated to the astonished Henry Mayhew how they processed information about historical figures, linearity, and causality acquired directly from books (by the literate amongst them), or indirectly (through collective readings), or through observing monuments and buildings which they mentally mapped and connected to rumour about wars, victories, or, most substantially, through connecting literal information to their experience of the law and modes of punishing (notably public hanging). They transported historical details to their fictions and to oral lore. They thus transformed novels about Tudor England (W. H. Ainsworth, *The Tower of London*, 1839–40) and the eighteenth century (Ainsworth's *Jack Sheppard*, 1839) and their extremely popular heroes into stories and shows relatable to their everyday routines and itineraries.[44] Some, stating they know 'nothing of history of the old times', were nevertheless familiar with the word itself, professed to an acquaintance with the revolutionary and Napoleonic wars, associating them with landmarks such as the Wellington Pillar at Charing Cross 'just by the candlesticks (fountain)'.[45] The literature and heroes these men and boys absorbed, admired, and assimilated were 'processed' through experiences of class and gender (the latter acquired within the masculine street culture of costermongers, apprentices, and labourers): historical felons like Dick Turpin and Sheppard became their cult heroes and dramatic realizations of all historical novels figuring crime, the gallows, or the guillotine became running best-sellers.

[43] Michèle Lamont, Review of de Certeau, *The Practice of Everyday Life*, in *American Journal of Sociology*, 93 (1987), 721–2.

[44] Henry Mayhew, *London Labour and the London Poor* (1850–1; repr. New York, 1968), iv. 391.

[45] Ibid. i. 473.

A few decades later, Edmund Stonelake, possessing of a greater degree of literacy (he was born after the 1870 Education Act), extracted his political education from Carlyle's *French Revolution*, describing the ferocity and the vivid descriptions of the guillotine and of the influences of the Revolution on peoples and countries struggling against the powerful to establish democracies.[46] And Elizabeth Bryson, born in 1880 to an impoverished bookkeeper, identified her first moment of defiance against hierarchy, against the powerful and against the stricture of her gender and poverty, with the instant at which her eyes rested on the lines describing sans-culotte defiance in Paris of 1793.[47]

The two-way travel of histories between their producers and consumers may be characterized by four modalities which readers may hold on to, to lead them along the long continuum treated in the book, and which may be added to the substance of the interpretations of the past (introduced earlier) and to the survey of changes. By modalities I mean the modes and manner in which patterns percolated within the culture of history, recurred, and repeated themselves throughout the period examined in this book.[48] The first modality is the resonance of themes and images through various forms and genres and across classes, evident in the theme and image of the dangerous past in which power is very central, and their association with sensation and horror. In its modification, which took place from the 1870s and 1880s and which may be connected to a juncture of changes in the Empire and the democratization of access to politics, the notion of the dangerous past is retained, but dangerous periods are attached to a readier acceptance of power, the state, and the Empire. The second modality concerns repetition in the patterns and dynamics of access to history and to knowledge about and usages of the past. Each new form emerging after 1800 did not replace but was added to older and traditional genres, modes, and forms which already existed in the urban environment and experience and was relatable to them. At the same time new forms presented breaks from the older ones. Thus waxworks presenting historical figures, rapidly gaining popularity after 1800, were a vestige of *ancien régime* aristocratic consumption and the plebeian culture of the fairground, but in their new garb, availability to urban spectators, and exploitation of modern forms of advertising, as well as in their relation to politics, they formed the prototype of the new commercial culture of history. In similar manner the generic forms of historical fiction of the 1830s, 1840s, and 1860s, especially historical crime novels and novels depicting historical monuments, drew on an older, eighteenth-century urban lore of crime; but they capitalized on the modernization of technologies of printing, engraving,

[46] Cited in Jonathan Rose, *The Intellectual Life of the British Working Classes* (New Haven, 2001), 43.

[47] Elizabeth Bryson, *Look Back in Wonder* (Dundee, 1966), 80–1.

[48] Rather than 'aspects ... which relate to ... mode, or manner or state of being, as distinct from ... substance or identity; the non-essential aspect or attribute of a concept of entity'. *Oxford English Dictionary* (Oxford, 1953, repr. 1961), vi. 567.

publishing, and distribution—from engraving on steel in 1822, making possible the production of hundreds of thousands of quality impressions cheaply, to stereotyping in 1827, facilitating the incorporation of images into texts directed at the hard of reading, to lithography, litho-tinting, and electrotyping and serialization.[49] The most successful new genres and forms developing during these decades circulated through these new apparatuses and included the topographical-historical novel (Ainsworth's, or Dickens's), the guidebook, and the 'live' experience of the dungeon—reconstructed in venues such as Tussaud's and the newly created 'national' monuments (notably the Tower of London) and in historical 'realizations' of historical texts on stage. The period from the 1890s, but most notably the 1930s, 1940s, and 1950s, saw the emergence of film, until this last decade the ultimate 'modern' form and technology. Historical films also represent the ultimate form of accretion. They were built on, and with the technologies and devices that developed in, the much older urban forms of producing moving images of the past, from the panoramas and phantasmagorias to theatricals, and even on novelistic techniques and conventions. But film also offered wholly new ways of looking at the past and producing it and new visual perceptions of history, and made it accessible to millions.

The last two modalities concern the scope and circulation of history and its availability and their relationship to democratization and definitions of national culture and identities. Third is the overarching trend towards the democratization of history, apparent in its diffusion across classes and culminating in its dispersal in and through the mass media during the early twentieth century, examined in the second half of the book. This democratization is of course related to the slow rise of urban democracy after 1867 and the slow development of a new kind of democracy, with the state playing a role in it as culture-provider from the 1940s. But democratization was inextricably linked to its very reverse, cultural distinction, admitting audiences into the culture of history, while making distinctions between them and sifting out some groups. Such distinctions operated to include and exclude classes or segments of them, genders, particular age groups, locales, and individuals. Reduced entry fees to workers after dark in Madame Tussaud's operated as a de facto form of separation between middle-class and working-class viewers. Stringent regulation of viewing and movement, operating in the Tower of London until the 1930s, effectively excluded adults and children from London's poorer areas from what they regarded as part of their history by right, and became the subject of locally and nationally organized protest. And the dynamics of democratization and distinction are also apparent in a tension, which the book records, between unities

[49] Patricia Anderson, *The Printed Image and the Transformation of Popular Culture 1790–1860* (Oxford, 1991), 2–3; Michael Twyman, *Printing 1770–1970* (London, 1970), 51–2; and Louis James, *Fiction for the Working Man, 1830–1850* (Oxford, 1963). For the relationship between technologies and forms of writing see Stuart Sillars, *Visualisation in Popular Fiction 1860–1960: Graphic Narratives, Fictional Images* (London, 1995).

in historical themes, interpretations, and images on the one hand, and the possibilities for individuals' choosing between and among the desirable version and images of the past.

The fourth modality concerns the scope and possibility for a national history. Virtually all studies of modern histories present them as constructs of modern nationalism (sometimes exclusively so) and the ultimate vehicle for the making of national identities. Histories have long been recognized to be creators of national identities and communities and their mobilizers.[50] In an overused phrase, narratives of history have the role of 'narrating nations'.[51] Like virtually all studies of English preoccupations with the past, this book endorses this premiss; it would be senseless to argue against it. But, as is clear from the aforesaid, it does not see the culture of history solely in terms of national consciousness, and I seek to go beyond generalities about histories and Englishness and to modify assumptions about the territories, borders, and individuals which made up national histories and indeed the limits of the term 'national' itself. Thus I identify and follow the group of the agents of Englishness, via English history, who were not 'purely' English. Madame Tussaud's Frenchness, her foreignness and exoticism, were at the heart of her prestige as the creator of the most popular history of the Revolution. The traffic between English and foreign traditions, the native and the international, apparent in her career and examined in Chapter 1, manifest a broader trend. English history was connected to developments within and the organization of production of cross-national histories, and as the nineteenth century progressed, the distribution and capitalization of these productions was globalized, a trend culminating in the cinema, but already apparent in the earlier markets for literary and theatrical productions. Moreover, the group of what I describe as the 'entrepreneurs' or 'impresarios of history', mediating between materials, audiences, senses of the past and experiences of the present, made a new kind of cultural group different from traditional cultural and social elites and included a vast number of 'outsiders' making their way into the centre.

STRUCTURE

The broad canvass of the culture of history—to appropriate the language of panorama and genre painting—and the long continuum covered determined the structuring and arrangement of the book. Though the narrative is not strictly

[50] Benedict Anderson, *Imagined Communities: Reflections on the Origin and Spread of Nationalism* (London, 1983; repr. 1991). Examples of studies of English histories as the embodiment of national identity include Mitchell, *Picturing the Past*, esp. pp. 1–19; Mandler, '"In the Olden Time"'; and Readman, 'The Place of the Past'.

[51] This phrase was coined by Homi Bhabha in reference to Ernest Renan. See 'Introduction: Narrating the Nation', in H. K. Bhabha (ed.), *Nation and Narration* (London, 1990), 1–7.

linear I roughly observe chronology and theme. The beginning and in many ways 'origin' of the new culture is the French Revolution, acting upon and releasing popular and collective forms of sensationalism and behaviour and shaping them anew. Part I then is devoted to productions of the Revolution and is organized around the sets of representations and sensations which these productions generated and exuded. The three chapters in it explore the perception of history as a place of horror, or rather pleasurable horror, and its real and metaphoric sites—the prison and dungeon, the guillotine and gallows—and connect these images and metaphors, and their uses, to the experience of modernity in the city. Madame Tussaud's museum, especially its Chamber of Horrors, examined as a part of a dense grid of historical objects—mainly wax models, but also relics and gadgets—lets on the entire culture of history, demonstrating the modalities detailed above. Tussaud's is also taken to represent the modes of visual access to and techniques of looking at the past in the mega-city. It particularly represents the detailed close look, below street level, at relics and vestiges of history. Chapters 2 and 3 move from objects and material representations of history, identified with popular culture, to two reflexive classical texts on the Revolution, Thomas Carlyle's *French Revolution*, published in 1837, the single most influential non-French text on the event, and Dickens's *A Tale of Two Cities*, appearing in 1859. The choice of these particular works by a cultural historian may court criticism. They may seem to qualify as 'literature' and therefore be the territory of the literary critic. More significant even, these exceptional texts may also seem to represent 'Culture' in a sense that is almost Arnoldian, and which is somewhat narrower than that used throughout the book.

However, one aim of this book is precisely to avoid the division of the culture of history into 'high' and 'low', leaving the former to non-historians and settling for 'majority cultures'. The last chapter focuses on historical operas and previous ones include references to genres like experimental biographies. And the 'great texts' selected here are not studied in isolation from culture but in the culture of history. Indeed they are treated as prime examples of the resonance of representations and sensations about the Revolution, or, for that matter, notions about the past, across genres and forms and across audiences, classes, and genders. Carlyle is connected to what I describe as historical 'city texts' and to the world of urban historical shows, especially that of panoramas, as well as to the technique of looking and form of spectatorship which competed with the dungeon or prison view of history: the bird's-eye view of the city—be it Paris or London—seeking control over history's chaos and unmanageability. Dickens's novel of the Revolution in these two cities is an exemplar of the mid-century urban history not only in its subject matter but also in its relation to the vast plebeian culture described by V. A. C. Gatrell as the culture of the gallows and, one may add, prison, reverberating in a vast literary and oral repertoire, in novels and in pictorial and theatrical 'realizations' (Martin Meisel's term), and, most important, in the cross-class spectacle of public hanging, present on the British urban scene until 1868.[52]

City, urban change and anxiety, and their relationship to the predominant notion of history as a place of danger is picked up in Part II, which is devoted to the nineteenth-century discovery of the Tudor era and the circulation and uses of its images and memories. The material and visual aspects of the past, together with the alternative modes and technologies of looking at it—the 'low' dungeon look and the panoramic view of history—are also picked up and followed in a detailed examination of new historical forms and genres defined during the late 1830s and early 1840s. These are the topographical historical novel, with a historical building for the main character (exemplified in the novels of Victor Hugo and Ainsworth), and the urban historical monument deemed 'national' and embodied in the Tower of London. I examine the related development of these forms and their social and political uses and meanings during the period following the setting of the Select Committee on National Monuments and Works of Art, a time rife with intense public agitation about and campaigns for democratic and cheap access to history. More broadly, this part touches on the relationship between the circulation of histories of the Tudors, the urban experiences followed in the previous chapter, and urban unrest (real or imagined) after the 1830s, thence between 1867 and the inter-war period.

Part II also makes a wider claim concerning the relationship between history, culture, and society by focusing on gender not only as a component of imagining the past, but also as a way to configure change and difference. Whereas Part I recovers the place of women as producers of popular histories and the impact of images of women and femininity on visions of the Revolution, Part II argues that gender—or representations of masculinity and femininity and of the differences between men and women—was vital to the very making of the uncosy and unconfident vision of history, as well as for its circulation across mixed audiences and age groups. The thread of gender is picked up in Parts III and IV, which recoup the second and third resurrections of the Elizabethan era, evolving around the image of a female monarch and connecting notions of power to modernity, during the inter-war period and around the Coronation year.

Part III takes the circulation of histories to the extended twentieth century, stretching from the 1870s and coinciding with the 'Age of Empire', global competition, and a centring of the monarchy within the growing democracy. The decades between the 1870s and 1900s form a divide between the early and mid-Victorian uses of the past and those more characteristic of the 'modern' century. But it is a porous divide, rather than an impenetrable and uncrossed barrier. Thus Chapters 6 and 7 recognize and map remains of the older urban

[52] V. A. C. Gatrell, *The Hanging Tree: Execution and the English People 1770–1868* (Oxford, 1994, repr. 1996), 56–90; Martin Meisel, *Realizations: Narrative, Pictorial and Theatrical Arts in Nineteenth-Century England* (Princeton, 1983).

forms and traces of the past like the novel, guidebook, and historical artefacts and monuments consumed and used in their environment. Its main focus, however, is the generic twentieth-century form of telling about the Tudor and mainly Elizabethan past, the film, which this part sets in the context of new forms of cultural capitalism whose saliency was a strong relationship to other mass media, like the press and radio, and to cross-national cultural exchange. Specifically, Part III focuses on the cycle of Tudor films produced between 1912 and 1953 in Britain and touches on their Hollywood connections and corollaries, to highlight the cross-Atlantic, imperial, and global aspect of 'national' histories. But it also carries on the motif of local urban consumption and of individual consumers' choices within the constraints of the 'big' political and economic change which affected cultural production. This part also examines in detail the input of brokers of the past on mass consumption of it, chiefly the input of film stars in the roles of monarchs, as interpreters of historical character and action, relating this role to the changes in the cultural roles of the British monarchy during the first half of the twentieth century.

The slightly shorter Part IV examines the last and most popular revival of the Revolution during roughly the same period, between its centenary in 1889 and the Second World War. It weighs the surviving motif of horror and older kinds of sensationalism alongside the new role of the Revolution and indeed of history as a source of glamour and a lifestyle fit for modernity and democracy. This new role parallels the changes in the image of the monarchy examined in the previous part and is also related to the juncture of politics and mass culture as manifest in the development of the media.

The twin themes of modernity and the democracy of the culture of history are brought together in the final chapter, which recovers the last Elizabethan revival before and during the year of Coronation in 1953. This chapter also ties together the 'popular' and minoritarian views of and on the monarchy and Empire and the interplay between individual producers and brokers of interpretations of the past (here musicians and composers, most notably Benjamin Britten but also the group which may be described as the publicists of New Elizabethanism, notably A. L. Rowse) and the state in its new role as distributor of the culture of history. Its material is music as a medium for the transmission of history and its focus is opera, the single most visual and spectacular form of music, and it anchors the discussion in the story of the production of the first historical state opera in Britain, Britten's *Gloriana*, produced for the Coronation.

The workings of history in culture, their dynamics and mechanism on the one hand and relationship to 'big change' on the other in urbanization, the diffusion of literary and visual culture and the media, modern technologies of seeing, and urban and imperial politics—all these are best followed sequentially. My ideal readers would proceed in this way and would thus gain the sense of resonance and of the growth of the culture of history by accretion and repetition in forms, uses, and repertoires, but also, and most importantly, of the changes in all of these. Readers who may find the journey too long or tedious, or experts in particular fields, like the nineteenth-century 'order of exhibition', the Victorian city, the film, or 'historical' vocal and instrumental music, may wish to proceed from the Introduction to specific Parts (in the instances given here: Chapter 1, Parts I–II, Parts III–IV and V). The beginnings of the different parts of the book would give them a rough sense of continuities within and breaks in the ways in which the past circulated in culture.

PART I

THE FRENCH CONNECTION: HISTORY AND CULTURE AFTER THE REVOLUTION

1

History as a Chamber of Horrors: The French Revolution at Madame Tussaud's

HEADS

Visitors to the Chamber of Horrors at Madame Tussaud's museum in London are invited to look at 'a history of crime and punishment'. They follow a one-way trail, modelled on a dungeon, making progress, or regress, from medieval instruments of torture to likenesses of notorious nineteenth- and twentieth-century murderers, posing in semblances of city yards and alleys, courtrooms and prisons. The last two figures in this urban trail are Dennis Andrew Nilsen, the Muswell Hill murderer, strangler of young men, necrophile and body-carver, convicted in 1983, and 'Tiger' Donald Nielson, kidnapper and killer, condemned in 1975. Practically adjoining them is a tableau of the assassinated Jean-Paul Marat, martyr of the French Revolution, in his tub, followed by revolutionary figures and relics, including a replica of the guillotine, complete with a basket-full of severed heads. The last exhibit visitors come upon is one of the collection's oldest prize items: a display of the 'heads' of five of the victims of the Great Terror of 1793–4. Three of the heads were modelled by Marie Tussaud herself from their bleeding originals, fresh from the guillotine, and had once belonged to three active promoters of the Terror: Jacques Hébert (1757–94), journalist and publisher of the radical *Père Duchesne*, the engine of sans-culotte revolutionary protest; Jean-Baptiste Carrier (1757–94), member of the Committee of Public Safety and executor of revolutionary justice in the city of Nantes, where he drowned thousands in *noyades*, or vessels with trapdoors, floating up the Loire, and Antoine-Quentin Fouquier-Tinville (1746–95), Public Prosecutor of the Revolutionary Tribunal. The two other, royal, heads, of Louis XVI and Marie-Antoinette, allegedly made by Marie Tussaud, had not been displayed during her lifetime and were first presented to London audiences in 1865. The heads still retain the realism which early and mid-nineteenth-century spectators looked for and found in wax figures. What more gruesomely real and exciting than the blood-dripping models displayed on pikes—a replica of the popular practice of parading heads in the streets after revolutionary executions? Protected by glass, like the rest of the collection's revolutionary wax effigies and 'relics', the heads literally are a showcase of one of the oldest and arguably most widely available and influential images of the French Revolution (see Fig. 3).

The proximity, contiguity even, of murder that is domestic in the sense that it is British and is carried in or from home, and 'foreign' political violence, is not simply a reminder that Tussaud's started in 1802 as the first museum of France's *ancien régime* and the Revolution. This proximity may also serve as a showcase of the new culture of history which evolved from the early nineteenth century. The early history of the collection—both the history of its development and organization, and that of its meanings for diverse and heterogeneous audiences and their uses of it, hones a few of the most prominent features of this culture: the usability of aspects of the past in an urban locale, the centrality and

Fig. 3. Madame Tussaud's Chamber of Horrors: the guillotined heads

enormous appeal of violence and crime in the democratized and highly commercialized vision of this past, the interplay between older traditions and patterns of cultural production and consumption and newer ones, and the appearance of an entrepreneur, an impresario of history as it were, utilizing popular demand for sensation and in turn shaping it. The collection was not just 'an exhibition, it was an institution' which represented and shaped popular notions of history by firmly anchoring them in aspects of nineteenth-century urban culture.[1] It adhered to the new forms of respectable leisure and circulated a conservative notion of the past with the monarchy, nation, and, later in the century, Empire at its centre. But it also drew on earlier and contemporary popular traditions in which crime was a centre of attention and public punishment, especially public execution, formed part of the experience of metropolitan life and its representation. Tussaud's biggest drawing force was, and probably still is, the uncomfortable, dark, and frightening images of history as a place of horror. And during the first three-quarters of the nineteenth century, horror, or rather 'horrors' in the plural, was not just a configuration for the Revolution and history, but constituted a set of attitudes and sensations in which repulsion, apprehension, and fear combined with attraction and delight. Dickens, who had been attracted by the tradition and lore about crime and criminals, and by the spectacle of punishment and death outside Tussaud's and inside it, fully appreciated this mixture and wrote in 1860 that this English institution had that 'profound and awful misery' which 'provides the Englishman with an entertainment which does not make him happy'.[2]

The following detailed examination of this showcase will highlight the ways in which the Revolution as represented and marketed by this 'English institution' admitted a sense of the past and historical consciousness into a cross-class field of historical representation, while preserving, or 'letting into', the uses of history older forms of sensationalism and consumption. This examination may puncture the alleged dichotomies which have bedevilled much of the historiography of popular culture, between popular and elite leisure and culture, between traditional and modern forms of display, and between pre-modern and modern forms of spectatorship. Madame Tussaud's takes these 'pairs' apart and challenges some assumptions about the production and consumption of culture. The origins of the collection were in the court culture of the *ancien régime* in France, in British aristocratic culture, and in the market for luxury goods and crafts, but the collection had also strong ties to the popular tradition of displaying wax models in fairs and open-air 'shows', especially in what Richard Altick described as the 'shows of London',[3] not to mention allegiances to that show which V. A. C. Gatrell has described as the cheapest and, until 1868, most easily

[1] George Augustus Sala, 'Historic Notes on Madame Tussaud', in *Madame Tussaud's Exhibition Guide* (London, 1905), 3.

[2] Charles Dickens, in *All the Year Round*, quoted in Pilbeam, *Madame Tussaud and the History of Waxworks*, 228.

[3] Altick, *The Shows of London*, 332–49.

accessible of urban shows: public hanging.[4] And the collection, from its very beginning, capitalized on popular tastes and on popular demand for public display of the criminal and his or her punishment. Finally, in its physical organization and structure, its advertising and marketing, Madame Tussaud's represents the trend towards the democratization of the historical museum during the first half of the nineteenth century: it was in principle open to all and allowed viewing that was free of direct monitoring and control. At the same time it and, more broadly, the new culture of history partly preserved what Pierre Bourdieu has famously called 'distinction': it reproduced difference in the disposition and social make-up of spectators, a difference related mainly to class, in directing access to culture and creating tastes for history.[5] Last but not least, Madame Tussaud's capitalized on and defined the contours of interest in the French Revolution as the grand modern historical event and, more broadly, history, associating the Revolution with disorder and crime while taming it and transforming it into an English event, a constitutive component of English popular culture. To comprehend the collection's role as transmitter of images of and sentiments about the Revolution and the power of both, we first need to consider its basis and that of wax modelling and wax modellers in traditional entertainment, craftsmanship, and entrepreneurship.

CEROPLASTIC CULTURE: TRADITION AND CULTURAL ENTERPRISE

In the metropolitan world of spectacle and entertainment, the exhibition of historical figures made of wax was no novelty. Nor was the art of wax modelling, known as 'ceroplastics'. Madame Tussaud's popularity during the nineteenth century is partly attributable to a firmly established taste for wax artefacts of a wide variety and for a multiplicity of uses: religious and secular, votive and decorative, pedagogic and prurient. By the end of the eighteenth century, when ceroplastic art had reached its apogee in western and central Europe, the special qualities which render wax a perfect medium for preparing figures and models had long been known.[6] The relatively cheap and available solid fatty substance of animal and vegetable origin is, unlike other oils and fats, free of glycerin and does not reject colouring matter; it can be melted in ordinary temperature, easily kneaded, then cut and shaped, and its texture and consistency modified by the

[4] Gatrell, *The Hanging Tree*, 56–80.

[5] Pierre Bourdieu, *Distinction: A Social Critique of the Judgment of Taste*, trans. Richard Nice (London, repr. 2000).

[6] E. J. Pyke, *A Biographical Dictionary of Wax Modellers* (Oxford, 1973; Supplement, London, 1981), pp. xxxv–xlii; Vanessa R. Schwartz, *Spectacular Realities: Early Mass Culture in Fin-de-Siècle Paris* (Berkeley, 1998), 92–4; Michel Lemire, *Artistes et mortels* (Paris, 1990).

addition of other matter. As wax absorbs light, it appears translucent and mobile, thus lifelike, possessing a verisimilitude that is enhanced by period clothing and human hair. Used by the Egyptians and the Greeks for funerary rites, wax modelling came to hold an important place in Rome, both in the domestic and the public sphere: *imagines*, or masks of ancestors, were displayed inside the Roman household, but could be exposed in public on ceremonial occasions. Significantly, the *ius imaginis* preserved the privilege of displaying artefacts (in what in effect had been the first wax museums) to patricians. Ceroplastics retained its religious and votive function in Christianity throughout the Middle Ages and the Reformation. Indeed even in Protestant countries the ceremonial uses of wax effigies died hard. As late as 1672, John Evelyn complained about the display, in Somerset House in London, of the Saviour and the Disciples 'in figures and puppets made as big as the life, of wax work, curiously clad and sitting round a large table', which 'all the City came to see'.[7] More widely accepted was the custom of modelling and displaying the effigies of dead royalty and the nobility. The funeral effigy of the Duchess of Richmond, commissioned from Mrs Goldsmith (first name unknown), a celebrated modeller and dealer in wax artefacts, drew large and admiring audiences.

Quite early on then, wax works and their display were associated with aristocratic consumption of luxuries. This was the case in France, where the production of such artefacts and their public exhibition were pursued under court patronage. The careers of both John Christopher Curtius, Marie Tussaud's adoptive (and most probably real) father, and her own were launched under the patronage of Versailles. Yet alongside aristocratic ceroplastic culture, and quite often in relation to it, there developed a popular taste for wax models, a taste strongly associated with cross-class urban traditions of entertainment and spectacle. The display of full-sized effigies and models became a regular fixture of Southwark Fair and St Bartholomew's Fair in Smithfield. Indoor exhibitions mushroomed in the Strand area, on Fleet Street, and in the Old Jewry, rather mixed neighbourhoods, where entertainment drew in varied and mixed audiences. Mrs Solomon's show on Fleet Street boasted in 1710 of a medley of tableaux, including the 'Fatal Scaffold, of Charles I, The Royal Seraglio of Mahomet the Third, the Rites of Moloch', complete with 'Cannanitish Ladies offering their first born to a burning Moloch' and, for a special treat, a mechanical model of Old Mother Shipton (the prophetess foreseeing Charles I's death), administering farewell kicks to patrons.[8] The indoor displays seem to have retained at least one characteristic of the display in the fair booth, the mingling together, jumbling even, of different sorts of exhibits, notably likenesses of royalty and other celebrities, mythical and extraordinary figures, wonders and other miscellanea. Mrs Solomon's recipe proved successful during

[7] Cited in Altick, *The Shows of London*, 50. [8] Ibid. 52.

the late 1780s (when Curtius and Tussaud launched their show in Paris) and was imitated in Mr and Mrs Sylvester's 'Cabinet of Royal Figures, Most Curiously Moulded in Wax, as Large as Nature', which the entrepreneurial couple showed in the Lyceum on the Strand, complete with the British and French monarchs, a Sleeping Beauty, and such luminaries as Voltaire and Warren Hastings (in that order).

It was the very diversity of artefacts of wax and their considerable expansion to the market of commercial entertainment that made wax modelling appealing to artists and dealers. Appeal probably lay in the combination of opportunity in a relatively open and not too hierarchical field and the association to 'the quality'. Typically the artist who produced for the popular shows worked on commission for aristocratic clients. Mrs Goldsmith's full-size effigy of the Duchess of Richmond and Lennox fetched a nice £200, a fact that both the shrewd artist and the press utilized to publicize exhibitions of her work.[9] Late eighteenth-century and early nineteenth-century ceroplastics thus presents a remarkable example of an open field of cultural production, lacking a rigid organization and hierarchy and subsequently exploitable by newcomers marginalized elsewhere. And this openness is pronounced in the fairly large number of women in all the stages and processes of production, distribution, and exhibition. Of the sixty-seven women wax modellers listed in E. J. Pyke, *Biographical Dictionary of Wax Modellers*, some thirty-six were active in Britain between the early eighteenth century and the late twentieth. The presence of women is particularly strong during the heyday of ceroplastic art in the second part of the eighteenth century and the first decades of the nineteenth century—when Marie Tussaud made her own career. The origins, upbringing, and aspiration of a considerable number of modellers were genteel and, in some cases, even aristocratic, and it is quite evident that their careers, even when these involved the public exhibition of their work for money, were quite acceptable. More importantly, a professional career in ceroplastics, because of its association with the aristocracy, was deemed womanly and even ladylike.

The life and career of Catherine Andras (1775–1860), Marie Tussaud's younger contemporary, is one example of the opportunities women could capitalize upon in the thriving market for products of wax. A disciple of James Tassie (1735–99), the celebrated gem engraver and modeller of profile medallions, Andras first specialized in small-scale pink-wax portraits and figures against a low-relief background, distinct luxury commodities. As the adopted daughter of miniature painter Joseph Bowyer, she had a good introduction into that circle of conspicuous consumers of applied arts who made up her distinguished clientele. During a long and fruitful career (she was productive until the age of 80), Andras modelled the portraits of politicians and artists including Charles James

[9] Pyke, *A Biographical Dictionary*, 'Goldsmith Mrs.', 55; and Pilbeam, *Madame Tussaud and the History of Waxworks*, 2, 11.

Fox, Pitt the Younger, the Duke of Wellington, the Polish republican general Kosciusko, Sir Walter Scott, and Mrs Searle. That her customers included John Wesley and Hannah More testifies that wax modelling was acceptable even in evangelical circles, usually condemning the plastic arts. With her appointment in 1802 as 'modeller in wax' to Queen Charlotte, Andras reached the top of her profession and secured a stream of lucrative commissions, including that of Lord Nelson's effigy for Westminster Abbey, her only surviving large-scale work. Throughout this genteel career, her work was displayed to varied publics, in a variety of venues.[10] Other modellers capitalized on their class, the elasticity of gender ideology, and the flexibility of the relationship between luxury and low consumers' culture. British aristocratic entrepreneurs included Mary Elizabeth, Countess of Denbigh (1798–1824), wife of the Seventh Earl of Denbigh, modeller of medium figures in high relief, the Honorable Mrs Anne Seymour (1794–1828), and Lady Diana Beauclerk (1734–1808), eldest daughter of Charles Spencer, Third Duke of Marlborough, the last two, like Andras, apprenticed to Tessie.[11] And Marie Tussaud herself, capitalizing on the aristocratic connection of ceroplastics, successfully embellished her biography with a career at Versailles as a tutor to Madame Elizabeth, France's Princess Royal and Louis XVI's sister.

Among the lives and careers of wax modellers, female and male, Tussaud's loom very large. For she was not simply a modeller and dealer but what I would call a cultural impresario, an entrepreneur making use of the political changes which impinged upon the production of wax artefacts and the massive growth of an urban cultural economy, and who came to mediate tastes for, and notions of, history. Her career has been recovered and eulogized time and again, during her lifetime in the memoirs she co-authored with Francis (François) Hervé, posthumously by her grand-nephew John Theodore Tussaud, and in numerous commercial publications including catalogues and guidebooks to the collection, in Pauline Chapman's biographies and, most recently, she has received academic attention by Pamela Pilbeam and Uta Kornmeier.[12] It may be useful briefly to discuss here the highlights of Marie Tussaud's career and focus on the period before the Revolution and the revolutionary years before looking closely at her reconstruction as England's custodian of the popular memory and history of this revolution.

[10] Pyke, *A Biographical Dictionary*, 'Andras, Catherine', 146–7.

[11] 'Denbigh, Countess'; 'Beauclerk, Lady Diana'; 'Seymour, Anne Damer', in Pyke, *A Biographical Dictionary*, 38, 11, 36.

[12] Marie Tussaud, *Madame Tussaud's Memoirs and Reminiscences of France, Forming an Abridged History of the French Revolution*, ed. Francis Hervé (London, 1838); John Theodore Tussaud, *The Romance of Madame Tussaud* (London, 1920); Pauline Chapman, *The French Revolution as Seen by Madame Tussaud* and *Madame Tussaud in England*; Anita Leslie and Pauline Chapman, *Madam Tussaud: Waxworker Extraordinary* (London, 1978). See also Pilbeam, and Uta Kornmeier, 'Madame Tussaud's as a Popular Pantheon', in Matthew Craske and Richard Wrigley (eds.), *Pantheons: The Transformation of a Manumental Idea* (London, 2004).

As virtually all of her biographers have noted, Marie Tussaud, née Grosholtz, had had an impeccable pedigree as a professional artist and show woman in the field of luxury applied arts, so characteristic of the culture and economy of the late *ancien régime*. The fact that her reputation and authority derived from her personal and professional experience of the French Revolution cannot be overstated. She was apprenticed in the art of ceroplastics by her father—posing as her uncle and adoptive parent—the physician and anatomist turned wax modeller Philippe Kreutz (Curtius), who had been summoned in 1776 to Paris by the prince de Conti. Still enjoying the patronage of the prince, Curtius exhibited his work at the Palais-Royal and, from 1782, in the more popular showroom at 52 Boulevard du Temple, where it became 'the greatest show of pre-revolutionary Paris'.[13] The eclectic collection was a cross-breed between models of celebrities and a display of criminals and crimes of notoriety, known as the *Caverne des grands voleurs*. In later years the idea of a cavern of crime and violence would become the nucleus of the concept of a Chamber of Horrors. Grosholtz, born in Berne in 1760, was brought to Paris by Curtius at the age of 6, apprenticed by him, and groomed to be the manageress of the two collections. She became adapt at different branches of ceroplastics such as portrait-making, the making of wax flora, and the moulding of full-size figures and was invited by Madame Elizabeth to Versailles. With the turn in politics in 1789, Curtius shrewdly and decisively severed his relations with the court and court patronage and called his niece to Paris, set on reconstructing new identities for himself and for her as republicans, patriots, and artists in the service of the people and the changing regime.[14] He claimed to have taken a part in the storming of the Bastille on 14 July 1789, joined the Jacobin Club and the National Guard, and was awarded with a mission to the Rhine. And he assiduously capitalized on his work relationship with eminent critics of the *ancien régime* like Rousseau, Voltaire, Benjamin Franklin, and the reforming Controller-General, Jacques Necker, to gain his way into the right political circles.

The very early days of the Revolution amply proved that Curtius's effigies had more to them than wax, and that they could be used symbolically and politically. Two days before the storming of the Bastille, crowds invaded his salon in the Palais-Royal, seized the busts of Necker and the revolutionary Duc d'Orléans, draped them in black, and paraded them before cheering multitudes. As the Revolution progressed, Curtius and Grosholtz received a steady stream of commissions from the General Assembly and, later, the Committee of Public Safety. The Great Terror of 1793–4 was good for ceroplastic business: the two artists moulded the death masks of an impressive gallery of executed public

[13] Quoted in Schwartz, *Spectacular Realities*, 93, and Charles Sherwood, *Farce and Fantasy: Popular Entertainment in Eighteenth-Century Paris* (Oxford, 1986).

[14] On the revolutionary careers of Curtius and Grosholtz see also David Bindman, *The Shadow of the Guillotine: Britain and the French Revolution* (London, 1989), 75–6 and Schwartz, *Spectacular Realities*, 92–7.

figures of varying political hue. Marie Grosholtz's own unfortunate models included Bernard René Jordan, Marquis de Launay, Jacques de Flesselles, Jean-Paul Marat, Fouquier-Tinville, Jean-Baptiste Carrier, and probably the Princess de Lamballe, the hated Superintendent of Marie-Antoinette's household, and Maximilien Robespierre.

But Grosholtz's own sympathies and ambitions during the Revolution are less transparent than her uncle's. This is mainly because of her effort, from about 1794, to sever herself from the Jacobin regime and her later attempt to construct a royalist and legitimist identity. The fact, or believable story, that Marie Grosholtz had been imprisoned and held in La Force prison for a good part of the Revolutionary Year II (1794) would certainly play in her favour in Britain, where Madame Tussaud (her married name, which she would keep after her separation from her husband) would market herself as a victim of the Revolution. Following the Jacobin demise and Curtius's death she served two other reigns which, albeit oligarchic, were decidedly non- (and even anti) monarchist: the Directory and Napoleon's Consulate. The service rendered to the First Consul eventually paid, when in 1801 he granted her permission to leave France for England. In later years Tussaud's collection in London would become the largest repository of Bonaparte's relics outside France and the site of a specifically English Napoleonic cult (see below). In 1801 or 1802, at the age of 41, Marie Tussaud embarked on her second, forty-nine-year English career, making her collection a national institution and remaking the French Revolution into an English event. Of the nearly five decades, she spent a little over three as an itinerant artist and show woman, perpetually on the move in England, Scotland, and Ireland with her growing collection, whose core remained the full-size figures brought by her from France and the revolutionary relics she and her sons collected. It was only in 1835 that the collection moved to London and, after changing location a few times, finally settled in the Bazaar on 38 Baker Street, which it was to occupy until 1884, when it moved to its permanent place on Marylebone Road.

FROM EXPERIENCE TO A HISTORY OF THE TERROR: THE MAKING OF AN IMPRESARIO OF HISTORY

From the very beginning of her career in Britain, Madame Tussaud's reputation and identity as a popular authority on French history derived from her personal experience of the four successive regimes between the 1770s and 1801. But it was the experience of the events of 1793–4 and the interpretation of this experience which dwarfed the rest and contributed to the making of the early collection into a museum of the Terror. As her biographers have noted, this long-standing reputation rested on popular identification of her with the old monarchy in

France and with the British monarchy. Yet her carefully constructed public identity and image as artist and popular historian had been quite equivocal. On the one hand, she had tried, from 1802, to detach herself from republicanism, revolution, and political change, and to associate the collection with the restored monarchy in France and on the rest of the Continent. On the other hand, her very status and the status of the collection as an English institution, cultivating an English sense of the past, derived from her foreignness and from the rendition of the revolutionary experience as a history of crime and retribution.

Experience was a composite construct. It included not only actual life, work, and travail during the revolutionary upheaval in France but also an assiduously marketed representation of Marie Tussaud's activities. Throughout the nineteenth century she was reproduced not as an active agent of the event but as a participant observer. It was her role as an 'eyewitness' to these great events that was constantly picked by herself and her contemporaries to mark her off from the historians of the time. Indeed being a witness to the Revolution made her a historian and her collection a history. This particular quality is succinctly described in her memoir, co-written with (and probably dictated to) Francis Hervé in 1838. Her role is advertised in the emblematic title: *Madame Tussaud's Memoirs and Reminiscences of France, Forming an Abridged History of the French Revolution*, and stated outright in the didactic Preface:

> It is hoped that the following pages may not only prove as interesting as one who has witnessed some of the most appalling scenes which modern times have presented, but that they may be found useful, as forming a concise history of the most striking events connected with the revolution.[15]

And again: 'she had been an eye-witness of those scenes upon which authors have generally written after the description of others'.[16] The constant resort to ocular metaphor, as well as the reference to sight and seeing, define the historian herself as both spectator ('witness') and producer of a spectacle, and her material (the revolutionary events) as a 'scene' that is to be revisualized and thus historicized.

To be sure, the metaphor of history as spectacle is not original, not even in relation to the French Revolution. Carlyle, as we shall see in the next chapter, used it amply in his history of the Revolution about the same time. But in Tussaud's and Hervé's use 'witnessing' acquires two meanings which connect the popular historian to two available and different traditions of history. The first tradition is the eighteenth-century plebeian lore about the spectacle and witnessing of public execution, where crowds watched the condemned on their last way to the gallows, a lore that persisted almost until the last third of the nineteenth century. I discuss this experience and its representations in connection

[15] Tussaud, *Madame Tussaud's Memoirs and Reminiscences*, ed. Hervé, p. i.
[16] Ibid. p. iii.

with images of the Revolution at some length in Chapter 3. Suffice it to say here that histories of crime and biographies of the condemned, describing their lives and 'witnessing' their trial and death, had been a staple in the older eighteenth-century plebeian urban print culture, ranging from traditional chapbooks to ballads. During the nineteenth century, these 'histories' filtered both 'down' to cheap-market crime and execution literature and 'up' to the historical novel of crime known as the 'Newgate novel'. Most important here, sight and witnessing, which had formed such a vital part of the culture of the gallows and its French revolutionary counterpart, the guillotine, were also integral to material representations of condemned criminals in wax. Madame Tussaud would capture the likeness of executed criminals in the same way that she had that of perpetrators or victims of the Terror at the moment of their death. The guillotine and 'horror' of the historical event could thus easily be connected with the spectacle at the gallows and with gallows culture. And her status as witness and one-time prisoner further authenticated the models themselves and the gallows/guillotine and prison view of historical events.

The second reference to history in the memoirs, guidebooks, and catalogues addresses written histories of the Revolution and changes in writing which Tussaud/Hervé think are desirable: the compression of written histories, or their 'abridgement', to a size accessible and easy to digest by the new kind of reader/spectator. Previous and contemporary histories of the Revolution were 'of so voluminous a character, as to deter those persons from reading them who cannot dispose of a large portion of their time, as also others who have not the inclination to encounter so elaborate a detail but yet would desire to be informed of the principal occurrences of so interesting an epoch in history'.[17] Such statements defined the readers of the memoir, and at least part of the prospective viewing public, as not belonging to the leisured or highly educated classes. They also locate Madame Tussaud herself in an ongoing historical discourse. The memoir was published just two years after the opening of the permanent exhibition in London, which it frankly promoted, and at the end of a decade that saw a new blaze of historians' interest in the Revolution. As Hedva Ben-Israel has argued, the July Revolution of 1830 and its aftermath, both in Paris and on the rest of the Continent, served to normalize the legacy of the great revolution of 1789–95.[18] And normalization, I would argue, had to do with the sense of a repetition, albeit in a minor key, of events that had already been seen. Put differently, the days of July 1830 were a condensed version of a part of the previous upheaval, without the momentous power of the original.

The February Paris revolution in 1848 and the wave of revolutions on the Continent that year augmented the sense of British observers that history was

[17] Ibid. p. i. [18] Ben-Israel, *English Historians on the French Revolution*, 98–110.

repeating itself for the third time and kindled sympathy and support amongst liberals and radicals. From the spring of 1848, as Margot Finn and others have shown, the revolutionary tide played a significant role in the realignment of British protest, evoking the great revolution, while generating the fears of conservatives, progressives, and the propertied.[19] The *Illustrated London News*, that chronicler of the metropolis's middle-class cultural life, referred to the 'third' French Revolution as 'the spectacle of a great and enlightened nation' and covered it in day-by-day reports and an abundance of illustrations in folio size which constantly and repeatedly invoked the great revolution of 1789–95. An illustration of 'The people in the Throne Room of the Tuileries' harks back to the storming of this palace in the summer of 1792, familiarizing readers with an action which had already occurred twice, while at the same time demonizing the lower classes of Paris. The same mixture of the sense of repetition and horror is produced by illustrations of the Chamber of Deputies, featuring protesters armed with makeshift weapons near the elected deputies, an invocation of the famous sans-culotte storming of the national Convention in 1793 and 1794.[20] This sense of the familiarity with the great historical events of the 'paradigmatic' revolution was of course fuelled by agitation, in Britain itself, for political reform, first after the passage of the Reform Act of 1832, then during the restless 1840s. Apprehension that a revolution might catch in Britain fuelled Tory historians' panic over the possible dangers of reform. Such an apprehension was integral to such multi-volume histories as Sir A. Alison's mammoth *History of Europe during the French Revolution*, appearing in ten volumes between 1832 and 1842. Other histories included G. P. R. James, *Lives of the Most Eminent Foreign Statesmen*, not to mention Carlyle's oeuvre, as well as a number of autobiographies and memoirs. Madame Tussaud's very reference to scholarly history and the mention of its partisanship marks off her own from it, yet at the same time appears to attach her to the 'serious' historical and literary debate on the Revolution. Indeed she claims her work to have a special authority, to do with the definition of the Revolution as a spectacle and that of her role in it as a surviving victim/eyewitness. Thus in her version the events are

> far better accredited when we hear them from the lips of one who was actually a spectator, and suffered from the decrees which deluged France with misery and blood. There are few persons now existing, who can give a more accurate account . . . her observations ever acute and circumstances brought her into contact with almost every remarkable character who figured in the revolutionary annals.[21]

[19] Margot C. Finn, *After Chartism: Class and Nation in English Radical Politics, 1848–1874* (Cambridge, 1993).

[20] *ILN*, 4 Mar. 1848, nos. 305–6, vol. xii, p. 127; 1 Apr. 1848, no. 310, vol. xii, p. 207; 15 Apr. 1848, no. 312, vol. xii.

[21] Tussaud, *Madame Tussaud's Memoirs and Reminiscences*, ed. Hervé, 3.

MOULDING THE TERROR: THE ORGANIZATION OF THE EXHIBITION

'Character' is shorthand for biography and is a key word in the reminiscences, which are loosely arranged around revolutionary biographical vignettes. The same biographical approach to history dominates the guidebooks and is behind the arrangement of the collection. Guidebooks from 1803 onwards were lists of figures as well as being compendia of brief biographies. Their titles are quite transparent and never fail to evoke Madame Tussaud's lineage and her pre-revolutionary connections. Note, for example, the title in 1826: *Biographical and Descriptive Sketches of the Whole Length Composition of Figures and other Works of Art Forming the Unrivalled Exhibition of Madame Tussaud (Niece of the Celebrated Curtius of Paris) and Artist to her Late Royal Highness Madame Elizabeth, Sister of Louis XVI.* The notion of history as the deeds of great men and a few great women was quite widespread at that time. In Madame Tussaud's the focus on the great event and great lives had (and still seems to have) two additional features. First is the lack and indeed independence of linearity and sequence. The second is a total and quite effective separation between the revolutionary sequel and the rest of French history, achieved by the treatment of revolutionary figures and their life stories as a separate category and their location in the separate collection, which from 1846 came to be known as the 'Chamber of Horrors'. These strategies have effectively meant the dehistoricization of the Revolution. For inside the museum the period from 1789 to 1795 was condensed into the short period of the Great Terror of 1793–4 and literally dissociated from what had preceded and what followed it. And the Terror lent the entire revolutionary era the aura of a crime, danger, and horror.

This dehistoricization of what was represented as a piece of history is quite apparent in the arrangement of the whole of the French figures in the collection. Over the years the number of figures and relics representing the *ancien régime*, the Revolution, and nineteenth-century French history did not increase significantly in proportion to the entire collection. But the separation between the disordered past and the rest of history remained a fixture. Thus in Maidstone in 1833 there were fourteen full-size figures and tableaux covering the *ancien régime*, the Consulate, and Empire out of a total of fifty-eight figures and tableaux (24 per cent). Revolutionary figures and tableaux numbered eight of the eighteen (or 44 per cent) figures in the separate collection, a significantly higher proportion.[22] In 1835 in Baker Street there were fourteen figures and tableaux

22 These and all the following figures have been drawn from the lists of wax figures compiled at the Archive, Madame Tussaud's London (MTA). MTA, 1833, List of Figures, Maidstone; and lists for 1835, 1837, Bazaar, London; 1848, Bazaar; Jan. 1851, Jan. 1852; July and Oct. 1857 and July 1858; 1888–9, Marylebone Road.

representing France's non-revolutionary history out of a total of sixty-three in the general collection (22 per cent) and eleven revolutionary items out of the nineteen (58 per cent) in the special collection, which had not yet received the name 'Chamber of Horrors'. In 1851, when a sumptuous 'Hall of Kings' was added to the museum, the proportion shrank to eighteen non-revolutionary French figures out of 136 in the Hall and the adjacent large rooms (13 per cent). In the centenary of the Revolution only twenty-eight of 288 figures (or a mere 10 per cent) in the various halls of the new location in Marylebone Road had to do with French history; over half represented the Napoleonic era, the Restoration, and the Second Empire. In the Chamber of Horrors the number shrank to twelve of eighty-one. Numerous objects (distinct form figures) representing the Napoleonic era were a separate category and were housed in the 'Golden Room' devoted to Bonaparte.

It was not the quantity of the exhibits that made the Revolution the showcase of the vision of history which the collection produced and propagated, but rather their arrangement in the museum's space, the construction of the biographies attached to them, and the set of contemporaries' sensations increasingly attached to both. The revolutionaries occupied the 'separate' or 'special room' together with violent and murderous publicly executed criminals. The idea of a separate exhibition within the larger collection drew on Curtius's original policy of distinguishing between the noble and celebrated (displayed in the Salon in the Palais-Royal) and the criminal (drawing mass audiences to the cavern on the Boulevard du Temple). Once in Britain, Marie Tussaud pursued the strategy of separating the 'great' from the notorious, drawing and capitalizing on the older forms of sensationalism and spectacle that had surrounded crime and judicial killing, and extending them to politics: revolutionaries were represented as criminals and the guillotine figured as a substitute gallows.[23] In 1826 visitors to the 'special room' could see the likeness of the assassinated Marat and the 'heads', as well as a tableau of the legendary and probably mythical Comte de Lorge, allegedly the longest-serving prisoner in the Bastille, in his cell, complete with chains and wax rats gorging on wax bread. The tableau would inspire Dickens; the Comte probably was the prototype for the character of Dr Manette in *A Tale of Two Cities*. Next to the Comte was an Egyptian mummy, a figure of Ravillac, Henry IV's assassin, and the shirt Henry 'had worn' when he had been stabbed. Regicide and political terror are joined with murder, as the figures of the Scottish serial killers and dealers in anatomical parts, Burke and Hare, were placed between that of Ravillac and a model of the Bastille.[24] This particular arrangement remained during the 1830s. By 1847 distinction between violence instigated by the state and 'private' murder, between popular, public disorder

[23] Chapman, *Madame Tussaud in England*, 24.

[24] *Biographical and Descriptive Sketches of the Whole Length Composition Figures and Other Works of Art Forming the Unrivalled Exhibition of Madame Tussaud* (1826), 35–40.

and individual transgression, crime and revolutionary politics—had become even thinner. In the separate collection, labelled a year earlier by *Punch* 'Chamber of Horrors', spectators passed from the Jacobin 'heads' to Ravillac, to the Scottish body-snatchers, then came directly upon a group of Old Bailey convicts, consisting of political conspirators and assassins and 'ordinary' murderers, and savoured the horror and thrill.[25] A *Punch* cartoon of 15 September 1849 captioned 'Madame Tussaud her Wax Werkes. Ye Chamber of Horrors!!' depicts a cluttered room, flanked with the heads and a replica of the Old Bailey, with a row of serial murderers standing in it. The crowd jamming the room consists of men, women, and children, facing the dock or poring over and literally hiding the tableau of the death of Marat. The slashing article attached to the cartoon is written in the form of an entry from the diary of a spectator, one Mr Pips, and is typical of *Punch*'s treatment of Tussaud's collection: 'Then to the Chamber of Horrors which my Wife did long to see most of all; . . . a Room like a dungeon where the Head of Robespierre, and other scoundrels of the French Revolution in wax, as though just cutt off ghastly and Plaster casts of fellows that have been hanged.'[26] This deliberate association between the female spectator and the sensational history of the Revolution (the cartoon too features women) is also typical. As I show later, Madame Tussaud's, like other museums and historical sites, was a heterosocial space, admitting mixed audiences. Unlike some of the older wax collections, which displayed nude and wax erotica, the new establishment determinedly guarded rules of respectability, shunning the display of the naked body (Marat's bare torso in his tub was the one exception). And unlike these older establishments it was deemed safe, and catered for, women and children and, indeed, the presence of women and families in shows and exhibitions reproducing the horrors and crimes of the past and present was sanctioned and deemed beneficial to the public at large. Pips lampoons the most recent attraction of the Chamber, the full-size model of the murderer James Bloomfield Rush and a replica of Rush farm, realistically restored 'as though the place were as famous as Waterloo'. 'Methinks it is of ill Consequence that there should be a Murderers Corner, wherein a villain may look to have his Figure put more certainly than a poet can to a Statue in the Abbey.'[27]

The analogy between the Chamber and a national monument (and the closest England had to a national pantheon) implies that the two sites are two complementary cultures and indeed two competing modes of popular memory and representation of the past. Notwithstanding the critique of the Chamber's glorification of crime, both *Punch* in the 1840s and other periodicals in the 1850s, notably Dickens's *Household Words* (from 1859 *All the Year Round*), rekindled popular attraction to the mixture of crime and history, danger and

[25] *Biographical and Descriptive Sketches of the Distinguished Characters which Compose the Unrivalled Exhibition of Madame Tussaud and Sons*, 'Chamber of Horrors' (1847), 27–8.
[26] MTA, press cuttings, *Punch*, 15 Sept. 1849. [27] Ibid.

sensationalism they so vehemently condemned. Inside the enlarged Chamber, which the Tussauds revamped in 1851, the line between 'private' crime and political violence was disappearing altogether. By 1860 Marat and the relics of the Revolution became surrounded by models of serial murderers. The model of the Bastille, which in English popular culture had initially stood for and symbolized coercion of any kind (it gave its name to the workhouses built after the New Poor Law of 1834), was placed next to the models of Stansfield Hall (the scene of the Rush murders) and Mrs Emley's house (where a number of murders took place). Next came a new full-size 'real' guillotine, complete with baskets receiving the chopped-off heads.[28] The guillotine was purchased in 1854 from Henri-Clément Sanson, of the Sanson dynasty of public executioners, Chief Executioner of Paris (just made redundant) and grandson of Charles-Henri Sanson, public executioner at the time of the Great Terror and whose cooperation Marie Tussaud and Curtius had enjoyed in 1793–4. It was displayed (and still is) with baskets full of severed heads. And it was the basis of a collection of instruments of killing and torture which the museum rapidly accumulated after the liquidation of the gallows and the older type of prison. Gallows, parts of historical prisons, notably Newgate, and even fittings of the Old Bailey, that symbol of the old penal system, were purchased between the 1850s and 1900s, together with instruments of torture.[29]

The awfulness and excitement of history as serial crime, a crime 'experienced' inside the Chamber, changed the meaning of the word horror itself. Its Latin original *horror* (plural *horrores*), denoting shaking, trembling, and shudder, associated with cold or 'chill', and extended to describe 'dread' and 'terror', proved untranslatable.[30] For 'shivering, by which it is translated, [was] too feeble an expression'.[31] And the physical sensations associated with the origin '[had] no actual synonyme [*sic*] in the English language'.[32] 'Horror' was rapidly anglicized. Until about the second quarter of the nineteenth century it denoted a physical sensation or feel, or even a kind of texture, usually shagginess or raggedness, and, increasingly, an inner sensation of repugnance or fear. When used in the plural, the word had often denoted a medical condition, a fit or, typically, *delirium tremens*, and referred to and was associated with drunkenness and alcoholism.[33] One such late use appears in Walter Besant's *The Demoniacs* in 1890.[34] All these meanings

[28] *Biographical and Descriptive Sketches of the Distinguished Characters which Compose the Unrivalled Exhibition and Historical Gallery of Madame Tussaud and Sons* (1869), 5.

[29] MTA, *Madame Tussaud and Sons' Catalogue*, 1872, 'Collection of Instruments of Torture'; Pilbeam, *Madame Tussaud and the History of Waxworks*, 179–80.

[30] C. T. Lewis, *An Elementary Latin Dictionary* (Oxford, 1891), 370.

[31] 'horror, n.' *Oxford English Dictionary*. MS slip, 1st edn. Superfluous. Oxford University Press Archives. Reproduced by permission. The citation is from *Monthly Magazine*, 54, p. 75.

[32] Ibid.

[33] *Oxford English Dictionary* (Oxford, 1933), v. 397. See also 1987 edn., p. 393.

[34] 'The common sort call them (the fits), simply, the Horrors', 'horror, n.': 'horrors' Oxford University Press Archives.

would persist until the end of the century. But from around the 1840s, 'horrors' acquired a new life and came to occupy a larger territory. Literally. The word was extended not just to feelings, indispositions, and emotions, but also to the material objects and places which were invested with the power of generating those sensations. The epithet 'Chamber of Horrors' stuck to Tussaud's, where the murderous and condemned, of the past and the present, were gazed and gaped at. But soon enough it was applied to parts of other museums, to Lloyd's Royal Exchange (on account of the notices of shipwrecks posted in it), and the warehouse at the public auctioneers Christie's.[35] Most significant, the sensations which proximity to places of horrors in the metropolis aroused now expanded to include not merely fear, repugnance, or disgust but kinds of pleasure which the spectacle of the horrid generated, such as thrill, joy, ridicule of the odd, grotesque, and awful, and wonder at the mystery of the dead or dying.[36] The winning combination of the horrible and pleasurable, so beloved by Dickens, and its association with a metropolitan and even imperial geography of sensationalism, persisted until the very end of the nineteenth century. In 1895 the *Success*, an Australian ex-convict vessel, retired from service as a floating imperial prison, moored in the East India Docks. The vessel was both an educative travelling exhibition of prison and policing and an awesome and thrilling reminder of the histories of its former criminal inhabitants. It virtually earned the title: 'Chamber of Horrors': '[It] had the distinction of housing some of the vilest scoundrels who ever lived, and which after exhibition in various Australian ports, has now been brought to England for the edification of the horror-loving Londoners.'[37]

In the long-term trend towards a 'criminalization' of the Revolution there is one break, between the early 1910s and late 1920s. This break may be attributed to the Tussauds' wish to incorporate the republican and Bonapartist tradition of Britain's chief ally in the First World War in a war-time version of the narrative of modern history. The war propaganda of the Entente pitted Franco-British liberty and democracy against German crimes and war horrors. During the war the revolutionary heads and the guillotine were moved to the Napoleon Rooms upstairs. By 1918 Fouquier-Tinville was found deserving enough to be installed next to Ferdinand de Lesseps, this paragon of Third Empire colonialism and Western technology. The Jacobin heads remained incorporated in the general narrative of French history until their final ejection to the Chamber of Horrors, after the rebuilding of the entire premises of the museum following the fire of 1927.[38]

35 'The flimsies record the lost and overdue vessels, and the place bears the gruesome and apt title "Chamber of Horrors" '; ibid.

36 Eric Partridge, *Slang and Unconventional English: Colloquialisms and Catch Phrases, Fossilized Jokes and Puns* (8th edn., London, 1984), 108 and 406; *Chambers's Twentieth-Century Dictionary*, ed. E. M. Kirkpatrick (Edinburgh, 1983), 510.

37 'horror, n'. (as in n. 31).

38 *Madame Tussaud and Sons, Catalogue for 1918–19*, 30: 1920; *Madame Tussaud and Sons, Official Guide and Catalogue*, 1928.

With the exception of this brief *entente cordiale*, the image of the first French republic as a site of crime and violence persisted. The written biographies of revolutionary figures, aimed at enhancing visual affect and augment in spectators the sensations associated with horror, stressed the villainy and criminality of republican leaders and of republican crowds. Thus the spectacle of a thrilling history of crime and punishment was designed to be experienced twice: through the cheap catalogues (in the form of biographical vignettes) read on the spot, and through looking. As Vanessa Schwartz and Kate Flint have indicated, and as Chapters 4 and 5 in this book amply demonstrate, the modern urban consumer of culture was assumed to have possessed a degree of literacy and to have travelled between literal and visual texts.[39] Cultural agents at large, and more specifically the impresarios of the burgeoning culture of spectacle and exhibition, assumed that reading (and a degree of knowledge acquired through it—in this case rudimentary knowledge of recent history) preceded 'seeing' and could 'programme' it. By the 1830s reading had become widespread among even the poorest in the metropolis and, as Louis James and Patricia Anderson have shown, the cultural horizon of the lower urban classes expanded enormously with the explosion of illustrated literature and journalism. The staple of this written culture was the complementary relationship of word and picture, or illustration.[40] This relationship characterized the broader urban culture which was a grid of references between written texts, pictorial images, and displayable objects described in these texts. The popular guidebook and catalogue massively resort to visual imagery, whose chief purpose is to 'illustrate' the historical objects, exhibited for all to see. The biographies did not carry drawings, but they provided concise historical information in a visual language. The relationship between reading a criminal history of the Revolution and 'seeing' the criminals, between text and the 'real', material bodies of dead historical agents, is well demonstrated in the representation of the three revolutionary figures best known in England: Maximilien Robespierre, Jean-Paul Marat, and Charlotte Corday.

'OF ALL THE HORRID MONSTERS': RECONSTRUCTING ROBESPIERRE

Of all the revolutionary figures, that of Maximilien Marie-Isidore de Robespierre (1758–94) probably aroused the greatest curiosity among nineteenth-century Britons. As Ben-Israel has noted, attitudes towards him wavered from unanimous horror, during the republican phase of the Revolution, to a nuanced and

[39] Schwartz, *Spectacular Realities*; Flint; *The Victorians and the Visual Imagination.*

[40] James, *Fiction for the Working Man*; Anderson, *The Printed Image and the Transformation of Popular Culture.*

rather complex approach towards the middle of the century.[41] Madame Tussaud's certainly did not reflect this shift and persisted in modelling him—figuratively and literally—not merely as murderous but also as monstrous. The visual language of the biographical sheets and catalogues is transparent. Significantly, their anti-revolutionary vocabulary is quite similar and almost interchangeable with that applied to crime. Robespierre, runs a typical text of 1826, had been a 'sanguinary demagogue', who

> employed the darkest intrigues to lead his opponents to the scaffold. Wishing to be declared a dictator, he hastened the death of the unfortunate Louis and his family... France was now filled with denunciations in every province and in every town tribunals were erected, which condemned alike the innocent and the guilty... Suspicious, timid and irresolute, the tyrant yet had sufficient art to interpret the machinations against his power, as treason against the republic, and to sacrifice his personal enemies as the most perfidious citizens in France... such was the influence of this monster, that France forgot the honor and religion at his command.[42]

In 1847, the wording is even stronger: 'Of all the horrid monsters who figured in the French Revolution none have descended to posterity with a name so abhorred as Robespierre... the crimes he committed were of so horrible a nature, that they have handed down his character to future ages, as the guiltiest of the guilty.'[43]

Five years later, Tussaud's *Economical Guide to London, Paris and Brussels Specifying the Cheapest Mode by which these Capitals May be Visited*, responding to the recent rise of popular tourism, advertises the Chamber of Horrors: 'Here are exact representations of many of the monsters of the French Revolution, Robespierre, Marat... from the casts taken by Madame Tussaud after they were decapitated.'[44] It is only towards the very end of the nineteenth century that the language of the biographies is mitigated. The evocation of revolutionary horrid monstrosity taps on popular sensationalism and fascination and obsession with the 'monstrous' and criminal. Human 'monsters' had been exhibited in popular fairs, 'peep shows', and 'raree shows' well before the nineteenth century and throughout this century became popular in ethnographic museums and exhibitions. Typically these monsters were 'freaks', with physiological deformities that rendered them exotic. Exoticism characterized colonial 'freaks' but could be easily applied to foreigners.[45] Robespierre and Fouquier-Tinville had the appeal of the human monster and criminal, but probably lacked the glamour of the well-known Newgate condemned whose fate did generate popular sympathy.

[41] Ben-Israel, *English Historians*, 165–70, 195–7.

[42] *Biographical and Descriptive Sketches* (1826), 35.

[43] *Biographical and Descriptive Sketches* (1847), 29–30.

[44] *Tussaud's Economical Guide to London, Paris and Brussels, Specifying the Cheapest Mode by which these Capitals May Be Visited* (London, 1852), 14.

[45] Raymond Corbey, 'Ethnographic Showcases, 1870–1930', in Jan Nederveen Pieterse and Bhikhu Parekh (eds.), *The Decolonization of Imagination: Culture, Knowledge and Power* (London and Atlantic Heights, NJ, 1995), 57–81.

Unlike the displayed English condemned, the French revolutionaries were, literally, de-formed, fragmented, and decapitated, as it was only their heads viewers could see (Robespierre's still is deformed by a scar).

It may well be argued that this kind of image was a popular and sensational version of Tory notions of the Revolution and Tory apprehension of political disorder and change. However, the popular image of Robespierre has one characteristic which marks it off from other conservative images: his sexualization and the association between lasciviousness and political motivation. Of course, an association between sexual and political transgression was a staple of anti-revolutionary propaganda from the very beginning of the events in France. Tory and evangelical writings made explicit analogies between disorderly and unregulated sexuality and gender and social disorder. The writings of Evangelicals like Hannah More and the vehement Tory reaction to Mary Wollstonecraft's writing on the Revolution, as well as her *Vindication of the Rights of Women* (dedicated to Talleyrand), are the most salient examples of this common association. Characteristically, as both Linda Colley and George Mosse have shown, it was women's transgression, rather than the disorderly behaviour of men, that conservative anti-revolutionism attacked.[46] The public and political activity of French women of all classes and parties, but especially of sans-culotte women, identified with extremist Jacobin politics, was condemned as particularly dangerous, as I show in the next two chapters. The sexualizing of male revolutionaries was less typical. More significant even, it was atypical of renditions of Robespierre. Even his most vehement detractors in England, who had stressed his dogmatism and cruelty, had commented on Robespierre's sexual morality and general incorruptibility. He was habitually described as virtuous, impeccable, and asexual. Thomas Carlyle's wonderful reference to him as 'Sea Green Incorruptible' immediately springs to mind.[47] It is against this backdrop that his sexualization, and that of all Jacobin males, acquires special meaning. In the Tussaud collection sensuality and lasciviousness were interpreted as the moving force of dangerous politics. The image of the revolutionary as a transgressor was effective because it was gendered and mediated through female figures cast as victims of the political upheaval. The point about Robespierre's own immorality was driven in through the full-size model of a sleeping Madame de Sainte-Amaranthe, allegedly a widow of a lieutenant in the guard of Louis XVI, 'killed at the attack on the Tuileries'. The royalist flower of female modesty rejected the Jacobin leader who had coveted her for a mistress and was therefore summarily brought to trial and guillotined. Unlike her persecutor, she has always been displayed in the main collection, together with other central female figures of the *ancien régime* like Marie-Antoinette herself and the Duchess of

46 Colley, *Britons*, 250–7; George L. Mosse, *Nationalism and Sexuality* (New York, 1985).

47 Thomas Carlyle, *The French Revolution, a History* (London, 1837; modern Library edn., New York, n.d.), 113, 320, 456.

Angoulême. And she is still to be found in the collection as a gently heaving 'sleeping beauty'.[48]

Female victimhood is further stressed by the association between virtuous aristocrats and the bourgeois Madame Tussaud: during much of the nineteenth century her own wax figure was placed together with the queen's at the head of the bed of the sleeping Madame de Sainte-Amaranthe. Moreover, she juxtaposed her own sexual innocence with the carnality of the male Jacobins. This juxtaposition is implied in her memoirs, in the episode of her being saved, from a fall, by Robespierre himself, during a tour of the dungeons of the Bastille, after the fortress's release on 14 July 1798. The future master of France (here inaccurately represented as partial to female youth and beauty) held the body of Marie Grosholtz to prevent her from falling and commented on the beauty of her neck—expressing his desire to save this part of her body from destruction. The reversal of the metaphor of the fall is probably unintended. But the prototypical character of the episode and similar ones is intentional, as well as the reversal of the relative roles of the powerful Robespierre and the powerless Grosholtz. The incident at the Bastille foretells the tyrant's doom and her control over his dead body: 'how little did Madame Tussaud then think that she should . . . have his severed head in her lap, in order to make a cast from it'. She allegedly took this cast, 'by order of the National Assembly', immediately after his execution.[49] The closeness of the victim and persecutor, between the perpetrator of the Great Terror and the woman involuntarily involved in it, is even more explicit in the interrelated biographies of Marat and his assassin Charlotte Corday, which in their turn are inextricable from Madame Tussaud's own.

'SHE LAID THE MONSTER DEAD AT HER FEET': MARAT'S DEATH

As with Robespierre, so with Jean-Paul Marat (1743–93): British history had moved from an almost unanimous condemnation in early writing on the Revolution towards a complex attitude. In popular political debate, notably in Chartist writing, Marat was presented as the 'friend of the people' (after his influential journal *L'ami du peuple*, appearing between September 1789 and September 1792 and his epithet) and became a model for a number of self-styled English and Irish republicans.[50] Madame Tussaud's was little affected by these subtle changes. Until the outbreak of the First World War the collection persisted in demonizing Marat the man and the politician. This demonization was potent because his assassination and the myth surrounding his death had, from

48 *Biographical and Descriptive Sketches* (1826), 26; (1847), 21.
49 Tussaud, *Madame Tussaud's Memoirs and Reminiscences*, ed. Hervé, 98.
50 Ben-Israel, *English Historians*, 98–115.

the start, been intertwined with the myth of Charlotte Corday, his assassin, so that their representations gendered the Revolution, its history and morals.

The assassination of Marat had attracted numerous artists, including Joseph Boze, Duplessis-Bertaux, who painted Corday calmly seated while awaiting her arrest, a number of anonymous French painters, and, most famously, Jacques-Louis David. In Britain, where Corday came to be an icon of 'good' Republicanism and anti-Jacobin liberty, she had a certain vogue immediately after the debacle of the 1848 revolution and the election of Louis Napoleon to France's President in December of that year. Her assassination of Marat and execution were popularized in biographical vignettes such as Julia Kavanagh, *The History of Women in France* (1850), and in historical paintings, notably Edward Matthew Ward's 'Charlotte Corday Led to her Execution', shown at the Royal Academy in 1852. Marie Tussaud's advantage over writers and artists was in the possibilities for naturalism and verisimilitude which her raw material offered, as well as in her first-hand acquaintance with the two protagonists while they had still been alive and after their violent death. She had access to Marat's corpse and Corday's severed head and claimed to have been summoned to the scene of the assassination to take Marat's mask. She took Corday's cast twice, once in prison and a second time, from the guillotined head, in the cemetery at La Madeleine. The tableau had been exhibited in Curtius's salon in Paris and brought by Madame Tussaud to Britain. Its location in the Chamber of Horrors and the printed versions of the assassination changed very little over time. Significantly, Marat's early career as a man of science and physician, including his long service to the *ancien régime*, were omitted from all the biographical vignettes and guidebooks. The fact that he had visited England frequently before the Revolution and had sought and received political asylum there too was omitted. Characteristic snippets from the biographical notes of 1826 depict him as 'one of the atrocious leaders of the Revolution', who

> Delighting in blood . . . promoted the murders of September [the September massacres of 1792] and, by repeated accusations, carried the most virtuous of the citizens to the Guillotine . . . This execrable wretch might still have added to the number of his victims, but a heroine rose in the world of his tyranny—Charlotte Corday and with a blow of the dagger she laid the monster at her feet.[51]

The allusion to the tyrant-slayers Deborah and Judith is quite transparent. What marks off descriptions of Marat from those of other revolutionaries is an excessive attention to physical detail that is unusual even for Madame Tussaud's writing and that initiated by the museum. The historical Marat easily rendered himself liable to such excess. He had cast himself as a revolutionary outcast who had abjured civility, domesticity, and middle-class values. As Simon Schama has elegantly put it, Marat had also 'made an art of this kind of confrontational

[51] *Biographical and Descriptive Sketches* (1826), 36.

ugliness'.[52] None of this was lost upon Marie Tussaud or her audiences. 'The worthless tyrant was in his person disagreeable and ferocious, he spoke with animation, but his looks betrayed the black purposes of his heart', states the biography of 1826. And, adds the memoir, he had been 'the most ferocious monster that the revolution ever produced'.[53] And there certainly had been none better qualified than Marie Tussaud herself to describe and judge him. For Marat had been a friend of Curtius and had sought asylum in his house (and hers) during the era of Girondin dominance. 'Short', 'with a fierce aspect', 'slovenly in dress', and 'dirty in person', 'coarse', and 'rude', Marat had affronted the young Marie Grosholtz's sense of propriety and modesty and, one might assume, those of her British middle-class patrons. His presence in her uncle's parlour and proximity to her are presented in the memoir as an assault. While haranguing on the Revolution, Marat rudely taps the young Marie on her shoulder with considerable 'roughness' and this infringement of decorum inside the middle-class house manifests 'some demonical possession'.[54] Yet the roughness makes the monster border on the ridiculous. The narrative of familiarity climaxes in the episode of the casting of the death mask, when an intimacy develops between the modeller and the cadaverous Marat and, vicariously, between him and the audience, aiming to produce 'horror': 'He [Marat] was still warm and his bleeding body and the cadaverous aspect of his almost diabolical features a picture replete with horror, and Madame Tussaud performed her task under the influence of the most painful emotions.'[55] This is exactly the kind of proximity between death and an implied eroticism that could appeal to Victorian audiences in the Chamber of Horrors and had been so central in the contemporary discourse on sexuality, violence, and death. This kind of titillation occasionally comes through and may be registered in descriptions of public executions, especially when the condemned are women, as Gatrell has argued.[56] But in the respectable Tussaud's collection the relationship between violent death and sexuality is reversed. It is not the women victims of terror who are eroticized but their male tormentors. The desexualizing of the dead female body and its obverse, the association between political corruption and male sexual corruption, is a testimony to the policy of keeping the collection respectable and compatible with Victorian morality. Victimization of women and their desexualization characterizes other contemporary historical displays, notably in the Victorian Tower of London, and will be touched on again in Chapter 4.

Madame Tussaud's Charlotte Corday presents an almost symmetrical opposite to Marat and, more broadly, to revolutionary men. She is heroic, a tyrant-slayer to Marat's tyrant, a modern Judith to his Holofernes, a beauty to the ugly beast, a paragon of female virtue to his sexuality, and a symbol of upright republicanism to his anarchism and extreme Jacobin politics. This

[52] Simon Schama, *Citizens: Chronicles of the French Revolution* (New York, 1989), 734.

[53] *Biographical and Descriptive Sketches* (1826), 37; Tussaud, *Madame Tussaud's Memoirs and Reminiscences*, ed. Hervé, 194–5.

[54] Ibid.

[55] Ibid. 199.

[56] Gatrell, *The Hanging Tree*, 264–5.

composite image clearly drew on conventional representations of Charlotte Corday in Britain, where she became an icon of liberty. Most British historians and biographers drew heavily on Alphonse de Lamartine's almost hagiographic rendering of her in his anti-Jacobin *Histoire des Girondins*. But sympathy with her cut across partisan politics and was never limited to supporters of Girondin politics, with which Corday had been identified. Though never a royalist icon, her kind of republicanism could be stomached and even idealized by staunch monarchists such as Madame Tussaud. Also noteworthy is the latter's admiration of Corday's 'unfeminine' characteristics and conduct, characteristics which are typically described in visual detail:

> [Madame Tussaud] found her a most interesting personage; she was tall and finely formed; her countenance had quite a noble expression; she had a beautiful colour, and her complexion was remarkably clear; her manners were extremely pleasing, and her deportment particularly graceful. Her mind was of a rather masculine order, fond of history, she had made it much her study, and naturally became deeply interested in the politics of her country; was a pure admirer of pure republican principles.[57]

THE GOLDEN ROOM: ANGLICIZING BONAPARTE

In contradistinction to the revolutionaries, Napoleon Bonaparte was admitted to Madame Tussaud's pantheon of heroes, and the entire period of his rule—from the first Directory through the Consulate and the First Empire until his final abdication in 1815—was painstakingly recovered for English audiences. The whole of this rule, but especially the decade of war between France and the Coalition headed by Britain, were represented and marketed as a part of the sequence of historical events from which the French Revolution was severed. By the middle of the nineteenth century, that most English institution was probably the world's biggest repository of Napoleonic memorabilia, far exceeding comparable collections in Bonapartist France and surpassing private British collections of Napoleoniana such as John Sainsbury's, which never enjoyed Tussaud's wide appeal.[58] Madame Tussaud, her sons, and later her grandsons helped initiate a popular cult of the emperor which anglicized Bonaparte, domesticated, and co-opted him in a British historical culture. Central to British politics during his rule, the deposed emperor was slowly rehabilitated and absorbed into popular culture after his demise and his cult had distinct material and commercial aspects as well as semi-religious ones. The museum became a shrine to his material remains. And as will become clear, these remains, like the emperor's death, were meant to produce responses that were quite different from those designed to be

[57] Tussaud, *Madame Tussaud's Memoirs and Reminiscences*, ed. Hervé, 338.

[58] On Sainsbury's collection see Stuart Semmel, *Napoleon and the British* (New Haven, 2004), 226–7.

generated by the revolutionaries/criminals. Here too was a lesson about crime and punishment, but this narrative was absorbed into a story of rise and decline which at one and the same time comfortably integrated Napoleon into England's military history and national mythology and, as Stuart Semmel has recently shown, rehabilitated him and made him 'inescapable in British culture'.[59]

The fact that Marie Tussaud's own career had been less embroiled in the Napoleonic regime than in the Revolution may account, albeit only partly, for her fascination with the Napoleonic phenomenon. She enjoyed the patronage of Josephine and, through her, that of the First Consul, who granted her permission to leave France for Britain before the collapse of the Peace of Amiens and the new outbreak of the Continental wars. Thus, at least in public opinion, she could not be directly connected with the anti-British regime which conspicuously lacked the legitimism of the traditional monarchy to which she consistently pledged her allegiance. Tableaux representing moments in the course of the rise and fall of Bonaparte became a fixture of the main collection from its early days in Britain. The tableaux of his coronation, based on David's famous painting, drew in large audiences well into the 1830s. It showed the Emperor, attired in the coronation robes, in the act of crowning himself, with Josephine kneeling beside him, surrounded by Cardinal Fesh, the Pope, and Roustan 'the loyal Mameluk'; the last figure, brought to London from the Paris salon, had an orientalist flavour which appealed to audiences. Orientalist stereotyping is apparent in the effusive report on the death of the original of the effigy of the 'loyal Mameluk', the 'historical' Roustan, in the *ILN* on 3 June 1846:

> Another name which belongs to history was just departed: it does not owe much perhaps to Clio, as to the muse, if there be one who presides over the recording of events by painting; in this respect, the name of Roustan, the Mameluke, is eminently historical. Who has not seen him amid the group of brilliant warriors of the staff always gathered round the Emperor in all the paintings of his battles . . . but writers neglect him.[60]

The 'history' of the faithful Mameluk echoes the earlier orientalist and exoticist strands in attitudes to Napoleon. The emperor himself had been exoticized. British political culture of the first half of the nineteenth century presents an extraordinary fascination with Napoleon's national and racial identity. Of Italian birth, but possessed of 'French national character', 'half African and half European', a 'Corsican Mulatto', a hybrid between Western ambition and Eastern rapacity, this identity was intriguingly undecidable. Apparent contradictions in his characterization point at a broader difficulty to classify Napoleon as simply a foe. Even before Waterloo he had been depicted as despot and emancipator, emperor and Jacobin (and even a democrat), as driven by boundless ambition, and the victim of his own power. After his exile to St Helena, his historical role and status became more disputable. This disputability

[59] Ibid. [60] *ILN*, 3 Jan. 1846, p. 5.

generated a cross-class appeal and even sympathy towards the fallen hero, mixed with curiosity about the strange and foreign. And the mingling of exoticism, pity, and awe was central to the process of Napoleon's integration in popular culture and may explain how he became 'unescapable in British culture precisely because he was so variously useful'.[61] The biographical vignettes and 'historical' publications distributed by the Tussauds use superlatives which stress Bonaparte's status in the popular historical imagination as a hero on a titanic scale; at the same time his fall from grandeur exudes pity. The biographies routinely assume prior knowledge about the contradictions within his life and meteoric rise and fall, even among the least educated:

> The incidents of his life are so well known to Europe, that it is unnecessary to detail them... No other age, nor country has produced a more astonishing man... unlike his person which was small, his mind was that of a giant. Like the eagles, his favourite emblem, he towered above the common race of men. But the sun of his glory which rose so bright, is set forever.[62]

Here lay part of Bonaparte's enduring attraction and the explanation for his incorporation in the historical imagination. The titan became a victim, 'an object of pity'. His role in European and English history was represented and celebrated in tableaux showing the 'principal actors of the War' (the Continental and Peninsular Wars of 1803–15) because his demise had been engineered by Britain. Unlike the Revolution, which, notwithstanding its 'domestication' in popular culture, still retained the notions of social danger and public and private crime (and would retain them till the end of the nineteenth century), the dead Bonaparte and the Napoleonic threat could be accommodated within an English narrative of victory, and appeal across parties and classes. Undoubtedly Bonaparte was completely anglicized. The new rooms, opened in 1843, were aggressively advertised as a storing place for the preservation of his relics, 'forming a series of national reminiscences of great interest'. The dead Emperor was not simply attached to a collective British memory. His history and that of his times 'is so much mixed up with this country as to be almost one'.[63] Or as the catalogue put it in 1869: 'It is almost needless to say that everything connected with the late Emperor Napoleon belongs to British History.'[64]

His naturalization as a British hero is easily discernible in the organization of the Museum's contents and space. The Tussauds made him not only an attractive part of a realistic spectacle, but the subject of a constantly expanding collection of memorabilia which grew into the world's main repository of Napoleonic objects. The collection, started in the 1800s, really took off in the early 1830s, with the move to London. That there was a market for such

61 Semmel, *Napoleon and the British*, 7 and 35.

62 *Bibliographical and Descriptive Sketches* (1826), 9.

63 'Madame Tussaud and Sons' New Room: Relics of the Emperor Napoleon' (1843), Pamphlet, MTA.

64 *Biographical and Descriptive Sketches* (1869), 30.

historical memorabilia is, in itself, proof of a widespread fascination with their subject, bordering on a 'Napoleon mania'. In 1834 the Tussauds purchased his Eagles in a public auction of 'Napoleon's Spoils', for a little over £12. In addition they acquired the carriage in which he had fled from Waterloo, assorted furniture kept by the emperor after his abdication, and items of dress and other personal paraphernalia, which made up the nucleus of Napoleon's Rooms. In 1847 the main room, the newly opened 'Golden Chamber', was advertised as a 'New Room with a camp bed, Regalia of France, the Coronation Robes of Napoleon and Josephine Bonaparte, Girandoles, Clock and Candelabra from Malmaison, the Figure of Napoleon from the best authority—David, the celebrated flag of Alba.'[65]

The imperial insignia were, or could be, presented and seen as trophies, collected by the victorious British. Yet the Tussauds were after more than just 'spoils' of wars and the insignia of public power. They obsessively acquired personal and everyday objects used by the emperor in his daily routine: his watch, his ring, dessert knife, fork, and spoon, a pair of socks, a Madras handkerchief, an under neck-handkerchief, a shirt, drawers, a toothbrush.[66] These ordinary everyday objects, all with a direct contact with the dead emperor's body, helped domesticate the recent historical drama and 'embody' the historical memory, all the while attaching the everyday to death. Significantly, the new national cult had distinct religious—almost Catholic—elements, remarkable in a Protestant country. Already in 1843, 'the counterpane of the camp bed on which he died, marked with his blood' drew thousands of visitors.[67] It added to the collection an aura of sanctity, making it a shrine as well as an *omnium gatherum* of things representing the glorious, the curious, and the mundane. A prize item, the Waterloo carriage, was acquired at bargain price from William Bullock, who had exhibited it at the Egyptian Hall, Piccadilly, where it had attracted some 800,000 visitors. The ever increasing collection was arranged in 'authentically' decorated rooms, designed in 1869 after the plans of the emperor's own artists, Sattey and Fontaine, at the cost of £13,000.[68]

The tableaux, trophies, and relics seemed real and convincing not only because of their high verisimilitude, but also and precisely because of the very materiality of the clutter of historical objects which were 'ordinary' things, belonging to those dead and alive. Thus unlike the world of the Revolution, which was recreated around the prison, the guillotine, and instruments of torture, the imperial world of Bonaparte had a material density about it which evoked everyday life in the past. This was by no means an ordinary life; but it contained enough material traces of the mundane and the usable, and their density was communicated through the sheer number of highly symbolic personal and public objects. As Asa Briggs has noted, the Victorian world was a distinctly material 'world of things'. Objects,

65 *Biographical and Descriptive Sketches* (1847), 26–7.
66 Madame Tussaud and Sons' New Room, Pamphlet (1843), MTA. 67 Ibid.
68 *Biographical and Descriptive Sketches* (1869), 30.

used and usable in everyday life, and an abundance of impractical gadgets inhabited both the Victorian middle-class house and the new 'world of exhibition', embodied in public museums and galleries and apotheosized in 'the great exhibition of things' in Crystal Palace in 1851.[69] The spread of mass consumption also began to fill the material world of the urban working classes with objects that had not been easily afforded before. The visibility of 'things' and their display to mass audiences was part and parcel of the new culture of commodity and mass consumption, characterized by new forms of advertising that catered for large and varied audiences of urban tourists. Exhibited objects thus were commodified and their commodification had to do with the symbolic value they contained rather than their purely economic value of exchange.[70] As commodities which had no tags and were not purchasable, these exhibits became fetishized commodities with a special aura. But the Napoleonic objects discussed here, just like the Tudor 'things' which jammed the Tower of London and will be discussed in Chapters 4 and 5, were neither commodities, nor fetishized objects, nor goods. These objects had a market value, a symbolic value, and use value. Amongst collectors (like the Tussauds themselves), authenticity and value were especially important and were constantly hyped as both a feature and a proof of historical status. A typical pamphlet reads:

> Madame Tussaud and Sons, anxious in everything in their power to render their exhibition interesting to their liberal supporters, respectfully state, that, in adding the relics of the Emperor Napoleon, they have had in view the instruction of Youth in particular, which is imbibed in everything connected with history; and as that of Napoleon is so much mixed up with this country as to be almost one, they have not hesitated in embarking a large sum to endeavor that gratification to their frequenters, knowing that relics, when well authenticated, bring the period to which they belong immediately to the imagination . . .[71]

The Tussauds had every displayed object confirmed as 'authentic' at the Court of Chancery, and traced and advertised the history of the ownership of newly acquired items.

To audiences the memorabilia symbolized an array of images, beliefs, and meanings that together made up the dense grid of a material historical culture, a proof of Britain's superiority and the all-inclusive character of English history—a history that could absorb that of the country's chief rival in a transnational pantheon. But these memorabilia had uses beyond the vaguely symbolic: they were physically accessible to visitors. Tussaud's allowed exhibits to be touched, thus becoming a very early example of 'hands on' history. Another such example is, of course, the Tower of London, where the materiality of most displayed

[69] Asa Briggs, *Victorian Things* (Chicago, 1989), 11–51, 53–102.

[70] On the symbolic value of commodities and on the exhibitionary order see Thomas Richards, *The Commodity Culture of Victorian England Advertising and Spectacle, 1851–1914* (London, 1991) and Tony Bennett, 'The Exhibitionary Complex', in Boswell and Evans (eds.), *Representing the Nation: A Reader*, 332–63.

[71] 'Madame Tussaud and Sons' New Room', MTA.

objects generated audiences' exchanges with traces of the past.[72] Napoleonic objects were not just touchable but usable. Visitors could climb into Napoleon's carriage and have a sit and make themselves comfortable in it, enacting the dramatic historical event yet making do with it within their own daily experience. Thus whole families picnicked in the carriage; others filched 'souvenirs'—stripes of its dark red upholstery.[73] The ordinariness of the response to Napoleon and its material aspects were astutely captured by and lampooned by Cruikshank in a couple of cartoons depicting the crowds covering the carriage at Bullock's rooms and the Tussauds' wax figures coming into life in a dance led by the emperor and Madame Tussaud herself in a plebeian saloon's setting.[74]

What smoothed Bonaparte's entry into and uses within British historical culture was the association between him and Britain's most illustrious military hero: Arthur Wellesley, Duke of Wellington. Like his French adversary the duke was the subject of spectacle. More significantly, he was a principal actor in the emerging metropolitan world of exhibitions and shows. A close look at their related roles and especially at Wellington's double role as spectator and the subject of historical spectacle may illustrate not only strategies of display but also common Victorian procedures of spectatorship. To this day, visitors may see a full-size model of the seated duke, gazing at the dying Napoleon. To early Victorian spectators he was easily visible—in image and real life. In the itinerant show in 1826 he was part of the 'Coronation Group'. In the collection's permanent London location in the Bazaar on Portman Square, the Duke was elevated to the centrepiece of the first tableau in the Great Room, 'in honour of Her Majesty and the Illustrious Duke of Wellington', showing the queen and Prince Albert 'offering to the hero the honours he so well deserves'.[75] Visitors of all classes were well aware that the duke's extraordinarily long career had been inextricably associated with Bonaparte's. Both were born on the same year, attended military schools, were their countries' chief soldiers, and made and 'un-made' each other. As the victor of the Peninsular Wars of 1804–14 and Waterloo in 1815, as Commander of the British occupying forces in France between 1815 and 1818, Wellington had been identified by contemporaries as the chief agent of the Emperor's demise and fall.[76] He had also been responsible for the moderate approach towards post-revolutionary France, which he saw as a part of the conservative Restoration policy on the Continent. In terms of domestic politics he had been, at least until the late 1830s, a staunch Tory, vehemently opposing reform, and had been identified in popular culture as a symbol of tyranny. His deep suspicion of urban mobs determined his trenchant objection to the democratization of access to such national monuments as the Tower of London.

[72] See Ch. 4, pp. 144–5. [73] Pilbeam, *Madame Tussaud*, 115. [74] Ibid. 110, 115.

[75] *Biographical and Descriptive Sketches* (1847), 26–7.

[76] Iain Pears, 'The Gentleman and the Hero: Wellington and Napoleon in the Nineteenth Century', in Roy Porter (ed.), *Myths of the English* (London, 1992), 216–36; Norman Gash (ed.), *Wellington: Studies in the Military and Political Career of the First Duke of Wellington* (Manchester, 1990); and Elizabeth Longford, *Wellington: the Years of the Sword* (London, 1969).

Yet already during his old age Wellington was transformed into a quintessential national historical hero and a symbol of the people. As an adulating *Gentleman's Magazine* put it in October 1852: 'In all that has singled out England from the nations of the world, the Duke of Wellington was emphatically an Englishman.'[77] And of all living politicians no other personified more the association between the present and the past. Alive, the duke was a monument of English history seen as a series of great military deeds and grandeur. Dead, he became an even more enshrined piece of history. His funeral was carefully constructed as a historical spectacle which combined a display of continuity on the one hand, drawing as it did on the funerals of Cromwell, Marlborough, and Nelson, and modernity on the other. The funeral was so full of allusions to the past that it was regarded by many as archaic and even anachronistic.[78] Over one and a half million spectators were brought to London by trains to watch the duke's departure to St Paul's Cathedral. The duke's and Britain's French connections were there for all to comment upon: twelve years earlier Bonaparte's ashes were ceremoniously put under the dome of Les Invalides. And Louis Napoleon, Bonaparte's nephew, would be crowned emperor of France a little less than a year after Wellington's death. Significantly, the duke's historical role was inextricable from the central role he played in the evolution of London to a centre of the culture of spectacle. The funeral trains unpacking their cargo in the city were quite reminiscent of the trains which had just unloaded the millions of spectators who had come for the Great Exhibition at the Crystal Palace. While alive he took an active part in the development of the very order of spectacle and exhibition, including the Great Exhibition. He was responsible for the establishment of the London Zoo in Regent's Park and supported all kinds of movements for the foundation of indoor museums. He himself was an exemplary spectator, regularly riding in the streets of the city and dropping into public places. Unlike the archetypal *flaneur*, or city stroller described in English and French urban texts, his perambulations were purposeful and his visits to public shows focused. As Richard Altick has wittily commented, the duke would have been the proverbial 'frequent visitor' of our era.[79] He was a faithful and useful patron of Madame Tussaud's, which he regularly visited, and had been immensely attracted to the French displays in the collection, most notably the Napoleonic ones. And visitors would come across him gazing at his dead

[77] *Gentleman's Magazine*, Oct. 1852, p. 423.

[78] Pears, 'The Gentleman and the Hero', 219–20.

[79] A shortlist of studies on the *flaneur* should include Walter Benjamin, *Charles Baudelaire: A Lyric Poet in the Era of High Capitalism*, trans. Harry Zohn (London, 1983); Keith Tester (ed.), *The Flaneur* (New York, 1994); Susan Buck-Morss, *The Dialectics of Seeing: Walter Benjamin and the Arcades Project* (Cambridge, Mass., 1989). For a consideration of the *flaneur* in the British context and especially in relation to London see Judith Walkowitz, *City of Dreadful Delight: Narratives of Sexual Danger in Late Victorian London* (Chicago, 1992), 15–41 and Nead, *Victorian Babylon*. Both provide a gender perspective.

adversary. Thus the duke was a visitor/spectator, while himself constituting a 'display', part of the historical spectacle (recall his various life-size effigies). And looking at the real-life duke was difficult to distinguish from gazing upon his likenesses. Quite often he could be looked at looking at his own wax image, or gazing upon other historical characters. Thus the very act of looking performed by a historical living symbol of British dominance not only sanctioned and ritualized the spectacle of history, but possibly transferred the duke's aura to Napoleon.[80]

CONSUMPTION AND DISTINCTION: AUDIENCES AND THE REVOLUTION

Clearly the Duke of Wellington does not represent the ordinary consumer of Tussaud's historical package; nor do the bouncing customers trying the springs of Napoleon's carriage and immortalized by Cruikshank. Although both types of spectators throw light on the relationship between historical objects, modes of seeing and making do with them, and cultural consumption, their roles need placing within broad and long-term patterns of access to the collection and spectators' experiences. Extant information that has survived in the Tussauds' records about attendance and early audiences is very rudimentary. Long-term sequences of actual figures of visitors are unavailable (partly due to the theft, some years ago, of the relevant ledger book) or patchy, and direct verifiable data are confined to the first itinerant years of Madame Tussaud and to the twentieth-century inter-war period.[81] It appears that the museum skirted the one million figure per year about the same time as the Tower of London did (around the end of the nineteenth century and the beginning of the twentieth), or a little later. The reopening of the rebuilt museum in 1928 after a fatal fire brought in 965,818 admittances and 235,322 admittances to the new cinema added to the premises, the former a peak figure which subsequently slightly slumped.[82] For the long stretch in between we may conjecture. But we may make use of the scattered evidence in the catalogues, guidebooks, and the press, which makes it possible to glean valuable details, adding up to a broad view of audience composition and habits, as well as pointing at the structure of the popular culture of history and at its accessibility to individuals, groups, and classes.

Marie Tussaud, her sons, and their descendants continuously sought royal and aristocratic patronage and clientele, as both were vital for securing commissions and safeguarding a royalist reputation. During its early decades the collection

80 Pilbeam, *Madame Tussaud*, 119.

81 Kornmeier's estimates for the 1800s is of 100 visitors per day and between fifty and 130 a day for the 1810s—perhaps impressive for a provincial venue of entertainment but rather poor in comparison with London shows. I am grateful to her for making the figures available to me.

82 Exhibition Admittances, MTA.

boasted the patronage of members of the royal family as well as generations of Bourbons—dead and alive, including ultra-conservatives like the Comte d'Artois, later Charles X (1821–30). The published list of patrons announcing the opening of the permanent show at the Bazaar boasts of the support of 'the Universities of Oxford and Cambridge; the Persian Princess; the Foreign ambassadors, and . . . most of the Nobility and Gentry' and, last, 'the Public', a somewhat hazy and mobile term.[83] High patronage of this kind was capitalized upon to manufacture a desirable snob appeal, to attract the middling sort in the early nineteenth century, and the respectable during the early Victorian era. Note the wording of the 1846 advertisement for a new tableau of court life: 'A magnificent display of court Dresses of surpassing richness, comprising 25 Ladies and Gentlemen's costumes intended to convey to the Middle Classes an idea of the Royal Splendour; a most splendid novelty and calculated to display to young persons much necessary instruction.' The all too obvious snob appeal was not lost on contemporary satirists. *Punch*, quicker than most to register the tonalities of middle-class language, trounced the Tussauds, suggesting that the collection would also 'include specimens of the Irish peasantry, the handloom weavers, and other starving portions of the population, all in their characteristic tatters; and also inmates of the various workhouses in the ignominious garb presented to them by the Poor Law'.[84]

Yet clearly audiences had never been comprised of the upper and middle classes alone. Ceroplastic culture is one exemplar of the overlapping of forms of 'high' and 'low' tastes and spectatorship. Already in Paris Curtius and Grosholtz had built on precisely this mixture of elite and popular entertainment. Once in Britain, the collection persistently catered for working-class audiences, which had developed a taste for wax shows in fairs and in indoor exhibits. It may appear that Tussaud's embodied the trend towards a democratization of the museum, conventionally seen now as a salient development of the latter. Put differently, the collection may be seen to have offered universal and indiscriminate access to the past. However, this democratization, noted by Schwartz and others, was quite limited. While the policy was to draw in plebeian audiences, distinctions were made between and among classes of spectators, cultural distinctions which corresponded, albeit not in a strictly reflective manner, to class differences and dispositions. Pierre Bourdieu's definition of 'distinction' may be usefully applied here critically and extended back in time, to the early and mid-nineteenth century, and 'spatially', across different forms and fields of culture.[85] The principal of distinction within culture and taste which, he has argued, separated 'high' elite culture from popular (and mainly workers') culture and

[83] 'The Opening of the Show in the Bazaar, Portman Square with New Decoration at the Golden Corinthian Room' (1837), Pamphlet, MTA.

[84] Cited in Leslie and Chapman, *Madame Tussaud*, 170–1.

[85] Schwartz, *Spectacular Realities*, 32. For Bourdieu see *Distinction* and Jen Webb, Tony Schirato, and Geoff Danaher, *Understanding Bourdieu* (London, 2002).

duplicated class difference, here did not operate within a quality 'high' culture of connoisseurs excluding the 'masses' (as undoubtedly would be the case in the twentieth-century museum of modern art which directly interested him), but within a popular culture of spectacle. Spectacle was thrown open to the 'respectable' and monitored the rest. At the same time that Tussaud's invited in working people, it created audience segregation and until the last third of the nineteenth century effectively limited, or perhaps even excluded, working people. These parallel processes of inclusion and exclusion are, as I argue throughout the book, a saliency of the democratized Victorian popular culture, more specifically of the culture of history.

Probably the simplest and most common form of exclusion and segregation between audiences was the invention of a working peoples' fee, which, in the first place, aimed at drawing them in. From their very beginnings in Britain, Madame Tussaud's introduced a flexible scale of fees which combined a working people's fee with flexible and long opening hours. It was among the first cultural institutions to offer the package of reduced admission fees and long opening hours to attract popular urban audiences. Late opening had long been a characteristic of popular venues such as the fair and the public house, but would be adopted only partially and rather belatedly in other London museums and in monuments. Thus in Portsmouth in 1830 (and most probably earlier) Tussaud's announced that

> considering that a large class of persons are unavoidably excluded from viewing the Collection, in consequence of the pressure of time, they have made arrangements to admit
>
> The Working Class
> During the Time the Exhibition Remains
> For Half Price
> From Quarter before nine till ten in the evening; By this arrangement sufficient time will be given for both classes to view the Collection without interfering with each other, and they hope that none but those situated will take advantage of it, as, if known, they will be refused.[86]

The reduced 'working class fee' amounted to 6*d.* The almost embarrassingly straightforward policy of segregation is somewhat complicated by the awareness that, quite commonly, it was the respectable middle-class audiences that benefited most from the attempts to attract urban workers and the urban poor to the newly emerging forms of spectacle aiming at cultural improvement. There hardly seems another way of interpreting the hope that 'none but those situated will take advantage of it'. And this interpretation may also be supported by what we know about the massive use middle-class audiences made of cheap and free days during the Great Exhibition.[87]

[86] 'Last Week but one Exhibition Promenade', Pamphlet, MTA.

[87] See Jeffrey A. Auerbach, 'Exhibiting the Nation: British National Identity and the Great Exhibition of 1851' (Ph.D. diss., Yale University, 1995) 314–23.

In 1852, following the renovation of the premises in Portman Square, the museum stayed open from eleven in the morning until eleven at night in the summer, and from seven in the morning until five in the afternoon, then from seven until ten in winter, and was easily accessible by public omnibuses, which carried huge advertisements hyping the show. The price, reduced to one shilling, plus an additional sixpence for the Napoleonic rooms and the Chamber of Horrors, with half price for children, was lower than the Tower's Armouries alone. Remarkably long opening hours made Tussaud's accessible in theory to the working classes, certainly to the respectable working classes, a fact recognized in the *Tussaud's Economical Guide to London*, which points out that the collection 'contains objects of interest to suit all tastes', adding that 'there is also among certain classes an intense curiosity to view the Chamber of Horrors'.[88] The curiosity of the uninitiated and unrespectable was lampooned by such observers as Dickens, who targeted not so much metropolitan lower-class audiences but provincial ones, as in the following pastiche, describing an uncouth youth consuming a pork pie in the French part of the Chamber of Horrors: 'His eye was on the model of Marat as assassinated in a bath and with this before him he could eat an under-done pork pie! It is the last straw that breaks the camel's back; it was this last horror that sent your eyewitness out of Madame Tussaud's as fast as his legs would carry him!'[89] What Dickens is disgusted at is not the persistence of habits and forms of conduct characteristic of more traditional urban culture (of all classes), where eating and drinking had not been rigorously separated from spectatorship and viewing. He is ostensibly appalled by the proximity of the everyday (eating) and the horrible: the pork pie and the likeness of the dead Marat. But it was precisely this kind of proximity which made the collection so appealing to audiences.

Distinction did not aim only at replicating social stratification, but was also used throughout the nineteenth century to elaborately reconstruct gender. The new commercial culture of history, indeed nineteenth-century urban culture itself, was potentially and, as this book seeks to show, in practice a gender-mixed one, inhabiting what G. J. Barker-Benfield has usefully described as a heterosexual space, open to both men and women.[90] Unlike specific spaces designed for urban consumers such as the shopping arcade and later in the nineteenth century the department store, which were increasingly feminized, the space of the public art gallery, the museum, the public park or garden (distinguished from the unrespectable pleasure gardens) and the monument was open to women and children. Although, as already mentioned, early wax shows were considered improper places for women, Tussaud's aura of respectability made it a safe place for women and children, mainly because it avoided anatomical and

[88] *Tussaud's Economical Guide to London, Paris and Brusselsn* (1852), 14.

[89] Pauline Chapman, *Madame Tussaud's Chamber of Horrors* (London, 1984), 86.

[90] G. J. Barker-Benfield, *The Culture of Sensibility: Sex and Society in Eighteenth-Century Britain* (Chicago, 1992), 95–6.

pornographic displays. Violence and horror crossed the gender barrier and the barrier of age. To be sure, the Chamber of Horrors was continuously and vehemently criticized for its unsavoury contents and apparent glorification of crime, most vigorously and continuously by *Punch* in 1846 and in Dickens's *Household Words* and *All the Year Round* between 1854 and 1860. But characteristically this kind of criticism was general, attacking the Chamber as unfit for all kinds of viewers. Moreover, the most vehement critics of violence were attracted to it. The awfulness of the Revolution and the Terror were at least as compelling as the military splendour of the First Empire. Precisely this mixture of attraction and repellence characterizes Dickens's obsession with the Chamber. As George Augustus Sala reported in 1884, Dickens continuously attempted to convince young reporters that they should spend the night there and record their impressions.[91]

Notwithstanding occasional criticism of certain revolutionary items, the underlying premiss that the Revolution was a horror and the past a site of violence was not shaken. Moreover, through representations of the Revolution, the irresistible appeal of horror was admitted into the spheres of respectability and was domesticated. From at least the 1830s, the collection in its entirety was developed as a family entertainment, offering instruction in history as well as entertainment. Illustrations repetitiously feature a mixed audience, of men, women, and young children (I have in mind the *Punch* illustration discussed earlier). From early on Tussaud's stressed the didactic and educational potential of the moralizing view of the past as a history of crime and punishment. Stress on the morals to be learnt from history served to counter accusations that the Chamber of Horrors corrupted youth. As early as 1826, the catalogue notes the educational potential of the museum: 'convey[ing] to the minds of young persons, such biographical knowledge—a branch of education universally allowed to be of the highest importance'. By the 1850s the deterring power of the spectacle of horror was stressed. Joseph Rendal Tussaud renamed the Chamber of Horrors 'The Chamber of Comparative Physiognomy', no doubt playing on the popularity and authority of physiognomy as a scientific method and register of inner morals.[92] As the century progressed family attendance was put to the fore in special children's catalogues. *A Visit to Madame Tussaud's* by J. E. Hawkins, issued in 1876, features Mabel and George visiting the museum with their mother. One illustration shows the figures of Marie-Antoinette and Louis XVI, flanked by Voltaire, a French Coquette, and Joan of Arc, gazed upon by the small family group and groups of children, unaccompanied by grown-ups, a sure sign of the safety of the museum. By the early twentieth century the Chamber of Horrors became utterly respectable and was deemed 'educational'. The latter role was sanctioned in April 1929 when the Instruction Film Company made a film,

[91] *ILN*, 19 July 1884, no. 2361, vol. lxxxv, p. 51.
[92] Chapman, *Madame Tussaud's Chamber of Horrors*, 83.

the first of many, entitled 'The Chamber of Horrors, Historical Crime and Punishment'.[93]

A showcase of the emerging culture of history, the Tussauds' collection may serve to illustrate the overlapping of different, albeit inseparable, older forms of sensationalism and spectatorship and newer modes of audience participation in and usages of the past. The collection drew on the economies of culture production and consumption that had developed in both the older culture of representation of old-regime Europe and the urban popular tradition of the eighteenth and early nineteenth centuries. And as the latter century progressed, it cultivated features of the commercialized culture of history which I call multiple or chain consumption and study in some detail in Parts II and III. Here we have noted the proximity, adjacency even, of reading and viewing histories of the Revolution and touching its material traces and relics. Moreover, these three related forms of use of the past were connected to the wide access to an urban repertoire of crime and punishment available to all classes, both a vast cross-class literary repertoire, describing histories of criminals and their punishment, and the visibility of the gallows and public executions. The evolving culture studied here also accommodated a combination of a cosmopolitan and transnational tradition (the art of ceroplastics, which proved popular both in Britain and France), thus expanding our notion of what constituted a national history, the exoticism of and fascination with a foreign history (the French past), and the complete and successful domestication of this history in the English past. For the Duke of Wellington to become a 'world historical' hero, there was a need of a Napoleon. Inside the Museum and outside it, the two figures became so complementary that they could 'cancel out' each other. The naturalization of French history became complete with the elevation of the foreign, female, and slightly exotic Madame Tussaud to a national institution. As the ever observant George Augustus Sala shrewdly put it in 1905: 'although the exhibition has long since come to be regarded as an essentially British Institution as English as the National Gallery or the Crystal Palace—what may be termed the nucleus of Madame Tussaud's is considerably older than the last century... with the episodes and personages of the Revolution, equally with the scenes and characters of the Consulate and Empire, the Exhibition must ever be indissolubly associated'.[94] Thus as much as the study of Madame Tussaud's history throws open definitions of popular history and popular culture, it opens up definitions of the national as native and admits the foreign, cosmopolitan, and global, as we shall also see in Part III. Last but first is the sustained appeal of the Revolution as an 'appalling' and

[93] *A Visit to Madame Tussaud's* (London, 1876), no pagination; Chapman, *Madame Tussaud's Chamber of Horrors*, 223.

[94] Sala, 'Historic Notes on Madame Tussaud', in *Madame Tussaud's Exhibition Guide*, 3.

horrifying place: the horror of history contained and represented in a chamber whose title carried this very adjective had the power of defining a mixture of attraction and repulsion. The uncomfortable, terrifying version of the past was so titillating because it could and was facilely associated with the social, with the urban display and spectacle of the criminal and his/her punishment.

2

History as a Panorama: Spectacle and the People in Thomas Carlyle, *The French Revolution*

CURTIUS'S BUSTS

If anyone would have recognized the role wax shows and models came to play in the expanding and democratized urban culture and in popular politics, it would have been Thomas Carlyle. For him, ominous historical changes, involving the appearance of new actors on a distinctly urban scene, begin in the French Revolution. He breaks off his account of the days before the storming of the Bastille, pauses and ruminates on the revolutionary crowd's parading Curtius's busts of Jacques Necker, France's Controller-General, and the Duc d'Orléans, the king's revolutionary brother. It is 12 July 1789 and France

> So long shaken and wind-parched, is probably at the right inflammable point. – As for poor Curtius, who, one grieves to think, might be but imperfectly paid, – he cannot make two words about his images. The Wax-bust of Necker, the Wax-bust of D'Orléans, helpers of France; these covered with crape, as in funeral procession, or after the manner of suppliants appealing to Heaven, to Earth, and Tartarus itself, a mixed multitude bears off. For a sign! As indeed man, with his singular imaginative faculties, can do little or nothing without signs: thus Turks took their Prophet's Banner; also Osier *Mannikins* have been burnt, and Necker's Portrait has erewhile figured, aloft on its perch. In this manner march they, a mixed, continually increasing multitude; armed with axes, staves and miscellanea; grim, many-sounding, through the streets.[1]

The passage, from his *French Revolution*, is located in the chapter entitled 'To Arms', immediately after a description of Camille Desmoulins, journalist, orator, and future Jacobin leader, haranguing an audience to invade the 'image shop' of the wax modeller and take over the streets of Paris.

Characteristically, Carlyle writes in the 'dramatic present' to convey to his readers the presence of the past. His eye, and that of the reader, roves across Paris, from the Palais-Royal to the Café de Foy, the scene of Desmoulins's

[1] All quotes are from Thomas Carlyle, *The French Revolution, a History*, I, V, IV, p. 140.

speech, to the Boulevard du Temple, the site of Curtius and Marie Tussaud's Caverne des Grands Voleurs, to the Tuileries Gardens, to the Hôtel de Ville. The stations in his urban panorama were, even as early as July 1789, venues of a new kind of popular politics as well as being places of entertainment and of the emerging consumption of culture that cut across social divides. The Palais-Royal was a hive of revolutionary propaganda and the centre of a highly politicized industry of pornography. The Boulevard du Temple, the scene of protest and fighting, was the abode of cheap shows and exhibitions—notably the 'original' Tussaud wax collection. The juncture of popular revolutionary action, urban spectacle, and forms of observation of the urban environment illustrates a broader preoccupation which informs the *French Revolution* and, more broadly, the early nineteenth-century culture of history. As with the material traces and representations of the Revolution in Tussaud's, so with Carlyle a main concern is the visual aspect of history and the role and function of the historians and their audiences as spectators and producers of spectacles. But Carlyle is not just an observer; he is a surveyor and a 'seer'. Nineteenth-century readers noted that his magisterial work was a scenic history with the characteristics of a panorama, or a period painting on a large scale, and that it abounded with ocular metaphor, thus engaging them in a collective experience of spectatorship, where the subject was gloomy and horrible. As Thackeray put it, on readers the book had the power of the 'gloomy rough Rembrandt-kind of reality... of historical painting'.[2] And Margaret Oliphant noted in 1892: 'We are made spectators rather than readers of the terrible developments, one after another, of each successive act of drama working blindly towards a denouement.'[3]

Recently, too, literary scholars have stressed the importance of the ocular in the rhetoric of the *French Revolution*, its narrative and, most important, the metaphor of the 'eye of history' and the notion of the historian's craft as an exercise of his faculty of sight and prophecy. Carlyle, as John Rosenberg has succinctly put it, is an 'ocular impresario'.[4] For a long while historians have given up on what was the single most influential Victorian text on the French Revolution.[5] In what follows I propose to approach this text as a cultural historian and locate its language and some central themes in it in the popular discussion about the Revolution, as well as in the preoccupation with the city during the first half of the nineteenth century. The magnitude of the event, its very status as the definitive historical moment, demanded the use of devices and

[2] Fred Kaplan, *Thomas Carlyle: A Biography* (Berkeley, repr. 1993), 244.

[3] Cited in D. J. Trela and Roger L. Tarr (eds.), *The Critical Response to Thomas Carlyle's Major Works* (Westport, Conn., 1997), 64.

[4] See e.g. John D. Rosenberg, *Carlyle and the Burden of History* (Cambridge, Mass., 1985); Mark Cumming, *A Disimprisoned Epic: Form and Vision in Carlyle's French Revolution* (Philadelphia, 1988); David Srensen, 'Carlyle's Method of History', *The Carlyle Society*, 9, sessions 1982–3 (Edinburgh).

[5] Exceptions include Ben-Israel, *English Historians on the French Revolution*, 127–48 and Burrow, 'Images of Time'.

technologies of spectatorship rather than simply reading. Such technologies were already accessible to readers in the late 1830s in the varied and immensely popular repertoire of panoramic exhibits which evolved in London from the early 1790s and then spread to the Continent. The panorama offered not only special techniques of looking and sightseeing, but would become a framework for historical thought that made it possible to make sense of the grand-scale, dramatic events that made the past. And as much as this form of description and display suited the event, so did the event itself serve Carlyle and his readers as a model for history at large. The panoramic approach to history, so different from the 'hands on' involved spectatorship offered in the Chamber of Horrors and discussed in Chapter 1, suggests another form of observing and ordering the rapidly changing time and urban scenery.

Carlyle and his early readers were experiencing a period of transition, including a stupendous urban growth, especially in London, whose population grew from just under a million on the eve of the first census in 1801 to a staggering 2,362,263 by that of 1851, the first census to reveal that England had become an urban society. The 1830s in particular were transitional in their shifts in political balances, climaxing in the Great Reform Bill, in changes in social legislation concerning rural labour, the poor, and municipal governance (London, of course, being an exception to the municipal legislation), and in the mounting of cross-class agitation that was primarily political. With these changes in the lived environments and in politics at home, and the beginning of a second revolutionary tide abroad (beginning in the Paris July 1830 Revolution and culminating in 1848), there was a need for new forms of looking at history. I begin with a discussion of the visual imagery of the *French Revolution*. I then relate it to the definition of the Revolution as 'sans culottic', an event of and for the people, and connect the popular stance of the work to the development of the panorama as an urban artefact and form of entertainment and to a growing obsession with urban crowds. As I show, Carlyle's fascination with ordinary people and the plebeian revolution influenced his panoramic approach to history. I then narrow the discussion to what I propose is the core of Carlyle's narrative and interpretation: the action of revolutionary women, who serve as shorthand for the Revolution itself and for the concern with urban disorder and violence.

'TOUT EST OPTIQUE': HISTORY AS A SPECTACLE

The visual character of the *French Revolution* has to do with Carlyle's belief that it was the ultimate historical event, a 'world historical' drama and the essence of the modern age. It was, he wrote to John Sterling in September 1833, 'the grand work of our era'.[6] Narrating it was, therefore, creating a repository of all historical knowledge and understanding. Yet though universal, the Revolution was of particular value to the English, as studying it held lessons that could guarantee a better understanding of the political and social unrest in a contemporary Britain on the brink of a revolution. Knowing about the sans-culottes was vital to becoming familiar with the lower classes at home and handling them properly. Paraphrasing Carlyle, 'our philosopher historian', John Forster wrote in the *Examiner* on 10 October 1838: 'that there be no second Sansculottism in our earth for a thousand years, let us understand well what the first was; and the rich and poor of us go and do OTHERWISE'.[7] Writing and reading history could be a useful prophylactic. Of course, the appropriation of the French Revolution, especially of the Terror and the attachment of both to sensations of 'horror'—this last compounding fear, awe, and attraction—was by no means peculiar to Carlyle. As argued in Chapter 1, it was central to the culture of history in which this event became rapidly 'anglicized'. What makes Carlyle so original is his identifying of the horror of the Revolution with the lower classes. And this amounts to his marginalizing institutions and actors which traditionally were allocated a central role in historical writing: states, forms and bodies of government, from the monarchy to the democratic republic, from royal councils to the array of representative bodies emerging after 1789, constitutions, and the European powers which, from 1792, engaged France in continuous wars.

To Carlyle the French Revolution, and indeed all history, was neither institutional nor state-centred, nor (what it had been to some of its stellar historians, including Burke) 'philosophical', unfolding the abstract ideas of the Enlightenment. It was 'sans-culottism'. And he made the urban lower classes not only his main subject but a main subject of history, vital for historical thought and writing. Yet this historicity, indeed the historicity of the Revolution, is often subordinated to and cancelled out by Carlyle's notion of it as a part of a grand design, a cosmic plan. Interpreting it thus makes him a prophet as well as a historian. These contradictory notions about the great event, about history and the historian, cohabit in the image of the writer/historian as an omniscient spectator, capable of commanding the entire revolutionary scene unhindered by limits of time and place. Carlyle's narrator is not limited by the need to take account of sequence, chronology, and causality. He moves freely between the past, present, and future, constructing his reader as a spectator, capable of a panoramic view. The opening paragraphs of the description of the procession of the 1,200 members of the Estates-General in Versailles on May 4 1789 is one example of his 'optics' (Carlyle's own term). The 'procession of processions'

[6] Cited in Lowell T. Fry, '"Great Burke", Thomas Carlyle and the French Revolution', in Lisa Plummer Crafton (ed.), *The French Revolution Debate in English Literature and Culture* (Westport, Conn., 1997), 83–106 at 84.

[7] *The Examiner*, 17 Sept., 10 Oct. 1837, pp. 596–8, 629–30.

is the first of numerous accounts of the advance, across place, of parades, cavalcades, trains of dignitaries, and ordinary people's progresses to create a sense of spectacle which involves certain procedures of looking. The passage is worth quoting at some length:

Versailles is a very sea of men. But above all, from the Church of St. Louis to the Church of Notre Dame; one vast suspended-billow of Life, – with *spray* [*sic*] scattered even to the chimney-tops! For on chimney-tops too, as over the roofs, and up thitherwards on every lamp-iron, sign-post, breakneck coign of vantage, sits patriotic Courage; and every window bursts with patriotic Beauty; for the Deputies are gathering at St. Louis Church; to march in procession to Notre-Dame, and hear sermon. Yes friends, ye may sit and look; bodily or in thought, all France, and all Europe, may sit and look; for it is a day like few others. Oh, one might weep like Xerxes: – So may serried rows sit perched there; like winged creatures, alighted out of Heaven: all these, and so many more that follow them, shall have wholly fled aloft again, vanishing into the blue Deep; and the memory of the day still be fresh. It is the baptism day of Democracy; sick Time has given it birth, the numbered months being run. The extreme-unction day of Feudalism! A super-annuated System of Society, decrepit with toils . . . and with profligacies, sensualities, and on the whole with dotage and senility, – is now to die; and so, with death-throes and birth-throes, a new one is to be born. What a work, o Earth and Heavens, what a work! Battles and Bloodshed, September massacres, Bridges of Lodi, retreats of Moscow, Waterloos, Peterloos, Tenpound Franchises, Tarbarrles and Guillotines; – and from this present date, if one might prophesy, some two centuries of it still to fight! Two centuries; hardly less; before Democracy go through its due, most baleful, stages of *Quackoracy*; and a pestilential World be burnt up, and have begun to grow green and young again.[8]

Carlyle positions his readers in 1837 in a variety of places that allows them multiple and simultaneous views of the grand occasion of May 1789. They are invited to look at it from roof tops, chimneys, and windows, in Paris and Versailles, as men and women. Direct address ('Ye friends'), deliberate use of the present tense, and constant sliding between different times break historical sequence and indeed serve to dehistoricize the panoramic view. The convocation of the Estates-General (the first since 1614), which marked the substitution of a constitutional monarchy for an absolute one, is 'seen' to have happened simultaneously on different registers of time, in the remote past (ancient Persia) and the near one, within the memory and actual life experience of readers. 1789 appears to take place together with the waves of violence and the establishment of the Republic in 1792, the Great Terror of 1793–4, Napoleon's victory in Lodi and his debacles in Russia and Waterloo, and, significantly for early Carlyle readers, popular protest and repression in Britain (the Peterloo massacre of 1819) and the passage of the Great Reform Act (implied in the reference to 'Tenpound Franchises'), five years before the publication of *The French Revolution*.

[8] *French Revolution*, I, IV, IV, pp. 106–7.

Moreover, different pasts easily slide into the future. In the march of deputies 'lies Futurity enough'. The Revolution is present—in the two senses of this last word: it is not a closed event with an end, but goes on and will go on into the future and it is visible everywhere. Carlyle thus disobeys those rules of sequence by which historians conventionally abide. The scale of the grand event justifies this disobedience, what Carlyle himself termed a 'wild savage book'.[9] Writing and reading his kind of history, indeed making sense of the French Revolution, necessitated not simply visualization but reliance upon technologies of seeing and forms of spectatorship. Carlyle's own point of view, the one which he identifies with the 'Eye of History', is, always, the bird's-eye view that gives him command of all that takes place 'on ground'. The reader/viewer shares the historian/prophet's position:

> suppose we too, good Reader, should, as now without miracle Muse Clio enables us, – make *our* station also on some coign of vantage; and glance momentarily over this Procession, and this Life-sea; with far other eyes than the rest do, – namely the prophetic? We can mount, and stand there, without fear of falling.[10]

The text swarms with references to such elevated 'stations', prominent spots offering panoramic views. In addition to the windows and roofs, overlooking the deputies' procession, galleries in the Constitutional Assembly, and later the Convention offer views of politicians and citizen's delegations. The coachman's seat in Louis's rolling carriage offers a point of view on his escape to Varennes, and lamp-posts offer another, on revolutionary crowds. Most favoured among these vantage points is the stylite pillar, conjuring the image of the historian and his reader as stylites. This image draws on the ascetics of the early Eastern Church, who led exemplary lives on top of pillars, offering religious instruction and spiritual guidance to their followers and most commonly identified in tradition with the model life of the Cilician saint Simeon Stylites (390–459). According to this tradition he lived on top of a pillar reaching the height of forty cubits to become the object of emulation and pilgrimage and, despite his isolation, exercised some influence within the world of orthodoxy.[11] Though wholly different from Abbot Samson in *Past and Present*, the esoteric stylite is the spiritual character that would appeal to Carlyle.

Carlyle's synoptic bird's-eye view is quite different from Tussaud's and that of Dickens, which is the focus of the next chapter. Tussaud's lumping together of revolutionary figures and traces, especially in the crammed Chamber of Horrors that was to develop into a replica of a dungeon, offered a limited vision at ground level, or even from below ground. Visitors to Tussaud's were not allowed the panoptic view which some recent scholars have attributed to nineteenth-century

[9] Letter to John Sterling dated Jan. 1837. Quoted in Fry, '"Great Burke"', 88.

[10] *French Revolution*, I, IV, IV, p. 108.

[11] F. L. Cross and E. A. Livingstone (eds.), *The Oxford Dictionary of the Christian Church* (2nd edn., Oxford, 1988), 1276.

museum audiences. Nor, as we shall see, are Dickens's readers privileged with the all-encompassing view that Carlyle's history unfolds. In both cases viewing hardly facilitated an ordering of the chaotic past: rather it involved partaking in the urban chaos. Carlyle represents a different way of looking at the urban past and present. He 'mixes' the two modes of looking at cities and experiencing them by combining an extraordinary density of details—available to walkers in the streets, or readers of some contemporary descriptions, and a panoramic look which, buttressed with the historian/prophet command, makes the *French Revolution* an attempt at a 'total history'. This combination of the panorama and the alley or street is unique to him. Moreover, throughout the text and again quite unusually, the panorama includes people and their culture, with a great sensitivity to both, and acknowledging that both came to their own with the political upheaval. As we shall see, characteristically the panoramic mode of looking and representation, in urban entertainment, architecture, and even in literature, kept a distance from human subjects, their problems, and culture.[12] Carlyle humanized the panoramic look.

First his attitude to revolutionary culture, which is, like the great event itself, popular in its symbolism and dynamism. The best example of the connection between politics and culture is to be found in the chapter entitled 'Flame Picture', which is a panoramic survey of various venues of popular entertainment and instruction in Paris, especially in its 'sans-culottic' parts. The surveyed landscape is dense with sights, exhibitions, displays of new technological innovations like the telegraph and the guillotine, drawing crowds. The list of 'sights' includes Jacques-Louis David's enormous outdoor plaster statues of the 'Sovereign People' at Pont Neuf and his huge 'Liberty' at the Place de la Révolution, the new Arts and Military Schools, Paris's twenty-three theatres, its Salons de dance, the Sections' committee rooms (meeting places of the core, sans-culotte militants), and the guillotine. Carlyle chooses to show two close-ups of this 'flame picture': the engineer Chappe's 'far writing' machine, the telegraph, and the factory for recycling wigs (of executed aristocrats) mentioned in the same breath with the tannery at Meudon, which anti-revolutionary propaganda described as a plant producing leather breeches out of human skins. Readers/spectators are offered a mock sightseeing of the revolutionary city. Their itinerary begins with a visit to the wonders of the new culture, its technology and machinery, proofs of the power of science and progress. It ends in violence and cannibalism (Carlyle's own terms). First the telegraph machine in the Bois de Vincennes, then the tannery are described in Carlylese swarming with direct speech (out of quotation marks), the 'dramatic present', and direct address.

[12] Donald Olsen, *The City as a Work of Art: London, Paris, Vienna* (New Haven, 1986), 21; Will Vaughan, 'London Topographers and Urban Change', in Ira Bruce Nadel and F. S. Schwarzbach (eds.), *Victorian Artists and the City: A Collection of Critical Essays* (New York, 1980), 106–25; Nord, *Walking the Victorian Streets*, 19–49.

What, for example, is this that Engineer Chappe is doing, in the Park of Vincennes? In the Park of Vincennes; and onwards, they say, in the Park of Lepelletier Saint-Fargeau the assassinated Deputy; and still onwards to the heights of Écouen and further, he has a scaffolding set up, has spots driven in; wooden arms with elbow joints are jerking and fugling in the air, in the most rapid mysterious manner! Citoyens run up, suspicious. Yes, O Citoyens, we are signalling: it is a device this, worthy of the Republic; a thing for what we will call *Far-Writing* without the aid of postbags; in Greek it shall be named Telegraph. – *Télégraphe sacré*![13]

And on the tannery, citing directly from his source, Montgaillard, to substantiate the gross fabrication, then reverting to his regular direct speech out of quotation marks, to deliver a summary that condemns the culture of progress as camouflage to 'natural' and unchanging cruelty:

History looking back over Cannibalism, throughout *Purchas's Pilgrims* and all early and late Records, will perhaps find no terrestrial Cannibalism of a sort, on the whole, so detestable. It is a manufactured, soft-feeling, quietly elegant sort; a sort *perfide*! Alas then, is man's civilization only a wrappage, through which the savage nature of him still burst, infernal as ever?[14]

The scenic history and Carlyle's uses of the panoramic look correspond to the emergence and meteoric rise of the panorama during the first half of the nineteenth century. The history of the panorama hones a radical break away from conventions of painting and viewing on the one hand and the rapid growth of a popular commercial urban culture on the other. Moreover, by the thirties what Stephan Oettermann has described as 'the culture of panoramas' offered audiences, as well as readers, a technique and procedures for approaching a variety of topics and fields of information and knowledge, including history and geography.[15]

SCENIC HISTORY AND THE CULTURE OF PANORAMAS

Practically invented and patented by the Scottish surveyor and landscape painter Robert Barker in June 1787, the first ever realistic painting on a cylindrical cycle was exhibited in Edinburgh then in London in the autumn of 1788. Initially, the new form had no word to describe it: it was invented, or rather appropriated, from the Greek, denoting 'all-embracing view', and was used on billposters to advertise Barker's painting of the view of London from the Albion Mills. In this narrow sense 'panorama' designated painterly depictions of landscape of 180 to 360 degrees and replaced the older 'prospect' and 'exhibition'. But it speedily entered common vocabulary and was applied not only to cylindrical canvases

[13] *French Revolution*, III, V, VII, p. 665.

[14] Ibid. 668.

[15] Oettermann, *The Panorama*. For Panoramas in Britain and especially in London see pp. 101–35. See also Hyde, *Panoramania*.

depicting cities, but to large-scale paintings, engravings, series of pictorial depictions with a unifying theme, pageants, theatrical performances, and, gradually, literary descriptions of magisterial scenes or conflicts. Curiously, 'panorama' also came to be used diminutively to denote ordinary or small-scale pictorial renditions of city spaces and historical scenes. Thus peep shows in fairs such as St Bartholomew's capitalized on the 'panorama' for advertising.

The principle of the panorama was emulated in a multiplicity of forms which sprouted in London and were immediately exported to cities on the Continent, and was accompanied by a bevy of neologisms. This included the moving panorama, occasionally described as the 'perstrephic', the 'diorama', the cyclorama, the padorama and pleorama, and the octorama. Such was the growth of all kinds of '-oramas' that a bemused contemporary noted in 1830 : 'The family of Ramas is already large, but it will soon increase to an extent which no verbal Malthus will be able either to limit or to predict, if its members are to be distinguished, like the Streets of Washington, by numerical prefixes.'[16] In the words of a comic song with a Jim Crow refrain, Britons were living in 'The Age of Panoramas'. The craze for the new form of entertainment bordered on 'Panoramania'.[17]

The novelty of cylindrical painting was, of course, that it broke the rule of forty-five (and at most sixty) degrees, which allowed a viewer to take in only as much as any painter could capture on canvas without moving the head. So that in a sense, the panorama stretched and challenged the limits of the scope and range of human sight, redefining perspective and indeed optics. Put differently, and as the term itself implies, it was an all-encompassing, unlimited rendition of an entire circumference, which could now be monitored and mastered. What enhanced the popular appeal of panoramas was the combination of this unlimitedness and the realism which characterized the productions of Barker himself, the map maker and watercolour sketcher Thomas Hornor (who in the mid-1820s embarked on producing a 46,000 square foot canvas presenting a view of London from the top of the dome of St Paul), and their many emulators. To accommodate such canvases and maximize the possibilities for their viewing, the early patent holders erected purpose-built places which immediately became London landmarks. Barker's panorama opened in 1794 on Leicester Square and was run by Robert Barker and Robert Burford, then was taken over by Henry Aston Barker and run by him until 1826. Hornor's plans for a sumptuous Rotunda in Regent's Park materialized in 1829 with the opening of the Coliseum.

These circular buildings, like their numerous imitations (some of which, especially those housing dioramas, drew on the model of the amphitheatre) were not just venues of entertainment: they redefined and formulated the conditions and procedures of viewing large-scale scenes, topics, and landscapes. Viewers

16 Altick, *The Shows of London*, 173.

17 Ibid. Hyde, *Panoramania*.

climbed flights of stairs, leading to circular platforms in the centre of the building, stopping on each platform to view the canvas hanging around the entire inner circumference of the rotunda, the sight facilitated by light from skylights in the dome (which itself was often an imitation of St Paul's'). Thus the unhindered bird's-eye view, unattainable in painting, and rarely possible 'in nature', was achieved. The special qualities of the panorama made it ideal for renditions of large and sprawling cities like London itself and Paris, serving as pictorial maps. Huge canvases depicting Paris in painstaking detail were exhibited in London in 1802, 1828, and 1832, drawing large audiences. Remote places and exotic ones too were 'panoramic' subjects, and their viewing was popularly seen as a substitute for travel.[18] But most relevant here, history, remote history, but especially that of the recent past still alive in collective memory, was a particularly appropriate subject for panoramas. Military campaigns of the Continental Wars, naval battles, and colonial wars drew patriotic crowds and were at one and the same time visual histories and documentary surveys (actually functioning like the illustrated journals of the time and weathering the competition of such journals like the *Illustrated London News*, which offered readers depictions of these topics). Thus the Panorama, Leicester Square, treated its audience to a Panorama of the Battle of Paris, signalling the termination of France's supremacy on the Continent, and a brochure which included a replica of the canvas as well as a 'descriptive panorama'. Scenes of the July Revolution of 1830, in various neigbourhoods of Paris, were available in diorama form at the Queen's Bazaar in 1832. The vogue of topographical and historical panoramas directly influenced genre painting, especially early Victorian historical painting, which was large-scale, manifesting what art historian Boase called 'the cult of enormity'.[19] And as Deborah Epstein Nord has demonstrated, the panoramic view and mode of looking deeply influenced literary representations of the city, especially London, during the first decades of the nineteenth century.[20]

The image of cities seen from a distance, ordered and controlled by the viewer's eye, expressed notions of grandeur, expansion, and metropolitan pride. It also hid, or cut out from view, poverty and social distress and the endemic problems of urbanization like congestion, pollution and disease, and violence. It is not a coincidence that the many-faceted panoramic culture outlined above reached its apogee during the heyday of London's rebuilding and planning on a grand scale in the Regency era and immediately afterwards, a rebuilding known as the era of 'metropolitan improvement'. Although only a fraction of the plan was actually carried out, it had a grandness, stateliness, and wholeness exactly like the spectacle of the panorama. And indeed the new venues of visual entertainment were built and located in the 'new' and grand London.[21] There certainly is

18 See e.g. Altick, *The Shows of London*, 203–10.
19 T. S. R. Boase, *English Art 1800–1870* (Oxford, 1959), 21.
20 Nord, *Walking the Victorian Streets*, 30–49.
21 Olsen, *The City as a Work of Art*; Roy Porter, *London: A Social History*, 194–225.

a fit between the large-scale painting, architecture, and planning and the widespread idea of the grand, dramatic, and paradigmatic historical event embodied in political upheavals such as the French Revolution. All these forms stress the magnitude and singularity of the subject, as well as acknowledging that these generic characteristics demand a special form of representation complete with techniques of observing and viewing. If the Revolution was everywhere and in 'everything' around (Lord Cockburn's words), then the panoramic survey, whether a pictorial or a literary one, was the most appropriate form to recover it.[22] The panorama then provided a way and specific means for making sense of and coming to terms with the constitutive moment in modern history, indeed with history.

It also provided means for observing and mastering the metropolis. It is quite significant that though the Revolution was by no means an exclusively urban event, it was the large-scale events that took place in France's cities and mainly in Paris that hooked the attention of nineteenth-century British historians and the audience at large. It is about Paris, rather than France, that Carlyle and Dickens write. It is on Paris that the *Illustrated London News* would concentrate in its coverage of the 1848 revolution, which it would interpret as a 'repeat' of the great revolution. The revolutionary crowds that attracted and repelled Carlyle and Dickens were seen and apprehended to be distinctly urban phenomena, a characteristic of metropolitan life and culture which they perceived as central to any analysis of history. Urban crowds of course formed the potential and often real audiences of the spectacles and shows embodied in such forms as the panorama, potential consumers of urban spectacles and monuments. Throughout the nineteenth century, but especially during the turbulent decades of the 1830s and 1840s, crowds and audiences were not only and simply 'real' entities, which mobilized to protest against specific politics or an economy, but also elaborate discursive constructions created by politicians and intellectuals. The much-feared Chartist crowd of 1848 and the 'shilling visitors' of the Great Exhibition in Crystal Palace in 1851 are examples of these constructions. Audiences were regarded as potential revolutionary mobs and deemed dangerous, not least because of the historical example set by the French Revolution. More broadly, the panorama provided terms, and an apparatus for, organizing and ordering not just the Western city, city crowds, and history, but the world at large. It is useful to note at this juncture that its principles were adopted in, and governed, the design of international and colonial exhibitions which followed the Great Exhibition. As Timothy Mitchell and Raymond Corbey have shown, these exhibitions were based on the panorama's positioning of the tourist/consumer in a privileged vantage point that enabled him or her to command and rule all that could be seen (the famous imperial viewing position).[23]

22 Henry Cockburn, *Memorials of his Time* (1856; Chicago, 1974), 73.

23 Timothy Mitchell, 'Orientalism and the Exhibitionary Order', in Nicholas Dirks (ed.), *Colonialism and Culture* (Ann Arbor, 1992), 289–319.

Carlyle's *French Revolution* aspired to be such a total picture of what he perceived as the total historical event, the *summa*, as it were, of all history. The panoramic 'eye of history' omniscient and omnipresent, and there to be shared by readers/consumers, was the means to master the detailed landscape of the Revolution.

THE BIG DEEP: THE SANS-CULOTTE REVOLUTION

The urban crowds, that site of rampant fears of disorder and social and political anxiety, were not merely present in the Revolution. To Carlyle they were its moving force and the essence of its history. Their importance is revealed in the subtitle of the first edition: *A History of Sans Culottism.* Their action and agency is far more significant than Enlightenment ideas, ideals, and political institutions. To be sure, he skips none of these factors; but he insists that 'The national assembly . . . goes its course; making the Constitution; but the Revolution goes its course.'[24] And far more explicitly:

> French Revolution means here the open violent Rebellion, and Victory, of disimprisoned Anarchy against corrupt worn-out Authority; how Anarchy breaks prison; bursts up from the infinite Deep, and rages uncontrollable, immeasurable, enveloping a world . . . The 'destructive wrath' of Sansculottism: this is what we speak, having unhappily no voice for singing.[25]

Carlyle's key term needs some elucidation, especially in view of the vast work on the sans-culottes over the last decades, and the shifts in the approaches to them in the historiography of the Revolution. By and large, interpretations of their power have swung from an economic-political Marxist to a revisionist interpretation, thence to a cultural one. According to the first, represented by such historians as Albert Sobul, the Parisian sans-culottes were the small artisan and shopkeeper stratum and responded to the pressure of modern forms of capitalism by developing a politics and agenda related to the Revolutionary Year II (1794). A revisionist reading of their action and platforms (by Michael Sonenscher or David Garrioch) would locate the emergence of their social identity before the Revolution in complex patterns of organization and kinship and in a pre-revolutionary democratic notion of society and property relations. With the linguistic, 'cultural' turn Revolution studies have taken, definitions of the sans-culottes have expanded to include their 'language of class', symbolism, and various representations of their revolutionary experiences. One could rather loosely define the sans-culottes as a popular movement that was mainly urban, with distinct ideology and language, with a solid—albeit temporary—base of power in the Sections of Paris and revolutionary army, and an agenda

[24] *French Revolution*, I, VI, I, p. 169. [25] Ibid., I, VI, I, p. 167.

stressing the right to subsistence, right to bear arms, and access to *political* citizenship.[26]

Carlyle's definition of them (and the array of Carlylese epithets he derived from the term) was, for his time, broad and innovative, signifying sometimes contradictory meanings. At base level it has the original literal and derogatory and gendered meaning which denotes lower-class men who donned pantaloons rather than culottes, or breeches. In this particular context, his repeated reference to the manufacturing of human skin breeches in Meudon is all the more lurid and macabre. More literally even, as David Lodge has noted, Carlyle used 'sans-culottes' and 'sans mentionables' interchangeably, thus referring to the ritual practice of publicly exposing the lower part of the body to shame exponents.[27] This associates sans-culottism with rough and degraded masculine sexuality. However, as I show later, the *French Revolution* identifies the Revolution itself and revolutionary violence as feminine and effeminizing. Somewhat more broadly, the term is attached to the collectivity of the oppressed and their violence. It is vital to stress here that Carlyle, who does not condone violence, causally relates it to *ancien régime* oppression, to poverty and dearth. The violent eruption is a direct consequence of the dire economic hardship before and during the Revolution. Hardship moves the people who, in their turn, move the events.

It would be, however, wholly inappropriate to describe the text as a social history, let alone as a history 'from below'. For if anything, this panorama literally is people's history 'from above'. The Revolution unfolds an ordained plan. Although Carlyle rejects 'ideological' or ideational interpretations which blamed abstract (and inhuman) ideas for violence and disorder in favour of an apparently social reading of the causes of the events in France, he sees all socio-political action and movements as motions in a divine, cosmic history, a history which, needless to say, is pre-ordained. The main tension in this narrative is between the social, which he never lets go, and the divine, between people's lives and deeds—usually missing from panoramic descriptions—and grand, inhuman design (sometimes 'nature'), both of which are described in apocalyptic terms, which his early readers found to be 'poetic' and epic, rather than strictly 'historical'. It is this tension that Carlyle uses to define the Revolution as a monumental force which is, at one and the same time, destructive and generative:

> it seemed that no Reality any longer existed, but only of Phantasms of realities . . . and men were buckram masks that went about becking and grimacing there, – on a sudden, the Earth yawns asunder, and amid Tartarean smoke, and glare of fierce brightness, rises Sansculottism, many-headed, fire breathing, and asks: 'What think ye of *me*? . . . ' Behold the World-Phoenix, in fire-consummation and fire-creation: wide are her fanning wings;

[26] For an introduction to the literature on the swings in the scholarship consult Gwynne Lewis, *The French Revolution: Rethinking the Debate* (London, 1993), esp. 72–106.

[27] David Lodge, 'The French Revolution and the Condition of England: Crowds and Power in the Early Victorian Novel', in Ceri Crossley and Ian Small (eds.), *The French Revolution and British Culture* (Oxford, 1989), 123–41.

loud in her death-melody, of battle-thunders and falling towns; skyward lashes the funeral flame, enveloping all things; it is the Death-Birth of a World![28]

Here the twisted use of classical allusions and associations is notable. The popular movement is a subterranean, organic force, associated with the mythological Tartarus, that part of the underworld where the wicked suffer punishment. But the allusion is twisted into a mock mythology in the question 'What think ye of *me*?'

To think of the sans-culottes is essential. Writing and comprehending their history is vitally necessary in the socially perturbed Britain, especially in its cities. Social unrest, which Carlyle would pin down to the effect of industrialization, urbanization, and the malaise of modernity, would become a main concern of his from the early 1830s, as would popular movements such as Chartism. And the study of what he undoubtedly regarded as the paradigmatic popular revolution carried lessons for his contemporary Britain. Put differently, learning the history of the Revolution and from it was a necessary prophylactic, aimed at preventing a similar outburst at home. Moreover, not only French history but universal history was the 'acting and counteracting' of ordinary, hard-up people. But again, the predetermined course of this action by cosmic forces and the human psyche *ipso facto* makes the Carlylean very definition of agency problematic and in fact dehistoricizes it. Nowhere is this double movement, on the one hand humanizing the dredges of society and on the other naturalizing their action and movement and regarding them as 'a genuine outburst of Nature . . . ', 'the portentous inevitable end of much, the miraculous beginning of much', as apparent as in Carlyle's treatment of women in the Revolution.[29]

THE INSURRECTION OF WOMEN

Sans-culottism has a gender: it is female and feminine. And since the book equates the Revolution itself with sans-culotte action, the sans-culotte women are elevated to a metaphor and a shorthand for the grand event. Their action apotheosizes this event as both historic and human, and 'natural'. Notwithstanding the centrality of gender in and to Carlyle's writing, this key aspect has been consistently ignored in the scholarship. Literary studies like Lodge's and Rosenberg's do note the role of women in pivotal chapters of the *French Revolution*, but they do not place gender as a framework for the text's dealing with society, disorder, and hierarchy. Feminist criticism and historiography has, after a brief interest in the early twentieth century (the writings of Violet Paget, known as Vernon Lee), virtually ignored this text and, for that matter, the bulk

[28] *French Revolution*, I, VI, I, p. 168. [29] Ibid., I, VI, I, p. 169.

of Carlyle's work.[30] Exceptions such as Catherine Hall's study of his colonial writing singled out masculinity for examination and are primarily biographical. Such neglect has to do partly with Carlyle's open misogyny and racism and partly with his domestic life and the domestic economy of the Carlyle household.[31] Introducing gender into our study of the single most influential Victorian historical text on the French Revolution is useful not only in and for itself, but for gaining a more complex insight into the broader nineteenth-century preoccupation with the disorder and horror in history.

In itself, the interest in revolutionary women was neither novel nor original—quite the contrary. Women's visibility in the public sphere and their gender-specific action had pricked the imagination of many English historians and writers. As Joan Landes and Lynn Hunt have shown for France and Linda Colley and Leonore Davidoff and Catherine Hall for Britain, by the 1830s the female revolutionary had come to occupy a privileged site in a discussion in which gender served as a reference to diverse political and social changes. Women's public power was not thought to have originated during the Revolution.[32] Indeed, throughout the last third of the eighteenth century, many British observers had commented on the inordinate and dangerous influence of aristocratic and bourgeois women within the *ancien régime*. These women came to symbolize both the travesty of the old absolute monarchy and its vulnerability. But it was after the outbreak of the Revolution that gender and female sexuality came to occupy a privileged place in both anti-revolutionary Tory and Evangelical discourse and in the Radical discussion of the events in France. The conspicuous presence of women in all kinds of revolutionary events, but particularly in mass urban events like the famous *journées*, was increasingly interpreted as the collapse of order and hierarchy. Edmund Burke's famous description of the market women's march on Versailles on 5 October 1789 became a set-piece which many later writers, including Carlyle, drew on in their renditions of the Revolution as a gender travesty and a travesty of all political order. To Burke, the *poissardes* were a threat to womanhood, to the domestic sphere, to the state, and to nature: 'furies of hell, in the abused shape of the vilest of women'.[33]

Such attitudes and the biographical approach shared by quite a few of Carlyle's predecessors made them naturalize the 'ordinary' revolutionary

[30] Lodge, 'The French Revolution and the Condition of England'; Rosenberg, *Carlyle and the Burden of History*.

[31] Catherine Hall, 'Competing Masculinities: Thomas Carlyle, John Stuart Mill and the Case of Governor Eyre', in *White, Male and Middle Class: Explorations in Feminism and History* (New York, 1992), 255–96.

[32] Colley, *Britons*, 252–7; Leonore Davidoff and Catherine Hall, *Family Fortunes: Men and Women of the English Middle Class, 1780–1850* (London, 1988). For France see Joan Landes, *Women and the Public Sphere in the Age of the French Revolution* (Ithaca, NY, 1993) and Lynn Hunt, *The Family Romance of the French Revolution* (Berkeley, 1992), 89–124, 151–93. See also Dominique Godineau, 'Masculine and Feminine Political Practice during the French Revolution, 1793—Year III', in Harriet B. Applewhite and Darline G. Levy (eds.), *Women and Politics in the Age of the Democratic Revolution* (Ann Arbor, 1993), 61–81.

[33] Quoted in Colley, *Britons*, 252.

woman and prefer the 'extraordinary' female hero, of a higher class and exceptional breeding, who could be cast as a victim of the Revolution. Heroines included Manon Philipon, better known as Madame Roland, a central figure in the Girondist party, and Charlotte Corday, whose political action and obvious crossing of the borderlines of gender were conveniently mitigated by their death. Both could easily be accommodated in conventional and, as Ben-Israel has noted, sentimental biographies and biographical vignettes. In 'biographies of emotion', most notably in those biographies produced by women writers from Mary Hays in *Female Biography* (1803) to Julia Kavanagh in *Women in France during the Eighteenth Century* (1850), and in the Tussauds' biographical vignettes, these female saints are elevated to paragons of the right sort of liberty (quite distinct from popular democracy) as well as of womanhood.[34] They are 'true' women, despite their forcefulness and political action and, in the case of Corday, violence. The female pantheon included Marie-Antoinette, whose alleged misconduct and corruption were easily expiated by her trial and martyrdom. The queen, far more than Louis XVI, stirred British readers and exhibition goers, as her exposure to violence, representing the exposure of all women to the violent upheaval, embodied the relationship between individuals, society, and disorder.

Carlyle too included mini-biographies in his book and treated his readers to detailed accounts of the queen's (and king's) trial. And, notwithstanding his vehement critique of Girondist politics, with which both Madame Roland and Corday were identified, he incorporated, emblematic portrayals of both (Corday's is a classic description of his usage of dialogue in direct speech out of quotes).[35] But these are not characteristic of the overall handling of women's action in the *French Revolution*. His interest in the event as a popular movement determined a preoccupation, an obsession even, with the role he assigned to women as a social group, a preoccupation that is in stark contrast to his interest in exceptional biographies and portraitures (I have in mind not only his biographies of Cromwell, Muhammad, and Friedrich II, but also his involvement in the establishment of the National Portrait Gallery). And as already implied, the 'insurgent women' are not just historical actors, they serve to define the scope, character, and threat of the Revolution.

Women's complex and privileged role in the text is manifest in a stress on everyday, historical detail that concerns a specific female suffering and experience of the Revolution. The extraordinary attention to the material aspects of this experience alters the conventions of the panorama, with its aloofness from social life and problems in the city. Ironically, the thickness of social detail also predates the much later interest of social and feminist historians in 'women and the French Revolution'. Yet Carlyle's apparent historicization of ordinary

[34] Ben-Israel, *English Historians*, 122–6.

[35] 'Charlotte Corday', *French Revolution*, III, IV, I, pp. 603–9. On Madame Roland see II, V, IX, pp. 424–5.

women is offset, though it is not completely cancelled out, by massive resort to mythology and a running association between women and the natural, rather than social (thence historical), world. The unsolved and unsolvable contradiction between historical action and what Carlyle and his contemporaries deemed female 'nature' is writ large in the chapter entitled 'The insurrection of Women', and which may be considered as the most important part of the entire work, a synecdoche of the *French Revolution*. The chapter opens the seventh book, closing Part I, and revolves around the march of Paris market women to Versailles to protest against the dearth of bread and the grain and food crisis of the autumn of 1789, as well as against royal intransigence. The celebrated march, which culminated in the women's invasion of the queen's private apartment, ended with a surrender of royalty and the ceremonial and highly symbolic removal of the royal couple and their children to the palace at the Louvre, a sign of their appropriation by the people of Paris. The event launches the popular insurrection in the form of the *journée*, or collective and typically armed protest with a defined economic or political agenda (or both). For Carlyle, the October march, the first in a succession of such *journées*, was a clear demonstration of the public power of women and their control over the city. His description of the background to the October days and the first revolutionary 'day' serves Carlyle in his overall analysis of the relationship between the constitutional revolution and the development of the limited monarchy (and, after the summer of 1792, the Republic) on the one hand and the popular revolution on the other. His signalling the women's resurrection also manifests an interest in 'conditions' and social problems which corresponds to his preoccupation with the 'condition of England'.

The visibility of women in a male urban space, their public speaking, and indeed their resort to violence is a result of 'conditions': poverty and dearth. Their hardship is different from and greater than men's and licenses a different anger and distinct forms of action. Thus 'The public-speaking woman at the Palais-Royal was not the only speaking one: – Men know not what the pantry is, when it grows empty; only house-mothers know. O women, wives of men that will only calculate and not act!'[36] There is no moralizing here. Female action and indeed violence are directly connected to women's role as mothers and within the household (which he compounds in the term 'house-mother'). These women's anger does not threaten home and hearth (the Burkean interpretation) but buttresses the family, as it is their place as mothers and wives, natural nurturer's, that mandates and legitimizes their violence. Thus the militants' invasion of the public and political sphere during the October Days was an extension of the kitchen and pantry, actually enhancing the borderlines of gender. The following paragraph is worth citing at length precisely because it combines the maternalist stance in Carlyle's interpretation and an extraordinary attention to physical and topographical detail concerning women's everyday life

[36] Ibid., I, VII, III, p. 197.

in an urban locale. It is this obsession with detail which breaks down the aloof and distant panoramic mode and complicates his more essentialist reiterations regarding female nature.

A thought, or dim raw-material of a thought, was fermenting all night, universally in the female head, and might explode. In squalid garret, on Monday Morning Maternity awakes, to hear children weeping for bread. Maternity must forth to the streets, to the herb-markets and Bakers'-queues; meets there with hunger-striken Maternity, sympathetic, exasperative. O we unhappy women! But, instead of Bakers'-queues, why not to Aristocrats' palaces, the root of the matter? *Allons*! Let us assemble. To the Hôtel-de-Ville; to Versailles! To the Lanterne! In one of the Guardhouses of Quartier Saint-Eustache, 'a young woman' seizes a drum, – for how shall National Guards give fire on women, on a young woman? The young woman seizes the drum; sets forth, beating it, 'uttering cries relative to the dearth of grains'. Descend, O mothers; descend, ye Judiths, to food and revenge! – All women gather and go; crowds storm all stairs, force out all women; the female Insurrectionary Force, according to Camille [Desmoulins] resembles the English Naval one; there is a universal 'Press of women'. Robust Dames of the Halle, slim Mantua-makers, assiduous, risen with the dawn; ancient Virginity tripping to matins; the Housemaid, with early broom; all must go. Rouse ye, O women; the laggard men will not act; they say, we ourselves may act![37]

The catalogue of women's occupations, the mention of places that were to become centres of militancy, the use of the dramatic present and direct, unquoted speech (with two exceptions which cite 'sources' for substantiation), all these enable Carlyle to speak in a female voice—significantly in the plural. And it is the many voices of women which apparently make for women's historicity and, by implication, the historicity of the sans-culottes in the text. Yet even as the omnipresent narrator 'sees' and speaks for the historical sans-culottes and sympathizes with them, he locates them outside history, in a world that oozes with myth and nature. Revealingly the entire passage is to be found in the chapter emblematically entitled 'The Menads' and which coins the epithets that would describe the women militants throughout the *French Revolution*. The resort to Greek mythology is by no means peculiar to Carlyle's writing on women. He ransacked classical epics and both Greek and Roman myth in search of such epithets that could be used rhetorically for characterization and dramatic effect. The work in its entirety literally swarms with classical allusions which are deliberately misplaced to produce satire and irony. For his descriptions of lower-class urban women Carlyle draws not on the epics, but on drama and Dionysian cults with their sexual symbolism. The very characterization of women as 'menads' and of the Revolution as 'menadic', thus female, is the most salient example of his rhetoric of gender. In Greek mythology and drama, the *maenades*, as quite a few of his middle-class readers would have known, are irrational and orgiastic female followers of Dionysus who play a central part in the cult of this

[37] Ibid., I, VII, IV, p. 199.

deity. Conventionally feasts for Dionysus had reversed sexual and gender roles in Greek societies of the classical era in which women had been segregated and excluded from public affairs and spaces. Dionysian and public female sexuality wholly violated domesticity, hierarchy, and so-called Apollonian religion, and had been associated with the absence of control of sexuality and, in Carlyle's interpretation, of all social control. Examples of representations of the *maenades* would include Euripides' *Bacchae* and Aristophanes' *Thesmophoriazusae* (*The Women Celebrating the Thesmophoria*) and *Ecclesiazusae* (*Women at the Assembly*).[38] The constant reference to popular female revolt as 'menadic' effectively naturalizes it. The sans-culotte women have historical attributes, but they are likened to a force of nature. Their insurrection is uncontrolled and indeed uncontrollable and incarnates the general revolutionary eruption in France, that 'inflammablest immeasurable Fire-work, generating, consuming itself'.[39]

The densest concentration of mythological images of disorder is reserved to those descriptions of the march in its final stages near and in Versailles and from it to Paris. As with the rendition of the progress of the Estates-General, so here the movement of crowds forms a spectacle: women are 'Sight of sights: Bacchantes', a 'menadic host', and their very real and historical hunger is, nevertheless, 'menadic hunger'.[40] And as their march progresses it is looked upon by terrified male spectators positioned to watch this panorama: 'men peer from windows'.[41] The most intense moment of the spectacle is the women's invasion of the National Assembly (previously the Estates-General and still convened in Versailles), a perfect example of the power of the popular revolution over the constitution and the State. The women set a parliament, a female assembly that is occasionally referred to as an assembly of apes (the reference to Erasmus is transparent) and it is the greatest imaginable contrast to a body of representatives. This is because throughout the French Revolution women were excluded from all elected national assemblies and the overwhelming majority of local ones, and, of course, from voting. As historians like Darline Levy, Harriet Applewhite, and Dominique Godineau (who analysed the same march on Versailles) have noted, women militants repeatedly invaded not only the streets of the capital, but such distinct political spaces as the houses of the National Assembly (later the Convention) and the royal palaces, thus actively interpreting notions of citizenship and extending its meaning beyond the strictly political.[42] In the *French Revolution* the description of this invasion takes a carnivalesque turn:

a Senate of Menads! For as Erasmus's Ape mimicked, say with wooden splint, Erasmus shaving, so do the Amazons hold, in mock majesty, some confused parody of National

38 Paul Harvey, *The Oxford Companion to Classical Literature* (Oxford, 1986), 152 and 428.
39 *French Revolution*, II, VII, IV, p. 198.
40 Ibid., I, VII, V, p. 201; I, VII, VI, pp. 205, 207.
41 Ibid., I, VII, V, p. 201.
42 See Darline G. Levy and Harriet B. Applewhite, 'Women, Radicalization, and the Fall of the French Monarchy', in Applewhite and Levy, *Women and Politics*, 81–109; Godineau, 'Masculine and Feminine'.

Assembly. They make motions; deliver speeches; pass enactments; productive at least of loud laughter. All galleries and benches are filled; a Strong Dame of the Market is in Mounier's [president of the Assembly] Chair . . . To such length have we got in regenerating France. Methinks the travail-throes are of the sharpest!—Menadism will not be restrained from occasional remarks; asks, 'What is the use of Penal Code? The thing we want is Bread.' Mirabeau turns round with lion-voiced rebuke; Menadism applauds him; but recommences. Thus they, chewing rough sausages, discussing the Penal Code, make night hideous.[43]

The women become a predetermined metaphor of the Revolution and its apotheosis. The victims of poverty, dearth, and oppression, they lead the popular insurrection, menacing order and culture. Their rise, the rise of the sans-culotte movement, is tied by Carlyle to the collapse of the non-functioning state and the constitution and their surrender to the force of the multitudes and to anarchy. And it is because the plebeian urban insurrection is represented as female that the male revolutionaries, representing the Jacobin phase and the terror, are feminized. Robespierre lacks clear marks of masculinity and his gender and even sex are quite blurred. His shrill voice, histrionic conduct, feminine body language, and sartorial extravagance all make him a man/woman. He is 'anxious, slight, ineffectual-looking', 'snuffing dimly the uncertain future times' with a 'complexion of multiplex atrabiliar colour, the final shade of which may be the pale sea-green. That greenish-coloured (*verdâtre*) individual'.[44] The priceless compound 'sea-green Robespierre', borrowed from Madame de Staël, is one of the tags Carlyle attaches to the leader's proper name. Robespierre's smallness, shrillness, and virulence too are constantly remarked upon. To enhance the effect of such an effeminacy, he is constantly paired with the only two revolutionary figures Carlyle admired as manly, heroic, and exemplary: Honoré-Gabriel Riqueti, Comte de Mirabeau, the prominent figure in the Assembly throughout the so-called 'first' revolution and until his death in 1791, and Georges Jacques Danton, the Jacobin leader, an architect of the terror and Minister of Justice of the Republic. Both, especially Mirabeau, were prominent figures within the elected assemblies, while at the same time being great orators and charismatic popular leaders. Both represented 'the people'—this notwithstanding Mirabeau's aristocratic origins. Both were marked out by their contemporaries for their rugged and gigantic physique, exactly the same kind of physique that Carlyle admired in men. And of the hundreds of revolutionary characters which he describes they are the closest to the kind of masculine hero he had depicted in *Sartor Resartus* and would celebrate in *Heroes and Hero Worship*. So Mirabeau is:

the Type-Frenchman of his epoch . . . He is French in his aspirations, acquisitions, in his virtues, in his vices; perhaps more French than any other man; – and intrinsically such a mass of manhood too. Mark him well . . . All manner of men he has gained . . . more especially all manner of women.[45]

[43] *French Revolution*, I, VII, VIII, pp. 214–15.
[44] Ibid., I, IV, IV, p. 113.
[45] Ibid., I, IV, IV, p. 110.

But they, like the sans-culottic revolution which they embody, stand for all that is human. The female/revolution is dangerous because unavoidable. It consumes itself to a total destruction that alone would build a new society and politics.

In previous Francophobe discourse on the Revolution, especially in popular writing and iconography, Frenchness was attached to vice, a sensuality bordering on depravity and moral lassitude. British moralists and writers of different political hues associated political anarchy with sexual disorder. Burke himself, Hannah More, John Andrews, and Thomas Gisborne come to mind.[46] In Carlyle's Mirabeau and Danton, voluptuousness is dissociated from effeminacy (the all too virtuous and unvirile Robespierre is the woman). These men are 'titanic': in sheer bulk, in their action, vision, and in their fury. Thus at the same time that they are the leaders of the Revolution and heroes of and for their times, they are led by the great upheaval and will be consumed and destroyed by it. Precisely like the sans-culottes. Danton especially is a 'Titan of Forlorn Hopes', a 'Mirabeau of the Sans Culottes', whose very life, revolutionary career, and final execution are likened to a 'gigantic mass, of valour, ostentation, fury, affection and wild revolutionary force and manhood . . . a very Man' who 'may live for some generations in the memory of men'.[47] Like the female sans-culottes, Carlyle's paragons of masculine heroics and leadership are not clean of the mock-heroic and the ridiculous, or, in unsurpassed Carlylese: the 'ludicro terrific'.

READING THE *FRENCH REVOLUTION*

The French Revolution was the subject of multiple readings, creating multiple effects on individuals and different readerships. Fortunately for the student of the consumption of culture, these readings may be reconstructed well beyond the limits of the upper and middle middle class. As recent studies have established, most notably Jonathan Rose's, Carlyle had had a special and enduring appeal to self-educated working-class audiences. Reading/viewing his panorama of the Revolution was inflected more by class and gender and less by politics and ideology, as nineteenth-century readers of different political convictions absorbed the book and made different uses of it. As will be seen, class, gender, and locale disposed readers towards reading and using the text, but they themselves saw the exceptional historical text as a means actually to divert from and circumvent the restrictions of class and gender. In some instances, Carlyle's human panorama made an actual difference in readers' lives.

Contemporary middle-class readers, and later audiences, were captured by the intended panoramic effect, designed to construct the reader as a viewer. They 'looked at' and 'saw' Carlyle's version of the Revolution. Some of the earliest

[46] Colley, *Britons*, 250–7. Mary Wollstonecraft's own sympathy with the Revolution was connected by her contemporaries and commentators, writing after her death, with her 'disorderly' sexual conduct.

[47] *French Revolution*, I, VI, III, p. 679.

readers settled into their position as spectators, surveying a panorama. The book, states an anonymous writer in the *Monthly Review* in August 1837, 'brings the actor and scenes described before the readers' eye'. Another writer, reviewing for the *Christian Examiner*, noted the historian's elevated view which enabled him to command the myriad events which themselves were illustrations of laws.[48] The panoramic view of history impressed readers and students of the *French Revolution* as late as the 1900s. One of the earliest detailed analyses of Carlyle's usage and elaboration of the bird's-eye view for dramatization and the creation of a desired readers' response is to be found in a little study by the feminist essayist, pacifist, writer, and art historian Violet Paget, better known as Vernon Lee, published in the *Contemporary Review* and forming a part of her 'Studies in Literary Psychology'. The book, she argues, 'forces us... to look down on the revolution from a skyey post of observation where He sits, like some belfry gargoyle overlooking a flattened city, and a mapped out country'. The 'skyey post', and the flattened landscape creating the impression of a painted map, are exactly what the creators of painted and literary panoramas aimed at.[49] The visual effects of the work gave the book its aesthetic and dramatic impact, but made it problematic as a history. Indeed, even those readers/writers who regarded the work as a great history, befitting the magnitude of the ultimate historical event, were aware that size and scope, the *French Revolution*'s claim on the totality of the historical work, could be the very opposite of history. As a very critical anonymous writer for the *Literary Gazette* put it in May 1837, 'There is nothing like a history of the events which took place.' Or, as the *Monthly Review* uncharitably stated in August of the same year, this new history 'never can be useful'.[50]

The working class's response to the book, and to Carlyle in general, was rather more complex in the sense that it forces us to rethink his classification as a 'conservative' and an authoritarian, and that of the text itself as 'anti'-revolutionary. Taking account of this response may also challenge some assumptions taken for granted in regard to the impact of a so-called 'conservative' (or radical) writing and culture on working-class life and politics. Considering the surprising number of working-class women and men who put on record their impression of Carlyle, we are reminded of Alton Locke's saying about the book in Charles Kingsley's Chartist novel of this title: 'I know no book, always exempting Milton, which at once so quickened and extended my poetical view of man and his history, as that great epic of modern days, Thomas Carlyle's French Revolution.'[51] *The French Revolution*, and Carlyle's work more broadly, meant widely different things to different working-class readers. He was the working-class, self-educated person's writer. And his significance for this type of reader differed from the effect on the middle-class

48 *Monthly Review*, NS 2 (Aug. 1837), 543; *Christian Examiner*, 23 Jan. 1838, p. 386.

49 Violet Paget, 'Carlyle and the Present Tense' ('Studies in Literary Psychology', iii), *Contemporary Review*, 85 (1904), 386–92 at 390–1.

50 Both cited in Trela and Tarr, *The Critical Response to Thomas Carlyle*, 50, 52.

51 Lodge, 'The French Revolution and the Condition of England', 129.

reviewer of the 1830s and 1840s, or the early 1900s. What appealed most to working-class readers of different genders and geographic origins were Carlyle's moral tone and his scathing contempt for authority. The effect he produced on them was not conservative: he did not cause them to 'read' the French Revolution and its lessons as a warning, but rather as a promise, and to develop a 'positive' and sympathetic view with the ordinary people of France. Moreover, the book and Carlyle's other histories invariably produced on working-class readers the effect of criticizing and even negating the industrial and capitalist system and certain aspects of modern urban life as well as the powers that be.

And *The French Revolution* not only awakened a sense of social injustice and inequality, but, for many readers, an exercise in self-emancipation. Edmund Stonelake, a miner in South Wales who had never heard of the French Revolution, obviously found it difficult to grapple with the Carlylese, which taxed even the early middle-class readers discussed above. But slowly the book grew on him and he derived from it not only a sense of the working man's self-dignity, but his own political education:

> I learned the causes which fomented the minds of the people and gave rise to the Revolution, how ferociously it was conducted, and how the proclaimed hero of today was carted away tomorrow in the tumbrels to a place where his noble head fell under the merciless guillotine. I could visualise the Foreign Legion swooping down upon a vast unsuspecting concourse of quiet people slashing all around them with swords and sabers, leaving the dead and the dying whilst they disappeared and pursued the remainder who were fleeing in terror. I learned also of the great influence the Revolution had on peoples and countries struggling to establish democratic principles in Government in various parts of the world.[52]

Before him G. J. Wardle, later Labour MP, was attracted to what he saw as Carlyle's moral uprightness and the latter's dictates about duty. And still earlier, bookbinder Fredrick Rogers looked unto the 'prophet' as a preacher of 'social righteousness'. Later Labour leaders with no religious inclinations (and therefore 'immune' to Carlyle's brand of Calvinism), admired, as Rose has shown, what they regarded as his call for social justice and the historical agency of the working man. A questionnaire, conducted after the 1906 elections by the *Review of Reviews* among the first large group of Labour MPs, asking them to name the books and authors which most profoundly influenced them, demonstrates the scope and extent of Carlyle's impact on the informed working-class reader/activist. He came fourth, after John Ruskin, Dickens, and the Bible (in this order), graded higher than Mill (scoring the seventh place), Shakespeare (a modest eighth), and Adam Smith (a mere seventeenth).[53] Conspicuously absent from the list is Karl Marx, a testimony to the character and political education of British labour. Equally conspicuous is the appeal of

[52] Edmund Stonelake, *The Autobiography of Edmund Stonelake*, ed. Anthony Mor-O'Brien (Brigend, 1981).

[53] Rose, *The Intellectual Life of the British Working Classes*, 41–2.

such writers as Carlyle, Dickens, and Scott, facilely dubbed 'conservative' and even reactionary, on the readers, among them Ben Tillett, Keir Hardie, and George Lansbury.

Quite a few, but not all, readers were aware of and disliked Carlyle's admiration of white supermen and denounced his racism.[54] It is easy to see why he would attract male autodidacts, some of whom left their class roots as labourers to become its representatives. They no longer worked with their hands—a central component of 'classic' working-class masculinity. In Carlyle and in the forms of action his text depicted, they could find a model. Carlyle saw himself as a worker and glorified labour, including manual labour and a rugged manliness. He was also a preacher and a teacher. He and his prose style could present the possibility of retaining a working man's masculine identity even after detachment from the material basis of this class. More revealing and more problematic than the attraction to working men of Carlyle's ideas about action, with its distinct masculine characteristics, is his long-standing appeal to some working-class female activists, most notably to avowed feminists (we saw his attraction to middle-class ones before). What could they make of his dense descriptions of women's daily life and their revolutionary action combined with his naturalization of women as 'menads'?

Mary Smith and Elizabeth Bryson, born six decades apart, exemplify feminist readings and, more broadly, the active and imaginative ways in which readers made use of and intervened in their historical texts. Smith, a shoemaker's daughter born in 1822, educated in a Methodist school and a voracious reader, discovered Carlyle while serving as governess in the house of a Scotby leather works owner, reading him against her employer's admonition about the danger in his works. She particularly cherished his ability to expose social 'shams' and found in him self-confidence, and for a while corresponded with both the Carlyles. She later became a local journalist and a campaigner for the Married Women's Property Bill, women's suffrage, and the repeal of the Contagious Diseases Acts. Elizabeth Bryson's autobiography describes the moment of self-discovery engendered by the reader's absorption of the words of the historical text in exactly the same phrases which Carlyle employs ironically to describe the sans-culottes' moment of self-recognition: 'Suddenly, blazing from the printed page, there *are* the words that we couldn't find. It is an exciting moment... "Who am I? The thing that can say I. Who am I, what is this ME?"'[55] Bryson 'reads out' of the text Carlyle's irony and his association between revolution, urban anarchy, and female sexuality. She 'reads into' it a promise for a gendered sense of self that cuts across, and out and away of, the limits of class.

54 Ibid. 47.

55 Mary Smith, *The Autobiography of Mary Smith, Schoolmistress and Nonconformist* (London, 1892), 160; Bryson cited in Rose, *The Intellectual Life*.

Like Bryson, Helen Crawfurd confesses to have owed her political and feminist awakening to *The French Revolution, Sartor Resartus*, and *Heroes and Hero Worship*—this last found difficult to stomach by some workers because of the kind of leadership it advocated. A baker's daughter from Glasgow, a convert to evangelicalism, and a missionary turned socialist and suffragette, Crawfurd would become a militant of the Women's Social and Political Union (WSPU) and was imprisoned in Holloway gaol. She attributes her growing sense of the oppression and deprivation of simple, ordinary women (and men) to her reading of Carlyle. Unlike her male contemporaries, which the *Review of Reviews* interviewed, Crawfurd did read and was influenced by Marx. Revealingly, she stresses that what she was later to read in Marx's writings she first discovered in Carlyle, who had exposed the shams of law, religion, and the old regime, kingship and queenship, and 'admired the worker'.[56] She even, and rather confusingly, claims to have got her sympathy towards slaves in North America from him. His sympathy towards slave owners and blunt denigration of 'niggers' before and after the Governor Eyre affair make such a declaration rather dubious. However, the point is not whether Crawfurd, Smith, or any of Carlyle's working-class readers got right his interpretation of the French Revolution, or, for that matter, his history and ideologies. The point is that these readers made active and independent uses of his text, using it in the imaginary and in their social life, drawing from it those ideas and impressions which held the most attraction for them. They were attracted by his humanizing of the panorama, that is the inclusion of an involved dense description of everyday detail and suffering in the grand-scale depiction of the past. They were drawn by his stress on the urban lower classes as active agents and the same mistrust of states and institutions equated with authority and power: they liked his denouncing of hierarchies derived from wealth and rank and what they identified as the 'worth' of a lower-class person and the channelling of this 'worth' into action.

Our paying attention to the varied uses these readers made of *The French Revolution* does not mean idealizing Carlyle or glossing over some of the unacceptable parts in his thinking and writing on race, and women and gender. Carlyle was no feminist and he was a racist. But some of his feminist readers appropriated his interpretation of the grand historical event in ways that Michel de Certeau would describe as active and 'imaginative': they 'used' him to help define their own way in life and politics, adopting what seemed useful. If anything, Carlyle did not make these working women and men 'conservative'—he had a share in their radicalization. Their investment in his history and the personal gains which some of them made by it may help historians today be more careful when we categorize some 'great texts' and make and unmake our canons of the influential histories. In the next chapter we turn to the other

[56] Mary Smith, *The Intellectual Life*, 44–5.

'great text' on the Revolution, Dickens's *A Tale of Two Cities*, which drew massively on Carlyle and represents yet another case of active reading and rewriting history. However, Dickens not only represents another mode of looking at the historical event which is distinct from the human panorama, he also exemplifies a different interpretation of the city and of history itself as an urban site.

3

The Past as an Urban Place: Mid-Victorian Images of Revolution and Governance

MID-CENTURY REVOLUTION HISTORIES AND THE CHANGE IN CITIES

We would expect the horror generated by the Revolution and the fascination with its violence to have lessened somewhat by the middle of the nineteenth century. This indeed is what some students of Victorian historiography and popular histories tell us, relating this change to a move away from the past and from historical genres to an interest in contemporary topics.[1] The supposed mid-Victorian distancing from history is also, and more broadly, associated with a change in elite and middle-class apprehension about a second, French-style revolution in Britain. Fears of urban anarchy, at their zenith during the 1830s and 1840s, gradually subsided after the debacle of Chartism and the repression, throughout the Continent, of the revolutionary upheaval of January–June 1848. The revolutionary potential, indeed the power of crowds, which preoccupied Carlyle in the late 1830s and obsessed later commentators, may seem to have abated in 1851, owing to the orderly conduct of the lower class of visitors to the Great Exhibition. A number of historians regard the period 'after Chartism' and the revolutionary upheaval as one of 'equipoise' and quiescence, following the disquiet of the thirties and forties.[2] To these historians as well as to quite a few students of culture, 1851 is a convenient signpost: heralding a feel of security, drawing on England's grandeur and technological superiority, the latter embodied in the epitome of the culture of spectacle, the Great 'Exhibition of all Things' at Crystal Palace.[3]

[1] Mitchell, *Picturing the Past*, 228–61. Ben-Israel points to the weakening of interest in the Revolution after 1848. Ben-Israel, *British Historians*, 215–23.

[2] Chiefly W. L. Burn, *The Age of Equipoise: A Study of the Mid-Victorian Generation* (New York, 1965). Burn's term fell out of grace but has remained a point of departure for reassessments of the mid-Victorians, most notably Martin Hewittt (ed.), *An Age of Equipoise? Reassessing Mid-Victorian Britain* (London, 2002).

[3] On the Great Exhibition as a divide see Jeffrey A. Aurbach, *The Great Exhibition of 1851: A Nation on Display* (New Haven, 1999); Peter H. Hoffenberg, *An Empire on Display: English, Indian and Australian Exhibitions from the Crystal Palace to the Great War* (Berkeley, 2001); and Richards, *The Commodity Culture of Victorian England.*

This chapter and Part II make the somewhat different argument that images of a violent revolution and indeed of the past as an unruly place of injustice, arbitrariness, and danger proved remarkably resilient throughout both the torrid 1840s and the mid-century decades of 'equipoise' and actually escalated during the late 1850s. Another argument is that the past was imagined as an *urban* country. As with the older representations, the mixture which Charles Dickens, one central perpetuator of the sense of the horrors of history and of the modern city, described as 'the attraction of repulsion'[4] proved irresistible to producers and consumers of the new culture of history. The mid-century productions of the Revolution held on firmly to the sense of the grandeur of the great historical event as a spectacle, a moral lesson, and a metaphor for history, a sense inherited from Carlyle, together with his images of the French people's suffering and of the arbitrariness of the violence, disorder, and anarchy of the revolutionary crowds. These mid-century productions also retained the popular fascination with the guillotine, epitomized in Madame Tussaud's display of the horrors of the Great Terror. Yet alongside these powerful images new ones became articulated around 1840, which crystallized in two inextricable metaphors of the prison and the scaffold or guillotine, and which came to dominate representations of the Tudors and the revolutionary era. In both cases violence was located within the orbit of the State, the law, and the nation: whether the Tudor state, constituting the symbol of a Protestant monarchy, or the *ancien régime* and the Jacobin republic in France. The new image was especially cultivated in two historical genres, which I call the 'urban history' and the 'topographical historical novel'.

The vision of the past as urban and arbitrary, and its disassociation from rural nostalgia and ideals, resonated with contemporary readers and spectators because they addressed, forcefully and directly, the mid-century sea changes in the urban experience, in the governance of the big city and the ruling of its multitudes, and in the very geography and morphology of urban Britain. These changes, which occurred most spectacularly in London between the mid-1850s and the 1870s, surpassed the processes of urban expansion briefly outlined in Chapter 2, and the two decades present one of the metropolis's most intense moments of modernity. One instance of the project of modernization was the establishment in 1855 of the Metropolitan Board of Works (MBW), the first London-wide local authority and the body most identified with the swing towards 'improvement', the rational solution to urban problems by the eradication of old infrastructures of drainage, lighting, roads, and transport, and the building of new ones. The overlapping of an urban vision of the past and the project of urban modernization cannot be overstated. This overlapping involved two apparently contradicting notions, each with its own vocabulary and set of terms: one was that of 'improvement', perceiving modernization as the rationalization and reorganizing of the built environment, and centred around construction on a massive scale to

[4] Cited in Jordan (ed.), *The Cambridge Companion to Charles Dickens*, 107.

guarantee the free circulation of people, goods, and waste through the city's arteries. The other notion of modernity recognized that change had its obverse in the dramatic project of demolition of old buildings, streets, and roads, the segregation of old parts of London, and the erosion of institutions, corporate rights, and privileges, and, last but not least, the eradication of popular public rituals involving crowd participation, such as fairs and public executions (the latter abolished only in 1868).[5]

Improvement and the demolition of places and remnants of an ever-present past made up what recent historians of urbanism have recognized as a distinctly British form of modernization, at its most characteristic in London. As Lynda Nead has usefully shown, London (not less than Paris) was the 'capital of the nineteenth century', representing complex forms of modernity which took place not according to a master plan to rationalize modern life and experience in the metropolis, but gradually, almost piecemeal. Moreover, the experience and representations of improvement drew on the past, whose traces in the urban landscape were ubiquitous, reminders of older forms and rhythms of life and leisure. So that mid-Victorian reformers, writers, and artists constantly made analogies with history, while seeking to sever from it the cities they experienced and imagined.[6] Again it was in London that forms of urban observation and seeing developed, some of them quite different from the panoramic view ordering the city and articulated in the earlier panoramas and in panoramic histories such as Carlyle's.[7]

This chapter examines the juncture of what I call 'the urban history of the Revolution', changes in the city, the production and consumption of an urban vision of the past, and of modes of observing and knowing the metropolis. I pay special attention to representations of the prison and scaffold, and their circulation and consumption by various audiences, because of their centrality to the popular image of the Revolution and in widespread concerns about the city. To focus the discussion, I use Charles Dickens's *A Tale of Two Cities*, published in 1859, as an anchor for a consideration of the broader issues, thus anticipating the later discussion of the theme of the prison and torture in historical monuments and literature during the 1840s. In methodology and strategy I follow Chapter 2, using the single 'great work' as a vantage point for a study of the culture of history. This may invite some historians' criticism: why select one text, and an over-researched novel at that, to study 'culture'? How may historians possibly benefit by perorating on great literary texts (not our métier)? What may we gainfully say about a vastly researched novel? As I point out in the Introduction, my purpose is to weld together the canonical and marginal texts and their varied

5 Nead, *Victorian Babylon*, 1–57, is the most original analysis of the mid-19th-c. modernization project in London.

6 Ibid. 6–9.

7 Nord, *Walking the Victorian Streets*, 1–15; Williams, *The Country and the City*, 156; Nead, *Victorian Babylon*.

uses in the culture of history and not give up on great texts. *A Tale of Two Cities* defuses divisions between 'high' and 'low', the merely literary and the spectacular, and was consumed by varied audiences. It not only circulated long-sustained images of the Revolution as an urban event, but also exemplified certain characters of the popular historical artefact such as multiple production and consumption.

PATTERNS OF CONSUMPTION AND PRODUCTION

A Tale of Two Cities was neither the first historical novel on the Revolution, nor necessarily the most original one. Following Carlyle's huge success with his history, quite a few prominent novelists tried their hand at fictionalizing segments of the grand event and its aftermath. Edward Bulwer-Lytton's mystical novel *Zanoni*, appearing as a three-decker in 1842, featured Paris in 1794 at the height of the Great Terror. Its climactic end, the immortal hero's self-sacrifice on the guillotine to save his beloved's life, undoubtedly inspired the end of Dickens's own revolutionary melodrama. Anthony Trollope's only historical novel, *La Vendée* (1850), featured the 1793 royalist rebellion in the north-west of France. Another three-decker, it was a publishing disaster, realizing the prognosis that Trollope's 'history was not worth a damn' and implying a decline of interest in historical fiction around the middle of the century.[8] Dickens's success where others failed must be attributed to the economics of the production and consumption of his work and, more generally, to his role as cultural entrepreneur, moving between and across forms like the novel and melodrama and between classes and groups of consumers. This success also has to do with his urban history's relationship to older popular urban genres, most notably genres popularizing crime, prison life, and the scaffold, and to the vast plebeian urban lore about crime and 'the hanging tree' which sustained these genres.

More 'democratic' in terms of access to readers than the previous major Revolution novels, *A Tale* was written to start off Dickens's 2*d.* weekly *All the Year Round* in April 1858, succeeding *Household Words*. One novelty of the new publication was its stress on long continuous fiction, a feature reinforced in the subtitle: 'The Story of Our Lives from Year to Year'.[9] Serialized history was made accessible to a large and diffuse audience, far more diffuse than the buyers of Bulwer-Lytton's or Trollope's historical three-deckers (or their subscription-library readers), considerably more heterogeneous than readers of part-issues. Sales of the first number, introducing the novel, reached 120,000.[10] Simultaneously, the novel appeared in eight monthly parts with a good wrapper design by

8 Anthony Trollope, *Autobiography* (1883; Oxford, 1989), 110–11.
9 Robert L. Patten, *Charles Dickens and his Publishers* (Oxford, 1978), 272–3.
10 Ibid. 276.

Browne, with two illustrations, preserving 'my old standing with my old public and the advantage (very necessary in this story) of having numbers of people who read it in no portions smaller than a monthly part'. Issue sales were not staggeringly high, with demand for back issues reaching 35,000 in June and the first three numbers selling 15,691 by late August. But they obviously catered for a more defined middle-class audience.[11] Of course, the apparatus for the simultaneous production of novel-length fiction in serial and book forms had been firmly established during the late 1830s. This multiple production made possible what may be described as multiple consumption, by different audiences. The production of *A Tale* was innovative in that it made available at one and the same time two forms of serialized history, at weekly and monthly intervals and in unusually small chunks (in book form the novel is considerably shorter than most of Dickens's works). This, together with the novel's drawing on popular crime genres, action, and melodrama, would make it appeal to plebeian audiences. Though the novel never figured in Dickens's public readings, it proved immediately successful as a dramatic spectacle, especially suited to the popular stage. Quick adaptations for the stage followed high upon the heels of the serial double run.[12] The first 'authorized' dramatization, by Tom Taylor, supervised by Dickens, premiered at the Lyceum as early as 28 January 1860 and had a respectable run of thirty-five performances. A fourth version (within about a year from the beginning of serialization) in four acts by Frederick Fox Cooper catered for working-class, largely East End and south of the river audiences. It premiered on 7 July at the Victoria Theatre, located opposite Waterloo Station, a popular venue, with a revealing change in the title: *The Tale of Two Cities: or, The Incarcerated Victim of the Bastille*, stressing strong ties to melodrama. Fox Cooper exploited the nineteenth-century theatre's capacity for spectacular pyrotechnic effects, complete with smokescreens, 'conflagration', and collapsing walls, driving home the spectacular elements in the novel itself. Stage versions of the play continued to be steady runners throughout the nineteenth century and during the first decades of the twentieth. Indeed the novel was consistently successful as a popular spectacle on stage, then on screen, a success that revealingly counters the rather disdainful attitude of specialists and of literary critics. One example of the popular appeal of the urban melodrama of the Revolution is its most influential and definitive stage adaptation by the Reverends Freeman Wills and Frederick Langbridge retitled *The Only Way*. The adaptation was commissioned by John Martin-Harvey, the celebrated actor and theatre entrepreneur, and premiered at the Lyceum in 1899, with Martin-Harvey in his life

[11] Ibid. 277.

[12] Philip Bolton probably has the most detailed list of stage dramatizations. Philip Bolton, *Dickens Dramatized* (Boston, 1987). Useful summaries of dramatizations of *A Tale of Two Cities* may be found in Malcolm Morley, 'The Stage Story of *A Tale of Two Cities*', *Dickensian*, 51 (1954), 34–40 and Carol Hanbery MacKay, '"Before the Curtain": Entrances to the Dickens Theatre', in ead. (ed.), *Dramatic Dickens* (Basingstoke and London, 1989), 1–10.

role as Sydney Carton, which he would perform for nearly forty years, last on 13 May 1939 at Newcastle upon Tyne. I shall discuss his version in detail later; here it suffices to stress the durability of the adaptations of the novel into stage spectacle and its consistent hold on varied audiences.

NEWGATE AND THE BASTILLE: URBAN HISTORY AS A HISTORY OF CRIME AND CAPITAL PUNISHMENT

Of course, the chronicle of publishing and of adaptations of the novel, in print and on stage, provides a rather general idea of the novel's status and popularity and, indirectly, of the sustained popularity of the Revolution as a theme in popular memory. But fully to account for the enduring success of the urban melodrama of the Revolution, we must trace Dickens's construction of an urban past that was distinct from the present, yet near enough to be still alive in the collective urban lore and in actual everyday experience. As envisioned by Dickens and as read, or viewed by early readers/audiences, *Two Cities* was a tale of imprisonment, incarceration, even live burial, and occasionally (and not necessarily, as we shall see) as a melodrama of sacrifice. This is what some of Dickens's own few notes disclose and the Fox Cooper version makes quite clear. In these early versions, the prison, and its complementary, the scaffold, are not just 'props' or settings in an urban background. Nor are they just symbols. To borrow from V. A. C. Gatrell's characterization of the latter in his study of the early modern and modern British 'culture of the scaffold', they have a totemic function, as exemplifying presences and signposts.[13] And, I argue, the prison and gallows were instrumental and even necessary for understanding the Revolution and making sense of history generally. Their role may not be overestimated. In the popular culture of history they configured, throughout most of the nineteenth century, the very memory of the past within remembrance: the last decades of the eighteenth century and the first of the nineteenth. This was an uncomfortable memory, one replete with violence, disorder, and infringements of and on freedom, a far cry from a historicist notion of English history as a progress towards and through freedom and prosperity.

Few contemporaries captured this role more succinctly and forcefully than Dickens himself. Already on 1 January 1853, well before hitting on the idea of devoting an entire novel to the Revolution, indeed well before acting in Wilkie Collins's drama of incarcerations *The Frozen Deep*, where the idea for a melodrama of incarceration probably had been conceived,[14] he published in

[13] Gatrell, *The Hanging Tree.*

[14] On the genealogy of the novel see Philip Collins, 'A Tale of Two Novels: *A Tale of Two Cities* and *Great Expectations* in Dickens's Career', *Dickens Studies Annual*, 2 (1972), 336–51; 378–81.

Household Words a little-remembered essay entitled 'Where We Stopped Growing'. The essay is notable not only for the direct association between the traditional British system of imprisonment and incarceration in the *ancien régime* in France, between revolutionary and British symbols of oppression, but also for the illuminating reference to the individual and collective faculties of memory and recall. Dickens describes experiences over which people, including himself, 'stopped growing', experiences first encountered in childhood and retaining their original meaning later in adult life, both the life of the individual and that of the collective. The two never-outgrown experiences are those of the Bastille and Newgate Prison:

> We have never outgrown the rugged walls of Newgate, or any other prison on the outside. All within, is still the same blank of remorse and misery . . . We have never outgrown the wicked old Bastille. Here in our mind at this present childish moment, is a distinct groundplan (wholly imaginative and resting on no sort of authority), of a mass of low vaulted passages with small black cobwebs hung like a veil from the arch, and the jailer's lamp will scarcely burn, was shut up, in black silence through many years, that old man of the affecting anecdote, who was at last set free.[15]

And who, even after his release, 'prayed to be shut up in his old dungeon till he died'.[16] The old prisoner may have indicated the figure of Dr Manette, the prisoner in the Bastille in the novel, or, for that matter, popular myths about the incarcerated living-dead man held at the Bastille and released on the event of its storming by the revolutionaries on 14 July 1789. The wax effigy of this figure had been displayed at Madame Tussaud's and was familiar to Dickens. More important than any of these details, however, is the association, analogy even, between Newgate and the Bastille.

By the 1850s, mention of Newgate carried a multiplicity of images with layers of literary-historical and visual traditions, traditions which themselves had been firmly planted in the collective urban experience and in urban spectacle. Both Dickens and his readers would have been steeped in these images and the host of associations which flowed from such a mention. His earliest piece on the prison, 'A Visit to Newgate', appeared in 1836 in the first series of *Sketches by Boz* and reported, as both Philip Collins and Deborah Epstein Nord have noted, in an almost deadpan tone the extraordinary impact of the place on very ordinary men and women, not entirely different from the readership of the new genre, the urban sketch, which Dickens redefined.[17] His only other historical novel, *Barnaby Rudge: A Tale of the Riots of 'Eighty* (1841), documenting the Gordon

[15] Charles Dickens, 'Where We Stopped Growing', *Household Words*, 1 Jan. 1853, in *Dent Uniform Edition of Dickens's Journalism*, iii, ed. Michael Slater (Columbus, Ohio, 1998), 112.

[16] Ibid.

[17] Philip Collins, *Dickens and Crime* (London, 1964), 33; Nord, *Walking the Victorian Streets*, 64. For an account of the history of publishing of the sketches see 'Introduction', *Sketches by Boz and Other Early Papers 1833–39* (*Dent Uniform Edition of Dickens Journalism*, i; Columbus, Ohio, 1994), pp. xi–xxii. See also 'a Visit to Newgate', 199–211.

Riots and, like *Two Cities*, fixing on urban rebellion, repression exercised by the state and the law, and the dynamics of crowds' responses to them, featured Newgate centrally and he already acquired his distinct 'penological' condemnatory tone towards the penal code and the prison system. However, the most widely effective and popular impact of his representations of this prison, crime, and punishment may be related to the writings closest to a distinct and recognizable genre, devoted entirely to crime, low life, and imprisonment and widely known as the 'Newgate novel'. Developed by Dickens himself and by writers who were also distinguished and successful historical novelists, such as Bulwer-Lytton and William Harrison Ainsworth, the genre thrived before the 1850s, reaching its apogee between 1830 and 1847. It was exactly at that time that Newgate fiction became the subject of a furious controversy (the 'Newgate controversy'), in which Dickens himself was cast as a purveyor of a literary cult of crime and criminal life.[18]

Newgate novels drew on a considerably broader and older oral and literary prison and crime lore, traceable from the early eighteenth century (and even earlier), when biographical vignettes of the Newgate condemned, drawn chiefly from the prison's *Calendar*, attracted popular interest. The most ambitious and most widely known *Calendar* was *The Malefactor's Register or New Newgate and Tyburn Calendar* of 1773, which catered for a genteel readership. Plebeian and considerably cheaper tales and histories of the imprisoned and condemned had been available from the sixteenth century in a multiplicity of texts and urban spectacles which thrived during the second half of the eighteenth century and the early nineteenth century. These included the traditional, subversive, and ribald flash ballads and gentler broadsides, pantomime and penny-gaff melodrama, and, from the 1830s, a vast repertoire of serialized fiction, typically setting criminal life in an urban and metropolitan locale, frequently in the past.[19]

But Newgate was not just a literary construct, or a symbol of oppression and unjust power (though it certainly had been both in the prison genres). It had a very material life and a presence in the changing landscape of the metropolis. It was a landmark, a site/sight with a history that the early and mid-Victorians could and did associate with a bloody past, yet could not easily extricate from the evolution of the 'modern' city. In a city that by the early nineteenth century had more prisons than any other in Europe, Newgate had enjoyed a privileged status as the place of incarceration of the condemned and of a spectacularly public judicial killing. It retained its status long after the modernization of the 'Bloody' penal 'Code' during the late 1830s and the contemporaneous reform of the prison (Dickens's own writings on Newgate date from after this modernization). Between 9 December 1783 (with the stopping of public executions at Tyburn)

[18] On the Newgate novel see Juliet John, *Dickens's Villains: Melodrama, Character, Popular Culture* (Oxford, 2001), 57–61 and Keith Hollingsworth, *The Newgate Novel, 1830–47: Bulwer, Ainsworth, Dickens and Thackeray* (Detroit, 1963).

[19] Gatrell, *The Hanging Tree*, 109–56.

and 25 May 1868, with consistency and regularity that had no parallel on the Continent, it was the locus of the scaffold. The visibility and spectacular aspects of the gallows, axe, and noose made them very familiar to English people across classes, as Gatrell has amply demonstrated. The last decades of the eighteenth century and early decades of the nineteenth were 'killing days', with hangings peaking during the revolutionary decades between the 1770s and 1830 (the very eve of the repeal of the Code). Of the 35,000 condemned, some 7,000 were not reprieved and were hanged before crowds. Over 139 were hanged in London between 1774 and 1777 (compared with thirty-two in Paris). During the 1820s, the annual average of metropolitan judicial killing stood at twenty-three. This ratio dropped dramatically with the repeal in 1837 of most capital statutes, but the scaffold remained a feature of London life and of the life of provincial assize places until the abolition of public execution in 1868.[20] Even throughout much of the mid-Victorian era, the scaffold attached to the prison was the most regular, cheapest urban spectacle. 'No ritual was so securely imbedded in metropolitan or provincial urban life.'[21] It was a ritual which drew substantial audiences, described and perceived as potentially dangerous crowds and endowed with the characteristics of crowds in political public gatherings. Political executions drew tens of thousands of spectators: that of the Cato Street Conspirators is reputed to have drawn 100,000. Murderers had a sustained appeal which did not decrease with time. The hangings of the Mannings in 1849, on the roof of Horsemonger Lane Prison, which Dickens witnessed from a house overlooking the gallows which he together with four friends secured for 10 guineas, drew a crowd of 30,000. The execution of Benjamin Rush in 1856 attracted thousands of provincials and tourists from London conveyed by special trains. That same year, some 50,000 came to watch Muller die.[22]

The outdoor public ritual at street level in the environs of Newgate and the Old Bailey and their larger perimeter had its indoor equivalent in Madame Tussaud's Chamber of Horrors and, to an extent, as Chapters 4 and 5 demonstrate, in the reconstructed and reopened Tower of London, where the axe, scaffold, and dungeon had held a central part since about 1840. Wax models or death masks of the hanged, like Rush and the Mannings, or the young François Courvoisier (whose crime was thought to have been generated by a Newgate novel and whose execution too Dickens had witnessed) were realistic reminders of the 'real' thing. Viewing them inside the museum was supplementary (and could be a substitute) to witnessing the much messier actual killing.[23] As with the Chamber of Horrors, so with the prison and scaffold: crime and ritual execution and death became the measure of the past and its relationship to the present. The old killing days of the late eighteenth century and the revolutionary decades were viewed as a distant

[20] Gatrell, *The Hanging Tree*, 6–10; App. 2, pp. 616–19; Emsley, *Crime and Society in England*, 148–93.

[21] Gatrell, *The Hanging Tree*, 30.

[22] Ibid. 56–7.

[23] Pilbeam, *Madame Tussaud*, 179.

country. In the same year that *Two Cities* saw publication, Walter Bagehot described this past as 'so far remote from us that we cannot comprehend it ever having existed'.[24] And yet what made the eighteenth century so fascinating was its very proximity to the modern experience, its existence as history within living memory, as well as the multiplicity of its traces. In this memory, noted Charles Philip in 1857 in his *Vacation Thoughts on Capital Punishment*, 'every page of our statue book smelt of blood'.[25]

Dickens's own preoccupation, obsession even, with the prison and the scaffold, and the ways in which he exploited both to reconfigure history, highlight the duality which is at the basis of a broader attitude to the recent past: a distancing entwined with a sense of closeness and familiarity. For him Newgate and the Bastille, the scaffold and the guillotine, were not just relics or horrifying curiosities of bygone days. They were 'lived' memories with a powerful materiality, as well as being the subject of social action which honed a mixture of humanitarian drives and social and political concerns and anxieties.[26] In most histories of the abolition of public executions, Dickens has a place of honour. Initially an abolitionist, campaigning for the total repeal of capital punishment, Dickens changed his mind and heart in the early 1840s to campaign against public executions. Thereafter it was to scaffold crowds and not to the scaffold itself that he objected. Not the death sentence and its instigators (so directly decried in *Barnaby Rudge*), but the visibility of capital punishment to urban spectators whom he deemed vulgar and subversive motivated his feelings. As John Bright put it, what Dickens was after was assassination as replacement of execution, 'a longing to put someone to death'.[27] Displacing outrage from the scaffold to scaffold crowds certainly did not prevent him from returning to the hangings in the same way he repeatedly returned to the Chamber of Horrors: to experience at first (or second) hand the pleasurable horrors of public death. His reports in 1840 of the vulgarity of spectators at the death of François Benjamin Courvoisier, or the 1849 eroticized description of the dangling body of the murderess Mrs Manning, disclose an unconcealed frisson at the scaffold: the pleasure of horror.

LONDON AND PARIS

The urban tale of imprisonment is set between 1775 (when, probably not coincidentally, *Barnaby Rudge* too begins) and the Paris September Massacres of 1792, with 1780 as an interim station, sliding back to the 1750s and 1760s and shifting between the two capital cities. When the tale opens, Dr Manette has

[24] Cited in Gatrell, *The Hanging Tree*, 11. [25] Ibid.
[26] Marius Kwint, 'Introduction: The Physical Past', in id., Christopher Breward, and Jeremy Aynsley (eds.), *Material Memories* (Oxford, 1999), 1–17.
[27] Cited in Jeremy Tambling, *Dickens, Violence and the Modern State: Dreams of the Scaffold* (London, 1995), 129.

been released, demented, from long imprisonment in the Bastille for attesting to the rape of a peasant and the killing of her brother by the St-Évremonde brothers, ultimate personification of *ancien régime* corruption and cruelty. Brought to London, he is resurrected to life by his daughter Lucie, living in a prosperous triangle with her and her husband, Charles Darnay, prodigal aristocrat and scion of the house of Évremonde. Darnay's return to Paris during the early days of the Republic brings on his arrest, imprisonment, second trial, and condemning to death on the guillotine. His rescue from death for the second time, by the wasted and tormented barrister Sydney Carton, provides a final scaffold scene modelled on the crucifixion. The selection of 'The Period' (the title chosen by Dickens for the famous first chapter) and handling of chronology follows Carlyle's periodization in the *French Revolution*, which, as the Preface stresses and as numerous genealogies of the novel have substantiated, was Dickens's main inspiration and source.[28] It is precisely this periodization that makes it possible to cast the English past (and, needless to say, the French one) as an unreformed and unjust country. Take, for example, the mock-history of eighteenth-century disorder, incompetence in governance, and a bloody legal system, climaxing in a thrashing of the 'Bloody Code' at the very beginning of the novel:

In England, there was scarcely an amount of order and protection to justify much national boasting. Daring burglaries by armed men, and highway robberies, took place in the capital itself every night; families were publicly cautioned not to go out of town without removing their furniture to the upholsterers' warehouses for security; the highwayman in the dark was a City tradesman in the light, and, being recognized . . . the Lord Mayor of London was made to stand and deliver on Turnham Green by one highwayman, who despoiled the illustrious creature in sight of all his retinue; prisoners in London gaols fought battles with their turnkeys, and the majesty of the law fired blunderbusses in among them, loaded with rounds of shot and ball; thieves snipped off diamond crosses from the necks of noble lords at Court drawing rooms; musketeers went into St. Giles's to search for contraband goods, and the mob fired on the musketeers, and the musketeers fired on the mob and nobody thought any of these occurrences much out of the common way. In the midst of them, the hangman ever busy and ever worse than useless, was in constant requisition; now stringing up low rows of miscellaneous criminals; now hanging a housebreaker on Saturday who had been taken on Tuesday; now, burning people in the hand at Newgate by the dozen, and now, burning pamphlets at the door of Westminster Hall; to-day taking the life of an atrocious murderer, and tomorrow of the wretched pilferer who had robbed a farmer's boy out of sixpence.[29]

The thickness of this mock telegraphic history of urban disorder is made up of its numerous references to just the kind of literature discussed earlier: the Georgian

[28] Carlyle's influence is studied in Michael Goldberg, *Carlyle and Dickens* (Athens, Ga., 1972) and Branwen Baily Pratt, 'Carlyle and Dickens: Heroes and Hero Worshippers', *Dickens Annual Studies*, 13 (1983), 233–46.

[29] Charles Dickens, *A Tale of Two Cities* (1859, repr. London, 1994), Bk. 1, ch. 1, pp. 14–15.

and early Victorian literature on highwaymen, robbers, and gallant thieves, as well as to the much broader scaffold culture. This 'history', which is repeated later in the novel, is certainly not a Whig survey of the recent past, distancing the 'bad old days' from a progressive present. 'Then' was much worse than 'now', but the present does not represent progress. Indeed the idea of progress and an optimistic, ameliorative view of history is rejected in favour of the notion that the eighteenth and nineteenth centuries are similar, that the past is interchangeable with 'the present period, that some of its authorities insisted on its being received, for good or evil, in the superlative degree of comparison only'.[30]

This famous utterance may well be, and has been, taken to convey a lack of real or serious interest in history. Additionally, Dickens's self-confessed adherence to 'the philosophy of Mr. Carlyle's wonderful book'[31] manifests itself in the view of disorder, social upheavals and revolutions as human and 'natural' occurrences. Finally, the story's strong redemptory and revivalist motifs, at their most pronounced in the life story, action, and self-sacrifice of the Christ-like Sydney Carton, move the novel further away from history to the ahistorical and moralistic. To these 'weaknesses' of the novel as a history has been added its perfunctory geography of the Revolution.[32] In contradistinction to Carlyle's topography of Paris and its vicinity and his precision as far as public places, interiors, routes, and itineraries are concerned, Dickens's Paris and the dilapidated French countryside are bland and, beyond some details, unspecified. Although his knowledge of London was immense, and his writing about it 'like a special correspondent for posterity', his topography of the metropolis in the novel too is often imprecise.[33]

But all these apparent 'weaknesses' do not necessarily indicate a mid-century turn away from history, or an interest in the past solely as a genealogy of the present. Rather, comparisons between the recent past and the present articulate the duality of attitudes to the past in the urban text. The past is distant enough to be considered foreign, yet, as far as the late eighteenth century is concerned, close enough to the modern urban experience and indeed ineradicable from modernity. At the time of the serialization, Paris was undergoing and London was to undergo a massive reconstruction, involving the demolition of neighbourhoods (some of them not just old, but historic), routes, and buildings. The rebuilding of parts of central Paris, under the auspices of Baron Haussmann, its *préfecteur de police*, was considered an exemplar of urban planning and rationalization and was associated (at least in Britain) with centralism and authoritative

30 Ibid. 13.

31 Preface to the first edition, Nov. 1859, *A Tale of Two Cities*, p. i.

32 Mitchell, *Picturing the Past*, 229, 231. The non-historicity of the novel and its theology are discussed in David Rosen, '"A Tale of Two Cities": Theology of Revolution', *Dickens Studies Annual*, 27 (1998), 171–85; Kenneth M. Sroka, 'A Tale of Two Gospels: Dickens and John', ibid. 145–69; and Michael Timko, 'Dickens, Carlyle and the Chaos of Being', ibid. 16 (1987), 1–15.

33 Walter Bagehot, 'Charles Dickens', *National Review*, 7 (Oct. 1858).

government.[34] London was embarking on its second modern period of 'improvements' (the first being the Regency project of building), including the construction of railways, routes, and thoroughfares on ground, and the massive works of construction underground, including the most modern civil engineering project ever, of constructing the metropolis's drainage and sewage system, the world's first underground railway, and an infrastructure of gas-supplies system, all carried on by the newly created 'Metropolitan Board of Works' (MBW, 1855).[35] Yet the more intense the project of modernization, the greater the disruption and urban wreckage it caused. Dickens, as a recorder of the transition of and in London, captured the havoc caused by the very agents of modernity, like the railway. His descriptions of its effect, most memorably that of the building of the London and Birmingham railway at Stagg's Gardens in North London in *Dombey and Son*, immediately springs to mind.[36]

Yet this demolition and the overall massive changes in the metropolis notwithstanding, the older, eighteenth-century city was present, easily visible and impossible to eradicate—in Paris, behind the façade of boulevards and the geometric grid of its centre, in London, in those parts of the city which escaped improvement and demolition, or were deemed too autonomous or too marginal to be touched. The City of London and the metropolis's eastern parts were still seen as ungovernable, impossible to master, and, increasingly in the case of the East End, dangerous to penetrate. The piecemeal nature of the modernization of London, the absence of a master plan for its rebuilding, not to mention the lack of a central modernizing agency and the mushrooming of 'bumbledom', were such that modern London retained its labyrinthine character and structurelessness.[37] City explorers, not least Dickens himself, were aware that London's disordered 'nooks, alleys', and yards were dominant alongside the city's newly opened arteries. Put slightly differently, the city's chaotic and disordered past was alive and visible in its outlay, development, and lack of central government and was part and parcel of its modernity. Its huge and unrestrained growth in terms of space and population (4,500,000 inhabitants in the early 1860s) seriously aggravated congestion and what numerous writers, painters, and photographers, not to mention health reformers, described as 'blockage', filth, disease and putrefaction, mortality and disturbance—all living proofs of the heritage of

[34] David H. Pinkney, *Napoleon III and the Rebuilding of Paris* (Princeton, 1958) remains valuable.

[35] Nead, *Victorian Babylon*. For the MBW see David Owen (ed.), with Roy MacLeod, *The Government of Victorian London, 1855–1899: The Metropolitan Board of Works, the Vestries and the City Corporation* (Cambridge, Mass., 1982). On sewage and drainage see Stephen Halliday, *The Great Stink of London: Sir Joseph Bazalgette and the Cleansing of the Victorian Metropolis* (London, 1999). On gas see Nead, 83–148 and Martin Daunton, 'The Material Politics of Natural Monopoly: Consuming Gas in Victorian Britain', in id. and Matthew Hilton (eds.), *The Politics of Consumption: Material Culture and Citizenship in Europe and America* (Oxford, 2001), 69–89.

[36] On Dickens's documentation of the wreckage and of the expansion and building of London see Baumgarten, 'Fictions of the City' and Nead, *Victorian Babylon*, 34–6.

[37] Porter, *London: A Social History*, 288–312.

urban history deteriorating in, and as a result of, the passage of time and the scale of urbanization.[38]

Thus though London's cityscape had changed considerably between the torrid 1770s and 1780s and the 'present time' of the late 1850s, the parts of it which the novel describes had not been significantly 'improved'. They could be easily recognizable by readers. Significantly the only part of the West End touched at all in the novel is Soho Square, off Oxford Street, where the abode of Dr Manette and his daughter Lucie is located. Soho, around the time of the Revolution a haven for French refugees, was largely untouched by the Regency improvements (which in fact cut it off from the West End) and those of the 1850s and 1860s. And Dickens makes it a rural haven, a *rus in urbe*, quite different from its condition in mid-century. It is in the significantly older, little-changed parts inside the City itself, its precincts and borders, that most of the English chapters of the tale are set. These parts remained landmarks of an older, historic way of life and could actually be 'experienced' and known in the everyday. Most celebrated and to Dickens most objectionable was Temple Bar, which would be removed only in 1878, and its environs, seen by the Victorians as a public nuisance, an obstruction to the flow of traffic and a symbol of the City's obstructionist powers and corruption (in the novel the place of Tellson's Bank). Other landmarks were Fleet Street, 'Hanging sword Alley' in Whitefriars, that notorious area of 'freedom', historically outside the authority of the City and a sanctuary of outlaws, long identified as an anarchic place, and the more respectable yet, to 1850s middle-class Londoners, reputedly subversive and even revolutionary Clerkenwell. Significantly, the former is the domicile of the semi-criminal Jerry Cruncher, odd-job man at Tellson's Bank and 'resurrectionist' (body snatcher), the latter of Jarvis Lorry, the Bank's chief clerk, a 'business man' and the Manettes' mainstay. Thus the novel's map of London is at one and the same time plebeian, and represents the crumbling of law, the legal system, and the state. The emblematic 'meeting places' of the law and crowds are the Old Bailey and the neighbourhood of Newgate, both the locus of arbitrary and miscarried justice.

This juncture of the plebeian and the authoritative, of the lower strata of the people and the state, is also central to the Paris parts of the novel. Here the centres of action before and during the Revolution are the plebeian faubourgs, chiefly the Faubourg Saint Antoine, from 1789 Paris's most radical area and the centre of sans-culotte political activity, and the city's prisons. Both are foci of historic action; both are, as we shall see, also symbolic. The hub of the plebeian city and of the people, who become the carriers of revolutionary vengeance, is the Defarge wine

38 On growth see Francis Sheppard, *London 1808–1870: The Infernal Wen* (London, 1971). On blockage and circulation see Richard Sennett, *Flesh and Stone: The Body and the City in Western Civilisation* (London, 1994), esp. Part III. On urban exploration see Alex Potts, 'Picturing the Metropolis: Images of London in the Nineteenth Century', *HWJ* 26 (Autumn 1988), 28–56. See also Nord, *Walking the Victorian Streets*.

shop, functioning as revolutionary headquarters presided over by the legendary Madame Defarge, surviving sister of Évremonde's victims, who becomes the architect of a terrible vengeance directed against Darnay and his household. Outside this bastion of sans-culottism, prisons abound and serve as twin places of Newgate: the Bastille, where Dr Manette had served a sentence of eighteen years and compiled his record of the misdeeds of the Marquis of Évremonde, and which the Defarges and their co-revolutionaries take over, the prisons of La Force and the Conciergerie, last stations of the condemned, and the abode of Darnay and his double, Carton. And overshadowing the entire city is of course the guillotine, duplicating the scaffold and gallows at Tyburn and Newgate.

In this tale of cities, the countryside is not a rural and pastoral pre-industrial haven but an impoverished and pauperized place breeding exploitation, starvation, and death. When the countryside is evoked, as in the few descriptions of the Évremondes' estate, village, and peasantry, it is markedly 'empty' and devoid of any specific landmarks and even names. This absence of topographic detail stands in marked contrast to Trollope's novel of the landed revolt in the Vendée in 1793, the most sustained challenge to the Revolution. *La Vendée* is set almost entirely in the rural province of Poitou, in the Bocage area, and has the territoriality and feel for the locale exemplified in the 'traditional' historical novel of Scott. Trollope's rural history abounds with elaborate topographic detail on market towns, grain-growing villages, and small urban centres like St. Florent, Châtillon, and Vihiers, and he hectors readers with painstaking detail on local ethnography and economy. His rather pedestrian descriptions of the country residences of the nobility of Poitou, notably the description of the Château de Durbellière, home of the uprising leader Henri Duvergier de La Rochejacquelein, present a stark contrast to Dickens's bland description of the nameless chateau of the Évremondes and their *hôtel* in Paris, both obviously standing for the corrupt *noblesse* anywhere and at any time, like the demonized marquis himself. Evidently Trollope's meticulous and somewhat overbearing attention to historical and topographical detail, highly appreciated in his political and local 'contemporary' novels, failed to establish him as a historical novelist.

The empty and dehistoricized countryside and the disorderly cityscape of Paris and London are dominated, and given sense and coherence, by the scaffold and the guillotine, which figure in the novel materially and symbolically, or 'by proxy'. In the village neigbouring the Marquis's château the scaffold is erected on the well used by the peasants, a reworking, one of many, of the crucifixion and of the symbolism of the Eucharist. The scaffold literally poisons the village's water and life.[39] And on the streets of Paris, spilled wine signifies blood. The revolutionaries erect the 'real' guillotine and mock ones, including the toy guillotines, manufactured by carpenters and given to little Lucie, the Darnays' child. In the London parts, there are no descriptions of actual scaffolds and

39 *A Tale of Two Cities*, Bk. 2, ch. 9, pp. 132–3; Bk. 2, ch. 16, p. 177.

executions (though there is an abundance of general references to them and to the 'Bloody Code'), but of symbolic ones, easily identifiable. Revealingly, in all of these descriptions it is not at the instrument of miscarried justice that Dickens's eye is directed, but at the crowds/spectators participating in the action of justice and vengeance. Summary justice, both before the Revolution and during it and, by implication, in 'the present time', is represented as the ultimate urban spectacle. And the Paris and London crowds watching it are not just observers but active participants and 'proxy' executioners. In the first 'execution', which is to be found in the chapter emblematically titled 'A Sight', the prisoner's dock at the Old Bailey with the accused Darnay who is as good as condemned is an 'object of all this staring and blaring'.

> Everybody present . . . stared at him. All the human breath in the place rolled at him, like a sea, or a wind, or a fire. Eager faces strained round pillars and corners, to get a sight of him; spectators in back rows stood up, not to miss a hair of him; people on the floor of the court laid their hands on the shoulders of the people before them, to help themselves, at anybody's cost, to a view of him—stood a tiptoe, got upon ledges, stood upon next to nothing . . . [40]

The object of the collective stare, the sight, is of course not Darnay the man but his hanged and mangled body: 'The accused, who was (and who knew he was) being mentally hanged, beheaded and quartered, by everybody there, neither flinched from the situation, nor assumed any theatrical air in it.'[41] The ocular language of the scene, with its constant reference to 'spectators' and spectacle, 'theater' and 'sight', will be familiar from my discussion of Carlyle's imagery of crowds. But Dickens's theatre of the scaffold and, later in the novel, of the guillotine is his own, registering his concerns about the social and political dangers of the scaffold. Magistrates, executioners, and a paranoid and inefficient government, whether the English government during the time of the American War and the Revolution or the French Republican government, are all dangerous and arbitrary; but the source of the most serious danger is the urban crowd of spectators. The crowds at political executions, at all executions, are the executioners. The scene of Darnay's second and third trials at the Revolutionary Tribunal in Paris duplicates the Old Bailey scene. And the final depiction of the crowd watching the progress of tumbrils to the guillotine and of sans-culottes presiding over their executions again fixes the active role of the former as both the instigators of violence and its consumers and monitors.

> As the somber wheels of the six carts go round, they seem to plough up a long crooked furrow among the populace in the streets. Ridges of faces are thrown to this side and to that, and the ploughs go steadily onward. So used are the regular inhabitants of the houses to the spectacle, that in the windows there are no people, and in some the occupation of the hands is not so much as suspended, while the Eyes survey the faces in

[40] Ibid., Bk. 2, ch. 2, p. 70. [41] Ibid. 71.

the tumbrels. Here and there, the inmate has visitors to see the sight; then he points his finger, with something of the complacency of a curator or authorised exponent, to this cart and to this, and seems to tell who sat here yesterday, and who there the day before.[42]

Again as with the Old Bailey scene and the original of the description of the journey to the guillotine in Carlyle, resort to ocular metaphor abounds. Again ritual political violence and its collective watching are associated with urban tourism and entertainment (not least with the new kind of museum). But Dickens's fictional-historical account of the scaffold and the guillotine is far more immediate than Carlyle's because it resonates with the contemporary and widely available experience of the scaffold. Moreover, in the fictional eighteenth-century crowd Dickens duplicates the crowds which he repeatedly attacked in his campaign against public executions. As already noted, it is the 'vulgar', inhuman behaviour of crowds that he objected to from the early 1840s, not the inhumanity of the punishment, nor, for that matter, the horror of crime. Note his reaction to the spectators at the Courvoisier execution, which he had attended in 1840 and where he could trace 'no emotion suitable to the occasion, . . . no sorrow, no salutary terror, no abhorrence, no seriousness; nothing but ribaldry, debauchery, levity, drunkenness, and flaunting vice in filthy other shapes'. Nine years later he used similar phrasing and much the same sentence structure in his characterization of the crowd at the execution of the Mannings on the roof of Horsemonger Lane prison.[43] Compare these descriptions with those of eighteenth-century crowds in general and revolutionary crowds in particular (at the guillotine, hanging the executed heads on lanterns, or dancing the *carmagnole*) and you will find them difficult to tell apart. Strong as Dickens's critique of the law and government, past and present, is, much of his anxiety of violence and the danger in the big city is projected away from the instrument of oppression and onto its watchers. This projection or displacement, which Gatrell has aptly described as an 'evasion' of the scaffold, may have expressed fear and mistrust of plebeian responses to the scaffold and more broadly to law and order, which were far more complex than the respectable and polite would allow.[44]

The mid-century anxiety about scaffold crowds and its resonance in the urban history of the Revolution are more intense than Carlyle's in another way, having to do with techniques of seeing and observation of the city scene. The two writers represent two different ways of 'seeing'. Carlyle's view, it will be recalled, is the bird's-eye view, of the omnipresent prophet, surveying from an altitude the revolutionary city as if it were a panorama. His panoramic view of history, as we have seen, responds to the rich repertoire of panoramas which thrived in London between the 1790s and 1830s. The panoramic view of the Revolution not only suited the magnitude of the world-historical event, it also made the chaotic Paris

42 *A Tale of Two Cities*, Bk. 3, ch. 15, p. 362.

43 Gatrell, *The Hanging Tree*, 60 and 605–6.

44 Ibid.

(and, by implication, England's potentially revolutionary big cities) manageable and possible to master. True, Carlyle 'humanized' the panoramic sight by including people and their suffering in it. However, the surveyor-prophet's eye made it possible to order history's chaos from a distance. Seeing in *Two Cities* is quite different and represents a different strategy of coming to terms with the changing urban environment and with history. London and Paris are observed and explored not from above but at street level; not by an omnipresent surveyor, but by walkers. Most characters in the novel are pedestrians, crossing London (Jarvis Lorry, the Crunchers) and Paris (the Defarges, Carton, and even the domestic Lucie Manette). What their walking reveals is a labyrinthine, dense city, too vast and chaotic to control. The descriptions of Fleet Street, the grimy and odorific environs of the Temple Bar, including the decomposing Tellson's Bank, the putrescent graveyard at St Pancras, where the elder Cruncher digs up graves—all these are more than matched by descriptions of the nooks and alleys, garrets and little shops at St Antoine or around the revolutionary prisons.

This kind of representation corresponds to the approach to modernity in a large body of urban texts produced during the middle decades of the nineteenth century, across different literary genres from the novel to the social ethnographic survey of the city, through pictorial images, to city mapping (especially in the new ordnance survey of London in the 1850s). What made these urban texts unique, as Nead and Nord have noted, is an awareness of the inadequacy and limits of the panoramic view.[45] The metropolis, especially one like London, or Paris before the modernization of its centre, did not yield to grand narratives of order. The felt need for a closer and more involved observation that would take into consideration both the metropolis's past and its problems in the present was not an exercise in aesthetics. It translated precisely the social and political concerns and anxieties wrought by urban development politics and discussed earlier.

WOMEN AND URBAN DISORDER

Gender is central to the imagining of the disordered city and the scaffold at its centre. Women in particular are represented as chief agents of disorder in its ultimate forms: the Revolution and the Terror. They are ubiquitous on the streets of plebeian Paris. They are conspicuous in the revolutionary tribunal and at the guillotine. Though they are occasionally cast as victims (Lucie Manette and the unnamed milliner condemned to death with Carton), it is primarily as active spectators of democratic justice in action and as avengers/executioners that they are depicted. Their centrality in the narrative and the Revolution are in stark contrast to the marginality of women in *Barnaby Rudge* and Dickens's gendered interpretation of the Gordon Riots. In the earlier novel, destruction of property

[45] Nead, *Victorian Babylon*; Nord, *Walking the Victorian Streets*.

and lives, pillage, and the challenge to authority and unjust law, as well as Lord Gordon's anti-Catholic agenda and his Protestant Associations, are all connected to and represented as a part of a plebeian masculine culture, in which the workshop, rituals of heavy drinking, and demonstrations of physical might are hermetically sealed to women of all classes. The mob's plebeian leaders Dennis the hangman and Hugh the Ostler, who is likened to a satyr, are emblems of this bacchanalian masculinity. Women are conspicuously absent from the streets of riotous London. When they are discernible among the rioters set on breaking into Newgate, it is as the relatives of felons, or as 'miserable women, cast out from the world'. Significantly, the former are disguised as men.[46] The ordinary working-class woman or artisan's wife has no place in the world of politics and protest. Mrs Varden's intervention in this world, in the form of an ignorant and misguided anti-popery, is utterly ridiculous.

In *A Tale of Two Cities* ordinary and respectable plebeian women are ubiquitous. Their role as the engine of violent change draws on Carlyle's *French Revolution*, which, as we saw in Chapter 2, represented them as the driving force of the vulcanic eruption of human 'nature', at the same time as historicizing them as carriers of sans-culottism. Dickens endows these women with other special powers: an extraordinary power to watch and observe the city, historical memory and recording. They are the *ancien régime* and Revolution's spectators and plebeian historians, as well as being the authentic voice of the French people.

The female spectators which the novel famously marked out are the 'knitters': the militants of Paris's sans-culotte quarters who, between 1792 and late 1794, regularly attended public executions while knitting. Dickens's depictions of the *tricoteuses*, especially his description of their 'chief', the manic knitter Therese Defarge, would become the novel's staple, its most sustained image across genres, notably on the screen. But already before the late 1850s the sans-culotte knitter had become a well-known symbol of the Great Terror. During the Revolution itself the term had designated a whole area of gender-specific forms of political action and violence which had developed in France's urban centres. The Revolution, especially in its Jacobin/democratic stage, excluded women from political citizenship, repeatedly seeking to curtail their mobility within the city's sites of government and political citizenship. Voteless, revolutionary women carved for themselves spaces and forms of activity that drew on traditional, *ancien régime* female protest but also expanded to new areas, thus redefining women's citizenship. They attended the quarter assemblies within the Paris Commune as well as all-female organizations and clubs. When these became outlawed by the Jacobin Republic in 1793, lower-class women continued their protest in the streets, ritually invaded the institutions apparently reserved for active (male) citizens, like the Convention and the Revolutionary Tribunal,

[46] Charles Dickens, *Barnaby Rudge; A Tale of the Riots of 'Eighty* (1841; Harmondsworth, 1997), ch. 63, p. 569.

routinely carrying arms. These activities, like the denouncing of suspects and the monitoring of the Revolution's justice at its ultimate site, the guillotine, were interpreted as a form of female citizenship. The knitters, as Dominique Godineau has pointed out, were *citoyennes tricoteuses.*[47] And knitting at the guillotine was loaded with symbolism across the Channel, because revolutionary and counter-revolutionary rhetoric defined knitting as the patriotic woman's domestic duty. The order for the *levée en masse*, establishing the first citizens' army in January 1793, and Jacobin utterances concerning the closing down of women's organizations, abundantly referred to their knitting as a service for their country. The *tricoteuses*, while apparently carrying on this duty within the gender boundaries of the Revolution, challenged the borderlines between the republican home and action outside it. For the militants dangerously expanded a traditional and acceptable activity to the public and political sphere. In 1837 Carlyle could assume that the image of the militants was widespread and he referred to them as 'The female Jacobins, famed *Tricoteuses* with knitting-needles'.[48]

In a novel strongly linked to crime fiction and to popular pastimes, there was considerably more room to elaborate on the available images of deviant female revolutionaries than in Carlyle's philosophical-historical work.[49] The militant knitters of 1792, both as a group and as individual characters (notably Madame Defarge) have distinct characteristics of melodrama, arguably the most popular form of theatre in the nineteenth century—particularly with the urban lower classes. Melodramatic conventions and aesthetics, familiar from and already circulating in the theatrical repertoire which both he and his readers shared, offered Dickens the possibility of depicting excessively passionate and violent models of female character and behaviour, sometimes deemed asocial, yet at the same time dramatizing concerns about the family, politics, and society. Revolutionary women like Madame Defarge and her chief aide, the eponymous 'Vengeance', who are cast as melodramatic villainesses, certainly threaten conformity. As city, or street, women, they differ widely from the archetypical and liminal Victorian outcast or streetwalker: the prostitute. They are, at one and the same time, of the republican city and its streets and outside it. They are agents of political change, but also the victims of history. It is *ancien régime* feudalism and the patriarchal prerogative of a villainous aristocracy which engender the transgression Madame Defarge embodies. She is the sister of the violated peasant girl, raped and murdered by the Évremondes, the daughter of a murdered serf and sister of another. Family melodrama fuels her republican rage and bloodiness. Indeed the theme

47 Dominique Godineau, *The Women of Paris and their Revolution*, trans. Katherine Streip (Berkeley, 1998).

48 Carlyle, *The French Revolution*, III, VII, IV, p. 710.

49 Their origins, especially those of Madame Defarge in *The French Revolution*, are discussed in Shifra Hochberg, 'Madame Defarge and a Possible Carlylean Source', *Dickensian*, 91 (1995), 99–101. For a different analysis see Barbara J. Black, 'A Sisterhood of Rage and Beauty: Dickens's Rosa Dartle, Miss Wade and Madame Defarge', *Dickens Studies Annual*, 26 (1998), 91–106.

of cross-class exploitation and violation is recognizable melodrama stuff. And Dickens used melodramatic effects, notably exaggeration, to dramatize her.

Exaggeration is apparent in the theatrical positioning of the 'sisterhood' of murderous knitters as spectators at the Place de Guillotine 'in front of [which], seated in chairs, as in a garden of public diversion, are a number of women, busily knitting', presided over by The Vengeance, Madame Defarge's aide-de-camp who guards her usual place for her.[50] The highly and overtly theatrical character of the collective of knitters also expresses wider topics with a history from before the Revolution like poverty and hunger, kinds of labour, and the deteriorating family economy, topics which were not foreign to novel-readers and melodrama-goers around the middle of the nineteenth century. Indeed the knitters and knitting become the dramatic thread tying together the various episodes of the history of the Revolution. The following description is strategically located in the sixteenth chapter, titled 'Still Knitting', in Book the Second, revealingly titled 'The Golden Thread'.[51] In it women's work in pre-revolutionary Paris prefigures their dangerous and highly politicized work during the Revolution:

In the evening, at which season of all others Saint Antoine turned himself inside out, and sat on door-steps and window-ledges, and came to the corners of vile streets and courts, for a breath of air, Madame Defarge with her work in her hand was accustomed to pass from place to place and from group to group: a missionary—there were many like her—such as the world will do well never to breed again. All the women knitted. They knitted worthless things; but, the mechanical work was a mechanical substitute for eating and drinking: the hands moved for the jaws and the digestive apparatus: if the bony fingers had been still, the stomachs would have been more famine-pinched. . . . And as Madame Defarge moved from group to group, all three went quicker and fiercer among every little knot of women that she had spoken with, and left behind . . . Darkness closed around, and then came the ringing of church bells and the distant beating of the military drums in the Palace Courtyard, as the women sat knitting, knitting. Darkness encompassed them. Another darkness was closing in as surely, when the church bells, then ringing pleasantly in many an airy steeple over France, should be melted into thunder cannon . . . So much was closing in about the women who sat knitting, that their very selves were closing in around a structure yet unbuilt, where they were to sit knitting, knitting, counting dropping heads.[52]

'Mechanical work', 'worth', and 'worthless work' ring with the vocabulary of the Victorian debate on women's work. In the debate the needleworker came to be a symbol not just of women's plight but also of that of poverty and dislocation in the city. An array of literary and pictorial genres, from the domestic novel and poetry to city ethnography and genre painting, abound with descriptions and analyses of all kinds of work with the needle, their 'worth' and relation to both

[50] *A Tale of Two Cities*, Bk. 3, ch. 14, p. 360.
[51] Ibid., Bk. 2, ch. 15, pp. 166–77.
[52] Ibid., Bk. 2, ch. 16, p. 187.

traditional domestic economy and to the competitive capitalism of the metropolis. A variety of needlework, including forms of sweating-work employed in knitting, stitching, and embroidery making, was increasingly associated with urban exploitation, displacement, and poverty.[53] Examples of these associations, as well as of that between needlework and the depressed occupations suffering the consequences of mechanization, are legion, and were widely available to contemporary readers across class and gender. Suffice it to mention here the 'Song of the Shirt', written in 1843 by Thomas Hood, paintings by G. F. Watts ('The Seamstress') and Richard Redgrave, and innumerable testimonies in pamphlets and committees on women's labour. And, of course, Dickens himself provided quite a few descriptions of debased female work at the needle.[54]

What distinguishes his rendering women's work in *Two Cities*, however, is its political and historical meaning. For it produces anger, political action, and historical memory and interpretation. Madame Defarge's compulsive knitting is a register of the history of the oppression of her own family and of that of entire classes: the peasantry and the urban poor. While managing the family wine shop, she incessantly knits, in a language and code that are her own, all the names, titles, deeds, and dates of the wrongs done to the people. Her annals of the *ancien régime* become the basis of violent action and the law of the Revolution. Put differently, the historical memory, represented as female, is 'translated' into revenge and destruction. Madame Defarge, a 'strong woman, a grand woman, a frightfully grand woman', is armed and violent.[55] In her manly hands knitting and the Revolution are transformed into an act of vengeance. Though her characterization draws on Carlyle, she is considerably more subversive than his revolutionary lower-class women. For they are depicted as mothers; she is neither mother nor wife. And she transforms the role of daughter and sister into a bloody rampage. For such a deviant militant (and historian) there is only one end in the revolutionary city melodrama: violent death.

Like Madame Defarge, Sydney Carton too is a borderline figure. A recognized type in melodrama, he is a version of the urban dandy and rake, living purposelessly on the edge of respectable society. Indeed readers could trace him back to a gallery of Georgian and Regency literary and theatrical city types which, like the popular prison and scaffold plots, were easily referable to early

53 On women's work, urbanization, and poverty and the woman worker as a 'problem' see Joan W. Scott, '"*L'Ouvrière! Mot impie, sordide*...": Women Workers and the Discourse of French Political Economy, 1840–1860', in ead., *Gender and the Politics of History* (New York, 1988), 139–67. On needlewomen see Lynn M. Alexander, *Women, Work and Representation: Needlewomen in Victorian Art and Literature* (Athens, Ohio, 2003). On the image of needlework and its use by Victorian women historians see Melman, 'Gender, History and Memory', 14–15.

54 Alexander, *Women, Work and Representation*, and Helene E. Roberts, 'Marriage, Redundancy or Sin: The Painter's View of Women in the First Twenty-Five Years of Victoria's Reign', in Martha Vicinus (ed.), *Suffer and Be Still: Women in the Victorian Age* (Bloomington, Ind., 1972), 45–77.

55 *A Tale of Two Cities*, Bk. 2, ch. 16, p. 187.

nineteenth-century urban genres depicting leisured ramblers, loiterers, and men-about-town in their experience of urban low life. The genre, highlighted in Pierce Egan's famous *Life in London, or The Day and Night Scenes of Jerry Hawthorne, Esq. and his Elegant Friend Corinthian Tom in Their Rambles and Sprees through the Metropolis* (1820), is a distinctly gendered one, representing a rough and hedonistic (and very public) image of masculinity, most probably directed at male audiences. The narrative of Carton's fall and rise through sacrifice represents another, much softer, masculinity, bourgeois, and, of course, Christ-like. Like the older urban types and like Madame Defarge, his domesticity is doubtful and destined to fail. Unlike her, he is 'rescued' by the sacrifice which entitles him vicariously to achieve a membership in a middle-class household and family—the Darnays'—by becoming Charles Darnay's double (and, by implication, Lucy's other husband) and a symbolic father to Lucy's child. Carton's transgression of class and gender codes is assimilated in the melodramatic narrative. Rather than disrupting the household he is absorbed into its ethos and morality. Madame Defarge's transgressions are too great to be contained in the urban history of the Revolution and the conventions of the urban genres which made up *Two Cities*—the prison tale, the melodrama, and urban ethnography.

HISTORICAL MELODRAMA ON STAGE

Madame Defarge's and Carton's gender and political transgressions fascinated contemporary readers and viewers.[56] And both, like the plebeian nineteenth-century London and revolutionary Paris, attracted by their power to repulse: Carton as the reformed rake, or prodigal, who dies gratuitously, and Madame Defarge as the militant who dies apparently accidentally. The popular appeal of both characters and indeed the appeal of the Revolution itself as a family melodrama, albeit a politicized one, is evident in the history of the novel on the popular stage before and after 1859. One of Dickens's most dramatic novels, *Two Cities* had had a dramatic life even before it was novelized. As a few of its students have pointed out, it had been conceived not just with the stage in mind, but in dramatic terms. Dickens himself was at pains to show the popular theatrical origins and connections of the drama of double identity, imprisonment, and sacrifice in the Preface, noting how this idea took over as he was acting in Wilkie Collins's play *The Frozen Deep*, making him identify with its central figure, Charles Wardur, one of Carton's prototypes.

[56] On the social potential of melodrama and Dickens's uses of it see John, *Dickens's Villains*, 42–70, and on melodrama's uses of the Newgate tale, 95–122. See also Peter Brooks, *The Melodramatic Imagination: Balzac, Henry James, Melodrama and the Mode of Excess* (New Haven, 1976) and Michael Hays and Anastasia Nikolopoulou (eds.), *Melodrama: The Cultural Emergence of a Genre* (Basingstoke, 1996).

Less known than the connection to Collins's melodrama, the novel drew heavily on historical melodrama which from the 1840s thrived across the Channel and which located the themes of doubling, incarceration, and sacrificial death in the reign of terror. The prototypical Revolution melodrama is the Elder Dumas's *Chevalier de la maison rouge*, published in 1847 and climaxing in the hero, Lorin, taking the place on the guillotine of a condemned aristocrat. An English version by Dion Boucicault, that master of Victorian theatrical spectacle, premiered at the Adelphi in 1853, featuring two of the leading theatrical entrepreneurs of the fifties who played crucial roles in the circulation of historical drama: the French actress Madame Celeste, later to become the first Madame Defarge on stage, and Benjamin Webster, later her and Dickens's rival. Even before the novel's first adaptation by the reigning dramatist of the day, Tom Taylor, premiered at the Lyceum, Webster released *The Dead Heart* by the fairly anonymous Watts Taylor before the conclusion of *Two Cities* on the guillotine, an end which the play seems to have anticipated. At least one more authorized stage version appeared in 1860, *The Tale of Two Cities; or the Incarcerated Victim of the Bastille* by Frederick Fox Cooper, premiering at the Victoria in June and immediately plagiarized by Henry J. Rivers. The first two versions became the basis of numerous adaptations which circulated in the West End and south of the Thames, in Edinburgh and in the provinces, and on the east coast of the United States. Both the number of adaptations and the rampant plagiarizing are proofs that there was a popular and varied market for Revolution melodrama which during the nineteenth century outlived that for the novel. The Lyceum version catered for mixed audiences, including holders of tickets for boxes at 2*s*., the pit at 1*s*., and the galleries at 6*d*., and affordable to the shop assistants, housemaids, cooks, and even to workers, described in Max Schlesinger's *Sauntering in and about London* (1853), and the Victoria was even more down-market.

The multiplicity and simultaneity of forms and genres of the urban text reflect and at the same time exemplify the consumption of history characterized not only by a variety of choice but also by the visual consumption noted in the previous two chapters. The stage adaptations had a multimedia effect. They were designed to be experienced both visually and aurally and were lavishly staged as spectacles with music, a genre halfway between the play and the music hall. Moreover, the adaptations dramatized history in the same way that earlier and contemporary presentations of historical objects and relics which dominated urban entertainment did. Like Madame Tussaud's and some panoramic representations of Paris, the stage versions of the 1860s and 1870s included many 'tableaux', representing revolutionary types and slices of revolutionary urban life: sans-culottes fraternizing in the streets, the Revolutionary Tribunal, and, of course, the guillotine. Moreover, the historical theatre drew lavishly on stage technologies and pyrotechnics borrowed from the diorama and phantasmagoria, also discussed in Chapter 2. In the Victoria in June 1860, audiences watched the chateau of the marquis St-Évremonde set on fire, the setting covered in real smoke and collapsing, every evening, as well as watching the marquis himself stabbed to death. And they were witnesses to crowd scenes played to the sounds of the revolutionary *carmagnole*, which could be from music sellers to be replayed and thus enact the story. The urban Revolution during its democratic phase, identified with the Terror, became alive on stage, drawing in the audiences and their senses of vision and hearing. 'We are', noted *The Era*,

> Now brought to the year 1793, and the excitement of the Revolution is portrayed in vivid colours. The rousing of the sections is made to take place outside the wine-shop of Defarge. The fiendish dance of the Carmagnole, for which the original music has been procured from the *Bibliothèque Imperiale*, is performed, with all its traditional accompaniments of fantastic movements and shrieking curses. The stage is filled by the infuriated populace, and the *tableau* at the conclusion is well arranged and impressive.[57]

So impressive indeed was action on the street and around the guillotine that the dialogue seemed quite redundant.[58] The riotous experience did not end with the show but could be extended and transferred to the home: Music 'arrangements for the pianoforte' of the wild *carmagnole*, clearly aimed at the genteel, could be had at London musical treasuries such as Davidson's.

Notwithstanding the massive appropriation of visual techniques from the culture of panoramas, the theatrical experience of the Revolution was not panoramic and did not endow viewers with the bird's-eye view of an ordered and even manageable city. What they witnessed on the stages of the Lyceum and the Victoria was a melodrama of family crime, punishment, and rewards moved to the street and set against street politics, action, and life. Almost all of the prototypical adaptations staged in Britain and the USA between 1860 and 1900 began with a prologue which enacted the scene of the Évremondes' crime against the Defarges. In virtually all adaptations until 1899, vindication of the family's honour literally moved the plot, thus placing Madame Defarge at centre stage and endowing her with roles she did not enjoy in the novel. In Cooper's production and Rivers's piratical duplication, she witnesses the marquis's murder on stage. As 'The Smoke clears away, discovering the street beyond [his mansion] crowded with People, who exclaim loudly "Extermination", she calls over her manic knitting: "burn! burn! burn! St. Évremonde! Sister, thou art avenged." '[59]

Madame Defarge's importance manifests a shift away from the novel's interest in middle-class domesticity (albeit a constantly threatened one) and towards a direct class conflict played out in the city and which duplicates tensions between genders. It is notable that some of the middle-class characters are marginalized or

57 'The Theatre & Co', *The Era*, 5 Feb. 1860.

58 Ibid.

59 Henry J. Rivers, *The Tale of Two Cities: A Drama in Three Acts and a Prologue Adapted from Mr. Charles Dickens's Story* (London, 1860), 44.

dropped altogether (the quintessentially middle-class Englishwoman Miss Pross, for example) and their appearance in the plays is rather gratuitous. On the other hand, aristocrats are brought to the fore in a conflict between them and 'the people', embodied in the Defarges—wife and husband, their sans-culotte comrades, and some of the British plebeian characters, who stand for true British nationalism. Lucie Manette's role is considerably pruned and she is a rather anaemic foil to the larger than life plebeian characters. Jerry Cruncher becomes a cockney spokesman for working-class practical common sense and fierce nationalism. Thus he shops in the Paris markets for food, fraternizes during revolutionary festivals with militant sans-culottes, yet condemns their violence in ultra-patriotic language:

'of all the ugly, black looking, out-at elbows, cut-throaty lots I *ever* see, this is the wust by a long chalk! Why the Gordon rioters was gen'lmen and ladies to 'em'. No wonder that the revolutionary are comparable to the Irish: 'Black guards sir. Talk o' Irish blackguard—that ain't to be sneezed at. But it's Lord Chesterfield alongside o' the French harticle.'[60]

Like the characters, the action itself and its solution shift away from the home to the pubic places of urban unrest and disorder: the street and marketplace, the wine shop/tavern, the revolutionary courtroom (a transplant of the Old Bailey complete with the dock and jury), and, of course, the guillotine. Domestic 'issues', including family loyalties and parenthood, notably motherhood, are turned into conflicts coloured with class antipathies. Thus when Lucie pleads with Madame Defarge as a 'sister woman' and 'a wife at least' she is angrily harangued that ' "All our lives we have seen our sister women suffer poverty, nakedness, hunger, thirst and misery of all kinds . . . judge you, is it likely that the trouble of one wife and mother should be so much to us now. Hark! The sacred music of my Vengeance! Come, husband to the Tribunal!" '[61]

The appeal of the character was enhanced by Madame Celeste's Frenchness and her costume, a female version of the official sans-culotte male: the Phrygian cap of liberty (over loose hair), a shirt with a band in the revolutionary tricolor across it, a striped skirt, probably in the tricolor too, and a dagger at her waist. She 'gave all the strong colouring of her part in earnest delivery and expressive action, which have made her embodiments always remarkable for force and intensity of dramatic illustration'.[62] Her origins, experience, and temper made her an appropriate interpreter of the historical theme and event she represented, and her role as broker of the past is comparable to that of Madame Tussaud. Madame Celeste/Defarge's dramatic death, not Carton's, formed the climax. In Dickens's and Taylor's version his sacrifice is rather muted. And in Fox Cooper,

[60] Tom Taylor, *A Tale of Two Cities, A Drama in Two Acts and a Prologue Adapted from the Story of that Name by Charles Dickens* (London, 1860), 40 and 42.
[61] Ibid. 45.
[62] *The Era*, 5 Feb. 1860.

undoubtedly catering for plebeian audiences, Carton does not die at all! After successfully doubling as Charles Darnay, he tricks Solomon Barsad, the British 'double' spy making a living as a *mouton de prison* (prison spy) in the service of the Jacobins, into death on the guillotine. These two endings completely defuse the original theme of sacrifice and resurrection; they also fit well with the tradition of crime and gallows culture which I discussed earlier. Here not the reformed hero but the criminal who collaborates with the arbitrary power of the police, the courts, and government—be it traditional or revolutionary power—gets to pay. Audiences responded to these changed endings with gusto, 'with vehement rounds of applauds' demanding repeating curtain rises.[63]

The middle-class familial and domestic stance of Dickens's history of the Revolution and the melodrama of Christian sacrifice reappeared only at the turn of the century and may be exactly located and dated in John Martin-Harvey's version, revealingly retitled *The Only Way*, premiering on 16 February 1899 at the Lyceum. Though written by the Reverends Freeman Wills and Frederick Langbridge, the play was the work of the actor-entrepreneur who specialized in romantic roles across the Atlantic and his female lead and real-life wife, Nina de Silva. The Martin-Harvey–de Silva version would become the definitive one, both on stage and, until 1935, on screen, and Martin-Harvey appeared in it 5,004 times until his death in 1944. The turn and interpretation he and his collaborators gave to the play may enhance our understanding of the mid-Victorian versions and their bearing on the popular stage and imagination. The single most significant change made by Martin-Harvey undoubtedly was the abolition of Madame Defarge. Her complete disappearance from the later stage version (she would return in the 1935 Hollywood screen version) is accompanied, and indeed complemented by, Carton's centrality and his transformation into a romantic and spiritual hero, whose romance and sacrifice overshadow the entire play.[64] She is partly replaced by a substitute working-class female character who incorporates a plebeian identity and evangelical sacrifice. Encouraged by Martin-Harvey and de Silva, the clergymen-writers developed the nameless and marginal seamstress executed on the guillotine, a symbol of the Terror's and indeed the Revolution's victimization of ordinary people, into a full-blown character, Mimi, after the female lead in *La Bohème*. The original Mimì of Giacomo Puccini's opera (1896) is tragically 'condemned' to an early death by poverty, illness, a dangerous bohemian life, and unrequited love. Her biography is not only plebeian but distinctly urban and set in the Latin Quarter during the 'second' French Revolution of 1830. Martin-Harvey had her transferred back to the time of the first revolution, and attached to her a biography combining low life bordering on

[63] *The Era*, 5 Feb. 1860.

[64] For the various stage and film versions from the 1890s see Michel Pointer (ed.) with Anthony Slide, *Charles Dickens on the Screen: The Film, Television and Video Adaptations* (London, 1996) and Jeffrey Richards, *Films and British National Identity: From Dickens to Dad's Army* (New York, 1997), 330–40.

the criminal and a rescue story. She is a child of the streets, with a past in the dark recesses of Paris, found in the 'kennels' and rescued by Carton. She becomes his servant, keeper, and confidante, travels with him to Paris, and takes on his side by volunteering to die with him on the guillotine.[65] The double sacrifice and romance twists Carton's motives and Dickens's in the original and, certainly, the motifs and drive of the mid-Victorian stage versions, where Carton did not need to die. The double bill on the guillotine could be seen as, literally, 'a marriage in heaven' and, of course, a cross-class marriage too, standing for social conciliation.

Such a conciliation, and the shift to romance, were hardly possible in the earlier versions, which were embedded in the earlier and generic forms of melodrama and prison and gallows lore. In Dickens's rendition and in the mid-century stage 'realizations', the moving force of the Revolution narrative was the anger embodied in female characters and the dynamics of the street. The melodrama of the guillotine moved by plebeian anger and intense spectacle and exaggeration were easily relatable to, and indeed resonated with, the vision of the gallows and prison as the sites of oppression and popular retaliation. The melodramatic mode suited the mid-century vision of a disorderly and uncomfortable past, a past which remained ineradicably present during the mid-century period of intensified 'progress' and improvement, and of the attempt at 'civilizing' the cross-class urban rituals focused around the gallows and prison. The popular interpretation of the Revolution and, indeed, of history as urban melodrama moved by plebeian anger and violence resonated not only because it expressed anxieties and fears of disorder that could not be expunged even with 'improvement'. This interpretation was of its time because it offered a comprehension of the great historical event which had a life and could be endowed with meaning within the social and the material life of readers and viewers. After 1868 the gallows were no longer a signpost of a bloody history and its analogous present. Their disappearance from public view almost coincided with the Second Reform Act, which formally at least constituted the beginning of urban democracy. One Reform Act later (1884), the calming down of strife between labour and capital, and London labour's conciliation with empire and nation, diffused the intensity of visions of a repeatable revolution. Hence the substitution of a romance of conciliation for Dickens's earlier melodrama of anger. At the same time the material forms and meanings of modernity in the city changed and these changes called for a different vision of modernity, which is mapped and explained later in the book. Now it is necessary to elaborate further on the early and mid-nineteenth-century notions of the past, in representations of the other privileged history, the Tudor era.

65 Freeman Wills and Frederick Langbridge, *The Only Way: A Dramatic Version in a Prologue and Four Acts of Charles Dickens' A Tale of Two Cities* (London, 1899; 1942), 20–1.

PART II

HISTORY AS A DUNGEON: TUDOR REVIVALS AND URBAN CULTURE

4

Who Owns the Tower of London? The Production and Consumptions of a Historical Monument, 1840–1940

INSCRIPTIONS

If 'everything' in the culture of history, 'not this or that thing, but literally everything, was soaked' in the one event of the French Revolution, then it was practically drenched in images and vestiges of the Tudor era.[1] The early and mid-Victorians discovered and appropriated an abundance of traces of Tudor life and culture, inscribed in the architecture of mansions, halls, churches, and cottages, in paintings of different scales, in objects, and in literature. Material traces were reproduced and percolated in and through antiquarian writing and a vast popular historical literature, the latter moulding a new kind of historical tourism, more plebeian than ever before. Like the French Revolution, the Tudor era made a privileged 'past', used by individuals, collectives, and institutions in relation to, and to make sense of, change in the modern urban environment and experience. Like the circulated images of the Revolution, popular renditions of the sixteenth century accommodated an urban vision of history, and history's configuration as a dungeon and a scaffold: a site of fascinating horror. This configuration connected the two privileged pasts in the popular imagination. Trust Dickens to pinpoint the connection. In *A Tale of Two Cities* he has Charles Darnay refer to the discovery of inscriptions on the walls of the Beauchamp Tower in the Tower of London, in the early 1790s, in a conversation with Dr Manette, the long-time prisoner in the Bastille and the scribe of a history of torture and oppression on that prison's walls.[2] Dickens accurately attributes the discovery to antiquarian interest in 'the old buildings' of London, 'the topic at hand'. Such an awareness of the topicality of the historical culture did not escape his Victorian readers. And they would also be aware of his visual metaphors, implying the ability freely to reach historical buildings and monuments.[3] In

[1] This is a paraphrase of Lord Cockburn. See Henry Cockburn, *Memorials of His Time*, 73.

[2] Dickens, *A Tale of Two Cities*, 106.

[3] Ibid. The earliest description of inscriptions probably dates back to 1800. See J. Brand, 'Account of the Inscriptions Discovered on the Walls of the Tower of London', *Archaeologica*, 13

1858, access to what would become Britain's star monument was restricted and the traces of the past on it and, by implication, history itself not easily 'seeable'.

The following two chapters map the productions of Tudor horror in an urban context, from the late 1830s and early 1840s until the twentieth-century inter-war period, by closely looking at the slow and protracted rise of this urban monument and its multiple consumptions. My stance is different from that of recent scholarship on Victorian resurrections of early modern England and the development of the Tudor heritage. This scholarship has stressed rural aspects of popular and populist imaginings of the 'Olden Time' (the extended sixteenth century), sometimes highlighting its organic and even folkish aspects and focusing on aspects like the rediscovery of the Tudor stately home, Tudor rural architecture, Tudor 'folk', choral, and instrumental music, and the reduplication of Tudor motifs in a rich popular print culture.[4] These examples of revival have usually been taken to produce a non-urban and non-industrial culture, fostering plebeian freedoms and a cross-class sociability that had preceded modernity. I wish to introduce another aspect of popular notions of the 'Olden Time' and 'merrie England' and, more broadly, of the complex configurations of the past, in which conflict, danger, and disorder were quite dominant. Together with the images of the dungeon and scaffold, I take up my earlier discussion of the technologies of looking and, more generally, spectatorship and visual consumption. I show how the two different urban modes of looking at and making sense of historical periods and events—the grand panoramic view and the limited, pedestrian look from the angle of the dungeon—were effectively combined in a widespread discussion, carried on, on a number of platforms, on the access of lookers, of different classes, genders, ages, and geographies, to the Tower. And I demonstrate how this combination of the panorama and dungeon, and of the two notions about looking, was appropriated by writers and illustrators, urban readers and tourists, in actual practices of sightseeing and in their varied experiences of the monument.

The Tower and the next two chapters also introduce into my discussion of the culture of history the state and bureaucracies, and their input into the manufacture of the past. Here the state is not just a powerful image of oppression (central to both Carlyle's panorama and Dickens's melodrama) or of grandeur. Central government, together with corporate bodies and interests and local metropolitan interests, were active agents engaged in restricting consumptions of history, enabling access to the past and grappling with mediators of taste for, and practical knowledge of, the past like antiquarians, authors, and illustrators, educators and reformers, not to mention readers and spectators actively engaging in 'making' the Tower.

(1800), 68–99; Raphael Samuel, 'The Tower of London', in *Island Stories: Unravelling Britain* (*Theatres of Memory*, ii), 101–25.

4 The best discussion of the 'Olden Time' is to be found in Mandler, '"In the Olden Time"'. See also Howkins, 'The Discovery of Rural England'.

At the centre of the first two parts of this chapter is looking at the Tower and, more broadly, at history. They focus on the physical conditions of sightseeing, the changes in tourism, and the discursive construction of spectatorship as a right. This discourse is tracked from the early nineteenth-century reformers' debate on rational recreation, through late Victorian preoccupations with free access to history, to their early twentieth-century offshoots. The idiom of the debates on spectatorship and free access resonated with the language of rational recreation through historical knowledge. Later in the nineteenth century this idiom rang with the vocabulary of citizenship, but citizenship conceived as an urban, or even local, entitlement rather than as a universal right. Yet, as I show, the reformist idiom and propaganda of improvement and rationality was dramatically, and I mean dramatically, transported by the imagery and language of horror which shaped crime culture and the metropolitan experience of crime, which the previous chapters began to outline. In the third part, I show how producers of historical novels and illustrations, notably the novelist William Harrison Ainsworth and the cartoonist and illustrator George Cruikshank, themselves campaigners for rational recreation, drew on the older lore of crime and prison to change the image of the Tower from one of a jumble of antiquities and curiosities to that of a dungeon. Their best-selling *Tower of London*, published in 1839–40, apparently a 'recreationist' document preaching free access to history, actually reshaped practices of sightseeing, especially the enactment and actual experience of horror of individual readers and tourists. The remainder of the chapter is about how the dungeon took control of popular images and of women and men's actual experiences of the monument, and figured in politicized protest against the control of tourism.

Chapter 5 draws on the novel, focusing on the construction of the female prisoner/victim, the ten-day Tudor queen Lady Jane Grey, in literary sources and historical paintings, to demonstrate the interaction of individuals' renditions of the theme and image of the prison and cultural formations like gender. I show the varied ways in which the very terms of historical memory of the Tudors, indeed history itself, were shaped by Victorian sensibilities and notions about femininity.

Though I am fully aware of and refer to different aspects of the making of the Tower, notably the grandeur of the state, empire, and of military power, or the awe inspired by the symbols of the monarchy and embodied in the Crown jewels and the Regalia, it is on the attraction of the prison, the block, and the scaffold that I focus. My selection is made by choice and not by default, and was dictated by the underlying themes of the book. Readers who find the former aspects somewhat muted may fill in the gap with the help of recent studies focusing on these angles.[5]

[5] Geoffrey Parnell, *English Heritage Book of the Tower of London* (London, 1993); John Charlton (ed.), *The Tower of London its History and Institutions* (London, 1978); Parnell, 'The Rise and Fall

SEEING THE TOWER (1): ACCESS AND THE CONDITION OF EARLY HISTORICAL TOURISM

In the eighteenth century the precincts known as the Tower of London housed a conglomeration of buildings and displays from the exotic Royal Menagerie, dating back to the twelfth century, collections of arms jumbled with curiosities, and wonders and exhibitions of symbols of the monarchy like the Crown jewels. This jumble reflected the piecemeal development of the place from the Norman Conquest (if not from an earlier time) as a system of defence for the capital that had originated from the original keep, and as a residence of the royal household and a centre of administration. Arms made up the core of accessible exhibits and the Tower is an early exemplar of a military museum or show, celebrating the power and continuity of the monarchy, initially for the exclusive inspection of the select few, and later for limited consumption. Exclusiveness, as both Tony Bennett and Krzysztof Pomian have noted, characterized the traditional *ancien régime* collections of objects and curiosities, which excluded all but the privileged and concealed even from those privileged spectators a great deal of what they had actually contained.[6] Parts of the Tower were exposed to tourists' gaze before it ceased to be a lived-in palace and it drew its first fee-paying visitors as early as 1599, becoming a tourist sight during the reign of Charles II, when themed displays of arms and the menagerie were designed to attract and entertain visitors. The Line of Kings, a row of figures representing the English monarchs, mounted on wooden horses and wearing their armour, could inspire curiosity and awe, augmented in the three armouries, which were rearranged during the early nineteenth century. The Kings were housed in a purpose-built New Horse Armoury in 1826; the Spanish Armoury, renamed Queen Elizabeth's Armoury in 1831 and containing the figures of the Queen, heavily bejewelled, on a horse and accompanied by her page; the Small Armoury; and the Artillery Room.

The status of the Tower as a place of great antiquity, a military museum of sorts, and an *omnium gatherum* of unsystematically arranged curiosities was further complicated by the fact that until well after the middle of the nineteenth century the collections cohabited with multiple administrative and military bodies.[7] The old historical buildings accommodated the Royal Mint (until 1812), the Records Office (until 1850), and, during the heavy militarization of the place during the eighteenth century, a huge arsenal of small arms and artillery, barracks, and, until 1855, the Office (later Board) of Ordnance, that

of the Tower of London', *History Today*, 42 (Mar. 1992), 13–20; and Howard Tomlinson, 'Ordnance Building at the Tower of London', *History Today*, 32 (Apr. 1982), 43–8.

[6] Bennett, *The Birth of the Museum*, 36–41. For the older collections and access to them see also Krzysztof Pomian, *Collectors and Curiosities: Paris and Venice 1500–1800* (Cambridge, 1990).

[7] For general histories of the Tower see Parnell, *English Heritage Book of the Tower*, and Charlton, *The Tower of London*. Parnell is useful on the medievalization of the Tower during the

gigantic department of state that served as war office and a board of munitions in one. This proximity, mixture even, of government and army on the one hand and a public and civic place of exhibition, displaying arms and 'instruments' of the monarchy—notably the jewels and Regalia—on the other hand, would persist until just after the end of the Second World War. Such proximity was crucial not only to the development of the Tower as a monument, but to other nineteenth- century venues of popular tourism like Dover and Edinburgh Castles, Chelsea Barracks, and Greenwich. In the Tower, the Armouries displayed a profusion of historical arms and other military exhibits which, during times of national emergency, reverted to their original use. Even 'modern' weapons were sumptuously exhibited in an ornamental manner which rendered them exotic and 'antique'. Thus from 1863 the first two floors of the restored White Tower housed the thousands of rifles for the Volunteers (later known as the Territorials), arranged into gigantic columns and enormous lamps made out of parts of weapons. With light filtering in from skylights, the sheer scale and fantastic display of arms in actual use diminished the space between a military life and the army, and military 'history', between the status of objects as displays and their role as everyday things, the museum and 'life'.

The usability of the antiquarian objects may be taken as characteristic of the democratic historical museum and we have seen this at work at Tussaud's. In the Tower, the displayed rifles and guns, exhibiting England's military might, could at any moment be pulled out by the Volunteers ('civic' soldiers) to defend the realm, and were for all to gaze upon. But the very active use of the Tower by army and government was also a major hindrance in its development as a historical monument for mass use. A host of government offices and boards and corporate bodies (until 1825 the warders, later to be replaced by veteran non-commissioned officers) maintained the place, had vested interests in it, and were the main beneficiaries from revenue from tourists. This partly explains why Tower tourism, which I later discuss in some detail, remained so encumbered for so long; why a historical place so early recognized as the 'epitome of national history',[8] took longer than most monuments to become accessible to masses of Britons. More important even, the central role initially played by the state and army continuously hampered access and the condition and right to 'see', the two other tags of the modern culture of spectacle.

Well before the nineteenth century seeing was conditioned and shaped by distinction between classes of spectators. But this familiar form of restriction,

18th and 19th cc. See also his 'Rise and Fall of the Tower of London'. On the Tower as royal menagerie see Phillip Drennon Thomas, 'The Tower of London's Royal Menagerie', *History Today*, 46 (Aug. 1996), 29–36. On Ordnance see Tomlinson, 'Ordnance Building at the Tower of London'.

[8] On changes in Tower tourism see Peter Hammond, '"Epitome of England's History": The Transformation of the Tower of London as Visitor Attraction in the Nineteenth Century', *Royal Armouries Yearbook*, 4 (1999), 144–74.

which we saw operated by the new kind of capitalist cultural entrepreneur, was here utilized by the state itself for political as well as social purposes. The most obvious and successful way of effectively making distinctions was, of course, the admission fee, and the Tower's remained, throughout the eighteenth and most of the nineteenth and early twentieth centuries, exorbitant. Scattered information for the period before 1836 may be gleaned from unofficial guidebooks published from the 1740s on. The miniature, 5 × 6 cm, literally Tom Thumb guide for children, subscribed to in 1741 by seventy-three boys and ninety girls, gives a reduced rate at *6d.* for the lions in the menagerie (a child's rate), an unimaginably expensive *2d.* for each of the main displays in the Spanish Armada, *3d.* for some of the items in the small armoury, and *2d.* for the train of artillery and Horse Armoury, with a final rip-off at the Regalia.[9] In 1796 the fee was a punishingly high *9d.* for the lions, 1*s.* for the elephants, and 1*s.* for the Spanish Armoury (inclusive of other armouries). From 1805, a hurried view of the 'ferocious Fanny', a lioness born and bred in the Tower, and of the African lions and tigers cost 1*s.*, and the armouries an inclusive 2*s.*[10] With the transfer of the animals to the Zoo at Regent's Park, the Armouries at 3*s.* and an extra to the warders were bad value for money, especially when compared with the free-admission monuments such as Greenwich Hospital's Chapel (with its painted ceiling), Hampton Court, and the National Gallery. Reduction in 1837 had an immediate and galvanizing effect on the scale of Tower tourism, as the returns of revenue published in the Report of the House of Commons Select Committee on National Monuments of 1841 shows. Numbers rose from some 10,986, who paid 3*s.* (the other half being privileged free admissions), to 42,212 in 1838–9, paying 1*s.*, doubling to 84,872 during 1839–40 at an inclusive *6d.*, with a further rise to 92,231 in 1840 and 107,267 visitors during 1841–2.[11] In themselves and compared with corporation-run monuments such as St Paul's Cathedral and the Abbey (the latter having a mere 37,456 visitors in 1840) this may look impressive. But non-paying galleries and museums such as the National Gallery had upwards of half a million visitors, Hampton Court 122,339, 'mostly of working class', and the British Museum attracted on one public (free) day in July 1838 a little over the Tower's annual turn. Following the fire on the Tower in October and November 1841, numbers dropped sharply, hitting bottom with 32,000 in 1850, picking up during the year of the Crystal Palace, with nearly a quarter of a million visitors and dropping yet again the

[9] *Curiosities in the Tower of London* (London, 1741), i. 96.

[10] *An Historical Description of the Tower of London and its Curiosities* (London, 1796), 1; *An Historical Description* (1806), 13.

[11] 'National Monuments and Works of Art: Report From the Select Committee on National Monuments, Minutes of Evidence 1841', *British Parliamentary Papers, Education and Fine Arts*, vol. 2 (Shannon, Ireland), 264. For slightly different figures see *Society for Obtaining Free Admission to National Monuments and Public Edifices Containing Works of Art. Report to the Committee* (London, 1839; 1841), 11.

following year. It is only from the late 1860s that an uphill trend may be detected, with a significant increase following the belated introduction of free days on Easter Monday, 1875. By 1901 the number of visitors rose to 462,000, the number of free visitors far outnumbering those paying.[12] Still, even with this 'jump' the Tower lagged behind other national sites and probably Madame Tussaud's too.[13]

The reformed fees could not possibly put the Tower within easy reach of the majority of the working classes. Even when inclusive cost (combining travel and refreshment) was not a deterrent, early closing at around four in the afternoon and closing on Sunday served as clear class markers. Hampton Court, open to the public free of charge from November 1838, offered Londoners a considerably better Tudor package. Its state apartments, preserving the feel of a lived-in palace, were opened until six in the evening during the summer and, most important for working-class tourists, it remained open on Saturday and half Sunday. And it was lack of class distinction which its authorities stressed in the palace's book of regulations: 'There is no distinction whatever as to the admittance, every one are enjoying the privilege of entering the rooms and of continuing in them till they are closed.'[14] Not only tradesmen but 'operatives' could afford organized tours from the poorer parts of London to the palace in 'vans; sometimes . . . 60, 70 and 80 vans a day, each van containing 30 persons; upon an average 25 persons'. Compared with this, the Tower, even at a reduced admission fee,[15] was 'a heavy tax on the working man, who might want to give his family the enjoyment of rational pleasure by a visit to the Tower',[16] as the *Penny Magazine* noted in language entirely characteristic of the reformist idiom of 'rational recreation'. Brought out by Charles Knight for the Society for the Diffusion of Useful Knowledge (SDUK), the magazine itself, with a 200,000-strong readership, served as a useful instrument of the movement for improvement through worthy recreation for the working classes.

The idea behind 'rational recreation', as Peter Bailey and others have noted, was that culture was the key to 'improvement' through self-regulation and, indirectly, to social and political order. Significantly, the movement targeted mainly working men, whom its propaganda constructed as family men and rational consumers of the new and essentially middle-class forms of culture which had evolved in the changing civic space: the museum, the public monument, and the library. The consumption of these places was widely represented not only as the very opposite of irrational traditional working-class

[12] PRO, WO, 94/22, 1837; Hammond, '"Epitome of England's History"', 165.

[13] For figures for Hampton Court see *British Parliamentary Papers, Education and Fine Arts*, 119. For the British Museum and National Gallery see pp. 176 and 180.

[14] *British Parliamentary Papers, Education and Fine Arts*, ii. 246.

[15] Ibid. 250. On popular tourism see Simon Thurley, *Hampton Court: A Social and Architectural History* (New Haven, 2003), 317–21.

[16] Hammond, '"Epitome of England's History"', 152.

consumption of leisure, but also as antidote to it. The museum, public library, and historical monuments were sources for useful instruction and pleasure which were to replace the pub, betting, the fair, and the pleasure garden.[17] In effect, the achievements of rational recreationists benefited middle-class men and women no less than they did working-class heads of families. Middle-class women are conspicuous in publications like the *Illustrated London News*, which consistently represented the new civilized space of the metropolis as a heterosocial space completely safe for respectable mothers of families and children. 'There is', propounded the *Illustrated* in 1848,

> not a more rational mode of passing the Easter Holiday in the metropolitan than in a visit to this famed prison-palace. Not so many years since, this was an expensive recreation, and of course, accessible only to the few. The judicious reduction of the admission money, to view what are popularly termed 'the curiosities' has however materially tended to increase the number of the visitors.

The *Illustrated* then cites the returns of visitors for the decade following the reform of the fees. The sketches attached to the article feature well-dressed women and children. It was precisely this class (and gendered) vision of the national historic culture that organizations like the Society for Obtaining Free Admission to National Monuments and Public Edifices Containing Works of Art propagated from the late 1820s until the late 1840s.[18]

The limited impact of early cultural reformism is fully borne out by the brief and effective free-admission campaign of 1874–5. This later campaign was local and cut across parties. Initiated by Liberal reformists like the writer and traveller William Hepworth Dixon, it was taken over by Conservative politicians like the jute manufacturer Charles Thompson Ritchie, and drew on direct working-class participation. Orchestrated by Tower Hamlets MPs returned with the election of Disraeli's second government, the campaign was publicized by the East London press, notably by avowedly Tory weeklies such as the *Tower Hamlets Independent* (*THI*) and the slightly more Liberal *East London Observer* (*ELO*). The campaign's rhetoric retains the earlier Liberal-radical notion of cultural improvement, but attaches it to the citizen working man's place in the nation and his uncontested right to history. Such rhetoric could have made particular sense after the Second Reform Act of 1867, adding borough householders and ten-pound renters to the electorate. 'At present,' opines the *THI* on 12 September 1874, 'the Tower, with its many reminiscences of the past, is closed to all but those who are in a position to pay the sixpences demanded for the privilege of entrée to the ancient fortress from which our hamlets take their name.' As Dixon argued in a local householders' meeting in formerly radical Clerkenwell: 'The working men

[17] Peter Bailey, *Leisure and Class in Victorian England: Rational Recreation and the Contest for Control, 1830–1885* (London, 1978), and *Popular Culture and Performance in the Victorian City* (Cambridge, 1998), 30–46. Bennett, *The Birth of the Museum*, 17–25.

[18] 'The Tower of London', *ILN*, 313, 22 Apr. 1848.

of England had a right of free ingress to the Tower, in order that they might there study the great points of their country's history.'[19] Significantly, as much as the working man's right is a national entitlement 'earned' through universal male vote, it is a local and urban one. Put another way, it is as an inhabitant of the East End of London that he (note the gendered language of the campaign) demands a share in that city's history: the Tower belongs, first and foremost, to its neighbourhood. 'This great national record should be freely unsealed, as was the case in France, in Russia, and in nearly all the European countries . . . If the working men of London wished earnestly to have the Tower of London thrown open, they would not be resisted by Mr. Disraeli who was anxious to be in sympathy and accord with the working man.'[20]

Localism, argues an *ELO* leader published on 12 September, 'must have the heartiest sympathy for every East Ender'. The local peoples' own monument is then compared with

> The Castle of Edinburgh, which stands in like relation to the Scottish capital that the Tower does to our metropolis, is wholly free to the public. No charge is made even to viewing the regalia . . . Now there would seem to be no reason why Edinburgh should be able to offer this boon to her citizens, while London lowers her greatest historical monument to the level of a waxwork exhibition, by exacting so much per head for admission to it.[21]

SEEING THE TOWER (2): HISTORY, SPECTATORSHIP, AND SOCIAL CONTROL

The campaigns, whether middle-class or cross-class and populist, for reformed tourism and cheap access to history were only partly about costs and prices. They were mainly about the freedom for uninhibited 'seeing'. What the early campaigners and ordinary visitors most resented about sightseeing at the Tower was the elaborate forms of surveillance, restriction, and regulation of sight and movement designed to monitor looking and public conduct. Restrictions on movement and sight were not entirely lifted before 1880 and seem to have become anachronistic much earlier. Multiform surveillance, which I examine in detail later, was wholly incompatible with novel notions about sightseeing and spectatorship in general, which were central to the new nineteenth-century exhibitionary order. The new kind of exhibition and spectacle, in theory democratic, was associated with a set of assumptions about the relationship between the spectator, his or her position in the place of exhibition, and their possibilities of freely looking at and taking in objects. The association between

[19] *THI*, 12 Sept. 1874; *ELO*, 26 Aug. 1874. [20] *ELO*, 26 Sept. 1874.
[21] See also *East End News*, 26 Mar. 1875, 2 Apr. 1875; *Eastern Post*, 27 Mar. 1875.

the freedom to view historical places, their unhindered consumption, and the viewer's sense of the national past is quite evident in the language of even the earliest surviving guidebooks. During the eighteenth century and the early nineteenth century this association is most apparent in the metaphor of the unimpeded look at curiosities. The children's 1741 booklet states that 'ill concerted / artless eyes Our British youth / shall now despise' and the book itself is likened to a transparent glass case: 'What features in / the Tower's are laid, / Are here— / as in a glass displayed.'[22] The Preface to a popular Tower guidebook, which remained unaltered between 1792 and the early 1830s, describes in detail the limits on useful and free sightseeing which tourists to the Tower had had to put up with:

The desire of searching ancient repositories for the antiquities of our country is allowed to be a laudable curiosity: to point them out therefore to the inquisitive, and to direct their attention ... cannot be denied their degree of merit. The Tower of London, for the antique remains that there are treasured up, has been, for many ages past, the common resort of foreigners as well as natives; but it is a general complaint, that the mind, being crowded with too many objects at once, cannot distinguish, amidst so great a variety, what is worthy to be dwelt upon, and what is of less note, and the hurry with which strangers are conducted by their guides from one curiosity to another, occasioned by the numbers that are hourly flocking there to be entertained, leaves the spectator no time to examine what he sees, nor fix in his memory half the objects that have attracted his attention.

The purpose of the guidebook is to amend the restrictions on seeing and 'imprint useful observation in the mind'.[23] Free viewing not only educated the eye and senses of the gazer, it could turn him or her into the participant in the national culture whom the advocates of rational recreation envisioned. The propaganda of the Society for Free Admission consistently associated free access to history with, on the one hand, the democratization of consumption—via the abolition of fees and the control on urban tourists—and, on the other hand, inclusion in the nation. Both the publications for tourists and the reformers' propaganda draw on the guidebook technique and on the 'rationalist' version of the ocular idiom and metaphor so widely available to early Victorians. In one of their meetings in 1837, the Liberal Irish MP and Society activist Thomas Wyse compared the system of exclusion from public monuments in British cities to a more democratic and truly nationalist approach on the Continent:

On coming up the Thames, that noblest of avenues to this great city, this metropolis of a world, and seeing on all sides works of public competitions and industry, those indications of national virtue and moral and intellectual excellence of their wealth and elegance without their too frequent accompaniment of abject slavery, it is impossible for an Englishman not to feel proud of his country ... But when we approach Westminster

[22] *Curiosities in the Tower*, p. vi.
[23] *An Historical Description of the Tower of London*, p. ii.

Abbey and St. Paul's and stand before our National Gallery conjured with the Royal Academy, we are obliged to alter our tone and say 'these, these do not belong to the nation; a reservation has been made in favour of class'. In vain we protest that the barbarous exclusion is not ours; that a corporation holds the keys, and hence the pity of our friends and the sneers of our enemies throughout Europe.[24]

Reduction of fees in itself did not democratize access to the nation's history. As popular pressure and demand to see the Tower increased, so did the policy of restriction and control. Most buildings were off-limits to most visitors. Moreover, to stem the flow of sightseers, they were allowed in the armouries in groups of twelve accompanied by warders, who hurried them through the jumble of unlabelled and unsystematically organized exhibits. During this stampede the usage of guidebooks was discouraged and sometimes forbidden. As W. Hume argued: 'the hurried progress through the collection of historical illustrations deprive it (the Armouries) of much of its utility to the spectator'.[25] On public holidays (which were not free before 1874), visitors had to be turned away not for a lack of place, but because monitored group visiting could not accommodate the rise in public demand and mass tourism. Between 1825 and 1855 the number of visitors was restricted and no more than 100 were allowed inside the Tower perimeter. The hundred-visitors rule was enforced by the Duke of Wellington throughout his long term as Constable of the Tower and reflects his own and a much broader fear of urban crowds before and after the passage of the Great Reform Bill. The fear that the new class of urban spectators might turn into a revolutionary mob increased during times of unrest such as the 1830s and 1840s. During the Chartist protest in London in 1848, the British Museum was closed and guarded by armed forces. The Tower, an arsenal-cum-museum, seemed much more exposed to popular violence. As the adamant Duke put it about a decade earlier: 'Who is to prevent some thousands with a shilling from going in there [the armouries] if they please and when there, doing what they please.'[26] The analogy between the Tower, a symbol of military and royal might, functioning as an arsenal, and the Bastille—that symbol of France's *ancien régime* and the Revolution—is quite transparent. Phobic suspicion of urban audiences and crowds, especially metropolitan ones, as we saw in Part I, long survived the late 1840s. The suspicion of Tower authorities and the central bureaucracies increased with every bout of metropolitan discontent. Lord De Ros's *Memorials of the Tower of London*, appearing on the eve of the Second Reform Bill and in the wake of popular agitation for it, is a case in point. In an attempt to vindicate the Duke of Wellington's restrictions on visitors, De Ros connects virtually every attempt at a revolt in London since the late eighteenth century to the Tower. From the Gordon Riots, through Colonel Despard's

[24] *Society for Obtaining Free Admission to National Monuments and Public Edifices, Report*, 29 May 1837.
[25] *Society for Obtaining Free Admission, Report*, 1839, p. 6.
[26] PRO, WO 94/18, 13 Sept. 1837.

aborted attempt, through the Burdett's Riots in 1816–17, through the so-called Thistlewood conspiracy, through pro-Reform demonstrations, to the Chartist demonstrations in 1848, he argues: 'There has never been any riot or serious disturbance in London, without some plan being laid by the ringleaders for the attack and seizure of the Tower, from the days of Jack Cade to the Chartist Riots of 1848.'[27]

Apprehension of the revolutionary potential of crowds of spectators may not be identified with officials' obstructionism, or with an ultra-conservatism such as the Duke's; it was shared by the majority of writers and entrepreneurs of culture discussed in the first part of the book and by numerous others. The democratization of visual consumption could be politically dangerous: plebeian crowds could turn into unruly ones, just like the crowds at public hangings, or Paris's revolutionary crowds from 1789 onwards. In 1851, for example, Whig and even Radical apprehension of the visitors purchasing the cheap, 'shilling ticket' to the Great Exhibition reached almost epidemic proportions, only to prove wholly unfounded.[28] Moreover, it was the fear of social and political disorder which in the first place propelled reformers' advocacy of improvement by rational recreation based upon free access to culture. Yet the logic of the demand for 'free admission' and the freedom of the look was the very opposite of bureaucratic restriction. The former assumed that freedom would bring on self-monitoring. There was no danger of crowds becoming a mob, because once inside the Tower they would become an audience, an amalgam of spectators/citizens. As John Bayley, considered to be the Tower's first historian, indignantly remarked in his *History of the Antiquities of the Tower of London* (1821–5): 'In other nations we find no impositions laid on admittance to national institutions and why should England descend from pre-eminence among nations? . . . the people should, under proper restriction, have access to the Armouries'.[29] The evidence submitted to the Commons' Select Committee proved that the fears about improper behaviour were baseless. And campaigners hoped that 'the good conduct of the increased number of visitors, will induce government to remove all impediments'.[30] Comparable reports on the conduct of plebeian crowds of 'the lower class' of urban tourists and of soldiers at Hampton Court confirmed their proper conduct, even when merrymaking on the palace's grounds. Drunkenness, when it occurred, was not harmful and slight disorders never developed to protest. Actually the new kind of cockney tourist was at least as well-behaved as the former, fee-paying, and occasionally dangerous visitor whose

[27] Lord De Ros, *Memorials of the Tower of London* (London, 1866), 62.

[28] On the shilling days see Aurbach, *The Great Exhibition of 1851*, esp. the chapter on 'Integration and Segregation'; Paul Greenhalgh, *Ephemeral Vistas: The Expositions Universelles, Great Exhibition and World Fairs, 1851–1939* (Manchester, 1988), 27–32; and Humphrey Jennings, *Pandaemonium 1660–1886: The Coming of the Machine as Seen by Contemporary Observers* (New York, 1985), 257–70.

[29] Hammond, '"Epitome of the England's History"', 147.

[30] *Committee for Obtaining Free Admission, Report* (1839), 7.

'finger went through one of the pictures, and the eye of Lord Darnley was picked up with a penknife'![31]

The public debate on looking may appear to demonstrate the move from direct state control to what has been recently described as the 'rule of freedom', individuals' self-regulation within the nineteenth-century liberal state, a form which reached its apogee on this state's chief arena: the modern city.[32] Such a shift from 'direct' to self-control would nicely fit with the influential interpretation of culture as an instrument of control—albeit an 'indirect' one, drawing on Foucault and discussed at some length in the Introduction. Direct control was resented because it was incompatible with the new kind of venue of culture like the museum, where practices of surveillance were undergoing radical change and embracing the twin ideas of a self-monitoring, self-regulating audience and the transparency of exhibits in the changed architecture and structuring of places of exhibition and spectacle. As Tony Bennett has noted, the model exhibition space drew on the amphitheatre, the open gallery, and the arcade, thus encouraging an uninterrupted bird's-eye view of the displays, but also a free circulation of looks.[33] Thus not only objects but viewers too were to become transparent and could be watched by their social peers or their social superiors.

But the history of the Tower and the debates over who owned its history, as well as that of practices of looking in and at it, resist the chronology of the narrative of control in its Foucauldian version, and some of the assumptions concerning the new uses of culture in the city. In the first place, direct surveillance persisted until almost the end of the nineteenth century and coincided with the heyday of urban liberalism. Secondly, the Tower represented the very opposite of liberal urban architecture, certainly that of the new kind of museum. The Armouries may be described as 'anti museum' or 'anti exhibition', rather like Madame Tussaud's Chamber of Horrors. By the late 1830s the deficiencies of direct control in the cramped and unsystematically organized exhibition spaces became glaring even to some Tower officials. And the testimonies collected by the 1841 committee bear witness to public awareness of the relationship between the control of space, movement, and a sense of the past. One in particular, given by the illustrator and engraver Robert William Buss, is worth quoting at length. Asked whether 'the system of exhibiting the armouries to the public is effective', he described in useful detail some modes and practices of viewing:

> The people were hurried through in gangs of from 20 to 30, and there was no time allowed for the investigation of any thing, whatever; in fact, they were obliged to attend to the warder, and if people had catalogues they might as well have kept them in their

[31] *Select Committee on National Monuments*, 250, 149.
[32] See Joyce, *The Rule of Freedom.*
[33] Bennett, *The Birth of the Museum*, 50–3.

pockets; when they wanted to read them in conjunction with the object they saw, of course they lagged behind, and then the warder would say, 'you must not do that; the catalogues are to be read at home; you must follow me, or you will lose a great deal'; and I was peculiarly struck by that, for I thought it a very odd mode of exhibiting national property.[34]

Buss connects the right and growing demand to see this 'national property' to the expansion of the market for historical artefacts and genres serving as mediators and arbiters of popular tastes for history. He shrewdly marks out at least three such related genres: antiquarian works on old buildings and sites, historical novels with a national place for the main character, and cheaply produced historical illustrations.

Even more shrewdly, Buss notices the multiple production of these genres, for different audiences:

You say the public taste of late has been directed to the study and examination of antiquities—how does that appear; what evidence have you to show that?

If we look at the publications which issue from the press daily, we shall find that they have that character, and unless there was a market for them they certainly would not be issued.

What publications do you allude to?

I should mention Mr. Ainsworth's 'Tower' [*The Tower of London*, 1840] as one certainly, in the form of a novel, that would be calculated to create an interest; then there are the histories of the Tower, which have been published in various forms; then there is Mr. Knight's 'London'; and throughout most of the periodicals there is a tone of inquiry into those matters.

Do you mean that of late the practice of cheap publications with cuts and descriptions of ancient buildings has become more general?

I do.[35]

The set of relationships between a literary historical corpus, the changes in the practices of historical tourism, and the shift in modes of looking and spectatorship is crucial and complex and does not yield to control narratives. The new culture of history, as I have argued so far, was characterized by the interrelatedness of genres and artefacts, the literary, visual, and material. Historical fiction and antiquarian writing were informed by urban spectacles and shows and their visual consumption, adopting an array of visual metaphors and drawing on repertoires of looking. In their turn, as we shall see, the literary forms boosted historical tourism and also constructed procedures of viewing historical sites. Nowhere is the interrelatedness between the varied texts and debates about the tourist's gaze in greater evidence than in the novel Buss refers to in his testimony as 'Mr. Ainsworth's Tower'. A co-production of William Harrison

[34] 'Minutes of Evidence', *Select Committee on National Monuments and Works of Art*, 273–4. See also pp. 264–5.

[35] Ibid. 274.

Ainsworth and George Cruikshank, the illustrated novel is the single most instructive example of the blurring of the borderline in Victorian popular culture between word and image, literary genres, the urban guidebook and the historical map, and between reader and tourist/spectator. Moreover, the book and its co-authors sprang from the rationalist reforming tradition seeking improvement of the city and citizens via culture. Yet they themselves drew upon the Gothic, as a metaphor, style, and repertoire, and used it to redefine the idiom and agenda of the reform of tourism and popular history. In the following we shall trace, through the biography of their book and its huge impact on the status of the Tower and the varied uses spectators made of both, the popular turn towards the Gothic and the dungeon.

THE TOWER OF LONDON: THE SOCIAL LIFE OF A BOOK

The *Tower of London's* spectacular success drew on its biography and long social life not only as an urban text but as an object, with a materiality of its own, a life that changed according to the varied uses masses of consumers made with and of it. Even earlier than the urban histories of the Revolution discussed in Chapter 3, the *Tower* drew upon that apparatus of book production and distribution conveniently described as the publishing revolution of the 1830s and 1840s, a revolution characterized by the multiple production (and consumption) of fiction. First appearing in thirteen monthly part-issues between January and December 1840 (the last issue being a double number), the work was the most lavishly illustrated literary production in numbers yet produced. It included forty-three drawings on steel and fifty-five woodcuts and cost five shillings, a sum which definitely put it out of the reach of working-class readers. Some idea of the range of sales may be gleaned from evidence about the June part, which sold 8,500 copies. And net profits for the writer and illustrator who were equal partners in the venture with Bentley, Britain's premier serial publisher, were some £1,551.[36] A lucrative leather-bound edition at a prohibitive 14*s.* 6*d.* followed immediately, down-market second and third editions appeared in 1842, a fourth edition in 1844, a fifth in 1845, and a sixth in 1853, when Ainsworth and Cruikshank had already lost most of their influence and status.

One piece of evidence of Ainsworth's success among lower classes of readers is the rampant plagiarism of his novels. As each issue or number of the *Tower* came out, it was immediately 'adapted'. Retitled *The Legend of the Tower*, it was

[36] I am indebted to Robert Patten for helping me estimate the number of copies sold. The figures indicating profits are from the Bentley Papers, British Library, Add. MS 46676-A(432), p. 26; Add. MS 46676-B, p. 46; Add. MS 46650.06. For a bibliography of the editions see Stewart M. Ellis, *William Harrison Ainsworth and his Friends* (London and New York, 1911), 406–20.

reissued as the original work of 'W. H. Hainsworth' by Edward Lloyd, owner of a chain of down-market newspapers and serial publications, king of the so-called Salisbury Presses, located around Leicester Square and catering for working-class readerships, and, later, sympathizer with Chartist causes. A first stage version, patched up quickly by T. P. Taylor (who eighteen years later would adapt *A Tale of Two Cities*) from the novel and Alexandre Dumas's *Mary Tudor*, was produced at the Adelphi even as the *Tower* was still being serialized. A later version by T. H. Higgie and T. H. Lacey, *The Tower of London or the Death Omen and the Fate of Lady Jane Grey*, was produced in 1850. The first American edition appeared almost simultaneously with the first serialization and later ones did well throughout the 1840s. French, German, Spanish, and Italian translations too did well during this decade. Cheap serializations, catering for working-class audiences, followed in the fifties in weekly penny numbers and, simultaneously, in five parts with wrappers, costing an affordable *6d.* Popular editions continued to have a good run in the 1870s, 1880s, and 1890s, and in the early 1900s.

The few literary historians and historians of Victorian publishing who have dignified the *Tower* with a genealogy have affiliated it with a particularly urban historical genre, the topographical-historical novel with a national monument, typically a historical building or site, for the main character and central theme.[37] As the next chapter shows in detail, the book had not one but several literary genealogies, and it was precisely Ainsworth and Cruikshank's unorthodox use of a number of urban, Gothic, and crime genres that made it such a success. At this point it is necessary to focus on their definition of procedures of historical sight-seeing and their break away from the rationalist discourse of recreation. Probably inspired by such urban texts as Victor Hugo, *Notre Dame de Paris* (1834) and Eugène Sue, *Les Mystères de Paris*, *The Tower* is the very first example in English of the topographical-historical novel that is both metropolitan and national, in that it elevates a site in the capital city to a symbolic site of English history. As a blueprint, it would be emulated by Ainsworth himself in a succession of novels on monuments, most notably *Old Saint Paul* (1841), and in non-fictional writings such as Charles Knight's *London*. The blueprint's popularity and influence lay in Ainsworth and Cruikshank's mobilization of the campaign for the democratization of culture via freer access to history effectively to subvert the Whig, ameliorist approach to history. The novel's idiom draws heavily, even extravagantly, on the discourse of rational recreation, which, it will be recalled, also marks the tourist literature of the time. As Ainsworth states in his Preface:

> This is the introduction to the public of some parts of the fortress at present closed to them. There seems no reason why admission should not be given, under certain

[37] George J. Worth, *William Harrison Ainsworth* (New York, 1972), 62–110, and Andrew Sanders, *The Victorian Historical Novel 1840–1880* (London, 1978), 32–47. On Ainsworth from the perspective of publishing, see John A. Sutherland, *Victorian Novelists and Publishers* (London, 1976), 152–4 and *Victorian Fiction: Writers, Publishers, Readers* (London, 1995), 98–9, 102, 106, 162.

restrictions, to that unequaled specimen of Norman architecture, Saint John's Chapel in the White Tower,—to the arched galleries above it,—to the noble council-chamber teeming with historical recollections,—to the vaulted passages—and to the winding staircases within the turrets . . . Nor is there strong reason why the prison-chamber in the Beauchamp Tower, now used as a mess-room, the walls of which, like a mystic scroll, are covered with inscriptions—each a tragic story in itself, and furnishing matter for abundant reflection—should not likewise be thrown open. Most of the old fortifications . . . are, of course, inaccessible . . . They are the property of the nation, and should be open to national inspection.[38]

The association of 'national inspection' and democratic access proved immediately successful, as Ainsworth and Cruikshank transformed their readers into spectators. From January 1840 the numbers of readers/visitors increased in relation to the appearance of the part issues. Of course substantial increase occurred earlier with the reduction of fees, but the jump of returns from January 1840 to early 1842 may be attributed to the book. Armed with the novel/ guidebook, the *6d.* tourists flocked to the Tower and demanded, as the warders themselves reported, to be taken to those inaccessible places described by Ainsworth and vividly illustrated by Cruikshank. The detailed historical map of the sixteenth-century Tower and the index attached to the first edition made it look like and be used as a guidebook cum antiquarian essay (see Fig. 4). The Committee on Monuments itself endowed the book with authority by citing Ainsworth as an expert witness. The book's demand for free access was immediately adopted in the thriving popular literature on the history of London. Knight's own *London*, published in 1841 and evidently inspired by the novel, sets out to describe 'what the Tower ought to be as a great national monument. In detailing to the reader the course which we intend to pursue in the treatment of the subject, we shall also very slightly indicate of our general views of what a government that rightly estimates the value of patriotic feelings ought to do'.[39] As late as 1875, the *East End News* proposed that Ainsworth's urge to unravel the whole of the Tower 'for view' be implemented.[40]

But the book did not just advertise the Tower and defend free rational viewing; it indelibly constructed the former as a site of imprisonment and torture and elevated the prison to a forceful image of the past, the monarchy, and the state. Of course, as Geoffrey Parnell has rightly insisted, the function of the place as a state prison was subsidiary and marginal to its role as royal residence, a military stronghold, and a centre of the administration.[41] But it was the dungeon metaphor/myth that gained popularity in the culture of history. By the 1820s and 1830s the theme of the prison and dungeon, followed in Chapter

[38] *Tower of London, A Historical Romance by William Harrison Ainsworth, Illustrated by George Cruikshank* (London, 1840; 1854), Preface, pp. iv–v.

[39] Charles Knight, *London*, 6 vols. (London, 1841–4), ii. 214.

[40] *EEN*, 2 Apr. 1875.

[41] Geoffrey Parnell, *The Tower of London, Past and Present* (London, 1999), 112–13.

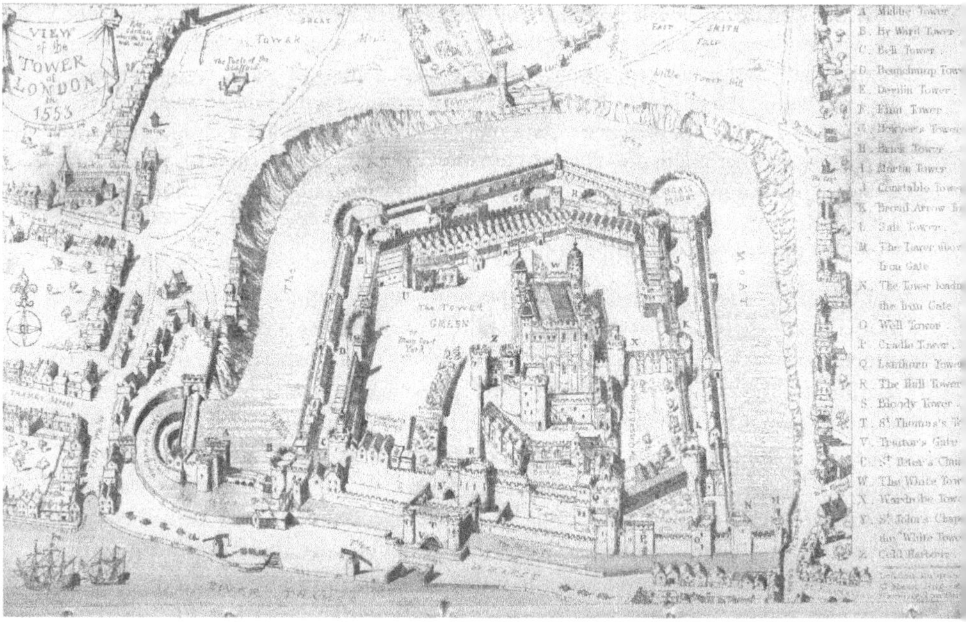

Fig. 4. 'View of the Tower of London in 1555' attached to *The Tower of London*. The improver's notion of access to the past, based on the idea of 'free looking', was overtaken by the idea of the prison and dungeon

3, began to percolate from popular histories of crime and the early novel of low life to antiquarian studies. Archaeologists and local historians cultivated the association between the dungeon and history. One example is John Bayley, mentioned earlier, Chief Clerk of the Records Office in the Tower, whose *History and Antiquities of the Tower of London with Biographical Anecdotes and Memoirs of Royal and Distinguished Persons* (1821 and 1825) is considered the first scholarly history of the place. Bayley ostensibly undertook to compile a chronicle of the Tower as a palace and fortress, but most of his text is devoted to 'an account of it as a state prison with biographical notices of the persons confined there'. That the topic was quite new is evident from his convoluted apology in the preface to the second volume, in which he admits to having indulged in describing the prisoners far more than was required by 'a work of this nature'.[42] Notwithstanding this *apologia*, the *History* contains detailed information on the subject, including reproductions of prisoners' inscriptions, which would so fascinate Dickens and his readers, and which Ainsworth would extensively draw on. The association of the Tower and, by implication, the monarchy and arbitrary violence is to be found even in mainstream Whig

[42] John Bayley, *The History and Antiquities of the Tower of London* (London, 1821), i, p. iii.

Fig. 5. The panorama and the dungeon from Ainsworth, *The Tower of London*, 1840. The novel insinuated the view from the dungeon into the panoramic view of history

historiography. Thus Henry Hallam's *Constitutional History of England*, appearing two years after Bayley's *History*, stresses that 'The rack seldom stood idle in the Tower for all the latter part of Elizabeth's reign'. Hallam makes the same analogy between the Tower and the Bastille, the Tudor arbitrary state and the *ancien régime* in France, that Wellington and Dickens would reiterate: 'that dark and gloomy pile affords associations not quite so numerous and recent as the Bastille did, yet enough to excite our hatred and horror'.[43]

Ainsworth and Cruikshank's most significant innovation is the formulation of practices of looking at the Tower/prison, which they recreate as a configuration of Tudor history by insinuating the subterranean and Gothic view of the prisoner into the rational look of the improvers, discussed earlier, and the tourist's panoramic view of the capital. The entire third chapter of the novel's Second Book is perhaps the best example of this very self-conscious attempt. In it Ainsworth has the emblematically British Gervase Winwike, one of the Tower's warders, act as guide (the warder's main function from the eighteenth century) to the nefarious Simon Renard, Spanish Ambassador to the Court of Mary Tudor. From the top of the White Tower they survey, unimpaired, the 'glorious panorama' of London and discuss the bloody history of England (see Fig. 5). The opening lines of their dialogue would be reproduced in guidebooks to the Tower, including the official guidebook, throughout the 1840s:

> 'There you behold the Tower of London', said Winwike, pointing downwards. 'And there I read the history of England', replied Renard. 'If it is written in those towers it is a dark and bloody history', replied the warder—'and yet your Excellency says truly. The building on which we stand, and those around us, are the best chronicles of our country.'[44]

It is precisely at this point that Ainsworth inserts, in parenthesis, a twenty-page history of the buildings of the Tower, drawing on a wealth of authorities, including such textbooks on torture and criminal law as D. Jardine's *A Reading on the Use of Torture in the Criminal Law of England Previous to the Commonwealth* (1837). He then interrupts the guidebook text to hammer down his association between the panorama and the dungeon, violence and national history:

> Viewed from the Summit of the White Tower, especially on the west, the fortress still offers a striking picture. In the middle of the sixteenth century, when its outer ramparts were strongly fortified—when a gleam of corslet and pike was reflected upon the dark waters of its moat—when the inner ballium walls were entire and unbroken, and its thirteen towers reared their embattled fronts—when within each of those towers state prisoners were immured—when its drawbridges were constantly raised, and its gates closed—when its palace still lodged a sovereign—when councils were held within its chambers—when its secret dungeons were crowded—when Tower Hill boasted a scaffold, and its soil was dyed with the richest and best blood of the land—when it numbered among its inferior officers, jailors, torturers, and an executioner—when all its terrible machinery was in readiness, and could be called into play at a moment's notice—when the steps of Traitor's Gate were worn by the feet of those who ascended them—when, on whichever side the gazer looked, the same stern prospect was presented—the palace, the fortress, the prison—a triple conjunction of fearful significance—when each structure

[43] Quoted in Hammond, '"Epitome of England's History"', 145.
[44] Ainsworth, *Tower of London*, 128.

had dark secrets to conceal—when beneath all these ramparts, towers and bulwarks, were subterranean passages and dungeons—*then*, indeed, it presented a striking picture both to the eye and mind.[45]

Slowly taking in what the eye commands, Renard and Ainsworth's reader/tourist finally fix their look on one particular object: 'The last object upon which his gaze rested was the scaffold. A sinister smile played upon his features as he gazed upon it. "There", he observed, "is the bloody sceptre by which England is ruled. From the palace to the prison is a step—from the prison to the scaffold another." '[46]

The apparent contrast between the Tower in 1840 and the sixteenth-century Tower, between the Tudor monarchy and the modern state, dissolves. By excessively using the relative adverb 'when' in an inordinately repetitious sentence, Ainsworth effectively blurs the distinction between the Tower and 'England': the site of unjust and bloody rule is an emblem of the monarchy and government in general. Most important, the grand-scale view, ostensibly similar to the visual experience at London's various panoramas and reworked in Carlyle's prophetic text on the Revolution, lacks order and instead hints at the inability to erase the unruly and arbitrary Tudor past and its relics from the sprawling labyrinthine metropolis. The unshackled tourist's eye is trained to 'see' disorder and arbitrariness, even as he or she is offered the vantage point of a panoramic view. Moreover, the eye is schooled in penetrating beneath surfaces and grids, to realize the subterranean Tower lives, a city underneath a city, as it were.

MAKING DO WITH THE TOWER: PROCEDURES

But how did actual readers/viewers make do with the language and notion of free and unhampered viewing of the violent and disorderly? How did they utilize and interpret the construct of Ainsworth and Cruikshank's version of the 'free spectator', and how indeed did this particular construct bear upon the limited albeit negotiable possibilities of actually 'seeing the Tower'? If we aim at connecting texts to their popular uses we must at least try to address these questions. I would argue that the vast corpus of historical writing on monuments produced during the first half of the nineteenth century made widely available an idiom which individuals could 'translate' into a 'tourist gaze'[47]—consisting of a repertoire of looking at urban historical traces, associating them with literary and pictorial images of history, and often competing with and effectively winning over both the official attempt at control and the agenda of rational reformism by introducing into them the sense of pleasurable horror.

45 Ibid. 140–1.

46 Ibid. 141.

47 See John Urry, *The Tourist Gaze: Leisure and Travel in Contemporary Societies* (London, 1990) and *Consuming Places* (London, 1995), 129–63.

Ainsworth's book had a central and even privileged place in the tourist's repertoire and its various uses teach us a great deal about broader procedures of Victorian 'making do' with culture. To begin with, the novel, appearing in thirteen issues—indeed, the genre of serial topographical-historical writing—transformed physical sightseeing by stretching the experience itself far beyond the actual moment of looking at the site, extending it to a year. Reading in many cases preceded and preconditioned the sightseeing itself. Moreover, serial reading of the densely illustrated text generated a repetitive visual pleasure, enhanced by anticipation during the block of time between numbers that set in motion what I would describe as serial viewing or serial spectatorship, in which the thrill of reading/watching the historical dungeon could be recapitulated and experienced again and again, privately or in group reading, at home and on the spot at the monument itself. Actual tourists during the 1840s, picking up on the text, demanded to be taken to the forbidden parts of the Tower now made familiar, especially the parts identified with imprisonment and torture. What they wanted to see above all were 'the dungeons and subterranean prisons' which Ainsworth had described and Cruikshank 'realized' (Martin Meisel's apt term) and which had been off-limits, rather than view the precincts of the site from elevated points.[48] And years after Ainsworth lost his position as one of Britain's top-selling historical novelists, he was recognized for having shaped urban sightseeing. As the *Pictorial World* put it, the public for which the Tower was first and foremost a dungeon were 'assisting in the illustrations of one of Mr. Ainsworth's novels'.[49]

It was the public's pressure that drove the Tower authorities into recognizing the potential of the prison myth. The official endorsement in 1841 of Ainsworth's identification between the Tower and England's 'bloody history' is one example. And there are numerous others. Official guidebooks began carrying an exhaustive description of the prisoners' inscriptions in the various buildings, which became accessible from the 1850s. The 1854 edition included a detailed four-page description of instruments of torture. A programme of repairs and restoration initially supervised by Gothic revival architect Anthony Salvin and meticulously described by Geoffrey Parnell gradually made the parts associated with the prison accessible to the public, the first among these being the Beauchamp Tower, which in 1851 was returned to 'its original and essential purpose of State prison'.[50] In 1850 the block was moved to the middle of Queen Elizabeth's Armoury for visitors to see and feel the edge of the axe 'for a pleasing thrill in the joints'. They could be locked in Walter Raleigh's cell and, the high point of the visit, given a hands-on show of the thumbscrew in action. The rediscovery of dungeons in the White Tower (following the removal of military stores from its basement in the 1850s) launched a new torture route, parts of it

48 Hammond, '"Epitome of England's History'", 160.

49 *Pictorial World*, 3 May 1874, p. 195.

50 PRO, WO 94/20, F233, 4 Dec. 1851.

subterranean, 'realizing' the prisoner's routes which Ainsworth and Cruikshank had made so visual. The route included St John's Chapel (which figures prominently in the novel), the Council Chamber, and 'Little Ease'—an infamous cell—in the White Tower, the Bloody Tower, the basement of the Wakefield Tower, parts of Beauchamp Tower, St Peter's Chapel, and the ramparts. Warders were instructed not only to escort sightseers along this itinerary but to respond to their interest, and they allowed racks, pincers, and thumbscrews to be applied—on demand. Significantly women's demand received the greatest attention. The illustrated press particularly relished the display of torture on young females. A number of illustrations depict them experiencing the thrill of mock pain with a male father figure 'witnessing' the enactment of torture: 'Papa the while improving the occasion and telling rosebud how thankful she ought to be that she was not born in the dark age.'[51] The *Illustrated London News* and *Pictorial World* of 1871 and 1874 carried illustrations of 'Holiday Sights: the Torture in Her Majesty's Tower' depicting young women having their fingers treated with the thumbscrew. George Bernard O'Neill, 'A Visit to the Tower', has a crowd of children—workers' children by their cloths, and better-dressed children and grown-ups, watch a girl being subjected to a mock execution. And Marshall Claxtone depicts a well-dressed 'lady' watched by a small crowd of female spectators with a warder instructing her how to put her head on the block.[52]

One may argue, of course, that these are representations of Tower visiting which may be approached as constructions of gender and class, rather than being indices to how actual women and men behaved in and 'took in' the Tower. However, audiences were willing participants in the hands-on historical melodrama which drew them in and made it possible to experience the horror of the dungeon and torture physically yet in a controlled manner as a 'thrill'. Interestingly, there are no available comments on squeamish responses (real horror). This was even more than Tussaud's relics of the Revolution and past acts of crime offered: in the Tower's torture route, instruments and objects acquired a 'usability' which was reinforced by the associations visitors brought with them to the historical place, inhabiting it with sensations.

By the 1880s and 1890s, the dungeon and dungeon tourism were taken on in vaudeville and the music hall, a sign that they had become highly conventionalized and commercialized. The Tower appears both in Gilbert and Sullivan's distinctly middle-class operetta *Yeoman of the Guard* and, more important here, on popular platforms catering for lower-class audiences. In 1899 the enormously successful Dan Leno sang H. Darnley's 'The Beefeater', printed on cheap sheets to be sung outside theatres and music halls. With asperity Darnley burlesques the combination of official resistance to a truly free access

[51] Hammond, '"Epitome of England's History'", 158; *ILN*, 30 Dec. 1851.
[52] Hammond, 170.

and official greed, manifest in the rapid commercialization of Britain's national monuments. First in good humour:

Chorus
It's a spleendid place to spend a happy day.
Old Tow'r of London! London!
Ev'rything is free, there's not a cent to pay;
But if you haven't got a bob or two you'd
Better stop away from the good
Old Tow'r of London! London!

Then in knockabout acerbic tone in the Beefeater monologue in the 'spoken' part:

Well ladies, I'll just point out one or two little items to you. First, you come to a little old man sitting at a little old gate who'll take a little old shilling from you; that's a very old custom and indicates that to-day is a free day... Now standing with your backs to the Refreshment Room, you get a beautiful view of the Tower; standing with your backs to the Tower, you get a lovely view of the—er, Refreshment Room. Coming back, and standing on the steps of the Refreshment Room, you get a fine view of the dungeons in which they put state prisoners—no matter what state they were in. At least, you don't exactly see the dungeons, but we have some very good photographs of them in the Refreshment Room at 6d each.[53]

LOCAL GESTURES: THE TOWER AND EAST LONDON

We should be wary of interpreting the conventionalizing of the dungeon, and the fact that it and the Tower made it to the music hall, as evidence that the debate on free access and individuals' creative uses of notions about it had no larger 'social' meaning and that they were depoliticized. Or, put in chronological terms, that early nineteenth-century protest subverted authority, whereas as the century progressed and access to monuments was democratized, the culture of history became one of acquiescence. Restrictions on access to the Tower persisted until the late 1930s and, as we shall see, it was between the late nineteenth century and the twentieth century inter-war period that debates on the right to see flared, developed into forms of collective action, and aligned around the contours of class and local interests.

After the Second Reform Bill and before the establishment of a London central government in the form of the London County Council (LCC), resentment of control manifested itself in a repertoire of collective political gestures with a special local stance. Although various shades of rhetoric presented

[53] 'The Beefeater, Written and Composed by H. Darnley and Sung by Dan Leno', *Vocal Music, 1890–99*, 56, 254.

the Tower as belonging to, and the 'epitome of the nation', geographically it was dangerously close to, if not a part of, the heart of East London. Maps of the LCC boroughs in 1888 locate it within the City of London, and bordering Stepney and Bethnal Green, areas which exactly at this period came to symbolize urban danger, destitution, and rampant crime. The Tower's presence in the East End did not mean that it was of it: it remained, for the majority of local people, *terra incognita*. Active segments of local audiences grew resentful of practices of control exercised in a city they considered their own, and on a territory which, by right, 'belonged' to them. They sometimes interpreted the new franchise of 1867 as a territorial and local right to free access to 'their' monument. And they interpreted the control which both the Tower's military authorities and central bureaucracy continued to exercise as an infringement of urban freedom, an infringement which had no parallel in other capitals. One example of the repertoire and language of protest is the response to the belated introduction of free visiting days in the 1870s, after a successful local campaign. Although free days in fact benefited a cross-class audience, they were presented throughout the Victorian era as a class 'concession', aimed at working people. But East Enders deemed the 'concession' an empty gesture, cancelled out by the continued practice of group tourism and the inconvenience which most non-paying visitors experienced. Already on the very first 'free' day, on Bank Holiday April 1875, thousands awaited their turn at the Tower's gates, a result of the 100-visitors rule. As both the local *Eastern Post* and the national *Daily News* indignantly reported a week later: 'Thousands who sacrificed a day's work for the sake of enjoying an edifying holiday, lost the results of both, by waiting hour after hour in hope of being admitted.'[54] Occasionally resentment generated public remonstrance, combining demonstrating, petition signing, and public speeches, all forms of protest drawing on the older reformist repertoire, but with a distinct local idiom. Thus on free day Saturday, 11 April 1880, a party of thirty

> were so annoyed at the absurd red tapism, that after being marshaled at a rapid rate through the Tower, and turned out at Wapping exit, they formed themselves into a meeting and waited until the arrival of other contingents. When some 156 persons were assembled, Mr. Henry Japson, of King David Lane, Shadwell, took the chair, and said that the concession to the public of opening the Tower free throughout England was not conceded until public opinion had, through the medium of the Press, made itself heard throughout England. Then and not until then were the public allowed to view gratis what belonged to them; but the grudging way in which the concession was given was perfectly disgraceful, and now that the public could get in free twice a week there were such shameful restrictions in use that a man quitted the Tower no wiser than he went in (Hear, hear) . . . men of sense who wished to penetrate deeply into the wonderful historical lore lying exposed there were hurried past every object of interest so quickly that they were quite unable to fix anything permanently upon their minds. (Hear, hear).[55]

[54] *Eastern Post*, 10 Apr. 1875. [55] *ELO*, 17 Apr. 1880, p. 5.

A petition, drawn up in pencil and produced on the spot, protested against visitors' 'being penned like sheep outside the waiting room and then marshaled like fools' through 'the finest historical relics in England'. 'Penning', like 'marshaling through' and 'hurrying', is associated with infringements of freedom (and, implicitly, with prison). Another demonstration took place on the same spot a fortnight later and made use of the same language of protest. Further petitions, publicized in the local press, brought on a discussion in the Commons in August 1880 and the final lifting of the regulation on numbers. Some seven years later, similar tactics and language were deployed in the local campaign to make the Tower Garden and Riverside Promenade freely accessible. In the summer of 1887, a petition, organized by a Mr Van Thal and signed by some 6,000 'inhabitants' of Whitechapel, recruiting the support of the Lord Mayor and presented by Samuel Montagu, MP to the War Office, stressed the right of these inhabitants, as well as of the 'neighbourhood' to take advantage of what by right was their recreation ground.[56]

Tension between Tower authorities and central government on the one hand, and civic and local interests on the other, between claims that the Tower belonged to the nation and the argument that it was 'of' its territory, would persist long after 1888. Although the later tensions and debates about who owned the Tower would replicate, as we shall see, earlier ones and draw on mid-Victorian procedures of protest, they were not just a replay of older forms but echoed inter-war discussion on the nature and trajectory of the culture of history as well as changes in education, especially the teaching of history, and in historical tourism. These changes are examined in detail in Part III. Here it suffices to fix on contemporaries' debates on the Tower as a site of concern about mass tourism, class, and the control over uses of history.

The single most important development during the early decades of the twentieth century seems to be the entry of the Tower, indeed of historical monuments and buildings, into the schoolroom. Historical tourism came to be regarded as part and parcel of a national history curriculum. This shift was accompanied by, indeed inseparable from, a concern about the working-class history pupil, both as a discursive construct, built up by educationalists, teachers, and local politicians and commercial interests, and an 'actual' tourist, conveyed to a historical place and then conducted through it. Already at the beginning of the twentieth century, schoolchildren of the poorer classes, under the local authority school system, were marked out and recognized to be a new and distinct audience. Schoolteachers, local education authorities, and, increasingly, the Board of Education, seem to have grasped the possibilities of utilizing the democratization of access to historical monuments, buildings, and museums as a lever in teaching and inculcating in children a 'national' history. Significantly, the study of history was seen as, first and foremost, visual and experiential, and only secondarily as a literary experience.

[56] *ELO*, 24 Apr. 1880, p. 5; 28 Aug. 1880, p. 5; 20 Aug. 1887, p. 4.

Of course, one of the main points of this book is that visualization of the past had been central to the culture of history from its very emergence. What seems to be novel in the twentieth-century debate on the ownership of and entitlement to history is the assumption that visual consumption and possession of the past suited most those considered to have the most limited access to literary culture: working-class children. Assumptions as to their limited capacities of learning led educators to stress their visual capabilities. As Charles H. Gascoine put it on 21 May 1919: 'The revised Regulations and Suggestions recently issued to teachers strongly advocate the beneficial results accruing to children (particularly those whose facilities for observation and reading are limited) from visits to places of historical interest.'[57] The association between visual consumption, visual capabilities, and limited literacy had been the logic behind a 1912 Board of Education circular recommending learning history by 'observation'. 'It is far more important', it had stated, 'if pupils should leave schools with their eyes trained to observe the historical remains which are to be found in almost every part of England, than that they should attempt to remember the whole of the political history, *much of which they cannot understand*' (emphasis mine).[58] Whereas the nineteenth-century notion of spectatorship propagated by reformers, writers, and illustrators postulated that seeing and reading were complementary, and that historical sightseeing was an extension of reading, some twentieth-century educationalists associated spectatorship with limited literacy. Revealingly, the association made in connection with objects and buildings is a focus of professional historians and film-makers' debates on historical films, studied in detail in Chapters 6 and 7. In both cases, the partly or uncomfortably literate are represented as highly and even exceptionally 'visual'.

There is a little more to Gascoine's argument than mere condescension and class prejudice: he utilized it in the campaign, generating in London and spreading to the provinces, to gain free admission for schoolchildren, as an entitlement to a free study of history via experience with physical traces. In the prolonged campaign for such an admission, teaching staffs, local authorities, and occasionally parents—supported, from the late twenties, by the burgeoning tourist industry—created ad hoc groups targeting central government, notably the Board of Works and Treasury, which persisted in denying access. The interaction of these various agents acting in culture demonstrates distinct languages of class, in addition to clarifying and historicizing notions about the modern state's manipulation of power to gain social control.

The first groups to have gained free admission were not necessarily the underprivileged and least literate. Quite the contrary. Without particular pressure Tower authorities granted 'concessions' to middle-class and deserving working-class children in 1889, admitting members of the Boys' and Girls'

57 PRO, OW AE1802/3, 3434; 791.

58 Trevelyan's testimony, 3 July 1912, Joint Committee on Ancient Monuments Consolidation and Amendment Bill, PP (1912–13).

Sunday Schools and choirs to the Armouries and the Regalia at half price.[59] Boys' Brigades and Boys' and Girls' Scout Brigades gained the same concession in 1910.[60] Significantly, this concession was extended only to large groups accompanied by an adult in an official capacity, and withheld from children accompanied by parents. Moreover, the two public free days granted in 1871 (one of these a Saturday) catered for adult working people and not for children. And when this concession was cut down in 1916 to one free day (the Saturday) it became quite meaningless. Even the grudgingly granted half price was over and above the reach of East End and poor north London families. As Mrs Piednue, Headmistress of the LCC Shepperton Road School in Islington, requesting free passage for some forty-five children on a payday, wrote to the Board of Works: 'The children have saved up money for their fare but are too poor to afford anything more. This is a poor school . . . and we were favoured with free pass three years ago.'[61] The Commissioner of Works was not to be budged. Gascoine touches in greater detail on the constraints put on poor children from Tottenham and their teachers, and is worth quoting at length:

> The journey [from Tottenham] to Liverpool Street Station, the walk through the City, the visit to London Bridge, and the ascent of the Monument were all thoroughly enjoyed and appreciated; but upon arrival at the Tower we were informed the full fees of admission were 1s. 9d. per person . . . Eventually we were, as a school party, allowed to enter at half-fees, but 10 1/2 d., to my boys meant much, and I venture to assert too much to expect from these children . . . I think I am speaking practically for all teachers when I ask you to use your influence on behalf of the boy or girl who is penalized by these charges.[62]

It took nearly a decade of the coordinated effort of educationalists, local schools, the LCC education officers, and the Board of Education finally to bend the Board of Works to admit elementary school children in groups not exceeding sixty, pending the success of 'an experimental period', these two conditions being reminiscent of the older restrictions on numbers. The most forceful argument for children's free access was that historical tourism was part of the ordinary curriculum, counted as attendance, and therefore must be free of charge, subject to the Education Act.[63] The argument itself drew on the, by then, fairly established set of assumptions about history's central place at school, study as a visual experience, and universal free education. But each of these assumptions, and the set in its entirety, was inflected by the principle of distinction which we have seen operating within the democratic culture of history, and each assumption reiterated views on economic, class, and regional difference. Moreover, the tension between democratization and the apparatuses of distinction remained high well after access and reduced fees were conceded to a

[59] PRO, WORK 14/952, July 1889. [60] Ibid., June 1910.
[61] WORK 14/2386, Oct. 1913. [62] Ibid., 21 May 1919. [63] Ibid., 11 Aug. 1919.

wide range of audiences and apparent decontrol replaced the old system of monitoring Tower tourists.

During the 1930s, questions like the numbers of visitors, their public conduct, and their claim on historical places flared up anew. The poor schoolchild remained the centrepiece of the debate. But distinction was made among groups of unprivileged children: the London poor, bred and educated in the city, now had uncontested claim on the Tower, whereas tourism of children from outside the metropolitan area was consistently obstructed. By the middle of the decade East End schools had fairly routinely extensive programmes of visiting historical landmarks within their immediate environs and, quite often, outside the perimeters of their locality. Typically such historical trips were sponsored by a variety of local or municipal and philanthropic interests, organizations, and funds (less typically by the Children's Holiday Fund). On 6 June 1935, the City of London Corporation organized and sponsored a trip of 120 pupils of Coleman's Street School to St Paul's Cathedral, to allow the children to participate in the celebration of the twenty-fifth anniversary of the accession of George V. They were allotted places inside the Cathedral to view ('from seats'!), the historic place and the Royal Procession, were provided with lunch and milk, and each was given a memento. Trips to the Tower were organized in December 1927 and November 1931. The monarchist and imperial tone, augmenting the history of the monarchy, was maintained in Coleman's programme of trips throughout the 1920s and 1930s, which supplemented history lessons with visits to the Imperial Institute, Guildhall (to celebrate Empire Day), and the Royal Exchange.[64]

Cubitt-Town School took to the Tower boys in groups of twenty, in February and March 1933, in January 1934, and again in March 1935.[65] Fairfield Road Boys' School, a secondary, non-paying school, organized an expedition, remembered in detail by W. G. Scotchmer, not least because it involved leaving the precincts of the children's own neighbourhood. Disembarking from the train at Fenchurch Street, they marched down Lloyds Avenue into Trinity Square, past the Royal Mint and onto the Tower, 'not forgetting to pause on the way to be shown the spot where Ann Bolegene [*sic*] was executed'. For the overwhelming majority of children this was their first encounter with the place: 'most of us being poor East End children had never seen this place before and we looked in wonder as Mr. Barnett described it's [*sic*] history'.[66] And wonder was mixed with fear at and awe of the dungeon and scaffold. From a distance of some sixty-eight years, Scotchmer still recalls that the 'experience was macabre and awe-inspiring'. Martin Smercovitch of Stepney Jewish School too remembers the

[64] LMA, EO/DIV5/COE/LB/3. [65] Ibid., EO/DIV5/CUB/LB/2.

[66] W. G. Scotchmer to Billie Melman and Katherine Bradley, 26 Mar. 2002. Author's collection. This and all contacts with memorialists cited below were made through 'Friends Reunited'.

thrill in the prison and the Crown jewels (as well as the bore of trudging from room to room).[67]

Evidently theirs and similar memories, culled from correspondence in early and mid-2002 with former East End schoolchildren concerning episodes of their schooling, are not without problems to historians. But the memories do help recoup a part of the experience of history in the everyday. Practically all memorialists acutely remembered their poverty, seen as a major hindrance to tourism. More important, their travel in time was experienced spatially and their visual memory of the historical defined and retained territorially, that is in connection with their moving across parts of East London. Commuting by the underground (so unusual for most), in unfamiliar roads and itineraries, was a modern experience of the metropolis. The children connected its materiality and everyday aspect to the strangeness of the past. In similar manner, other former schoolchildren noted the famous artificial beach, also known as the Children's Beach, ceremoniously opened on the foreshore of the Tower on 23 July 1934 by George V, for East London residents and specifically for local children.[68] The Tower and the beach were often regarded as a local territory, an extended playground of sorts, even by those who did not pass through the walls.[69]

The provincial juvenile tourist, and his or her right of 'seeing' the country's historical centre, was more easily contested than his metropolitan counterpart. The appearance of massive school tourism from outside London and the discursive reconstruction of the provincial pupil-tourist of the poorer class both evolved during, yet notwithstanding, the slump and one of the worst periods of unemployment. These did not seriously affect working-class schoolroom rail tourism to the metropolis. This branch of historical tourism seems to have boomed before the Second World War. Indeed the mass-tourism market was becoming differentiated, targeting schoolchildren as a large group of potential culture consumers. London's historical landmarks were an attractive package, thanks to cheap rail fares and the close cooperation of 'clients' (school boards mainly) and culture distributors, especially local and regional travel agencies. Agencies like Richards aggressively sold the 'Tower' to tens of thousands of Lancashire children and children from the Midlands, thus effectively changing the social and regional composition of historical tourism. On 1 May 1934, 2,330 schoolchildren from Stockport visited the Tower; on 4 May some 2,000 from Derby and 1,300 from Henley, and on 5 May 1,480 from Leeds. On a busy 8 June, Richards brought over 5,000 from Oldham and 450 from Darien, on 13 and 14 June 1,600 from Bolton, and on 21 June some 3,300 from Blackburn.[70] Both Richards and the schools authorities built on Friday cheap travel. But

67 Martin Smercovitch to Melman and Bradley, 10 Sept. 2002. Author's collection.

68 Denis Hogarth to Melman and Bradley, 2 Apr. 2002; Renee Jaffa, née Purkis, 22 Mar. 2002; Sidney Curtis, formerly Sklarsh, 21 Mar. 2002, ibid.

69 Gilda O'Neill, *My East End: Memories of Life in Cockney London* (Harmondsworth, 2000), 113.

70 PRO, WORK, 14/2836, Charles Richards Limited, Correspondence with Office of Works.

Friday was full-fee day and, we may safely conjecture, one on which less well-off local and provincial audiences, especially school audiences, were effectively excluded from the Tower. In the long negotiation over access and facilities that ensued, Lancashire local authorities, together with Lancashire-based Richards, stressed the marginalization of the new kind of historical tourists. Their class, low economic status, and very distance from the metropolis justified an effort to include them in the central culture of history. As the Education Committee County Borough of Blackburn stressed:

> Blackburn [was high] in the list of towns where unemployment was severe and . . . many of the children are taking part in the educational visit to London only at great sacrifice by the parents. The payment of small extra charge in many cases would be absolutely impossible, and thus the visit to the Tower must be shut out of the program for many of the scholars. This course would mar the whole of the London visit, for the Tower of London undoubtedly to provincial children is 'London'.[71]

A few days later, the argument was forcefully rephrased in the Commons: 'The denial of this concession is regarded by Lancashire parents as the refusal to their children of a privilege long enjoyed by the children of London and the Home Counties.'[72]

Tower authorities and the Office of Works could not, and, it seems, would not, cope with provincial mass tourism. And it was not solely the sheer numbers of rail excursionists which terrified officials but also (and perhaps mostly) the new type of visitors. Thus where local authorities and the tourist business employed and capitalized on the language of free access to an education in history and stressed the relationship between such an access and mass consumption, government posited 'education' and cheap visual consumption as contradictory phenomena. Mass excursion history travel was not educational but commercial, especially when it involved juvenile travellers. A letter dated 4 September 1934 from A. S. Williams, Receiver of Fees, to the Resident Governor of the Tower says it all:

> During the past summer, advantage has been taken by some of the Tourist Agencies and Railway Companies for dumping into the Tower hoards of children on a Friday from the North of England under the guise of as [*sic*] Educational Tour for their profit. The itinerary of these Tours including free access to St. Paul, Westminster Abbey and other places of interest in London. These parties cause a great deal of congestion at the Tower exhibits and are a source of considerable inconvenience and annoyance to the general paying public.[73]

And an earlier memorandum, in addition to conventional remarks on congestion and inconvenience, comments on the mass 'partaking' of luncheons packed in

[71] Ibid., 9 May 1934, 'Letter to the Secretary, Office of Works'.
[72] Ibid., 14 May 1934, Captain Elliston to the First Commissioner of Works.
[73] Ibid., 4 Sept. 1934.

industrially made cardboard cake boxes! 'The result of depositing 3,000 card boxes in and about the receptacles for litter can be imagined.'[74]

The point of course is not whether mass historical tourism was 'educational', or whether the outlay and structure of the buildings, especially of such attractions as the Bloody Tower and the Armouries, made tourism on such scale impossible. What is notable is the suspicion of juvenile crowds from outside London. Such habits as eating in public, condoned in local school groups, became threatening when practised by the masses of northern children. Comments on their eating habits rehearse Victorian disgust of public, lower-class eating in places of exhibition. Similarly, the strategy proposed and implemented by the Office of Works to cope with the rapid expansion of mass tourism was quite old and drew on early Victorian policies and traditions of control. Ruling that the so-called 'educational visits to historical buildings' were not educational at all, the Office of Works stipulated that no more than 100 children from any one grant-aided school would be admitted on any one day into the Tower, and that any application from such a school should be approved by the Office. Probably inadvertently, the new rule evoked the Duke of Wellington's much older, paranoid 'hundred visitors' rule.[75]

The protracted story of the making and consumptions of the Tower may serve as interim conclusion and a guide to mapping the broader landscape of popular culture and tourism. The significant point about the Tower's making is that it took so long, longer indeed than most other landmarks in and around the metropolis, to become massively accessible. Undoubtedly universal access was delayed and hindered by the state and delay had to do with the Tower's position and military functions. Notwithstanding the delaying role played by government from the 1830s, this story does not yield to a facile narrative of state intransigence and restriction of consumption versus popular demand, bordering on subversion. Government and governmental attitudes were not monolithic and at times (during the inter-war period, for example) certainly reflected departmental rivalry. More usefully we may point at patterns of access and processes of appropriation, discernible in the broader culture of history and noted in the previous chapters. First is serial, or chain, consumption: 'buyers' of the Tower package consumed more than one form of popular history. Thus the topographical-historical novel, especially Ainsworth's *Tower of London*, activated visual forms of access to history, notably tourism. These in turn encouraged the commercialization of history, recognized and practised by reluctant though greedy enough authorities. As Charles Knight noted, after the fire which consumed the Great-Store House in 1841, the authorities offered for sale remnants and exhibits rescued from this fire at affordable prices, thus making the entire

[74] PRO, WORK, 14/2836, Mr. Donoghue, 'Memorandum re a Proposed Visit of 5,000 Children from Oldham'.

[75] Ibid., 1935, Circular 1128.

Tower 'an emporium of history'.[76] Commercialization, combined with a reluctance to facilitate access to historical monuments and objects, is also apparent in the struggle over schools entry. A second pattern has to do with the tension between the democratization of history and distinction. Cultural reformism, the basis of the various movements for free 'seeing' of national monuments, premissed universal access to history as a means to both self-improvement and forms of citizenship. But the principle of access operated in tandem with the exclusion along the lines of class, locale, and age. Protest directed against exclusion also made distinction into a principle of operation, constructing the desired receivers of history around ideas connected to locale and class (in the campaigns of the 1870s and 1880s, and the 1930s). A third and related pattern is the relationship between constriction and the choice and operation of individuals making do with the Tower and a host of images of the Tudor monarchy connected with it. Within the limits put on access, seeing, and movement, individuals made do by appropriating procedures of visiting and experiencing the place. Last but first is the relationship between the halted democratization of the Tower and its image as a prison/dungeon, which runs throughout the entire period examined here, peaking between the 1830s and the 1870s but persisting well into the twentieth century. During the nineteenth century the dungeon served as organizing metaphor of the Tudor past. And although the Tower accommodated other traces and images of the power of the monarchy and military grandeur, it was the Tudor horror which had the largest appeal to varied audiences. Horror, as a compound of sensations of fear, awe, and 'thrill' which could be experienced around the dungeons and was endowed with symbolism, drew on the older sensationalism and representations of the prison and gallows. The dungeon as a place and an image, and the idea behind forms and practices of looking at and experiencing the past, insinuated themselves, through literary genres, into the idiom of improvement. Dixon's adoption of the dungeon as the chief metaphor for reform is just one exemplar of the surviving power of the Gothic idiom. In *Her Majesty's Tower* (1869–70), a typical reformist text, he preaches the need for an 'educational movement' based on free access to the past. But he admits the prison and dungeon as metaphors for this past and constructs the entire collection around 'lives of prisoners', much like the older sensationalist novel.[77] It is specifically in constructions and uses of the dungeon, as we shall now see, that gender played a major role.

[76] Knight, *London*, iii. 263.
[77] Cited in Hammond, '"Epitome of England's History,"' 162.

5

Lady Jane: Torture, Gender, and the Reinvention of the Tudors

RACKS

During the second half of the nineteenth century several miniature racks with miniature women stretched on them were made for display in the Tower. A surviving photograph of one of these exhibits, taken by Benjamin Stone in 1898, shows what appears like a doll, in a shirt-gown that reveals the legs from beneath the knees, so that the legs, tied to rollers, are clearly shown (see Fig. 6). In point of fact there had been only one recorded racking of a woman in the Tower, that of the poet and radical Protestant Anne Askew (1521–46), known mainly for her posthumous *Examinations*, the record of her interrogations. Incarcerated in the Tower, where she was tortured by Sir Richard Rich and Lord Chancellor Thomas Wriothesly, and burnt at Smithfield on 16 July 1546, the 'heretical' Askew instantaneously became a martyr.[1] The miniature racks look like toys—wooden cradles with puppets ensconced in them, an indication perhaps of how domesticated the theme of torture became during the mid-nineteenth century. The miniatures also illustrate how themes and images of punishment by imprisonment and of violence incurred upon the body became gendered—most specifically, how in the popular culture of history, punishment, and victimhood came to be identified with women.

Chapters 1–4 have discussed the interrelated democratization of access to historical monuments (albeit a democratization marked by exclusion and a system of distinction) and the growing appeal of the past as a time and place of violent conflict and arbitrariness, set in an urban environment. The main loci of this past were the dungeon and scaffold, which not only configured history but also shaped the modes of 'seeing' it. This chapter is about the Tower/dungeon as a gendered place. By this I mean not only that famous female prisoners, interrogated and executed in the Tower, held a special fascination for modern audiences and that these audiences themselves included women. I stake a broader claim that gender, or notions about and representations and definitions of femininity and the relative

[1] Parnell, *The Tower of London*, 80.

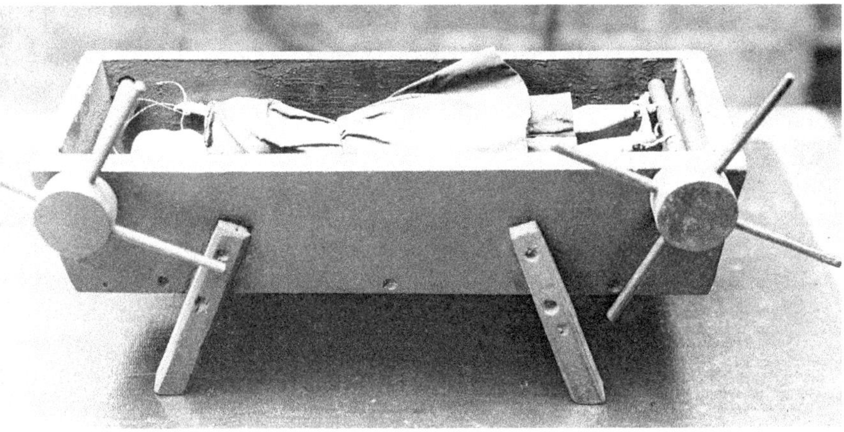

Fig. 6. A miniature rack at the Tower, nineteenth century

representations of masculinity, as well as of the differences between women and men, shaped the very imagining of the past and the terms of its comprehension as a site of conflicts, hierarchies, power, and imprisonment.

Most recent studies of Victorian tourism and the Victorian interest in the 'Olden Time' have paid attention to the representation of women in historical texts and illustrations and their roles as readers and sightseers. Little attention, however, has been paid to gender as a configuration of the differences and similarities between the past and modernity.[2] In the following I seek to show how closely tied the early and mid-Victorian visions of the dungeon, power, and the state were to notions of femininity and masculinity. I argue that the powerful and pervasive image of the dungeon available from the rich lore of crime and prison, and which I have discussed earlier, was feminized and domesticated in the early 1840s, and that this feminization made horror easier to digest and more respectable. At the same time the home/prison was not imagined as a separate female entity but was attached to the image of the emerging powerful Tudor state. Thus the stories and representations of women's torture and imprisonment offered not only legitimate delight at the horrible; they attached this feeling to the contemporary preoccupation with the 'woman's question': the discussion about the cultural, social, and legal limits on women, women's sexuality, and their role in the family. While the images of women's imprisonment certainly transposed prejudices of gender hierarchies onto depictions of the past, these images were also potentially anti-authoritarian in their tying of domestic hierarchies to hierarchy and power within the early state.

[2] There are mentions of women visitors in Mandler's useful account of popular tourism during the age of post-war affluence in *The Fall and Rise of the Stately Home*, 71–109, 386–7. See also p. 122. For representations of women see Mitchell, *Picturing the Past*, 136–7, 155–6.

The Tower of London, whose role in the debate on access to the Tower has been discussed in detail in Chapter 4, serves here as anchor and starting point for the discussion of the role of gender in the culture of history. The novel broke away from the model of prison history by introducing a female prisoner, and a royal one at that—Lady Jane Grey. Reproduction of notions of femininity in her image travelled between adjacent historical genres such as the novel itself and its imitations, drama and historical painting, and social uses of modes of observation and viewing of the prison. To highlight the change in the image of history as a prison/dungeon and in the broad prison lore which the novel inaugurated, I begin by briefly looking at its predecessor, the Newgate story and its uses by and meanings for urban audiences. I focus on the genre's greatest commercial success, *Jack Sheppard*, co-produced by Ainsworth and Cruikshank less than a year before they embarked on writing and illustrating the *Tower*. I then look at the feminization of the prison in the latter novel and relate it to the broader theme of the female prisoner in domestic genres such as the Gothic novel. The appeal of the feminization of horror is then traced in other adjacent historical genres from antiquarian writing to large-scale historical painting.

MASCULINE PRISON HISTORIES: JACK SHEPPARD

The early Victorian historical fiction on prison and prisoners, and in particular *Jack Sheppard*, illustrate that percolation of the older, eighteenth-century lore on criminals, public execution, and the condemned into generic early Victorian serial fiction, where it was turned into a popular vision of history. John Sheppard himself (1702–24), the famous Spitalfields apprentice turned felon and six-time runaway prisoner, was the stuff of plebeian historical narratives even before his riotous execution in November 1724 in Tyburn.[3] His London life, travails in a workhouse, six incarcerations, and six audacious de-incarcerations made him an icon. Even the earliest works on his life—appearing before his execution and running into six editions—were ordered into a 'history' and subsequent works purported to be 'histories', biographies, and 'memories', claiming veracity and authenticity. 'His deeds became Common Discourse of the Whole Nation.' But he gained popularity especially among the 'Common People' [*sic*], who grew 'mad about him'.[4] His history became etched on the popular urban memory as both an extraordinary biography and as a representation of a collective urban experience of work, poverty, and encounters with authority. In flash ballads and ballad opera (most notably Gay's *Beggar's Opera* of 1728), in pastiche and

[3] On the historical Jack Sheppard see Christopher Hibbert, *The Road to Tyburn: The Story of Jack Sheppard and the Eighteenth-Century Underworld* (Harmondsworth, 2001) and Peter Linebaugh, *The London Hanged: Crime and Civil Society in the Eighteenth Century* (2nd edn., London, 2003), 7–42.

[4] Cited from the anonymous *History* in Linebaugh, ibid. 31–2.

pantomime, in popular illustrations and in moralistic cartoon art, even in particular forms of slang like navy parlance, Jack Sheppard had become firmly established as a symbol of the dangers of urban life, and the liberties and oppression they presented.

Although Sheppard's status as a popular icon remained intact throughout the eighteenth century, it was during the late 1830s that interest in him exploded into a collective frenzy, a 'Sheppard phenomenon'.[5] The frenzy was part of an ongoing controversy on Newgate novels, raging between 1830 and 1847, a period when a cross-class and obsessive interest in prison fiction coincided with a political debate on the penal system, culminating in campaigns during the thirties to reform the 'Bloody Code', its abolition, and the appearance of the early penitentiaries. Indeed already the first Newgate novel, Bulwer-Lytton's *Paul Clifford* (1830), was outspokenly and clearly reformist in its use of crime fiction to press for a change in the treatment of the criminal and socially marginal. The debate and campaigns for reform coincided with broader changes in the state's involvement in the lives of the urban poor and working classes, most evident in the New Poor Law (1834), as well as with urban workers' agitation for reform throughout the 1830s and 1840s. The juncture of urban social unrest, changes in the means and mechanisms for social control, and the availability of a new cultural apparatus for the serial production, distribution, and consumption of the illustrated novel, may account for the renewed Sheppard frenzy, but only partly. Like the other Newgate novelists and illustrators, Ainsworth and Cruikshank drew heavily on the older ballad tradition and on flash, materializing their fascination with urban low-life literature. Cruikshank's fascination dates back to 1821, when he had cooperated with Pierce Egan on *Life in London* (1821). Ainsworth's was enhanced by his taste for antiquarianism and an interest in the Gothic, already apparent in his first successful historical novel of eighteenth-century banditry and highway robbery *Rookwood* (1834). *Sheppard*'s serialization in *Bentley's Magazine* between January 1839 and February 1840 was a sensational success, augmented by a simultaneous 'realization' of the book's illustrations at the Adelphi, repeated publications in book form, and at least seven pastiches appearing before 1850.[6]

The novel's huge success lay in its recovery of a past that was 'low' and plebeian, and in the firm location of this past in an urban and distinctly metropolitan setting. The early Victorians could perceive the early eighteenth century as modern: it presented the political Settlement and compromise, economic recovery apparent in growing consumption, and urban growth and the problems accompanying it, especially in London. Yet there was a gap between this era and the age of industrial capitalism and democratic revolutions after the

[5] Meisel, *Realizations*, 265.

[6] The best available account of Cruikshank's career and his cooperation with Ainsworth is Robert L. Patten, *George Cruikshank's Life, Time and Art*, 2 vols. (Cambridge, Mass., 1996). For the co-production of *The Tower of London* see ii: *1835–78*, 129–52.

1760s. Unlike the late Georgian and Regency periods, the early Georgians were not within living memory: they were remote enough to be subjected to Ainsworth's antiquarianism, yet close enough to the lived world of his readers to require a recognizable authenticity and an immediacy in representations. The mixture of the strangeness of this past and its familiarity is especially manifest in the treatment of disorder, conflict, and crime, which are elevated to the tag of the unreformed eighteenth century. Earlier fictionalizing of historical criminals had been typically set in picturesque and exotic settings (as in J. R. Planché's 1829 Italianate *Massaroni*), or in rural and peripheral ones (as in Scott's narratives of outlawry and Ainsworth's own *Rookwood*). *Sheppard* and its hero were entirely urban, native, and imaginable within its readers' social reality. Its hero was, quite distinctly, a Londoner. The novel presented a metropolitan biography and *Bildung* that could also be read as a social history of skilled trades and occupations, of the relationship between labour and capital, and of an age group and gender. As a juvenile male and idle apprentice on the run, Jack embodies the most volatile early modern urban type. A native of Spitalfields, in the early eighteenth century still the heart of silk manufacture associated with skilled labour and luxury consumption, Jack grew up at the Bishopsgate Workhouse, became apprenticed to a carpenter, and ran away to become a thief and a felon. But he is not just an elaboration on the Hogarthian, eighteenth-century theme of the apprentice sliding down from industry to idleness, then to prison and the gallows. His life and labour were easily associated and even comparable with the dislocations experienced by working people during the volatile 1830s and early 1840s. These two decades saw instability in some of the older London trades, an instability wrought by the impact of industrial capitalism on the small and highly specialized manufacture in certain areas of the metropolis. Spitalfields and its speciality, highly skilled handloom weaving, were disastrously hit by the mechanization of textile production. Carpentry and the manufacture of luxury furniture, Sheppard's own trade, too suffered from a growing gap between capital and labour. These economic dislocations generated degrees of unionization and political metropolitan working men's associations, culminating in London Chartism.[7]

It is no wonder that the novel's mythologizing of a 'low' biography set in a locale so easily familiar to plebeian readerships made middle-class reviewers apprehensive and, occasionally, even paranoid. For here was a historical character and a historical model representing urban danger—moral, social, and possibly political danger. As a disapproving reviewer for the *Atheneum* put it, the novel was a dangerous response to 'the struggle for existence', urbanization, and 'the routine habits of sordid industry'.[8] On the one hand, it encouraged the cheap sensationalism to be derived from the exploits of such a hero and, on the other, it

[7] On economic dislocations during the 1830s and 1840s and trades' collective action see David Goodway, *London Chartism 1838–1848* (Cambridge, 1982).

[8] Cited in Meisel, *Realizations*, 266.

generated 'brooding over the elementary principles of social existence, and... heaving with all passions incident to the first crude conceptions of the most stirring truths'.[9] Morality and order were in imminent danger—such a danger that the Lord Chamberlain ultimately forbade stage adaptations of the novel or any piece glorifying prison-breaking.

READING PRISON HISTORIES: JACK SHEPPARD AS A COLLECTIVE EXPERIENCE

Jack Sheppard and its version of the past as a story of imprisonment and escapes resonated with cross-class publics. But it made history especially appealing and easily consumable for urban workers and the urban poor, particularly to young and juvenile working-class males. As R. H. Horne, of the Children's Employment Commission (quoted by Engels) reported: 'Among all those who had never heard such names as St Paul, Moses, Solomon, etc. there was a general knowledge of the character and course of life of Dick Turpin, the highwayman, and more particularly of Jack Sheppard, the robber and prison-breaker.'[10] The journeyman engineer and autodidact Thomas Wright, who wholly disapproved of prison novels, condemned the equivalents of *Sheppard* as 'thief literature' which set a ruinous model for 'hundreds of boys, planning some scheme for becoming "boy house-breakers" or "boy highwaymen"'.[11]

Jack Sheppard was relatable to and usable in the imaginary and social world of young urban males, who could enact his life within the cityscapes familiar to them and in their individual and collective imaginary. Moreover, the masculine melodrama of incarceration and escape engaged readers, viewers, and listeners in a large repertoire of experiencing the popular historical text. This repertoire included literal and oral reading, watching, performing and dramatizing and, sometimes, a mixture of all of these forms. The experience could be individual, but its more characteristic form was collective. The variety of the repertoire is recorded in Mayhew's *London Labour and the London Poor*. Significantly, a substantial part of the life stories told by (or attributed to) boy inmates of the casual wards of London workhouses is taken by what are apparently their own detailed accounts of their access to, and diverse and extraordinarily imaginative uses of, *Jack Sheppard* or other novels by Ainsworth and Cruikshank. The accounts point not only at the wide circulation and impact of the definitive historical prison novel, but also at its co-production and consumption by

9 Ibid.

10 Friedrich Engels, *The Condition of the Working Class in England* (1844; repr. St. Albans, 1982), 142.

11 *Some Habits and Customs of the Working Classes by a Journeyman Engineer*, published anonymously and attributed to Thomas Wright (1867; repr. New York, 1967), 183.

the uncomfortably literate and semi-literate. Mayhew's interviewees either read the novel themselves or heard readers discuss it, or they participated in a dramatization of the story. Reproduction was not simply a repetition but a reworking and resetting of the narrative. One 16-year-old vagrant, a native of Wisbech in Cambridgeshire, settling to a precarious life on the streets of East London,

> never read Jack Sheppard—that is, I haven't read the big book that's written about him; but I've often heard the boys and men talk about it at the lodging-houses and other places. When they haven't their bellies and money to think about they sometimes talk about books; but for such book as them—that's as 'Jack'—I haven't a partiality.[12]

Inmates of the casual wards 'told stories', though 'not such stories as Dick Turpin or Jack Sheppard, or things that's in history, but inventions'. Yet the 'invention', narrated in a young vagrant's voice and given by Mayhew 'to show what are the objects of admiration with these vagrants', features 'Jack', a young runaway thief, as its main character, a nameless 'gentleman', and another nameless and stereotyped 'parson', both of whom Jack outwits, manipulates, and robs to 'give it all to the poor'.[13] Another young vagrant, a native of Manchester and formerly a spinner, is reported to 'have read "Jack Sheppard" through in three volumes; and I used to tell stories out of that sometimes. We all told in our turns. We generally began—"Once upon a time, and a very good time it was, though it was neither in your time, nor my time, nor nobody else's time". The best man in the story is always called Jack.'[14]

Even if we maintain that the voices sounded here are not 'authentic' and that Mayhew's juvenile vagrants, like other 'street folk' in his tetralogy, are discursive constructions rather than mere reflections of real-life people, we have to allow authority to his rendering of the uses of literacy and of history within the culture of poverty he describes. Clearly in this culture reading is neither solitary nor silent, but preserves some of the practices of an oral tradition. The production and the consumption of historical literature, of any kind of literature, do not make a 'binominal set' comprising two discrete kinds of activity. Indeed the difference between these activities diminishes.[15] Reading is a collective and mutual activity in which readers, or those read to about the historical Jack Sheppard, become co-producers of history. Mayhew's information about active listening is corroborated by other Victorian recorders and ethnographers of pastimes among the poor. Here the historical novel itself is retold by the collectivity of narrators/listeners who assimilate the text and process it, retell and change it, while preserving some, to them, very relevant features: Jack's occupation, a loose connection to an unspecified past associated with a notion that there is a 'history', and a plot built around the subversion of social authority and hierarchy.

[12] Mayhew, *London Labour and the London Poor*, iii. 388–9. [13] Ibid. 389.
[14] Ibid. 390. [15] De Certeau, *The Practice of Everyday Life*, 168.

Of course active reading, what Michel de Certeau has described as the reproduction of books by readers, was not peculiar to casual readers with limited literacy, but characterized reading of serialized literature throughout the nineteenth century.[16] But as Jonathan Rose has recently shown, collective and 'oral reading', that is reciting to the partially literate or illiterate, persisted throughout the nineteenth century and well into the twentieth century. It was the collectiveness of this pursuit that made it so widely acceptable to working-class audiences and, as Rose convincingly demonstrates, turned reading into a legitimate and desirable pastime.[17] I would extend the definition of 'oral reading' to describe the habitual and free movement of the consumer of literature between the written text and practices characteristic of popular forms of performance like the recitation of stories and ballads, or the street show. This movement is intrinsic to the processing of the historical story of crime embodied in *Jack Sheppard*. Mayhew's interviewees add up the novel, written materials (the numerous written publications featuring Sheppard), illustrations and cheap pictorial representations of the historical Sheppard, and make use of their sum in accordance with their own experience. This creative movement also involved watching the 'realizations' of tableaux vivants, drawing on Cruikshank's illustrations and first staged at the *Adelphi* to riotous acclaim on 28 October 1839, running for 121 performances and followed by six other stage adaptations in this year alone.[18] The sense of immediacy and veracity was enhanced by the awesome reproduction of the condemned prisoner's cell, as well as that of London scenes by night. To add piquancy to the sensation of horror, a woman, the actress Mary Anne Keeley (1808–99), appeared in the title role, her best-known part. This kind of male impersonation suggests that like Sheppard's social class, his gender too was mobile. Playbills and advertisements made much of the female Sheppard in breeches.[19]

The variety and simultaneity of histories featuring Jack Sheppard and other outlaws show that older practices of reading and traditional forms of literary consumption survived into the decades of and after the revolution in fiction and the fiction industry. The readers discussed here continued to read 'intensively' rather than 'extensively', that is they returned to a known and limited repertoire of fiction which they mastered in connection with their ability to read.[20] Oral reading coexisted with a 'literal' one, with viewing the

[16] Ibid. 131–77 and esp. 165–77.

[17] Rose, *The Intellectual Life of the British Working Classes*, 83–91.

[18] Meisel, *Realizations*, 271–9.

[19] On her performance, career, and impersonations of male characters see Walter Goodman, *The Keeleys on the Stage and at Home* (London, 1895). On Jack Sheppard see Theodore J. Seward, Alfred L. Nelson, and Gilbert B. Cross (eds.), *The Adelphi Calendar Project 1806–50: Sans Pareil Theatre 1806–19/Adelphi Theatre 1819–50* (Westport, Conn., 1990). The project is most easily accessible at www.emich.edu/public/english/adelphi_calendar/acphome.htm. See particularly 'Calendar for 1838–9'.

[20] On the overlapping of traditional and 'modern' readings see Martin Lyons, 'New Readers in the Nineteenth Century: Women, Children, Workers', in Roger Chartier and Guglielmo Cavallo (eds.), *A History of Reading in the West* (Philadelphia, 1999), 78–92.

illustrations and seeing the staged tableaux vivants. However, these older forms persisted in conjunction with the newly invented cheap serial novel and improved illustration. Moreover, the spectacle of the prison itself, in the text and on stage, could easily be connected to the larger, live spectacle. The reforms of the penal system and of policing (culminating in the creation of the penitentiary and the Metropolitan Police) did not eradicate the high visibility of the prison and gallows in the urban landscape, or their sustained drawing power, examined in Chapter 3. The new serialized prison histories were relatable to contemporary crime and to punishment in its ultimate form of public judicial killing. Only a few months after the initial serialization of *Jack Sheppard*, François Benjamin Courvoisier, the Swiss-born butler to Lord William Russell, killed his master in his bed and robbed him. This servant's transgression, fatally directed at his master, was attributed to the influence of Ainsworth and Cruikshank's novel. The connection made between the novel and real crime that could be perceived as social crime exemplifies the growing apprehension of middle- and upper-class contemporaries about the popularity of Newgate fiction. Apprehension of history becoming a model for the everyday is also manifest in Thomas Wright's observation that 'thief novels' had an influence tantamount to that of street life and 'real' crime.[21] The obverse of such an apprehension is the enormous interest in the trial, as in the novel, of cross-class audiences but, most markedly, plebeian ones. 30,000 people watched Courvoisier's execution, which Thackeray memorably described in his 'Going to See a Man Hanged', respectfully, as he reports (and Thackeray was no fan of the Newgate cult).[22] Courvoisier's chillingly realistic death mask, a memento and relic of the execution, was immediately put on exhibit at Madame Tussaud's, where it would remain until the 1920s. The Sheppard phenomenon demonstrates not only the percolation of the prison theme into a variety of traditional and modern forms of culture consumption, but also the appeal of a configuration of the past that suggested to contemporaries that, despite its apparent strangeness, the gap between it and the modern age was bridgeable both in the imaginary and the social worlds.

HISTORY AS A PRISON: GENDER AND DOMESTICITY IN THE TOWER OF LONDON

In *The Tower of London*, appearing just a few months after *Sheppard*, the prison narrative is significantly altered in two ways. First, while the prison and scaffold remain the organizing images of history, they are severed from Newgate and relocated in the palace. This spatial move is accompanied with a temporal one,

21 [Wright], *Some Habits and Customs of the Working Classes*, 183.

22 William Makepeace Thackeray, 'Going to See a Man Hanged', *Fraser's Magazine*, 22 (Aug. 1840), 150–8.

from the era of the Hanoverian, compromise state to the rising of the national Protestant monarchy embodied in the late Tudors. Discipline and imprisonment are 'centred' and their objects are no longer London labourers and the London poor and marginal but the good and great, and the locus of prison is the very heart of the state and nation, emblematically represented in the Tower of London. That Ainsworth is quite conscious about this shift is evident from his unrelenting hectoring of readers/viewers to look at the royal palace and fortress as a huge gaol and execution ground, full of 'dungeons' and 'subterranean passages' and inhabited by 'jailors' and 'prisoners', torturers, and the tortured 'immured' in the huge edifice's barely visible recesses.[23] This vast vocabulary of imprisonment could be easily recognized not only by readers of prison fiction, but also by the public familiar with the props and settings of the Gothic novel, which conventionally used the dungeon, as well as exotic and ancient buildings, as metaphor for the social and economic condition of its characters.[24]

The novel's second main break away from the prison narrative and plot is its re-employment of gender to renarrate and innovatively represent the prison image. The *Tower of London* feminizes the history of the prison and scaffold and, indeed, the past itself, and offers a domestic version of violence and punishment as a substitute for the androcentric Newgate novel, with the rough lower class and the anarchical masculinity it constructs. The masculine criminal biography was also in distinct opposition to model middle-class male *Bildung*, which posited work, orderliness, and responsibility for dependants (women, children, and employees), godliness, domesticity, and self-discipline at its centre.[25] To be sure, women were not excluded from crime fiction, nor even from the Newgate novel. Edward Bulwer-Lytton's *Lucretia, Or the Children of the Night* (1846), one of this genre's most scandalous exemplars, has a female mass murderess by poison as its main character, emblematically named after the infamous female Borgia. However, with her exception, the female figures in histories of crime and imprisonment are quite subsidiary or marginal, and even Lucretia is an imaginary figure, dissociated from prison life and, unlike the male protagonists of the novel, not drawn from the *Newgate Calendar.*[26]

Ainsworth and Cruikshank replace the boyish male figure with a young woman and insert romance and domesticity at the very centre of the prison plot. As the didactic 'Introduction', which appeared in December 1840 together with

23 *The Tower of London*, Preface, p. iii.

24 The best introduction to the themes and metaphors of the Gothic novel is Eve Sedgwick Kosofsky, *The Coherence of Gothic Conventions* (New York; repr. 1986).

25 On this kind of *Bildung* see Hall, 'Competing Masculinities'. For lower middle-class masculinities in model biographies of artisans and engineers see Moshe Elhanati, 'Engineers and Gentlemen: The Engineering Press and Cultural Discourse—from Technological Optimism to Gentlemanly Capitalism, England 1840–70' (MA thesis, Tel Aviv University, 2001).

26 This is in contradistinction to at least one of the male protagonists, for whom Bulwer-Lytton drew on the Calendar. See John Sutherland, *The Longman Companion to Victorian Fiction* (London, 1988), 386.

the novel's last instalment, puts it, they wished 'to make the Tower of London—the proudest monument of antiquity, considered with reference to historical associations, which this country or any other possesses,—the groundwork of a Romance'. And Cruikshank, claiming to be the originator of the idea of the novel, would assert in 1872 that its novelty was in devising a story of the Tower as a prison 'with some of the incidents of the life of Lady Jane Grey'.[27] The novel may not be bracketed as a 'women's novel', nor as a particularly 'genteel' story directed specifically at and therefore appealing particularly to middle-class readers. One characteristic of the popular historical novel and, indeed, of the popular culture of history, is what may be aptly described as its 'heterosocial' character and its catering for a heterosocial audience, comprising men and women.[28] Mayhew's 17-year-old vagrant, obviously an avid reader of Ainsworth, claims that 'I liked "Windsor Castle", and "The Tower"—they're by the same name. I liked "Windsor Castle", and all about Henry VIII and Hern the hunter. It's a book that's connected with history, and that's a good thing in it.'[29] Notwithstanding such evidence about its appeal across gender and outside middle-class audiences, the *Tower* effectively constructs a domestic and 'respectable' version of the motif of the prison, one that, as I proceed to show in detail, seeks to lure middle-class female readers. More important even, the feminization of the dungeon and its domestication insert horror into the 'home', thus preserving and even reinforcing the images of the past as a site of conflict, violence, and imprisonment. The domestic version, as we shall see, presented a view of the past that was more pessimistic than the masculine one. The former narrative offered forms of deincarceration and escape which were more passive than Jack Sheppard's self-release. On a political level, too, it was removed from the Whig notion of progress from a turbid past to a lighter and hopeful present.

Picking Lady Jane Grey for the heroine amounted to more than just substituting a female prisoner for a male one. Her short and ill-fated term as queen combined the idea of a Protestant monarchy—albeit one that was not 'constitutional', or based on popular consent—and the image of female victimhood. The great-granddaughter of Henry VII, granddaughter of his second daughter Mary and daughter of Frances, Duchess of Suffolk, Lady Jane was a puppet sovereign representing the interests of her powerful father-in-law, the Duke of Northumberland. Her youth, descent, and place in the succession through the female line, and her exploitation by some of the most powerful men of the realm, all made her an appealing symbol of feminine powerlessness that could attract middle-class Victorian readers. Her piety and adherence to the national religion, as well as her eventual execution, made her doubly appealing (see Fig. 7). Even her learning—remarkable for a woman of her time, in that Lady Jane mastered Latin and Greek and probably had had a smattering of some

27 *The Tower of London*, Preface, p. iii; Patten, *George Cruikshank's Life*, 133.
28 Here I draw on Barker-Benfield, *The Culture of Sensibility*.
29 Mayhew, *London Labour and the London Poor*, iii. 389.

Fig. 7. 'Lady Jane Grey's Execution', by Cruikshank, in *The Tower of London.* The feminized dungeon and gallows lore located violence in a symbolic site of the state and monarchy and related the theme of imprisonment to the contemporary debates on the position of women

oriental languages—could be represented favourably. Indeed in nineteenth-century discourse on gender and education, which labelled classical philology as a distinctly male branch of knowledge and its mastery by women as dangerous to their femininity, she occupied a special place. Her learning became a part of her image as a paragon of female virtues and contemporaries stressed the gap between the humanist classical education of exceptional Tudor women and the total lack of education in the classics in the education for contemporary women. As Lord De Ros would put it in 1860:

> The extraordinary learning and acquirements of Lady Jane Grey increased the general sympathy for her fate, nor is it very easy in these days to realize the early progress of so young a lady in classical studies. But so many other women of high rank who lived about that period, were distinguished for what would now be regarded as an abstruse education.[30]

Her classical education, that epitome of Victorian men's civic education, was condonable because it remained within the home. And it did not mar Lady Jane's simple religious faith and she prepared for death 'so religious and pure'. The image of the Christian female scholar was circulated in a few paintings featuring Lady Jane at her studies, most notably Charles Robert Leslie, *Lady Jane Grey 'who at her chamber sat nursing with Plato'* (1848) and John Calcott Horsley, *Lady Jane Grey and Roger Ascham* (1867). These and other paintings were reproduced in prints, easily obtainable by middle-class readers. Such paintings and prints, circulating the image of female learning within a domestic setting, well served painters and engravers such as L. Stocks, who, working from pictorial representations, produced moderately priced images of the learned queen.

Even more than Lady Jane's learning and faith, it was the combination of an utter and gender-specific powerlessness and queenship that made her ten-day 'rule' such an attractive episode in the history of the Tower. Other royal female prisoners could easily be cast as sexually impure (Anne Boleyn) or as all too powerful (Elizabeth I). Both are briefly portrayed in the novel, Elizabeth not quite favourably. As Rohan Amanda Maitzen has argued, Victorian historians, biographers, and novelists found a powerful female monarch like Elizabeth to be a rather problematic figure because of her crossing of the borderlines of gender and her special status as an unmarried and childless queen.[31] Elizabeth's complementary female figure, Mary Stuart, the centre of a distinctly English cult and a version of 'national romance' (Jayne Elizabeth Lewis's term) presented a highly eroticized image of motherhood and female desire, not easily reconcilable with the domestic ethos.[32] The young Lady Jane, asexual, a newly wedded

[30] Lord De Ros, *Memorials of the Tower*, 89.

[31] Rohan Amanda Maitzen, *Gender, Genre and Victorian Historical Writing* (New York, 1998), 123–36.

[32] Jayne Elizabeth Lewis, *Mary Queen of Scots: Romance and the Nation* (London 1998; repr. 2004), 1–13, 147–201.

child-wife, the daughter of powerful patriarchs—her father and father-in-law (the all-powerful Northumberland)—their proxy and victim, did not threaten the dominant early nineteenth-century ideology of womanhood and the family, though she did challenge it, as we shall see later.

The novel covers the seven months and two days, between Lady Jane's entry into the Tower as Queen, on 10 July 1553, and her execution on Tower Green on 12 February 1554. This turbulent time includes her ten-day reign as the figurehead of the Northumberland cabal, her escape from the Tower, the coronation and early reign of Mary, Lady Jane's release and further imprisonment after being implicated in the Wyatt Rebellion, and her trial and execution. The narrative is somewhat artificially divided into two 'books', the first covering Lady Jane's reign, the second Mary's early rule until Jane's execution. The politics of the succession and the state are intertwined with domestic politics and the story of love, marital disillusionment, and conciliation. Lady Jane's ill-omened marriage to Sir Guilford Dudley, Northumberland's fourth son, is marked by a conflict between her notion of her role as monarch and a wife's duty to her husband and his lineage. To this conflict is added another equally powerful one, between Lady Jane's set of 'new' loyalties to the succession (even if this is embodied in the Roman Catholic Mary), to England, and to the reformed faith on the one hand, and Dudley's allegiance to the older lineage and an aristocratic patriarchy on the other.

The intermixture of politics, domesticity, and romance is driven forth in a number of prison subplots to do with female incarceration, torture, and sexual exploitation. Looked upon by Ainsworth's many critics as yet another example of his disjointed narrative, these subplots effectively replicate the main story of the powerlessness and confinement of the female historic character. The main secondary story is the romance of Cicely/Angela and Cuthbert Cholmondeley, Dudley's squire. The aristocratic Angela is the daughter of Sir Alberic Mountjoy, who had been attainted and executed for heresy and high treason during the reign of Henry VIII, and Lady Alexia, who upon her husband's death had been arbitrarily detained in the Tower's dungeons by the sadistic Lawrence Nightgall. Separated from her newly born daughter and 'immured' in solitary confinement (the allusion to live burial is obvious), Lady Alexia loses her sanity and becomes completely deranged. Her own and Lady Jane's imprisonment are duplicated in that of Lady Alexia's daughter, Cicely/Angela, whom Nightgall also detains and harasses. The release he offers her—in the form of marriage to him—is another form of sexual bondage and imprisonment, which she refuses. The story of her eventual escape, through deliverance by and eventual marriage to the worthy Cholmondeley (who himself is subjected to torture and extortion), is an overdone rescue narrative in which the female prisoner is passive. This passivity, so different from the lower-class male prisoner's escape in the Newgate novel, is parallel to that of Lady Jane's own 'rescue' from subjection and conflict through self-sacrifice and a martyr's death. Domestic and political power and imprisonment also generously pepper the novel's handling of Mary Tudor. She is manipulated by her male advisers into imprisoning Lady Jane and is herself 'imprisoned' in her infatuation with Sir Thomas Courtenay, a romantic connection which implies at her own future bondage as the wife of Philip of Spain. Parallel to the multiple plots of high romance runs an intricate story of 'low' romance and domesticity, centred on the royal dwarf Xit who, it unbelievably transpires, is 'Narcissus Le Grand', scion of Anne Boleyn's groom and Jane, Queen Mary's fool.

These interrelated and rather messy domestic melodramas of female incarceration draw on and tease out a broader fascination with the female prisoner among early and mid-nineteenth-century audiences. For although she was absent from the masculine Newgate tale (Lucretia, the heroine of Bulwer-Lytton's eponymous novel, is not sent to prison, and her incarceration in an asylum is only implied at the end), this figure had been undoubtedly recognizable as an established literary theme and metaphor. Her origins lay in Gothic fiction, which served both Ainsworth and Cruikshank not only as a depot of props and settings, but also, and more importantly, as a reservoir of images of violence and harassment, exercised especially upon women. In the original Gothic, dating back to the late eighteenth century, and in its descendant, the popular Horror Gothic of the 1840s—usually described as 'Late Gothic'—the young female captive, confined to a dungeon, was a predetermined metaphor of the larger constrictions on women in society. As Sandra Gilbert and Susan Gubar have noted, the metaphor of female imprisonment was not peculiar to the unrealistic Gothic tale but pervaded the domestic novel as well, and was to become one of its dominant themes.[33] The respectable house, like the dungeon, the subterranean passage, and the cell in an exotic castle, was a widely used trope for the enclosure of women in private spaces. In fact, Gilbert and Gubar argue, anxiety about such a constriction was to become the central theme of both 'general' genres and the so-called 'female Gothic', a rather broad term defining women's writing on female domesticity within the house as a condition of imprisonment or captivity.[34] As the vast historiography on the Victorians and gender has amply shown, confinement and imprisonment as metaphors for the condition of women—especially married ones—were all-pervasive and informed debates about their social life, legal status, and economic conditions. The domestication of the dungeon was in unison with the larger preoccupation with the controls on women and their sexuality in an urban environment.[35]

[33] On the conventions of Gothic literature see Kosofsky, *The Coherence of Gothic Conventions*, 9–37. On the metaphor of women's incarceration see Sandra M. Gilbert and Susan Gubar, *The Madwoman in the Attic: The Woman Writer and the Nineteenth-Century Literary Imagination* (New Haven, 1984), 129–43, 445–58.

[34] Ibid.

[35] Carol Christ, 'Victorian Masculinity and the Angel in the House', in Martha Vicinus (ed.), *A Widening Sphere: Changing Roles of Victorian Women* (London, 1980), 146–63.

This 'soft' horror was effectively achieved with the aid of verbal and visual realism, transported from the urban guidebook as well as the domestic melodrama. Thus an abundance of topographic and architectural detail on both the Tower's contemporary condition and its condition during the sixteenth century validates some of the flimsier parts of the fantastic prison subplots. The Angela–Cholmondeley plot is buttressed by descriptions of their interrogation and torture—especially racking—in 'torture rooms', as well as by a tour of the Tower's subterranean parts, which the readers are able vicariously to make with the victims and their torturers (and which tourists actually made, as we have seen). There is, however, a perceptible difference between representations of men's and women's torture. The former is very graphic and rich in physical detail, the latter reports the use of actual force indirectly (as is the case with Angela and Alexia), or refers to forms of violence which apparently are not physical and are not directly suffered by the female body. These include the constriction of movement and access to space, various forms of surveillance, and a harassment bent on infringing religious and personal liberty. These latter infringements are carried out by the representatives of the state and the Church (as is the case with Lady Jane). Compare, for example, the following assortment of the episodes of Cholmondeley's and Dudley's torture and imprisonment with Cicely's:

> The first object that caught Cholmondeley's gaze on entering the fatal chamber, was a figure, covered from head to foot in a blood-coloured cloth. The sufferer, whoever he was, had just been released from the torture... Horror-stricken at the sight, and filled with the conviction from the mystery observed, and the stature of the veiled person, that it was Lord Guilford Dudley, Cholmondeley uttered his name in a tone of piercing anguish... how changed since Cholmondeley had seen him last—how ghastly, how distorted, how death-like, were his features![36]

> Cholmondeley was then seized by Wolfytt and the others, and thrown upon his back on the floor. He made no resistance, well knowing it would be useless; and he determined, even if he should expire under the torture, to let no expression of anguish escape him.... the sharpness of the suffering to which he was subjected by the remorseless Nightgall, was such as few could have withstood... 'Go on', cried Nightgall. 'Turn the rollers round once more.'[37]

> His muscles were so strained that he was unable to move, and every bone in his body appeared broken. The thought, however, that Cicely was alive, and in the power of his hated rival, tormented him more sharply than his bodily suffering... While thus tortured in body and mind, the door of his cell was opened, and Nightgall entered, dragging after him a female.[38]

The 'female', it transpires, is the harassed and emaciated Cicely/Angela, still technically intact, whom Nightgall had jailed to harass to compliance by

[36] *The Tower of London*, 371. [37] Ibid. 372. [38] Ibid.

a legalized rape in the form of forcible marriage. Her refusal of such a marriage would mean a continuous state of imprisonment and concubinage. In stark contrast to the persecution of her male counterpart, her suffering is not visualized. Readers are not allowed to 'see' brute force exercised upon her body (see Fig. 8).

The cause of such reticence has to do with the conventions and assumed expectations of readers about femininity and female sexuality, expectations

Fig. 8. Male prisoner in the dungeon, by Cruikshank, in *The Tower of London*. Direct, physical violence was 'reserved' to male prisoners and indirect harassment to females, observing middle-class notions about gender

which fed upon the debate on women, and on Ainsworth and Cruikshank's own expectations, to broaden the masculine and plebeian hard core of enthusiastic readers of the prison novel. Author and illustrator were addressing a wide and heterogeneous audience consisting of women and men, children and adults. That *The Tower* qualified as a reading matter fit and actually actively catering for women and families is evident from the centrality of romance and domesticity in it. Its function as a guidebook too classified it as fit for readers of both genders and all ages. Significantly, there is a fit between the assumed reading public, constructed and addressed by the writer and cartoonist, and the visual tourists, assumed to have had an interest in visiting the 'real' Tower and comprising middle-class women and men and respectable, rather than 'rough', working men and their families. And as argued in this book, this fit is a saliency of popular culture in which spaces and artefacts were heterosocial in that they were designed to cater for and accommodate, and did accommodate, both female and male consumers. It was the need to appeal to middle-class female readers and a family audience that may account for Ainsworth and Cruikshank's attempt to make horror compatible with the Victorian cult of domesticity. But by feminizing the prison and fixing on a female prisoner's body, which is literally absent from rough descriptions of torture, they also insert violence into the domestic version of history.

The prison image is popular not just in the sense that it is plebeian and 'rough', but in that it percolates outside a defined class and 'upwards' to the respectable working-class and middle-class imaginary and to the political debate on women's 'social body'.[39] Thus there is no reference whatsoever to physical coercion in relation to the imprisonment of Jane Grey. Nor should there be one: the historical Lady Jane was not exposed to this kind of violence. Indeed, both writer and illustrator, in accordance with the material available to them about her incarceration, trial, and execution, put forward the relative comfort afforded her even within her prison's walls. Moreover, the text and the illustrations accompanying it—both the woodcuts and the steel engravings—produce an image of her life in and experience of a feminized and domesticated prison. This domestication is apparent in the parts of the novel which chronicle Lady Jane's confinement in the Martin Tower, her final station before her execution. Known by the 1840s as the Jewel Tower, after the Regalia kept in it and exhibited to the public, the former Martin Tower was to undergo reparations and have an annex (the new Jewel House) built against its south side. During the production of the novel parts of the original building, including some of its architectural landmarks, were concealed by later additions and other parts were inaccessible to the public. In accordance with his wish to make visible and accessible those parts of the Tower from which the public was still excluded, Ainsworth offers a particularly detailed description of the Martin Tower, with

[39] On the social body see Mary Poovey, *Making a Social Body: British Cultural Formation 1830–1864* (Chicago, 1995).

reference to its architecture, inner partition, and the building's history as a prison. He includes a list of its most famous prisoners and their fates, and reference to the ghosts believed to inhabit the place.[40]

What is noteworthy about Lady Jane's prison surroundings is not the abundance of guidebook detail itself (characteristic of the entire book and designed to meet the expectations of readers and sightseers), but their homeliness and sacredness. Drawing on the dominant metaphor of female imprisonment, Ainsworth capitalizes on the female Gothic's chief assumption: women's constriction is not confined to actual imprisonment but exists everywhere. This was also the assumption of early feminist and reformist debates on the rights of married women.[41] Inside the Martin Tower, Lady Jane is freer than she had been during her term of 'liberty' in Northumberland's household—a liberty in name only. For the powerless sovereign was confined by law and marital status as well as by her condition as daughter (the biological daughter of Suffolk and Northumberland's surrogate one) and was a prisoner in all but name. Physical imprisonment liberates her. This paradox of female liberty in bondage is elevated to a national and religious symbol. Lady Jane is represented as an emblem of national and religious freedom. These reversals of the prison trope are inseparable from the changes in the image of the Tower:

> Jane's present prison was far more commodious than her former place of confinement in the Brick Tower, and by Mary's express injunctions, every attention consistent with her situation was shown her. Strange as it may seem, she felt easier, if not happier, than she had done during the latter part of the period of her liberation. Then she was dissatisfied with herself, anxious for her husband, certain of the failure of his enterprise, and almost desiring this failure,—now, the worst was past. No longer agitated by the affairs of the world, she could suffer with patience, and devote herself only to God. Alone within her prison-chamber, she prayed with more fervour than she had been able to do for months; and the soothing effect it produced, was such, that she felt almost grateful for her chastening. 'I am better able to bear misfortune than prosperity', she murmured.[42]

Entirely occupying her time with her devotions, she is transformed in her new prison from a scholar to a saint, from a girl to a woman whose 'features resumed their wonted serene and seraphic expression'.[43] As both a mere decor and a protagonist, the Martin Tower differs from those parts of the Tower associated with male prisoners and other female prisoners. The prison space occupied by Lady Jane is clear of any physical evidence of bloodiness. It is also, as I already noted, highly domesticated, being described as a 'chamber' and an 'apartment'.[44] Its femininity and decorousness are enhanced in Cruikshank's

40 *The Tower of London*, 386–7.
41 Poovey, *Uneven Developments: The Ideological Work of Gender in Mid-Victorian England* (Chicago, 1988), 51–89.
42 *The Tower of London*, 388.
43 Ibid. 389.
44 Ibid. 370–85.

Fig. 9. The lived-in Martin Tower, by Cruikshank, in *The Tower of London*. The woodcuts, like Ainsworth's text, feminized and domesticated the dungeon

wood engravings, which depict the early Victorian interiors of a chamber in the Martin Tower and of the entrance hall to it—both occupied in the 1840s by the Keeper of Jewels. The homeliness and comfort which the knick-knacks of a lived-in space suggest actually run counter to the atmosphere conveyed in the rest of the woodcuts, thus making Lady Jane's residence even more special. For Cruikshank used their linearity and static nature to represent the neglect and lacklustre appearance of the interior and exterior parts of the Tower in the present, while reserving steel etchings for illustrations depicting these same spaces during the Tudor period. The steels, with their curves, reproduced a dynamic past, vividly contrasted with a deadly and unchanging present, thus reversing the hierarchies of commonplace historical narratives, especially in the Whig versions of history[45] (see Fig. 9).

Respectable imprisonment, embodied in the homely chambers dangerously and intriguingly located inside the dungeon, has its complementary 'plebeian'

[45] 'Chamber in the Martin, or Jewel Tower', ibid. 384; 'Entrance Hall in the Martin, or Jewel Tower', 387. In both instances the furnishing is quite contemporary.

side in an abundance of verbal and pictorial descriptions of the domestic life of 'common' Tudor people. This life and material culture is centred in the Stone-Kitchen, representing the early modern equivalent to 'downstairs' and oozing gregariousness. The kitchen is populated with a crowd of domestics, cooks, bakers, pantlers, and entertainers, most notably dwarfs and giants. Its ribald conviviality was wholly in line with the early interest in 'Merrie England' of an 'Olden Time', which reached its apogee between the 1830s and 1860s. Popular antiquarianism epitomized in Charles Knight's historical and topographical publications and in such texts as Joseph Nash's multi-volume *Mansions of England in Olden Times*—published between 1839 and 1849, reprinted immediately upon production in the *Saturday Magazine*, then copied and miscopied through the popular prints—encouraged picturesque representations of sociability under the Tudors, and stressed free communication between social groups rather than hierarchy and 'order'. Peter Mandler has noted that this evocation of Tudor, or 'Merrie England' as a 'social England', suggests, and suggested to the Victorians, social harmony and even equality, embodied in a commonality of culture—both material and literary.[46] Thus Nash's crowded and vernacular mansions represent a popular and potentially radical notion of history at the same time as suggesting an early nineteenth-century social compromise between and across classes, and even harmony.[47] This image of history as a gregarious place is closely related to a hankering after a rural and pre-modern tradition.

And yet the sprouting literature of the dungeon, whether the Newgate novels or the Tudor ones, was neither a celebration of harmony nor a depiction of social compromise. Ainsworth's penchant for plebeian conviviality notwithstanding, what really fascinates him is the social danger in disorder and violence, which are set not in rural mansions but in urban sites. History 'happens' in early Georgian London or in the crowded commercial Tudor city with the Tower for its centre. His prototypical Georgian and Tudor novels, most notably *The Tower*, brim with urban conflict and violence, both domestic and political.[48] And this tension is quite apparent in both the home and the early state, apotheosized in the dungeon and the scaffold. In the novel these tensions, as well as the overlapping of the apparently separate spaces of private and public, are authenticated not only in the domestication of the dungeon discussed earlier, but also in the detailed study of the inscriptions of former prisoners and Lady Jane's own inscribing on them.[49] This, of course, is also a direct reference to the immense interest in prisoners' inscriptions which Dickens would record in *A Tale of Two Cities* (see Ch. 4), as well as to the growing body of antiquarian literature on these inscriptions.

[46] Mandler, *The Fall and Rise of the Stately Home*, 21–71.
[47] See as an example of this interpretation Mandler, '"In the Olden Time"'.
[48] These and some of his other most popular works are about London. Examples include *Old Saint Paul* (1841) and *The Lord Mayor of London, Or City Life in the Last Century* (1862).
[49] *The Tower of London*, 391.

CHALLENGING VICTORIAN NOTIONS OF GENDER

The feminization of the Tower does not cut the female prisoner down to a conventional feminine stereotype. Indeed Lady Jane's transformation into a saint involves various inroads on Victorian gender ideology, endowing her with kinds of liberty and autonomy which the novel denies her outside the Tower. These freedoms include demonstrations of filial disobedience and an infringement of her duties as a wife, as well as the ability to speak up on matters of state and theology considered as 'masculine'. Thus Ainsworth composes a number of written-in dialogues between Lady Jane and Roman Catholic and Protestant divines and scholars, drawing on her interrogation before, during, and after the trial. Among her partners in these dialogues are Bishop Gardiner, Mary's Lord Chancellor and one of the architects of the Catholic restoration, and Feckenham, Mary's confessor, and, on the Protestant side, the humanist Roger Ascham. Significantly, Ascham idolizes her for her piety as much as, and even more than, for her learning and humanist education and pronounces her to be 'a believer in the gospel, and upholder of its doctrines . . . a beacon and a guiding star of the whole Protestant Church'.[50] Such female piety could well compensate for Lady Jane's representation as a theologian, holding her own in disputes regarding the Sacraments and other issues of dogma with the representatives of the Church, and which erodes the Victorian notion of female pietism as a practical 'religion of the heart' only, which circumvents or bypasses theological matters and concentrates on emotion and the daily activity of the true Christian woman.[51]

Greater and more direct transgressions of the borderlines of gender are attributed to the two other Tudor monarchs who figure in the novel marginally. The marginalization of the powerful female monarch in the novel manifests her marginality in the early Victorian image of the Tudors, which fixed on the pre-Elizabethans rather than on the Elizabethan era itself and on Mary Stuart rather than on Elizabeth. Elizabeth's move from the periphery to the centre of the culture of history would occur only during the late nineteenth century and would climax during the first half of the twentieth, in the modern or New Elizabethanism which is explored in detail in Parts III and V. Early and sporadic popular interest in Elizabeth was censorious and was shaped by the same gendered world-view which shaped Lady Jane as a historical heroine/victim. The unmarried and childless Elizabeth in the role of an aggressive Protestant prince and defender of the realm and Protestantism was in a league completely different from the vulnerable Lady Jane and the Roman Catholic and 'Spanish' Mary Tudor, and the Roman Catholic and highly sexualized Mary Stuart.[52] Elizabeth could not be contained within

[50] Ibid. 390. [51] On gender and religion see Davidoff and Hall, *Family Fortunes*.

[52] Maitzen, *Gender, Genre and Victorian Historical Writing*; Melman, 'Gender, History and Memory'.

the image of the prisoner. Nor could her long and on the whole stable reign be accommodated to images of the monarchy as unstable and even anarchic. Lady Jane's vulnerable youth, powerlessness, and asexuality may have evoked the youth of the young Victoria, crowned barely two years before the beginning of the serialization and apparently dependent upon older male councillors.

Revealingly, in the novel Elizabeth's 'masculine' martial and political traits are attached to Mary, who becomes a compound figure of them both. Ainsworth chose to anglicize Mary and her leaning towards the Catholic powers as allies. This anglicization could accord with the first months of her rule, before the marriage to Philip and Catholic repression of Protestants. In his rendition of the Wyatt Rebellion and its suppression, Ainsworth even has Mary deliver some of Elizabeth's most famous speeches, including the Tilbury speech of August 1588, and some of her early addresses to the Commons delegations concerning the question of marriage and succession. As is well known, in such public addresses—some of which were delivered rather late in her reign, Elizabeth fashioned for herself an identity that blurred the distinctions between male and female, king and queen, drawing on the memory of her father yet wrapping her 'male' persona in reference to her bodily weakness as a woman. This, of course, is the point of the Tilbury speech, made in connection with the imminent threat of the Armada.[53] Ainsworth interpolates a loose version of the speech in the description of the much earlier events of 1554 and has Mary deliver it. The historical Mary never made an official address in public. Moreover, in the novel, the queen's very appearance, her manner of speech, and constant reference to Henry VIII accord with Elizabethan self-fashioning and not with Mary Tudor's 'female' and weak public persona. Ainsworth's Mary cuts a public and military figure and exhorts her soldiers to fight 'for the daughter of the Eighth Henry, whose august spirit is abroad to watch over and direct them':

> her whole countenance underwent a change; and those who remembered her kingly sire, recognized his most terrible expression, and felt the same awe they had formerly experienced in his presence.
>
> 'Oh! that I had been born a man!' she cried, 'that with my own hand I might punish those traitors. But they shall find, though they have a woman to deal with, they have no feeble and faint hearted antagonist. I cannot wield a sword; but I will stand by those who can.'[54]

The masculinization of Mary notwithstanding, 'her' speech is a rather muted version of that available at the time of the Tilbury speech, and she a weaker version of the patriot monarch.

[53] Carole Levin, *The Heart and Stomach of a King: Elizabeth I and the Politics of Sex and Power* (Philadelphia, 1994; repr. 1996), 121–49; Leah S. Marcus, 'Erasing the Stigma of Daughterhood: Mary I, Elizabeth I and Henry VIII', in Lynda E. Boose and Betty S. Flowers (eds.), *Daughters and Fathers* (Baltimore, 1989), 384–400.

[54] *Tower of London*, 322.

The gender differences and hierarchies stand for broader inequalities: the confinement and final execution of Lady Jane, like the torture and constrictions to which all the novel's female characters are subjected, are signposts of a broader conflict and a regime of oppression. Thus although the domesticated prison narrative with its gallery of Tudor women may seem conservative in comparison with the earlier male version of the prison histories, the former did hold a subversive and even explosive potential. As Ainsworth and Cruikshank and their readers were well aware, the combination of romance and the gallows did not diminish the image of the Tower as an emblem of violence and injustice but enhanced it. Moreover, it made possible a reading of the history of the modern state and the monarchy, not as the progress of the rule of the English constitution, but as a saga of domestic misrule and arbitrariness. A great deal of Lady Jane's popular appeal to certain audiences, for example to working-class autodidacts, lay in her role as the saintly female victim of a corrupt rule. One example of this appeal is an address, delivered on 28 November 1878 to the Young Men's Association in Albany, which the Association later printed. The address depicts the Tower as the bloody sacrificial ground of popular freedom in an insatiably cruel state and monarchy. In an 'England governed for centuries by the caprice and self-interests of its monarchs, without any settled policy or fixed principle', where even 'parliaments were subservient executors of the King's will', freedom fighters were 'dispatched to the Tower for not recognising the supremacy of the king'.[55] Lady Jane herself stood in a long succession of such revolutionaries against political and religious despotism! Despite her youth she was steadfast 'and displayed a sublimity of soul which still continues to attract the attention of all mankind. Certainly this was the most wonderful spectacle of which history has made record . . . The nation was embellished by her life and its government was stained by her death.'[56]

The feminized image of the prison travelled between such didactic prose, antiquarian writing, the novel and its popular dramatic realizations, and imitations like *The Traitor's Gate, or the Tower of London in 1553* (1850) and Higgie and Lacey, *The Tower of London, or the Death Omen and the Faith of Queen Jane* (1850).[57] But it is at a contemporary generic middle-class form that we need to look for proof of Lady Jane Grey's instrumentality in the domestication of the prison and the block. Already in 1792 she was painted by James E. Northcote for Bowyer's Historic Gallery. In 1806–7 John Singleton Copley produced *The Offer of the Crown to Lady Jane Grey*. But it was only after 1827 that Lady Jane became a figure of intense interest to historical painters and engravers. C. R. Leslie's *Lady Jane Grey Prevailed upon to Accept the Crown*,

55 Hamilton Harris, *The Tower of London: An Address Delivered before the Young Men Association, in the City of Albany* (Albany, 1878), 13.

56 Ibid. 17.

57 The Camden Society published manuscripts relating to Jane Grey, including *The Chronicles of Queen Jane and the Two Years of Queen Mary . . . Written by a Resident of the Tower of London*, ed. J. V. Nichols (London, 1850).

painted this year for the Duke of Bedford, inaugurated what Roy Strong has described as a painterly cult of Lady Jane. Between 1827 and the 1870s some twenty-four paintings of her were exhibited at the Royal Academy and these were reproduced in prints and engravings.[58] Again the fit between the pictorial and the literary is conspicuous. The historical painters and novelists draw on each other's materials, subjects, and texts. And again, historical images travel across class. The Royal Academy paintings and the mass-produced engravings focus on exactly the same motifs as Ainsworth: Lady Jane's learning and piety, her imprisonment, and the scene of her execution. This last theme drew the greatest attention and was to prove exceptionally marketable. William James Grant, whose *Tower February 1553: the Last Reliques*, exhibited in 1861 at the Royal Academy and engraved in the *Art Journal*, depicts Lady Jane with her ladies-in-waiting and her gaoler in the gaoler's house on Tower Green and features the same combination of small domestic detail and horror which characterizes Ainsworth's prose and Cruikshank's engraving. The victim kneels at the centre of the room, attended by her ladies, the gaoler, and her pet raven, the last no doubt a reference to the new tradition, established by the novel, of keeping at least five ravens nesting on the Green. But the scene of Lady Jane's serene departure to the block is interrupted by the images of an axe and a rope seen at the bottom of the painting.

Paul Delaroche, *The Execution of Lady Jane Grey*, painted and first exhibited in the Paris Salon in 1834, brought over to England in 1870, and remaining in private hands until 1902, when it was bequeathed to the National Gallery, surpassed all other painterly renditions of the death scene and influenced most British artists approaching the theme. This influence itself points at patterns of consumption characterizing the evolving culture of history. The painting was not publicly exhibited to British audiences during the nineteenth century and its availability during the twentieth century too was very chequered, having been officially declared a 'total loss' in 1928 and put on display as a curiosity only in 1975. But it was not the original work of art but its reproduction which acquainted consumers in Britain and the USA with Delaroche's rendition of the young queen's death. By the mid-1830s the Paris Maison Goupil, which handled his originals, vigorously promoted the distribution of their prints. By the mid-1830s, as Stephen Bann has recently established, Delaroche was the most extensively reproduced painter of his age, not only in France but in English-speaking countries.[59] Significantly, Delaroche was known for his large-scale canvases. And large-scale painterly rendition of scenes from the past was also characteristic of the panorama and its multiple subsidiary forms. Delaroche preferred to tackle landmark events, especially crises of the monarchy (preferably the English one) as domestic and intimate episodes or situations, focusing

[58] For a checklist of these historical theme paintings see Strong, *And When Did You Last See Your Father?*, 161.

[59] Stephen Bann, *Paul Delaroche: History Painted* (London, 1997), 15–16.

on personal tragedy. He had an inclination towards victims and losers, the vanquished, rather than victors in English history. The group of Salon paintings which made his early (and short-lived) fame featured distinctly English historical and mainly royal subjects, associating them with death, failure, or victimhood. Among these paintings were *The Death of Elizabeth* (1827), *The Princes in the Tower* and *Cromwell* (1831), probably the nineteenth-century's single most widely reproduced painting on a historical theme, *Lady Jane Grey* (1834), and *Strafford* (1837).

Of monumental scale, *Lady Jane Grey* is what I described earlier as a 'panorama of the dungeon', and is thus comparable to Ainsworth's later rendition of the tourist's gaze at the Tower. The painting presents a helpless prisoner, being prepared for execution on the block in an enclosed space and not (as she had been) on Tower Green, groping her way from darkness in the background of the painting towards light and the spectators. She is aided (as, according to tradition, she had not been) by the Lieutenant of the Tower. Attired in an informal white and light garment (historically wrong), which leaves her arms, neck, and shoulders exposed, her body could transmit to Victorian viewers that mixture of juvenile female vulnerability and purified and diluted sexuality which violent death could make all the more appealing. At the same time the blindfolded female victim and the figures surrounding her, particularly that of the guiding Lieutenant, communicated a traditional Christian theme of martyrdom. Jane Grey the Protestant martyr is denied the power of sight. The two other female figures, her ladies, too do not 'see' her on the block (one averts her face and the other is painted with her back to the viewer). We may safely assume that this 'blindness' was not lost on contemporary audiences. In itself the motif of the blind Christian was not particularly 'feminine'. Delaroche's models (notably Rubens) depicted male saints symbolically devoid of sight and heroism.[60] But the fact that he chose to feminize these models and set traditional religious painting in a specific historical framework in domestic detail is testimony to his awareness of changing tastes and expectations of contemporary audiences. What viewers themselves are 'blind to' is, of course, the execution itself: the feminization of the dungeon and the block and their move into the heart of respectable debates on domesticity dictated eradication of the moment of death (like torture) from the spectacle.

The appeal of Lady Jane and, indeed, of the feminized prison narrative as a configuration of the past, was in the plurality of interpretations which both offered to different writers and artists and to different audiences. This plurality differentiates this narrative from the older Newgate story and its early Victorian version, which excluded women and resonated with male audiences. In Ainsworth and Cruikshank's novel and in a variety of adjacent texts and images, she stood simultaneously for the modern monarchy and faith, yet also for

[60] On his usages of religious models see ibid. 126–8.

popular disapproval and mistrust of the state. She symbolized female duty and disobedience, domesticity and subjection, as well as the dangers the home incurred for women and children. Her inferiority and suppression marked broader injustices and conflicts. Cutting across these different and coexisting interpretations is the indissoluble association between the female icon and the image of history as a site of arbitrariness and instability, between the imprisoned woman and English subjects. Lady Jane became the Tower's most favoured prisoner and victim, surpassing all others. 'Fewer victims of a harsh and cruel exercise of the laws . . . have excited more interest; whose innocence, purity and vulnerability all combine to render her story one of the saddest of those which stain the annals of the Tower . . . '.[61]

The feminization of the motif and image of the prison and the dungeon, and their subsequent respectability and centring as dominant metaphors for history, are also quite apparent in the actual procedures of historical tourism and sightseeing, discussed in detail in Chapter 4. With the rapid commercialization of the Tower, its authorities capitalized on the popular fascination with women as the object of torture, making this torture the subject of 'hands on' spectatorship, where readers and tourists were active consumers of the prison. In the Tower, as we have seen, women and children became the favoured co-performers in 'shows' of torture and mock executions.[62] The insertion of a historical female figure into a rough and masculine genre (and 'roughness' spelled out both a social masculinity and a class) did not just produce a 'soft' respectable Gothic; it gave horror a new lease of life and, paradoxically, fixed it more firmly across class. The direction of the civilizing process, to use Norbert Elias's well-known term, may teach us about the way the culture of history circulated.[63] It was a hybrid that comfortably accommodated popular and more genteel notions about authority and power which were imagined in terms of gender. Most important, it used gender to mark not just differences between the pasts (the Georgian and Tudor) and the present, but also disturbing similarities between them.

[61] De Ros, *Memorials*, 89. [62] See Ch. 4, pp. 144–5.

[63] Norbert Elias, *The Civilizing Process: Sociogenetic and Psychogenetic Investigations*, rev. edn., ed. Eric Dunning, Johan Goudsblom, and Stephen Mennell (Oxford, 2000).

PART III

ELIZABETHAN REVIVALS, CONSUMPTION, AND MASS DEMOCRACY IN THE MODERN CENTURY

6

Buy Tudor: The Historical Film and History as a Mass Commodity

THE NEW HISTORIES OF THE ELIZABETHAN AGE: CONTINUITIES AND CHANGES

Over a century after the early Victorian popular discovery of the Tudors, the historian A. L. Rowse commented on the continuous life of the Elizabethan Age in the social and imaginary lives of modern English men and women. Writing in 1950, a few months before the Festival of Britain and two years away from the accession of Elizabeth II, which he would christen 'the New Elizabethan Age', Rowse ruminated about the ubiquity and visibility of the Elizabethans. 'The Elizabethan Age', he enthused, 'is not something dead and apart from us; it is alive and all round and within us. Wherever one goes in England there are the visible memorials of what those men and women were when they were alive.'[1]

What is noteworthy about Rowse's comment is neither his definition of popular history as a material memory, nor his alertness to historical memory as part of the everyday—both these notions had been staples of the Victorian usages of the past discussed in Parts I and II—but a confident acknowledgement that the Elizabethan Age was the uncontested and privileged past for twentieth-century English people. Rowse is at the tail of a long and sometimes protracted development, beginning in the 1870s, of a history of Elizabeth I and the Elizabethans as a history for a modern and democratized culture, accessible through new forms of mass communication.[2] Known for his popular work on Elizabethan Cornwall, the structure of Elizabethan society, Elizabethan art and literature (including, of course, his controversial studies of Shakespeare), as well as for the contradictions within his ideology and politics, Rowse was one of the architects of the popular revival of Elizabethanism during the first half of the

[1] A. L. Rowse, *The England of Elizabeth: The Structure of Society* (London, 1950), 1.

[2] Rowse summarizes the attitudes of Victorian historians to Elizabeth I in 'Queen Elizabeth and the English Historians', in *An Elizabethan Garland* (London, 1953), 29–55. *The Garland* was produced for the Coronation.

twentieth century and a major contributor to the cult of the 'New Elizabethans' in the early 1950s (see Ch. 9).[3]

The shift of interest from the early monarchs and decades of the Tudor era, which had generated a mixture of pleasure and horror amongst the early and mid-Victorians, to the reign of Elizabeth as an iconic past, a source, model, and tag of Englishness, registers certain broader changes in the popular culture of history. From the last quarter of the nineteenth century the powerful notion of the past as a place of instability and violence loses some of its grip on the historical imagination and another notion, attaching to history a feel of security and comfort, emerges. Yet the construction and multiple productions of an Elizabethan 'golden age' did not supplant the earlier construct of English history as a violent and unsafe place. Notions and ideas of instability and arbitrariness would persist, as the remainder of this book will demonstrate, well into the second half of the twentieth century. And the newer images would not eradicate the pleasure in and fascination with the horrors of the past. We only have to consider how tremendously popular the Tower of London and Madame Tussaud's remained throughout the twentieth century and still remain. However, from the 1870s until about 1953, a new cluster of images, which depart from the older powerful metaphors of the prison, the dungeon, and the scaffold, emerge around a newly evolving notion of the Age of Elizabeth as a privileged past deemed relevant to a new kind of politics and culture.

Within this notion and cluster three particular themes and sets of perceptions loom large. First is a change in popular attitudes to power and authority, attitudes which become more positive than the older popular resentment of authority apotheosized in the vision of the prison and dungeon. Power and authority now become embodied in the Elizabethan state and government, often, in the most literal sense, in the monarch herself, who is increasingly represented as the site and symbol of English liberties and freedoms rather than their oppressor. Second, and no less important than the relationship between power, freedom, and the person of the monarch, is the association between them and the military maritime empire. Glorification of the maritime empire and Elizabethan colonial adventure may be traced back to adventure fiction of the 1850s, to action historical novels like Charles Kingsley's aggressively expansionist *Westward Ho* (1855), and the appearance of the very first volumes of James Anthony Froude's monumental *History of England from the Death of Cardinal Wolsey to the Defeat of the Spanish Armada* between 1854 and 1856. But it was the last volumes of Froude's opus which virtually established a popular history of Elizabeth I as a history of colonialism. Some of his later work, notably *English Seamen in the Sixteenth Century*, written between 1892 and 1894 and

[3] 'Contradictions' is taken from Richard Ollard's sympathetic description of Rowse. See Ollard, *A Man of Contradictions: A Life of A. L. Rowse* (Harmondsworth, 2000). On Rowse's life work on the Elizabethans see pp. 223–31, 232–42. See also his edition of *The Diaries of A. L. Rowse* (Harmondsworth, 2003).

published posthumously, celebrated the Elizabethan seaman/colonizer, eulogized about the same time in Sir Henry Newbolt's nautical historical ballads, of which 'Drake's Drum', appearing in his 1897 *Admirals and Verses*, is one example.

The third change, which is directly related to the second, concerns the geography of the vision of England which the new popular Elizabethanism projected. Chapters 2 to 5 have stressed how city, rather than Country, figured prominently in Victorian imaginings of the past as a place of horror and violence, and how notions about the early Tudors were shaped by urban literary and visual forms of sensationalism, urban technologies of seeing, and urban spectatorship. The new popular Elizabethanism presents a more inclusive, more latitudinarian geography: the city and especially the sites of power in it are still central, but this is a palatial and imperial city. And seaports, the sea itself, coasts, and oceans are richly symbolic Elizabethan places. Additionally, the new form of Tudorism, as Alun Howkins, Georgina Doyle, and Paul Readman have noted, did not exclude cults of rusticity (inherited from older notions of 'Merrie England'), a sense of localism and *Heimat* patriotism, and a hankering after authentic and organic forms of labour and life.[4] Rowse himself exemplifies this latitudinarian geography. His early historical work and best-selling autobiography, *A Cornish Childhood* (1942), would lovingly evoke a rural England. After the Second World War he converted to what may be described as radical ruralism and criticized city life under what he regarded as a collectivist regime. But he hankered after earlier urban and metropolitan life in the Elizabethan era.[5]

These significant changes, which reached their apogee during the first half of the twentieth century, may be related, albeit not exclusively or causally, to the slow democratization of politics from the Second, 1867 Reform Bill onwards, and to the rise of the new, formal empire based on direct control and drawing on wide popular consent and Britain's rise to the position of a world power. More significant even, within the culture of history the status of the Elizabethan monarchy and empire gained in inverse relation to Britain's decline from world power and that of the monarchy. For the palmiest days of popular and mass-consumed narratives of Elizabethan might and prosperity coincided not with the scramble for territories between 1878 and 1914 but with the contraction of the empire and its gradual decline after the end of the First World War. The two decades which saw the emergence of the most widely accessible images of Elizabeth I and the Elizabethan empire were the 1930s, which witnessed an acute danger to liberal democracies from the rising dictatorships, and the 1950s, which

[4] Howkins, 'The Discovery of Rural England', 72–4, and Readman, 'The Place of the Past in English Culture'.

[5] I am grateful to Reba Soffer for suggesting the term 'radical ruralism' to describe his move towards an anti-modernist, anti-collectivist, and occasionally anti-urban ideology during the late 1940s and early 1950s. For the work on Cornwall see Ollard, *A Man of Contradictions*, 145–57.

saw Britain's final collapse as empire and decline to a second-grade power. More significant even, the privileging of the Elizabethan Age over other historical periods and the centring of the monarchy in the popular historical imagination coincided with a fundamental change in the image and role of the monarchy in modern British culture and in its actual status. Beginning in 1877 the monarch, now Empress of India (Kaisar-I-Hind), was becoming the head of a nation and a world empire. Yet Victoria's enhanced status, and the appeal and popularity of some of her descendants (in stark difference from the remarkable lack of popularity of some of her predecessors), as well as the spectacularization of the monarchy through the invention of a new ceremonial tradition, in reality marked the monarch's withdrawal and eventual retirement from governance and politics. This retirement, accompanied by the development of an elaborate and unique public ritual of royalty, has been memorably described by David Cannadine as the monarchy's slide into 'decorative and integrative impotence'.[6] Revealingly, the recovery, in the popular culture of history, of the period that had witnessed the rise of the first 'national' monarchy with claims to an absolute power and an overseas empire based on might rather than freedoms, occurs at the time of the decline of this institution and Britain's own slow abdication of a position of military and diplomatic supremacy.

But the monarchy's loss of power and concomitant spectacularization by no means signalled loss of a cultural role. As the next two chapters demonstrate, the new popular histories carved roles for the monarchy as the centre of a past worthy of remembering, attaching it to interest in a modern, highly visible, and commodified monarchy.

The spectacle of the imperial democratized monarchy was produced and staged in a new kind of imperial and metropolitan city. Imperial London, the 'world city', presented from the 1870s and 1880s a kind of modern urbanism which was quite different from that of the previous decades, discussed in the previous chapters. Though still suffering (at least until 1888) from lack of central governance and consistent planning policies, its imperial buildings and streets, port and docks were rebuilt and improved, as Jonathan Schneer has demonstrated.[7]

But these three changes on their own do not sufficiently account for the shifts in popular histories outlined above. And it would be misleading and rather simplistic to interpret the shifts in popular narratives and interpretations of the past solely as 'reflections' of material changes in politics and power: this would be to reduce culture to an epiphenomenon of political transition. For the new cluster of images of the monarchy and Empire flourishing in and around the

[6] David Cannadine, 'The Context, Performance and Meaning of Ritual: The British Monarchy and the "Invention of Tradition", c.1820–1977', in Eric Hobsbawm and Terence Ranger (eds.), *The Invention of Tradition* (Cambridge, 1983), 101–65.

[7] Jonathan Schneer, *London 1900: The Imperial Metropolis* (New Haven, 1999). See especially pp. 17–37.

newly invented Elizabethans to become the most powerful and, by far, longest-enduring symbols of English history, an entirely new form of telling about the past, with a set of novel technologies of representation and spectatorship, new forms of perception, and a new apparatus of production and distribution was needed: the historical film. Though originating in the early days of the film industry, this new form of history came into its own in the early 1930s, at precisely the same time that the film became the most popular form of entertainment in Britain. During this decade cinema-going became 'the essential social habit of the age', with attendance rising from 907 million a year in 1935 to 946 million in 1940, with some 23 million weekly admissions in Britain's 4,480 cinemas by early 1939.[8] Film production and film consumption represent quantitative and structural sea changes in what D. L. LeMahieu has described as a 'culture for democracy'. This was a common mass culture analogous to political democratization in its universal availability and accessibility. In theory at least the three new forms of media—the film and the mass-circulation newspaper, both evolving from the 1890s but making their fullest impact during the inter-war period, and the wireless (making an appearance in the early 1920s)—cut through class, gender, and regional differences and created a common repertoire and interests interpretable in different ways and forms by various audiences and new verbal, visual, and aural languages of communication.[9] It was the particular juncture of world and national political and cultural developments, most notably the developments in mass culture and consumption and 'the social habit' of the age, which accounts for the unprecedented commodification of the culture of history and the emergence of new areas of interest and tastes within it.

Of course, the democratization of this culture may be traced back to the early nineteenth-century plebeian oral and written histories examined earlier. But this lore and the cross-class visual sensationalism of the early and mid-Victorian era were not universally accessible and had nothing of the power and influence of the new mass media. The film made history 'democratic' in the sense that access to it was cheap, affordable, available to unprecedentedly vast audiences, regardless of class, gender, and age, and less easily pliable (though by no means immune) to mechanisms of distinction than other older and contemporary cultural forms. Historical films, with the aid of the popular press, changed the focus and areas of interest within popular history. The films made the monarchy, represented as 'national' and popular, into its central agent of change at a time when the

[8] On the scope of film-going see Ross McKibbin's section on 'The Cinema and the English', in id., *Classes and Cultures*, 419–57; Richards, *The Age of the Dream Palace*; Anthony Aldgate and Jeffrey Richards, *Britain Can Take it: The British Cinema in the Second World War* (Oxford, 1986); and Sarah Street, *British National Cinema* (London, 1997).

[9] D. L. LeMahieu, *A Culture for Democracy: Mass Communication and the Cultivated Mind in Britain between the Wars* (Oxford, 1988). On the structural changes in the common culture see also Billie Melman, *Women and the Popular Imagination in the Twenties: Flappers and Nymphs* (London, 1988).

monarchy enjoyed a 'cultural centrality to British life possessed by hardly any other British political institution'.[10]

The new form and technologies retained some of the central characteristics of the traditions of spectacle and viewing which had developed between the 1800s and 1870s and that were examined earlier. Not least among these was the combination of sight and movement ('moving picture') experimented with in the array of panoramic genres such as the diorama, cyclorama, phantasmagoria, and the magic lantern, from all of which cinematography developed.[11] Characteristically, the same city venues which had accommodated the variegated Victorian panoramas and shows in the first decades of the twentieth century would host the newer form of visual entertainment. Film may be connected even to wax museums. The Lumière brothers' first films were shown in Paris at the Musée Grevin, located in the *passage de panoramas* and most famous for its collection of waxworks. And the renovated Madame Tussaud's in London, redone in 1927, included a cinema hall seating over 1,000, which was appropriately inaugurated with the screening of a historical film. The genealogy of visual entertainments so firmly entrenched in the metropolis is inextricable from the development of imperial culture. For the panoramic mode of viewing, and later cinematography, was a way and mode of representing, making sense of, and coming to terms with the Empire and with colonial subjects. As Timothy Mitchell, Raymond Corbey, and Ella Shohat have demonstrated, first the panoramas, then films, were colonial forms of looking at exotic 'other' worlds far away and establishing national and racial hierarchies. Films became showcases of the world, condensing and ordering it while keeping imperial hierarchies in place.[12] And cinematography particularly suited such historical genres as the Tudor action story or romance, which focused on the Empire and maritime adventure.

In the following I discuss film as the transmitter and arbiter of the popular interest in the Elizabethans and, more broadly, as the transmitter of a mass culture of history in the twentieth century. Chapter 6 deals with the genre of Tudor films and indeed with the historical film itself as a commodity, examining its distribution, marketing, and advertising, the debate on its mass availability, and consumers' actual choices of uses of the past in the everyday. Chapter 7 focuses on the new group of historical impresarios, or brokers of senses of the past, mainly film stars and producers, and on the ways in which they developed new visual and verbal interpretations of the Elizabethans and the monarchy. In this chapter I seek to historicize (and contest) some widespread assumptions with

[10] McKibbin, *Classes and Cultures*, 7.

[11] On this genealogy of the film see Simon During, *Modern Enchantments: The Cultural Power of Secular Magic* (Cambridge, Mass., 2002).

[12] Timothy Mitchell, 'Orientalism and the Exhibitionary Order'; Raymond Corbey, 'Ethnographic Showcases'; and Ella Shohat and Robert Stam, *Unthinking Eurocentrism: Multiculturalism and the Media* (London, 1994).

regard to the relationship between film spectatorship, popular culture, class, politics, and gender.

THE TUDOR FILMS: A MAP

Within the new genre of the historical film, films featuring Tudor times and especially the Tudor monarchs, known as 'Tudor films', or as the 'Tudor sequel', acquired a special role. Contemporaries saw them not just as representative of a new genre, but as a generic artefact, inaugurating an entirely new filmic genre and a new form of history for the masses. This form, some of its advocates and numerous detractors argued, engaged vast majorities in dialogues with the past, issuing literally millions an invitation to a slice of history. Rather conveniently for the lexicographer of popular histories and culture, the appearance of the new kind of visual history may be exactly dated to 2 January 1912 and the release of *Les Amours de la Reine Elizabeth*, the first long historical feature film (four reels), starring Sarah Bernhardt in her film debut and produced by Adolph Zukor and Famous Players (later to become Paramount), and first screened in New York to captivated audiences.[13] Coincidentally perhaps, the first film on Elizabeth I was not only an international venture and the 'first big-time feature', but also inaugurated the system of distribution in theatres in the US and Britain, syndicating sales and advertising. Upon its twenty-fifth anniversary, the trade and fan press appropriately celebrated its historic release as the beginning of 'The Elizabethan Era and its new course of industry... wherein [occurred] the beginning of Mass Selling Pictures' and the 'launch [of] the first organised method of distributing important pictures'.[14]

The association between the historical genre, its selling apparatus, and the new mass culture is noteworthy. But *Reine Elizabeth*, marketed to English-speaking audiences as *Queen Elizabeth*, and small-scale British productions featuring episodes in Tudor history that followed it, did not make up a defined body of films. It would take two decades for the substantive body of Tudor films, or a Tudor cycle, to emerge. Launched in 1933 with *The Private Life of Henry VIII*, the first British film to have been defined as a history film, the first great success of the British motion-picture industry and the first (and for years) only British-made film to have become an international office-box triumph, the cycle had had a long and thriving life, ending in 1953 with the release of *Young Bess*, coinciding with the coronation of Elizabeth II and national euphoria about a 'second Elizabethan Age'. During the interval there appeared at least ten major films with the Tudor monarchy (overwhelmingly Elizabeth's reign) for main subject, most

[13] On this first version see Charles Ford, 'Sarah Bernhardt, Notes on a Dying Legend', *Films in Review*, 5, no. 10 (Dec. 1954), 515–19 at 516–18, and Albert Hilliard Hughes, 'Sarah Bernhardt on the Screen', *The Silent Picture*, 7, no. 26 (Summer 1970), 9–10.

[14] *Motion Picture Herald*, 2 Jan. 1937.

of them with naval and imperial history as a side or central issue. *Tudor Rose*, released by Gainsborough in 1936, featuring Lady Jane Grey's ten-day reign, was the only one to revolve around the dungeon as a central metaphor and motif. Alexander Korda's London Films' *Fire Over England*, celebrating the victory over the Armada, cashed in on Korda's earlier success with *Henry VIII* and on the popularity of this familiar subject and was to become the prototype film on Elizabeth I. RKO's *Mary of Scotland* was released a few months later and Warner Bros.' *The Private Lifes of Elizabeth and Essex* followed in 1939. Two swash-buckling melodramas, featuring the queen's sea dogs and thus combining monarchy and maritime empire, appeared in 1936 (ABPC's *Drake of England*) and 1941 (Warner's *Sea Hawk*). The Coronation brought on a 'rush' on the first Elizabethans, resulting in three major Hollywood productions, collectively labelled 'Coronatiana': MGM's all-British cast *Young Bess* (1953), Twentieth Century Fox's *The Virgin Queen* (1955), and British-produced, Walt Disney distributed *The Sword and the Rose.*[15] This shortlist reflects a central feature of inter-war popular culture, at its most pronounced in the film industry: its global aspect, manifest in Anglo-American cooperation in production, marketing, and advertising, and a strong European input in filming technologies and visual aesthetics. The global and distinctly American aspect of the economy of the new iconic national history and its implication for our considerations of the term 'English histories' are both examined in detail in the next chapter. Here it suffices to note this aspect before considering the local mechanisms of mass distribution, the British debate on the film, and British audiences' responses.

PACKAGING ELIZABETH R: THE TUDOR FILMS AND BRITISH AUDIENCES

Though a mass commodity, far surpassing in appeal and reach the cross-class character of the older, nineteenth-century sensationalist histories, the film was packaged, sold, and distributed to varied audiences, differing according to locale, class, gender, and age. The cinema was a part of a common popular culture, but 'Films, films, films', as J. B. Priestley, echoing many other contemporaries, noted, became the characteristic and most predominant form of working-class entertainment, rapidly replacing older forms of urban spectacle.[16] And, we may add, the historical film replaced and became a substitute for the plethora of panoramic historical shows, exhibitions, and theatrical 'realizations', investigated in Parts I and II, which had been so conspicuous in the nineteenth-century city and which had paved the way for the newer form. Priestley's impressionistic remarks are borne out by the numerous audience surveys, conducted throughout

[15] James Morgan, 'Coronatiana U.S.A', *Sight and Sound* (1953), 43–7.
[16] J. B. Priestley, *English Journey* (London, 1933), 121.

the inter-war years and the Second World War. Albeit 'general', the patterns of attendance demonstrated in these surveys also bear upon the consumption of particular genres like the historical 'biopic', or historical biography focusing on royalty and on other prominent historical figures.[17] The so-called 'typical consumer', which surveyors describe as a 'film enthusiast', habitually attending the cinema more than once a week, was a young working-class woman, quite often in her teens. This kind of enthusiast made up 61 per cent of all cinema goers in 1943, as against only 39 per cent men, according to the Wartime Social Survey.[18] A plethora of national and local surveys, meticulously studied by film historians like Jeffrey Richards and others, corroborate the broader socio-economic profile of cinema-going as a female rather than male social activity, urban rather than rural, typifying lower rather than higher income groups and poorer (and even distressed) areas and London, rather than other and more affluent parts of Britain, and youth rather than the old.

Patterns of preferences for historical films are more difficult to extract.[19] But small-scale studies like the MO survey in Bolton in 1938, surveys based on the examinations of box-office returns in London, and fractions of evidence from national surveys indicate that slightly more women than men were attracted to historical films proper. Costume dramas with history for a background, such as the lavish Gainsborough melodramas of the mid- and late forties and which, strictly speaking, do not 'qualify' as historical biopics, drew predominantly female audiences.[20] However, it was the assumed rather than actual presence of women and youth of both genders that is meaningful for our comprehension of the elaborate machinery of production and marketing of the Tudor films, and indeed of historical movies. This machinery and the international apparatus of advertising and distribution appended to it aimed at international (notably British and American) cross-class audiences, but targeted female viewers and schoolchildren as the quintessential consumers of historical spectacle. The interplay between national and local audiences, between the mass and sectors within it, characterizes the elaborate marketing campaigns of virtually all the Tudor films. Notwithstanding the strong American influence on the distribution in Britain even of British-made films (not to mention the Hollywood

[17] For a history of the genre and the term see George F. Custen, *Bio/Pics: How Hollywood Constructed Public History* (New Brunswick, NJ, 1996).

[18] Louis Moss and Kathleen Box, *The Cinema Audience: An Enquiry Made by the Wartime Social Survey for the Ministry of Information*, New series, no. 37B (June–July 1943).

[19] Sidney Bernstein, *Film Questionnaire Report* (London, 1947). Bernstein's data shows age rather than gender difference, with historical films ranking sixth in the scale of preferences of both women and men under 21 and fifth in that of the over 21. His samples are very small and their value is limited. Corroborating non-quantitative data supports the assumption about the predominance of women as viewers of historical films. See Richards, *The Age of the Dream Palace*, 258–9 and Harper, *Picturing the Past*, 11–12, 137.

[20] Harper, *Picturing the Past* and 'Historical Pleasures: Gainsborough Costume Melodrama', in Christine Gledhill (ed.), *Home is Where the Heart Is: Studies in Melodrama and the Woman's Film* (London, 1987), 167–97; George F. Custen, *Bio/Pics*, esp. 2–17.

productions), advertisers and distributors had to rely on local theatres and their links to the community, trade, and commerce and on local access to consumer goods. The campaign to launch *Fire Over England* and the film's biography demonstrate just this interplay. Marketed and seen as the most monarchist and patriotic film of the 1930s, the decade ridden with international conflict, it was produced by a multinational team firmly positioned in Britain and identifying with its national agenda and publicized by US United Artists. But its 'buyers' (local theatres) and actual consumers were local. The film was a package, compounding a ticket to a slice of the nation's past and holding the promise to a world of consumers' goods, some of them cheap and quite a few affordable in any urban locality.

From the start, publicity tie-ups and advertisements connected the attendance of the film to the consumption of mass-produced commodities and artefacts, from mock Tudor furniture, women's and men's fashions and Tudor accessories and trinkets, to processed 'Tudor' foods, toys, and games. Attending the film was meant to be a part, the activator, as it were, of what I described earlier as 'chain consumption'. One prize example of this kind of association is the linking of the film's central image of fire and cigarette consumption. In its narrowest and most literal sense, the fire and flames referred to the 'fire ships', the celebrated eight vessels converted in July 1588 into mobile incendiary devices and sent floating towards the remains of the Spanish Armada. In popular lore and in the film, fire also referred to the beacons believed to have been lighted at that time along the eastern English coast to warn against a Spanish invasion, a symbol of national resistance to occupation. Since the story of the Armada was a part of school curricula, both references were familiar to virtually all viewers. But viewers easily made analogues between the time of national emergency during the 1580s and the Nazi peril to Britain and Western liberal democracy during the late 1930s. Publicity aids, sent around to buyers in special kits, made the most of the fire motif in posters, programmes, and announcements to the press. And advertisers were quick to seize upon the wide resonance and market value of the incendiary trope, devising 'tie-ups' and 'links' to the tobacco and cigarette industry and to manufacturers of lighting aids like matches and electric lighters. United Artists together with Platinum Products Ltd, chief manufacturers in Britain of the Lektrolite 'flameless lighter', issued advertisements featuring stills showing actor Raymond Massey in the villain role of King Philip II of Spain and, by way of analogy, emblem of German and Italian aggression and dictatorship, using the lighter.[21] Massey's suave and slightly exotic appearance and his record in roles of villains made him the perfect model for the advertised commodity. This and similar advertisements were distributed to tobacconists, 'fancy stores', and 'gentlemen's outfitters', clearly categorizing the Lektrolite device and the film as gendered luxurious commodities offering men history and a lifestyle. Matches,

[21] 'Fire Over England: National and Local Tie-Ups', BFI.

clearly associable with the fire metaphor, were a different kind of commodity: very cheap, genderless, and usable in virtually all working-class households. The image of Elizabeth on matchboxes is a perfect example of a practical use made of the Tudors. In fact Elizabeth matchboxes had been in use before the release of the film. They were listed as 'sources' of information on the Armada episode by the groups of school girls who had cooperated with educationalist Frances Consitt on a school documentary on the Armada, together with a respectable list of history books.[22]

The visual pleasures and compound of associations and national memory which *Fire Over England* offered was extended, via goods, to the everyday and to such ordinary activities as the consumption of 'necessaries' like food and drink. Advertisements for the film and for popular soups feature Flora Robson in her role as the queen, feeding Morton Selten in his role as the veteran Robert Cecil, Lord Burghley, broth from a spoon (see Fig. 10).[23] The caption reads 'A and B', allowing local buyers sufficient room for manoeuvre. Conserved and tinned foods were becoming cheap and affordable even to the very poor, yet, notwithstanding their availability, they were considered as 'treats' and were associated by working-class consumers (and especially working-class women) with luxury and leisure. The implication that majesty considered mass-produced industrial food to be nourishing was modern in that it attached the great historical personage to mass consumption (see Fig. 11).

Consumption and relationship to the nation were gendered and domesticated: the monarch who sponsored and encouraged maritime power and expansion was marketed as a woman engaged in domestic activities. The combination of imperial charisma and domesticity which characterizes the advertising campaigns featured centrally in the contemporary coverage of the modern monarchy in the daily press of the 1920s and 1930s. Newspapers like the *Daily Mail*, *Daily Express*, and *Daily Mirror* covered in word and images the pursuits, rounds, and itineraries of royals in Britain and the Empire, virtually making some of these royals (Edward VIII, for example) into glamorous stars as well as national icons. The films on the historical monarchy not only overlapped but were continuous with the centring of the contemporary monarchy in mass culture.

The gendering of the films, apparent in their advertising, manifests the tension between the catering for common, mass needs and aspirations and sectional ones. The films were not categorized as 'women's films' and were never bracketed together with female genres such as the Hollywood melodramas and Gainsborough costume dramas. But the Tudor cycle unavoidably *was* about women in power. Together with a cluster of films focusing on the monarchy in Europe, it faithfully recorded the unusual concentration of female monarchs

[22] 'Scenario of a Film on the Spanish Armada Written by 4th Form Girls, Aged 14', in Frances Consitt, *The Value of Films in History Teaching, Being the Report of the Enquiry Conducted Under the Auspices of the Historical Association* (London, 1931), 401.

[23] 'Fire Over England, Tie-Ups', BFI.

Fig. 10. 'If his appetite is poor give him A and B soups'. Publicity tie-up, *Fire Over England* (1936). Film offered a visual consumption of the past compounded with that of modern, everyday goods, available to all. Advertisements, like the films, associated the monarchy with this kind of modernity

Fig. 11. The Queen feeding Lord Burghley broth, in *Fire Over England.* The film conjured up the image of a domestic and democratic queen, herself a consumer of everyday goods

Fig. 12. 'Fit for a Queen! "Fitalls" Shoes'. Publicity tie-up, *Fire Over England.* Women were especially targeted by the film industry as a distinct group of consumers of history via films

during the sixteenth century and throughout the early modern period. The biopics on Christina of Sweden and Catherine the Great immediately spring to mind. Of the ten films mentioned above, seven are about queens and only one features a male monarch in the title role.

Naturally the film industry and the advertising machinery were acutely aware of women's rising power as consumers. Thus the female viewer is targeted and offered her ticket to the Tudor empire and monarchy and an access to 'Elizabethan' goods. Advertisements for 'Fitalls' shoes 'Fit for Queens' feature stills of the rising star Vivien Leigh as Lady Cynthia (one of the Queen's maids of honour), fitting her mistress's foot with a slipper (see Fig. 12). A toothpaste advertisement, guaranteeing perfect white teeth, has the exotic Tamara Desni in the role of the Spanish Elena, flashing duly white teeth.[24]

But the most explicit connection between the democratization of access to history, 'democratic' consumption, and gender is to be found in the hyping of the film through the enormous coverage and publicity lavished on the costumes of the female leads. Costumes and fashions had a major role in historical films.

[24] 'Fire Over England, Tie-Ups', BFI.

To paraphrase Pam Cook, history was often identified, even equated with, costume, which during the 1930s developed into a major index of historical accuracy.[25] Professional historians as well as film critics latched onto dress as a chief sign of truthfulness and authenticity. Thus Flora Robson's elaborate gear and make-up in *Fire*, and Charles Laughton's as Henry in *Henry VIII*, awarded both films accolades for historical faithfulness. For the film and fashion industry, and the numerous film and fashion magazines, the Tudor and indeed historical film was the activator of female consumption. The *News of the World* put this point of view bluntly: history became a mere excuse for selling and buying beauty aids.[26] This rather narrow and simple-minded notion of the historical film smacks of the traditional and widespread equation between women and uncontrolled consumption. Revealingly women's consumption of history via films and via the accessory mass industries of cosmetics and dress was occasionally blamed for the ahistorical character of the new medium. Women's quintessential love of fashion interfered with accuracy and faithfulness to the past. Film stars were as guilty as their audiences. As *Sight and Sound* confidently pontificated in 1939, 'No actress will willingly wear an unbecoming dress' which would have 'a deforming influence of the contemporary'.[27] As this and the following chapters show, neither female stars nor female audiences surrendered history for fashion. Indeed quite a few among the former painstakingly sought and adopted accurate dress. Yet this kind of condescending journalese does point to the alarm the democratization of history through film and its relationship to other forms of mass consumption raised among contemporaries.

The tying together of Tudor dress and the fashions of the thirties and forties may seem the very reverse of the common linkage made between the historical film and mass consumption of staple goods like foods, light, and industrially produced clothes. In the first place, Tudor dress denoted the remoteness of the past, its foreignness, rather than usefulness in daily life. The elaborateness of the ruff, for example, distinguished it from modern fashions and made it out of tune with ready-made cheap women's clothing. Thus sumptuous dress on the screen could hardly be hyped as a commodity at a time of slump and soaring unemployment. What seems to be at work here is the pillaging of the past and that effort to promote and sell a hybrid style, combining mock Elizabethan designs and the modern and industrial, thus 'translating' the material aspects of history into the usefully modern and everyday (see Fig. 13). Take for instance a typical 'tie-up' advertised in press releases and taken up by the film-fans magazines:

> Flora Robson's costumes, created from old prints and seventeenth century [*sic*] designs, show the queen very richly bejeweled ... René Hubert thinks the big, square cut stones,

[25] Pam Cook, *Fashioning the Nation: Costume and Identity in British Cinema* (London, 1996).
[26] Quoted in Harper, *Picturing the Past*, 57.
[27] James Laver, 'Dates and Dresses', *Sight and Sound*, 8, no. 30 (Summer 1939), 50–1.

Fig. 13. History as fashion: Flora Robson as Elizabeth I, in *Fire Over England.* Elaborate early modern dress was constantly connected by the film industry with modern fashions and the fashion industry

and large ear-rings will be worn, while as in Elizabethan times, jewelry will be used to decorate hair. Short shoulder-length Tudor veils might be worn from the back of the hat with great effect. He also thinks that this great film will result in the adoption of richer materials for dresses, such as brocades, velvets, embroidered and decorated stitched fabrics . . . [28]

To temper the total impracticality of Tudor modes and textiles (implied in the reference to processes of production that are neither industrial nor mass, such as stitching and embroidery), there is a special paragraph subtitled 'Simple Styles':

During his researches for the film he (Hubert) found the court ladies of Elizabeth's time wore a small jeweled mirror from a chain at their waist. Mirrors, which came in those days from Italy, were most expensive. Why not, for modern wear, a small vanity case, worn the same way? Every vanity article is [not] so modern as it appears, for the popular 'flap-jack' powder case now so widely used was carried by 17th [*sic*] century English ladies. The adoption of such fashions, will also have effect . . . on hair dressing. Women will adopt softer hair lines of more feminine appeal. Curls will be small and close to the head.[29]

Significantly, the reference to Tudor items as 'modern' in this and interchangeable advertisements appears in down-market fan magazines. It is precisely here that some of the central notions of mass-consumed history and fashion lie.

[28] 'Fire Over England, Tie-Ups'. [29] Ibid.

Both are meant to be obtainable by all. Both blur distinctions between and mix 'high' and 'low', luxury and necessity, the cosmopolitan *haute couture* and ready-made synthetic garments, cheaply produced by the textile industry after the First World War and superficially blurring class distinctions. Finally, the very process of production of historical material (Hubert is a 'researcher') overlaps with that of goods.

By the release of MGM's technicolor *Young Bess* in 1953, marking the end of the Tudor film cycle, the monarchy and consumer goods were considerably easier to market across the Atlantic, but especially in Britain. The film, which took several years to make, duplicates the pattern of chain production and consumption exemplified by *Fire Over England.* Both films were free adaptations of popular novels, the older film of Alfred Edward Woodley Mason's novel of the same title, and the new biopic of Margaret Irwin's best-selling 1944 novel, launching her trilogy about Elizabeth I's adolescence and early womanhood prior to her coronation. The film's release in the Coronation year was opportune. The coronation of the second Elizabeth created an unprecedented national euphoria and international news, inaugurating hopes for a 'New Elizabethan Age' of prosperity and national pride. 1953 seemed to have duplicated 1558 and the coronation of a Protestant people's monarch after a period of strife. Britain of 1952 and 1953 was slowly released by the newly elected Conservative government from wartime austerity and the restraints on consumption and seemed to contemporaries to have embarked on the road to material prosperity and a degree of affluence, distributed as never before across classes. Decontrolling of consumption, prosperity, and conciliation, heralded in the 1951 Festival of Britain, now appeared to have materialized. The exceptionally long delay between the death of George VI and the Coronation (apparently duplicating the delay between Mary Tudor's death and the anointment of Elizabeth I) provided a sixteen months' run-up to June 1953, allowing a wave of spending that could easily be connected to, justified, and represented as loyalty to country and the monarchy. As the Annual Register put it, Britain was practising 'a religion of royalism'.[30] And, we might add, of post-war consumption. Finally, 1953 exemplifies the role of the mass media in the making of the monarchy: the advent of affluence and nationality coincided with the appearance of another wholly new apparatus of popular entertainment and spectatorship: television. The Coronation was broadcast on TV across the world and in Britain 'a nation mortgaged itself' to purchase or hire the new appliance, which made possible a new experience of history and the monarchy in the private space of the home. An estimate of twenty-six million in the UK alone watched the ceremony on 2 June for at least half a day. It is probably more than just a coincidence that the heyday of historical films of the monarchy came to a close exactly when television became a mass commodity.

[30] Quoted in Ben Pimlott, *The Queen: A Biography of Elizabeth II* (New York, 1997), 178.

The sense of continuity and security which the popular press and officialdom drummed up was seized upon by the film industry in Hollywood and in Britain and the advertising business. The release of Coronation films featuring Elizabeth I was referred to as 'Pomp, Splendour, Drama, Spectacle, Intrigue! Everything that made the bold and gold era so magnificent for the first Queen Elizabeth . . . is here!'[31]

What transported 'there'—the sixteenth century—'here' was the apparent confusion between the film star, the historical figure of the first Elizabeth, and the 'real life' monarch/celebrity Elizabeth Windsor. Before her coronation she was represented as, first and foremost, a mother and wife, a 'womanly woman' to Prince Philip's 'manly man'. And she still retained her wartime image as the people's princess, doing her duty to the nation. At the same time Elizabeth was consistently portrayed in the media as a glamorous star, possessing the star's magical aura. The combination of stardom and royalty characterizes her entire performance in public before and during the Coronation and is captured by commentators who likened the ceremony itself to a costume drama (and thus to a historical film). As Cecil Beaton, the photographer of royalty and film stars, noted, proceeding to elaborate on her dress: 'The Queen wore gold and stolid white. The long red velvet train, miniver-edged, splendid against the gold and scarlet setting, her stance, with rigid little head and well-curled hair around Queen Victoria's Crown, was marvelously set' and her eyes 'are not those of a busy harassed person . . . a slight suggestion of a smile lightens the otherwise cumbrous mouth.'[32] Beaton's impression of the Coronation as a fashion parade cum historical spectacle, and of the queen as a star/monarch, is echoed in numerous other reports. As Ben Pimlott has noted, there had not been similar comment on her male predecessors. The fact that *Young Bess* featured the young Elizabeth I rather than the mature or aged monarch of *Fire* and the other film versions made possible the sexualization of this monarch. A virgin, the Tudor princess could be marketed as an adolescent with a budding sexuality tolerated and whitewashed despite the relationship between her and the much older and married Thomas Seymour, which constitutes one of the film's main plots. The film was sold as romance, rather than a story of implied adultery, precisely because of the analogue to the young married Elizabeth II. Moreover, MGM and advertisers conflated the two queens and the film star by hyping the two leads, Jean Simmons as the young Elizabeth Tudor and Stewart Granger as Thomas Seymour, who were married to each other in real life. The ambitious and adulterous Seymour could be presented as the princess's 'husband'. And the sexual attraction between them was cemented by fervent belief in the navy and in England's future as a maritime empire.

These conflations of film and history, the past and present queens and the film's star, Tudor ritual and queenship, and the decorative pomp of the

[31] Poster. '"Young Bess", Tie Ups', Press Book, BFI.

[32] Pimlott, *The Queen*, 190.

Coronation year 1953 explain the emphasis on luxury in the campaign of *Young Bess*. Unlike the advertising campaigns of the thirties, it did not link the viewing of the historical film to the consumption of necessities but to an apparently more conspicuous kind of consumption, suitable to the more affluent fifties. Now typical tie-ups offered buyers display kits with replicas of jewels, regalia, and court robes, a direct reference to the Coronation. One such tie-up advertises 'Outstanding Accessories for an Outstanding Film! Crown Jewels Available! Including Crowns of Both Elizabeths!' The price list includes:

> The Crown of England-St. Edward (set with diamonds, rubies, sapphires and pearls) (This is the Crown used in the actual Crowning of Elizabeth II) 2 20
> Imperial State Crown (set with 2,783 diamonds and many other jewels including the Black Prince's Ruby) 2 20[33]

Worn by Elizabeth II during the drive following the Coronation. The Royal Sceptre, Sword of State, Orb of England, Queen's Orb, and Order of Garter Star (most of them becoming regalia after the Tudors) were to be had for 1*s*. 10*d*. each, as were Elizabeth the Queen Mother's Crown (containing the Koh-i-noor) and Elizabethan costumes for both women and men, 'available for theatre and street ballyhoo'.[34] Replica regalia signalled that the very symbols of the magic of the monarchy were duplicable, could be endlessly reproduced, and were available to all, hence that the monarchy itself was 'democratic' and egalitarian. The regalia became rather popular and could be purchased locally or hired for neighbourhood celebrations of the Coronation, even before the release of the film. Such cheap reproductions of royal insignia had little chance of appealing to mature audiences—female or male. But they could be utilized in selling the film to one specific large sector of film-goers which the Tudor film had targeted from its very beginning and which became the subject of a long and heated public controversy over historical films: children and adolescents.

A TUDOR SCHOOL PACKAGE: HISTORICAL EDUCATION AND CONSUMPTION

Viewing the historical film was an age-related experience. Throughout the first half of the twentieth century adolescents and children, very often visiting the cinema on their own, formed the most distinctive group of film consumers besides the young female enthusiasts. The two groups made up the hard core of film consumers. The availability of an expanding body of films with history for their material and subject to a mass of working-class children and youth with a limited access to the past (and whose right to such an access, as Chapter 4 has

[33] 'Showmanship: Ideas, Tie-Ups [*Young Bess*], Tips for Ticket-Selling', BFI. [34] Ibid.

shown, was still debated) generated a controversy about history teaching, education, and national identity. Indeed the controversy, which had begun in the late twenties, became particularly vehement after the launching of the Tudor cycle with *The Private Life of Henry VIII* in 1933 and did not abate until 1953. What the controversy touched upon was a set of much broader issues: what was history? Who owned it and who set its rules and standards? Was it quintessentially literal or could its visual experience and learning be pedagogically beneficial? Finally, who were entitled to produce it: members of a professional guild, film-makers, or participant audiences making do with images of the past? Professional historians, educators, and film-makers sounded their views on these matters on different platforms, from the official publications of the Historical Association (HA) to the down-market fan magazines. The democratization of access to history offered by film alarmed historians—a term used here inclusively and designating both academics focused on research and university teaching and history schoolteachers, who made up the overwhelming majority of the HA. The association was sometimes acting as a self-appointed body of custodians for a field which had still not completed the process of academization and professionalization, continuously seeking to mobilize film-makers and government in defence of notions of accuracy and historical veracity. As Sue Harper has demonstrated, the association succeeded in putting some strictures on teaching films and features.[35] To many such historians the new kind of film was a debased form of history, distorting the past, and particularly pernicious because it was so widely available to the defenceless consumer/spectator: the working-class child and adolescent in the classroom and outside it.

It is no mere coincidence that the furore over historical films took place in exactly the same decades as the protracted debate on children's admission to national monuments such as the Tower of London (see Ch. 4). In both instances, the schoolchild was constructed as an embodiment of the characteristics of the mass audience of historical spectacle: an exceptional ability to comprehend history visually (and its obverse, the incapacity for literary comprehension), ignorance about the past, and a failure to discriminate between 'real history' (facts) and fantasy. As G. Hankin, chair of the Historical Association's Film Committee, bluntly put it: 'They have a limited background and vocabulary... they are accustomed to a very simple type of spoken word.'[36] Charles Petrie, serving between 1933 and 1939 as chairman of the History and Arts Committee of the British Film Institute (BFI), was even franker when in the mid-thirties he recommended the use in the classroom of silent films only—extant and newly reproduced ones!—so as to enhance the history teachers' own voice and his or her authority.[37] His idea of forgoing voice and returning to the

[35] See a useful summary of 'Highbrow Interventions: The Historical Association and its Friends', in Harper, *Picturing the Past*, 64–77.

[36] Ibid. 66.

[37] Ibid. 68.

visual image implies the long-standing set of beliefs about the predominantly ocular faculties of poorer children. But it was precisely this compound of strong visual perception and what the historians regarded as a limited literacy which made cinema audiences, especially juvenile ones, ideal receptors of information and images transmitted through the cinema and the film—a valued (albeit often grudgingly) pedagogic instrument. And it was for the historian to monitor, vet, and regulate the production and viewing of both feature films and documentaries set in the past.

The HA was the first nationwide organization to have sought control over commercial films, establishing a Film Enquiry Committee as early as 1927 and appointing Frances Consitt two years later to investigate the uses of historical feature films in schools. Consitt's *Value of Films in History Teaching*, financed by the Carnegie Foundation and distributed in 10,000 copies in 1932, characteristically attributes the effectiveness of the historical feature to working-class children's visual competence. What distinguishes her association between sense-perception and class from that of her contemporaries is the belief that the working-class child was a creative spectator, actively sharing in the process of imagining the past. Moreover, rather inclusively Consitt defined history as a storage of popular images and notions, accumulated unconsciously and activated and released by a shock, or shocks of recognition triggered by the visual pleasure the film generated. And unlike the majority of her contemporaries at the association, she approved of films such as *Henry VIII*. These views were too radical for the HA and were dropped from the toned-down published report. The association did not censor Consitt's acknowledgement of the pedagogic value of the historical film or her advocacy of visual learning. What they could not stomach was the view that the study of history was in effect an act of the active popular imagination and that even the less initiated could take part in it. This, of course, impinged on the role and status of the trained professionals and such democratization was resented as dangerous to historians and spectators alike. The HA annual meeting of 1935, devoted almost entirely to the 'falseness' of historical films, passed the resolution that: 'This meeting of the Historical Association is gravely concerned at the effect on children and adults purporting to represent historical personages which are being shown in picture palaces, and considers that steps should be taken to assist teachers and others to estimate the accuracy of such films.'[38] The purported 'historical personages' undoubtedly were Henry VIII and his wives in Korda's smash hit, which historians roundly condemned as inaccurate, false, and lacking reverence for the monarchy.

But the HA did more than just consider steps to assist teachers in dealing with the allure of the commercial film. It sought to influence the work of semi-professional organizations mediating between the film industry and government.

[38] See a useful summary of 'Highbrow Interventions: The Historical Association and its Friends', in Harper, *Picturing the Past*, 66.

Hankin, in addition to chairing the ambitious Film Committee, was Her Majesty's Inspector in History at the Board of Education and Chairman of the BBC History Programmes Subcommittee for Schools. And he and a number of other historians sat on the British Film Institute Education Committee, serving to liaise between the BFI and the Board of Education, and later initiating and actually ruling the institution's History and Art Committee with a few other historians. The BFI platform, *Sight and Sound*, was continuously used as sounding board for their views on films and audiences and a Tory notion about history, politics, and class. In an early piece, entitled 'Can History Be Taught by Film' and published two years before the HA's resolution, only classroom historical documents are deemed compatible with the procedures of study and methodologies practised in the humanities. The full-fledged commercial feature 'has no business to educate' and is damaging to the easily impressed and excitable.[39]

Film biographies, the material of the Tudor cycle and practically the only kind of historical features made at the time, are regarded as particularly pernicious. This damning view is repeatedly reiterated by Petrie in his advocacy of academic control of film production, aired in a 1935 pamphlet entitled *The Historical Film*, originally published in *The Nineteenth Century and After*, and two years later in *History Teaching Films*, the HA's guidelines to the BFI. Conceding (in a rather self-congratulatory tone) that standards of accuracy have improved thanks to the role of mediating bodies liaising between experts (historians) and film-makers, Petrie still regards the commercial feature as second-rate history: 'The entertainment film is to the teaching film what the historical novel is to the text-book, and just as no one would confuse the function of the latter, so those of the former must be kept distinct.'[40] It was not only the sins against accuracy that put off activist historians but the film's handling of time, sequence, linearity, and causality. These subverted Petrie's Whig notion of history as a 'progress', a linear and ameliorative process. Cinematography opted for episodes, impressions, and 'events', rather than grand-line processes. These notions are quite in tune with those of the rank and file of the HA, in which only a minority of social and economic historians abandoned linearity for structure. Significantly, critics of the historical feature film considered it more suited to subjects in social and economic history, less subject to the rules of sequence than the still dominant political and constitutional history and, of course, not as respectable as these latter fields. 'Let [a film] begin with a hand significantly making an entry in what is now called the Doomsday Book', opines *Sight and Sound* in 1933, not with an episode concerning a great historical personage.[41]

One should not overstate the case for the actual influence of historians' organizations. Some professional historians unwittingly let their respectability as

[39] *Sight and Sound*, 2, no. 7 (1933), 91–2.

[40] Charles Petrie, 'The Historical Film', pamphlet reprinted from *The Nineteenth Century and After*, 117 (May 1935), 4.

[41] *Sight and Sound*, 2, no. 7, p. 92.

experts be used—and abused—by the British Board of Film Censors (BBFC), the Ministry of Information, and occasionally the Foreign Office to enforce censorship and control over the substance and tone of films. The BBFC in particular used the association's seal to interfere with the scripts of most of the Tudor films. And the real scope of their actual influence on government film policies is quite doubtful. Even more doubtful is the experts' leverage in the industry itself, where views about such issues as accuracy and sequence were sometimes far more sophisticated and complex than those advocated by the experts themselves, and audience's responses were held in greater respect. Indeed historians and teachers of history counted more as consumers and as the activators of juvenile consumption than as experts. For the transatlantic film industry was quick to discover not only the huge potential of child and adolescent consumption, but also that of the education system as an efficient agent in the new market for history. In this sense the Tudor films were treated as a gold mine. *Henry VIII* was ostracized by experts for its frivolity and lack of reverence for the monarchy, as much as for inaccuracies. But the rest of the Tudor sequence enjoyed a good reputation among teachers and historians. *Fire Over England* in particular was deemed worthy and patriotic. It is on the list of school outings of East End schools, together with exhibitions and metropolitan landmarks. Denis Hogarth, a former student, remembered an outing to a local cinema to see it 'all about the attempted invasion by the Spanish Armada. This was preceded by a patriotic address from the headmaster.'[42]

It was precisely this kind of collective and organized viewing that advertisers and distributors were after. A typical address to buyers and exhibitors states:

> The stirring story of the 16th century bears a 'u' censor certificate and provides a valuable opportunity for tying-up schools, etc. Go to the masters and registrars as well as the Heads of literature and English history and arrange with them to have the picture . . . arrange a special rate for school parties and as the majority of scholars come to the theatre in the late afternoon you will get the fullest advantage . . . at the slackest period of the day.[43]

Exhibitors were armed with viewing and teaching kits and aids, including colouring books, glossy postcards, and Armada mazes. By 1953 learning and play kits had become richer in contents, and the advertisers' text brimming with references to the monarchy and the Coronation. A pro-forma letter to history teachers, headmasters, and local school authorities is worth quoting:

> Dear Sir (or Madame)
> With the coronation of HER Majesty Queen Elizabeth II so fresh in the memory of us all, it is with great pride and pleasure that we bring to your notice a film of the first Queen Elizabeth. ON [to be filled in] we are presenting M-G-M's Technicolor screen version of Margaret Irwin's novel Young Bess. With its historical and literary connections and with

[42] Correspondence with the author. [43] 'Young Bess', 'Schools', BFI.

the reconstruction of the glowing tapestry of Tudor England, we feel that you and your pupils will find this production of great interest.

We should be delighted to arrange special matinees for your pupils should such a scheme meet your approval, and we would like to draw your attention to the special articles and illustrations designed to promote class-room interest.[44]

Features on all the Tudor kings and queens and on the English Reformation were appended to quizzes on sixteenth-century history and it is clear that advertisers made use of primers and other school texts. 'Name in order, the wives of Henry VIII ... What had the second and third wives of Henry in common? The first and fourth?' are typical questions.[45] Building on the huge success of its school campaign for *Ivanhoe*, MGM also targeted youth organizations, including Boy Scouts, the Boys' Brigade, and Sea Cadets—the latter no doubt tied up to the 'sea interest' in the film.[46] The rather glaring absence of girls' organizations in the lists of tie-ups of a film about queenship and female adolescence (and at the time of the accession of a queen) may not be taken to indicate gender bias. Elizabeth I and II were not marketed as 'women's queens' but as national symbols of a reconciled, sturdy, and military empire. And it may be recalled that no Tudor film was packaged and seen as a generically feminine artefact. It is quite possible that the rather open-ended image of the young queen was thought to have appealed to both genders.

BUYING TUDOR: AUDIENCE RESPONSES AND USES

The construction of viewers may not be taken as a 'reflection' of 'real' consumers of the historical film package. Buyers of the ticket to the past played a variety of roles that were quite different from those in which the experts on history and film-marketing had cast them. As *Film Weekly*, commenting on the furore over the aesthetic and historical value of *Henry VIII*, put it on 30 June 1933, 'The public is much more discriminating than highbrow critics would have us believe'.[47] Of course, the magazine itself formed a part of the industry's apparatus of publicity and marketing and had special stakes in conveying a flattering image of the cinema-going public. However, the information culled from autobiographical evidence as well as classroom surveys with regard to spectatorship and, more important, individuals' processing and appropriation of the historical materials offered to them, substantiates the claim for discrimination and what may be regarded as an active consumption of the historical culture. One primary source for recouping the variety of uses made of film is the collection of about two hundred 'motion picture autobiographies' obtained

[44] 'Young Bess', 'The Historical and Literary Background', ibid.
[45] 'Young Bess', 'Questionnaire', ibid. [46] 'Schools', ibid.
[47] Cited in Harper, *Picturing the Past*, 57.

through a series of competitions in *Picturegoer* and serving as a basis for J. P. Mayer's studies in the sociology of film audiences. Based on comparable studies in Germany, most notably Charlotte Buehler and Herbert Blumer's, Mayer sought to bolster surveys of the aggregate and 'mass' with insights into the habits and social ways of individuals. Though at least in two of the competitions participants were asked to answer standard specific questions, in what eventually formed the nucleus of the study they were generally guided to write anonymous film autobiographies, covering a variety of subjects, from personal histories of film-going, through personal preferences of films, genres, and stars, to sensations, 'temptations and ambitions' generated by viewing.[48]

Although published in 1947 and written during the war, the autobiographies recover what may be described as film-goers' life stories, thus covering the 1930s and, in a few cases, the 1920s and 1910s. In one life story, the respondent, a 47-year-old housewife and fiction writer, the daughter of a solicitor, testifies to have seen the 'developments of films from the beginning', the beginning significantly being *Queen Elizabeth* with Bernhardt.[49] Her age and class, however, make this particular respondent rather untypical, as typically, and most relevant for this chapter, the majority of respondents were working class or of working-class origins and included women and men between their late teens and mid-twenties at the time of writing. Virtually all testify that film-going was a lifelong habit regularly practised throughout their years at school and, in the overwhelming majority of cases, acquired from infancy. The mobility of working-class children and their knowledge about films may be striking to us today, as even very young ones visited the cinema accompanied by mates their age or on their own ('picking up' an adult, usually a woman, with other children to accompany them inside the hall, where they would not be let in on their own). No less striking is the absence of effective differentiation between children's, juvenile, and 'general' movies, notwithstanding the existence of the classification into 'u' and 'a' films. Thus historical films, even films like *Henry VIII* and *The Private Lives of Elizabeth and Essex*, which critics bracketed as salacious, were accessible to—and in fact seen—by the very young.

Actually viewers' overall definition of the role and function of the historical film was quite similar to those of the gatekeepers of culture. It was a useful aid, a pedagogic medium that, wisely used, would bring history to those less acquainted with it. As a 25-year-old engineering draughtsman perceptively put it: 'Not only documentary films, or other academic features, but films with an educational slant could be shewn in schools. What more delightful way of learning could there be than seeing?' Historical biographies in particular provided a way of learning about the past. Their particular value, thought a

[48] J. P. Mayer, *British Cinemas and their Audiences: Sociological Studies* (London, 1948), 13–14. See also his *Sociology of Film: Studies and Documents* (2nd edn., London, 1948).

[49] Mayer, *British Cinemas and their Audiences*, 120.

16-year-old clerk, was precisely in 'blending entertainment with education to a certain extent . . . a good method of acquainting the public with great men and good literature'.[50] Remarks on accuracy in historical detail and faithfulness to the period represented would have dumbfounded some of the fanatics of the HA. A lavish production of costumes and props alone could not satisfy veteran viewers like the 19-year-old clerk, the daughter of an electrical engineer and a housewife, who wrote:

I still like historical films but now for their history, not their costumes, although my interest in history had often made me wonder why film-makers must always introduce inaccuracies—nearly in every case, unnecessarily. Why make Queen Elizabeth a sloppy emotional woman when the quality for which she was noted was that her supreme love was England and she was a Queen more than a woman. But in *Elizabeth and Essex* she was pictured as deeply in love with Essex—the one love of her life—and finally she made the supreme sacrifice for England with great emotion—nonsense! Elizabeth loved only herself, she may have liked lovers to satisfy her vanity but she would have sacrificed everything she loved without a second's thought for the throne and power.[51]

Elsewhere, too, viewers express irritation about the blowing up of the Essex episode to a full-blooded romance. As a 23-and-a-half-year-old housewife, the daughter of a railway worker and 'of fairly well-to do farmer', argues:

My husband and myself like historical romances, if not too far fetched. That is, we enjoyed *Elizabeth and Essex* and *Henry VIII* . . . We really enjoyed *Robin Hood* because we had not expected it to be believable. I think that is the main difference—we hate films that are supposed to be authentic and are not intelligently presented and hate films that are frankly incredible, but good entertainment.[52]

The easy confidence of these respondents as regards historical detail and believable plot no doubt comes from a degree of previous acquaintance with Tudors and especially Elizabethan episodes and characters, which, by the thirties, had already been firmly grafted on the popular memory. In the prologue to his sequel on *The England of Elizabeth*, appropriately titled 'A Living Age', Rowse compiled a list of its evidences in 'our living experience . . . conscious tradition' as well as the unconscious memory, the heart, and the blood. One could, of course, argue that this organicist view of the diffusion of history cannot be taken as indicative of popular approaches to and uses of the Elizabethans and that his notions of history as part of a great unconscious are, and were at their time, highly debatable. However, his claim that the Elizabethans became highly familiar across class and region and that 'She [Elizabeth] is by far the best remembered figure of any that sat on the English throne [and] thousands of simple people who can hardly remember any other monarch have heard of her' is more to the point (if slightly condescending).[53] The dense grid of this available

[50] Ibid. 223, 161. [51] Ibid. 69. [52] Ibid. 205.
[53] Rowse, *The England of Elizabeth*, 13.

Tudor lore was contained in the myriad forms of literature and iconography for all tastes, in architecture and the landscape, in literature and in music. Of course, Elizabethan drama and portraits of the Tudor kings, such as Holbein's paintings of Henry VIII, exhibited at the National Gallery and used for reference in the films themselves, may not have been easily accessible to working-class adults and adolescents. But reproductions of historical biography, fiction on the Tudors, and painterly representations of period dress and furniture—consistently and widely reproduced in mass distribution fan-magazines such as *Picturegoer*—were. Conventionally the 'release' (the term seems apt here) of such histories was orchestrated by the film industry itself and coordinated with the publicity machine. Thus the debut of *Fire Over England* was preceded and accompanied by a stream of publications on the reign of Elizabeth I, and that of *Elizabeth and Essex* generated a spate of fiction on the romance of the Queen and the Earl. But their frankly commercial character notwithstanding, these reproduced histories did make rudimentary information about the past easily available.

The Tudors were also conspicuous in the everyday material world of adults, children, and adolescents, in objects and buildings which yielded information that could be and was variably processed and utilized. Apart from monumental landmarks in and around Greater London, such as the Tower and Hampton Court (a working-class resort since the 1840s), and the spreading imitation 'Tudor' or 'Merrie England' building in suburbs and estates, there were small, cheap, and mobile objects that offered bits and pieces of information on the sixteenth century. These industrially mass-produced objects served to distribute and multiply historical images. One example of the creative uses made of such carriers of information by children is to be found in an appendix to Consitt's report on history in the schoolroom. Consitt helped a group of 14-year-old girl fourth-formers write a scenario for a 'good film' on the Armada. The subject itself figured prominently in curricula and the girls had no difficulty drawing on reading lists provided by their history mistress and popular novels. For details on Elizabethan dress they drew on matchboxes and cigarette cards featuring the queen's portrait.[54] Their usage of this variety of materials, easily collected from both literary and material histories readily available to them, and used to create their own linear narrative of the story of the threat of invasion and the victory over the Armada, may be usefully likened to a 'bricolage', that ensemble of processed materials found in a culture and reused in a new context and form to make a meaning, or tell a story. The girls transported stories and materials such as images on matchboxes used in the everyday into the medium of a documentary 'study film'. Consitt was quite surprised at their practical knowledge about the Elizabethans, as well as at their mastering of the technical vocabulary and know-how of film photography (scenes, cuts, short, medium, and long

[54] 'Scenario of a Film on the Spanish Armada', in Consitt, *The Value of Films in History Teaching*, App. C, p. 401.

shots, etc.). They created a narrative of imperial greatness and national success by applying their imagination to the materials amassed and to the technology of film. As they themselves testified: 'here we let our imagination run riot'.[55]

For working-class children, especially boys, cigarette cards were a source of information, available from the 1890s. Originally serving to stiffen the paper cigarette packet and especially as 'strengtheners' for the weak blends packets (five for one penny), the cards soon appeared as series, featuring a wide range of topics. W. D. & H. O. 'Kings and Queens of England', featuring the Tudor monarchs, were one of the most famous and popular series. Ships and maritime history, empire and military uniform also made standard topics. Cheap collectibles, sometimes the working-class child's only valuable collectibles, these were used by these children as games, objects of exchange—sometimes, as Gilda O'Neill has noted, as actual currency (in London's East End), and as sources of information about history.[56] Indeed like the matchboxes, the cards were hands-on history. Their usage by children is memorably recovered by Robert Roberts in his *The Classic Slum*, where he describes how working-class boys in the poorest areas of Salford carried the cards about them, collected them using a variety of forms of exchange, from swapping to gambling (through games) to enrich their collections and knowledge. As he puts it: ' "Programmed" learning and visual aid, too, came to the child in the shape of cigarette card series. The value of the "fag" card ... as a conveyor of up-to-date information was enormous ... it developed into offering a panorama of the world at large.'[57] His usage of 'visual aid' and 'panorama' is revealing, evoking as it does both the repertoire of representations and techniques of looking which had become so familiar to urban audiences during the nineteenth century (see Ch. 2) and the widespread association between visual learning and social class.

Common usages of everyday objects and materials for the processing of history and as preparatory material for film-viewing were inflected by gender as well as by class. Gender further shaped the appropriation of history in the imaginary and in fantasy. The evidence on middle-class girls' imaginative dramatization of the reign of Elizabeth, documented by Consitt, is one example of uses in the imaginary of objects and materials, interpreted with the aid and through the medium of film. Alison Light has described the complex responses of two generations of working-class women in Portsmouth to the *Young Bess* trilogy in novel and film form. The trilogy, appearing during and immediately after the war, offered visions of a powerful female monarch unbounded by domesticity and seeming to subvert some current ideologies. These fantasies of liberation, affordable through the consumption of books and films, served to weld a monarchism of sorts to an adherence to Labour, democracy, and modernity. Moreover, the pleasures which popular Elizabethanism offered to this generation

55 Ibid.

56 O'Neill, *My East End*, 110. She draws on oral testimonies.

57 Robert Roberts, *The Classic Slum: Salford Life in the First Quarter of the Century* (Manchester, 1971), 134–5.

of women were passed on by them to a post-war child, growing up in the sixties, and served to bridge a generational gap caused by difference in education.[58]

The gender inflection is further corroborated by Mass Observation work based on essays collected in 1937 in two fee-paying Boys' Schools in Westhoughton near Bolton and an unidentified town near Middlesborough. The boys were familiar with the Tudors and made repeated analogues between Britain's foreign policy during the sixteenth century and that of the present. In this sense their enthusiasm about the first empire was no different from the passion Consitt's girl fourth-formers showed for the Armada. But the boys' preference was clearly for masculine imperial heroes. Of the 512 boys invited to write on 'The Finest Person that Ever Lived', two only considered Queen Bess to have qualified for the superlative, compared with the twenty-three who reckoned Francis Drake to be worthy of it. Drake, in fact, was the second runner-up in the category of military men, beaten only by Lord Nelson, and overall an impressive fourth runner. But then only fourteen essays deemed women 'the greatest person' and five of them were on 'my mother'.[59] Elizabeth I was valued for reasons very similar to those given by the contemporary film viewers whom Mayer studied. As one 15-year-old notes: 'She ruled as well as any man ever has done . . . she has [*sic*] no thought for the feelings of any person, and I think that sometimes she could be described as unscrupulous.'[60] Or, as he bluntly put it, she would do all the things that 'a King would normally'. To be sure, children in fee-paying schools do not represent the working-class juvenile film-goer, or the working-class child. Indeed we may safely assume that the former got a richer and fuller 'history kit'. Yet it is evident that his or her counterpart did not come to the film unequipped. The curricula, the schoolroom evidence, the glamourizing of the Tudors in the film-fans magazines, and the accessible and conspicuous traces of the sixteenth century in different areas of material culture all add up to an available storage which supplied and pre-programmed film-viewers who 'bought' the Tudor package marketed by the British and American film industries.

Of course 'buying' slices of the past via films was not free of constrictions, to do with the structural changes in the mass media, which were completed by the early 1930s. Not least among these changes are the convergence of film and the daily press in what may be described as 'analogous coverage' of historical themes and personages, notably monarchs, and contemporary ones—the Royal Family. Another change is the early globalization of the production and its concentration. Films were produced in Britain or Hollywood. In both cases, distribution, advertising, and the construction of history's consumers, notably of the two groups among them traditionally considered to be susceptible to manipulation

[58] Alison Light, '"Young Bess": Historical Novels and Growing Up', *Feminist Review*, 33 (Autumn 1989), 57–71.

[59] On the essays see MO extracts, MO, 'Children's Essays, 1937: "The Finest Person that Ever Lived', prepared by Paul A. Thomas.

[60] MO, Children and Education, 4, F.

by the media—women and schoolchildren—were centrally directed. However, concentration of the new industry and its 'universality' were interfered with and actually operated through local factors of demand. Moreover, structural change certainly did not preclude active and discriminate consumption and inventive usages of the past by individuals. The historical film, notwithstanding its 'exoticism' and the remoteness of the world it showed, was not taken in by spectators solely as a form of escape. The power of histories on the screen lay in that they were seen as continuous with, rather than completely separate from, the familiar social world which abounded with 'first hand' 'evidences' and 'memorials' (Rowse's terms) of the Tudors and mainly the Elizabethans and recycled and reproduced remnants of the past which preprogrammed viewers. The role of mass-produced objects as transmitters of preparatory information too is vital (Consitt's example comes to mind here). Viewers could 'set back' celluloid historical personages in the contemporary and modern material world. And it is this contiguity, as much as the strangeness, that made it possible for viewers/consumers to sift away what they deemed 'unbelievable' and fantastic (or unattractive) from the conceivable and compatible with their own imaginary and social life. This ability is manifest in the young clerk's reference to the way in which as a younger child she had used to dress up in bits and pieces that imitated the period of a favourite costume drama, as 'make believe' and 'unreal'.[61] Like other viewers she defended a separation between fantasy and the 'real world', with the latter accommodating a past that was different but seemed 'real'. In similar manner the early monarchs and empire represented in the films were connected to the contemporary monarchy, which the popular media made more transparent than ever before.

[61] Mayer, *British Cinemas*, 69, for her view on the wholesale application of cinema histories to real life.

7

The Queen's Two Bodies and the King's Body: History, Monarchy, and Stardom, 1933–1953

THE NEW VIEW OF THE PAST: AN OUTLINE

In early May 1936, a special premiere of *Tudor Rose* took place in the Tower of London. The film was embraced by officialdom and the gatekeepers of history as serious and duly respectful of the monarchy, and was well liked by audiences. The venue of the premiere was more than appropriate for a film on the ten-day rule and execution of Lady Jane Grey. Austerely produced and directed by Michel Balcon and George Stevenson, it represented history as a repressive place ridden with violence and a monarchy devoid of splendour and power.[1] Starred in by the child-actor Nova Pilbeam as the 16-year-old victim/queen, the film harked back to the early Victorian Tower lore manufactured by the novelists and antiquaries, amply discussed in Chapters 4 and 5 (see Fig. 14).

Tudor Rose is an exception rather than the rule of the new historical film. But it may usefully serve us to highlight the points of this form's departures from the older repertoire on the historical monarchy and the new centring of the monarchy within film and in the democratized inter-war culture. The film makes use of the dungeon and prison as organizing metaphors of history; it pessimistically represents history as a place of insecurity and disorder and as the site of oppression. And it projects a gloomy view of high politics and intrigues. Like the Tower novels, stories, and visualizations of the early and mid-nineteenth century, it uses gender as a pointer to social and cultural hierarchies and to difference between the past and the present. The Tudor-film cycle as a corpus of recycled and recyclable images of history separates from this view of the past. It casts the monarchy as the central agent and mover of English might, creates an attractive past with degrees of glamour, and completely breaks away from conservative notions of gender, using the male and female monarch, especially the latter, innovatively to reinterpret the relationships between political power, public action, and domesticity. Finally, the cycle as a whole demonstrates the

[1] *Daily Telegraph*, 8 May 1936. See also Harper, *Picturing the Past*, 35–6.

Fig. 14. The execution of Lady Jane Grey, in *Tudor Rose* (1936). The dungeon view of the past persevered well into the 1930s

crucial role of a new set of brokers of popular history, most notably the film stars. Stars, especially female stars—both British and Hollywood actresses—became conduits to the past, arbiters between modern images of the monarchy, notions about modernity and gender, and the historical personages they figuratively and literally embodied. And stars also came to embody a new kind of historical authority. Chapter 6 touched on the largely unsuccessful interventions of parts of the historical establishment in the workings of the apparatuses of film production and distribution and in consumers' approaches to and uses of the cinema. Here I look at the interventions of stars in the debate on history and at how these interventions bore on the circulation of images of the past and its uses and interpretations. Stardom made history glamorous and attached it to contemporary notions of celebrity and social leadership, as well as to the processes of the modernization of the monarchy within democracy. At the same time the female and male stars who 'incorporated' majesty and the monarchy were not glamorous in the orthodox sense of this term in studies of film and the media. They were neither objects of scopophilic pleasure and desire (Sigmund Freud's term, famously used by feminist film theorist Laura Mulvey), nor just objects of visual consumption, exploited by a capitalist system of culture production.[2] They had considerable stakes in shaping mass-consumed history, using for their new interpretations a patchwork of materials pilfered from professional historians, novelists, and even highly experimental 'psychohistory' drawing on Freudian psychology.

I begin by following the build-up of stars as mediators between audiences and the past, discussing their uses of historical materials, interpretations of them, and the filmic representations of the early modern monarchs. I then focus on the new interpretations of gender and power formulated in the films, interpretations which I relate to the contemporary debates on both, and to the new role carved out for the modern monarchy.

MAKING ELIZABETH/MAKING HENRY: STARS AS HISTORIANS

It is revealing that contemporaries, including historians, tended to append the terms 'history' and 'historical' to the stars of the Tudor films as well as to the films themselves. Of course, these historians as well as critics searched for and gauged accuracy in plots, portraiture of character, decor, and props. But the capacity to probe into the life and mind of historical heroes and heroines, as well as to interpret them, was sought for in the actor or actress. Their role on screen and sometimes off it easily collapsed into that of the historian. As LeMahieu has noted, the early cinema created a new form of celebrity, considerably more potent than earlier types of fame, not least by conflating the screen and public persona of stars and their apparently 'real life' selves.[3] The historic Elizabeth and Henry VIII were conflated with the personae of the stars in their roles. This constant shifting of roles from historical person to star to historian, and the blurring of the borderlines between the three entities, are conspicuous in views and assessments of Flora Robson in the role of the queen in *Fire Over England.* The film was never the blockbuster that *Henry VIII* succeeded in becoming, and Robson was never ranked as 'star' on popularity lists.[4] But there is no doubt that her appearance in the film immediately became the model and the film itself a reference for all future interpretations of the

[2] Laura Mulvey, 'Visual Pleasure and Narrative Cinema', *Screen*, 16, no. 3 (Autumn 1975), 6–18 and 'Afterthoughts on "Visual Pleasure and Narrative Cinema" Inspired by *Duel in the Sun*', *Framework*, 6, nos. 15–17 (1981), 12–15. See also *Visual and Other Pleasures* (Basingstoke and Bloomington, Ind., 1989).

[3] LeMahieu, *A Culture for Democracy*, 46–7. On the confusion between realness and fiction in popular fiction see Michael Saler, ' "Clap if you Believe in Sherlock Holmes" ': Mass Culture and the Re-Enchantment of Modernity, c.1890–c.1940', *Historical Journal*, 46 (2003), 599–623.

[4] For assessments of the popularity of films see John Sedgwick, *Popular Filmgoing in 1930s Britain: A Choice of Pleasure* (Exeter, 2000) and the useful application of his 'POPSTAT' index.

reign of Elizabeth I. The film's lease of life was extended by the inclusion of Robson in cameo roles of the queen in two other productions, the *Sea Hawk* and the war propaganda film *The Lion Has Wings.*

Professional historians, including some of the leading lights of the HA, were quick to describe her interpretation as good history, at the same time identifying the actress with the queen. A review by F. J. C. Hearnshaw and J. E. Neale, published in the *School Master*, then in *Sight and Sound*, is worth quoting. Neale, A. E. Pollard's successor at University College London, was an authority on Tudor government and on Elizabeth I as well as being the author of a widely read 1933 biography of the queen. Hearnshaw, Emeritus Professor of History, also at UCL, was President of the HA and became deeply involved in the campaign to reform the historical film. Like other historians and activists at the association, both acknowledged the potential of the new genre and the new medium. Like A. L. Rowse (and unlike some of their contemporaries), the two were alive to the need to popularize and democratize history. Neale wrote his *Elizabeth I* 'for a particular occasion and a particular public', the occasion being the fourth centenary of the queen's birth, and addressed 'the public [as] a body of lay men and women interested in the great historical personality'.[5] From exactly this notion of history as a biography he maintained that 'No one will go wrong who takes his idea of the historical Elizabeth from Flora Robson. Her interpretation, even her words, ring true: and indeed sometimes as in the supreme moment at Tilbury, her words are the very words spoken by Elizabeth.' As an interpreter of the past she surpassed Charles Laughton in *Henry VIII* and rendered the entire Elizabethan era a seriousness that was its due. 'Unlike the famous film of Henry VIII, there is no burlesque license taken with the queen. Miss Flora Robson's interpretation of Elizabeth is serious, highly skilled and, at times, intensely moving.'[6] Praise of her skills as interpreter and historian is conspicuous in reviews in the general press and in film magazines. The downmarket *Film Weekly* remarks that Robson 'plays Elizabeth so timely, and with such an understanding of character that she assumes first importance' and notes how this transforms a film intended as a swashbuckling romance into a historical character study and a drama of high politics and the empire.[7] The trade publication *Film Monthly Bulletin* marks out her portrayal of an 'entirely realistic character' and authoritative playing in a 'powerful study in queenship'.[8] As one adulating feature put it: 'probably never before in the history of the screen has the portrayal of a historical character been backed by greater knowledge and study'.[9] American reviewers, rather severe on the technical aspects of the production and sometimes on the abundance of historical detail which so delighted British experts, were quite

[5] J. E. Neale, *Queen Elizabeth I* (London, 1934; repr. Harmondsworth, 1961), Preface.

[6] *Sight and Sound*, 6, no. 22 (Summer 1937).

[7] *Film Weekly*, 27 Feb. 1937, p. 32.

[8] *Monthly Film Bulletin*, 4, no. 39 (1937), 52.

[9] *Film Weekly*, 8 Aug. 1936, p. 10.

unanimous in their praise of Robson. As the *New York Times* noted, she presented the queen as 'she must have been'. Farther away from the East coast and the New York scene, newspapers like the *Richmond New Leader* enthused about how the actress 'handles the queen from the scholarly point of view', and even Hollywood was satisfied that 'we are not only looking at history: we are looking at it being made' and interpreted in terms accessible to 'America's Main Street'.[10] Robson herself and some of the reviewers made much of how she clashed with the film's American director, William K. Howard, over precisely the issue of the accessibility of serious history to popular audiences.[11] As I show later, she succeeded in expanding and redefining Elizabeth's role and place on screen.

Not only experts and the press, but Robson too, like a few other actors in the roles of early modern monarchs, cultivated the image of the star as an expert maker of national history, combining on screen the roles of researcher, authoritative biographer, student of character, and interpreter of the past. Note her articulation of the star as mediator between audience and the historical texts she selects, narrates, and re-presents:

> The film story deals with only one year of Elizabeth's life, that is the year 1587–88. But this was in many ways the most eventfully symbolical year of her reign—the 'cause and effect' period of the Spanish Armada. My characterisation is really a cameo portrait of what Elizabeth stood for, rather than a biographical survey. It will show her in the autumn of her life as a woman, yet in full possession of her powers as monarch. She is the pivot, the mistress of ceremonies, around whom was woven a romance that is historically inaccurate, but well within the bounds of dramatic license. The zeal she showed in retaining her popularity with her subjects was matched by her anxiety for their welfare. That is why her reign marked the real rise of England to prestige and power, and became known as the golden age of our history. With all her foibles Elizabeth taught her people to worship an ideal.[12]

Robson's analysis is noteworthy not only for her resort to a vocabulary that is compatible with that of contemporary professional historians, but also for being publicized by a mass-distribution fan magazine like *Film Weekly*. What she outlines is a succession of procedures which historians pursue and that include selection (picking 'only one year of Elizabeth's life'), a search for causation ('cause and effect'), and representation of the selected fragment of the past for an interpretation of a broader period of time (by 'cameo portrait'). Moreover, she is aware of Elizabeth's own genius mastery of the art of spectacle and image-building. The analysis is far more than just a hyping device but actually sums up Robson's self-preparation for the role and interpretation of it. Like Charles Laughton, Robson drew on her background in the classical theatre, not least in

[10] Cited in Kenneth Barrow, *Flora: An Appreciation of the Life and Work of Dame Flora Robson* (London, 1981), 131, *Hollywood Spectator*, 16 June 1937, p. 7.

[11] Barrow, ibid. 102–3.

[12] *Film Weekly*, 8 Aug. 1936.

the roles of Tudor queens. She had played Elizabeth in Arthur Bryant, *The Golden Hind*, both on stage and in a radio play, and had done Mary Stuart in a play by Wilfrid Grantham. In E. A. W. Mason's original, a cloak-and-dagger melodrama, Elizabeth's role is limited and the story of the Armada subsidiary to that of the adventures of Michael Ingolby, the young seaman and the queen's faithful emissary to Philip II. In the film adaptation by the renowned novelist and playwright Clemence Dane (Winifred Ashton), the queen's role was savagely pruned in the interest of adventure and romance. Though on stage Dane created roles for strong historical women, most notably her version of Elizabeth in the highly experimental *Will Shakespeare* (1921), her rendition of women on screen was rather conventional. Robson, however, succeeded in virtually remaking this role, thus remaking the film into a story about the monarchy's golden age, royal authority, power, and gender. Dane included only a fraction of one public speech by the queen, a toned-down sample of the Tilbury speech, and omitted the reference to Elizabeth's male stomach and spirit in a frail female body, the queen's most celebrated utterance. Robson, on the other hand, interpreted the unabridged speech, which she had discovered in Neale's writings, as a key to the queen's persona, used a 1631 version of it (by Lionel Sharp), and successfully introduced it during rehearsal.[13] Her intervention convinced Howard to augment the part of the queen, thus effectively cutting down on those of the film's intended romantic stars Laurence Olivier as Ingolby and Vivien Leigh as Cynthia, and trimming the love story.

Robson's interventions, her refashioning of Elizabeth (Stephen Greenblatt's term, coined regarding the Elizabethans, seems apt here) throws new light on the role of stars in historical films and indeed on their broader cultural role, and may even challenge a few assumptions about individual agency vis-à-vis structure in the highly capitalized film industry.[14] Conventionally the stars of the classical film period, between the two world wars, have been critically regarded as pawns in a system that moulded them into commodified icons. They have also been seen as the creations of film-makers—producers and the great directors, or auteurs, thus as being mere vessels, the transmitters of these auteurs' ideas. In historic roles the persona of the star is completely cut off from the original. She or he does not represent a historic person, or for that matter any person, but becomes a 'mask', an icon which covers 'an essence' and arouses in audiences 'the deepest ecstasy'. This is how Roland Barthes describes Greta Garbo in the role of the seventeenth-century Swedish Queen Christina in the 1933 film.[15] Film theory and criticism, not least feminist theory, have also come to regard the female film star as the embodiment of these related processes of commodification and the erasure of the actors from artistic production. Moreover, in feminist

[13] Barrow, *Flora*, 103.

[14] See Stephen Greenblatt, *Renaissance Self-Fashioning from More to Shakespeare* (Chicago, 1980).

[15] Roland Barthes, *Mythologies*, trans. Annette Lavers (New York, 1972), 56–8.

tradition the woman star is also seen as an object of collective desire. She is the source of a particular kind of visual pleasure, described by Laura Mulvey as 'scopophilic', that is sexual and fetishistic by nature.[16] This paradigm of female stardom and male spectatorship has been applied to Hollywood stars in historical roles, most notably to Marlene Dietrich as Catherine the Great (in *The Scarlet Empress*, 1934) and Garbo herself as Queen Christina. Tough students of film have been well aware that there was no star system in Britain to create Hollywood-style actors completely subject to the rule of studios and powerful producers; they have continuously marginalized the role of actresses in British productions and, most relevant here, in historical productions.[17] For example, Anna Neagle, in her roles as Queen Victoria (in *Victoria the Great*, 1937) and *Nell Gwyn* (1934), is seen as the creation of Herbert Wilcox. Similarly, Elizabeth Bergner as Catherine the Great is allocated a somewhat subsidiary role in Korda and Paul Czinner's 1943 version.

Robson's active role in defining and interpreting Elizabeth confounds this set of assumptions about female stardom. She not only regarded herself as an authority on the queen but succeeded in carving out a model of roles featuring female monarchs and rulers, known as 'Flora Robson parts'.[18] Typically these roles featured older powerful women who could not easily be cast as objects of desire—though they were not desexualized. In Wilcox's *Catherine the Great* Robson played an authoritarian and lascivious Empress Elizabeth (of Russia) and in *Thirty-Five Days in Peking* an autocratic and corrupt Tzu Hsi. The combination of age, power, and a sexuality that was neither alluring nor fertile, once represented as both accurately 'historical' and as a character study, extracted Robson from prescribed and conventional female roles on screen and lent her liberties as the interpreter and even co-author of the script. Such liberties were not peculiar to British productions. Even Hollywood conglomerates such as Warner Bros., notorious for their autocratic star system, allowed actors in historical roles degrees of autonomy in interpreting character and period. Bette Davis, Robson's successor in the role of the aging Elizabeth in *Elizabeth and Essex* and *The Virgin Queen*, is just the case in point. Davis, who was Warner's chief female star, had had a limited power as a contract actress and this power was further curbed with a court ruling which compelled her to comply with the company. Nevertheless she exercised considerable freedom in the two productions, intervening in their direction and the interpretation of the queen. Significantly, for reference texts she used not only Lytton Strachey's *Elizabeth and Essex* and Maxwell Anderson's stage-play version of it, but also *Fire Over England* and *Henry VIII*, thus

[16] For Mulvey see n. 2. See also Mary Ann Doane, 'The Economy of Desire: The Commodity Form in/of the Cinema', *Quarterly Review of Film and Video*', 11 (1989), 22–33 (1989); Tania Modelski, *Loving with a Vengeance: Mass-Produced Fantasies for Women* (London, 1982).

[17] On the problematic of this marginalization and its implications for the study of actual audiences see Jackie Stacey, *Star-Gazing: Hollywood Cinema and Female Spectatorship* (London, 1994; repr. 1998), 1–49.

[18] Jeffrey Richards, 'Dame Flora's Crowning Glory', *Daily Telegraph*, 1 June 1990, p. 14.

endowing both films with the status of reference texts.[19] And like Robson she was immediately accorded the status of authoritative historian—so much so that the *New York Times* crowned the film 'Queen Bette's picture'.[20]

One notable difference between the making of Robson's persona as star/historian and Davis's is in the usage of class. Robson, like numerous other British film actors and actresses between the world wars, was fashioned by the publicity machine as a working-class woman and Elizabeth I as the people's queen, a monarch whose power derived from consent and approval. This particular fashioning influenced her status as an interpreter of the past and, more broadly, the notion of history which the British-made Tudor films propagated. It was the notion which I have described as 'a history for democracy', with a monarchy based on plebeian consent and trust at its centre and also implying that the past is accessible to and interpretable by all. The conflating of images of actress, 'real person', and queen was the co-production or invention of Robson and the film magazines, a co-production exemplifying the convergence of film and the popular press during the inter-war years. Invention in more than one sense: in the first place, Robson came from a middle-class Scottish background and had trained for the classical theatre; secondly, the working-class image for a star in a historical role was a novelty because this kind of role had been allotted to middle-class actors and actresses with a mastery of standard English in an upper-class accent acquired 'in life' and professional training in and allegiance to the theatre and literature—both distinctly middle-class. Working-class stars appeared in genres like the musical films, melodramas, or comedies derived from working-class forms of entertainment and lore. The allegiance of these stars was not to the theatre and the novel but to the performative traditions of the vaudeville, the review, and the music hall.[21] Gracie Fields and George Formby would be the most salient examples of popular British stardom.

Robson's invented working-class biography responded to the collective biography of many of her prospective viewers. It camouflaged her origins and blurred her period in RADA and in the theatre while at the same time blowing out of proportion her brief experience of unemployment, the latter perfectly in tune with the serious slump of the mid-thirties. 'Just like Lizzie Doaks of Clapham South', Robson 'found herself well and truly broke. Unwilling to borrow, unable to accept any stage engagement... Miss Robson settled down to the business of making her own bed, cooking her own breakfast, sweeping her own stairs. But didn't like it much.'[22] It was precisely the ordinariness of this kind of South London life that could have made them and

[19] On Davis see Alexander Walker, *Bette Davis* (London, 1986), 104–8, 160–2.

[20] *New York Times*, 2 Dec. 1939. See also *Today's Cinema*, 13 Mar. 1940.

[21] Andrew Higson, *Waving the Flag: Constructing a National Cinema in Britain* (Oxford, 1995), esp. 98–130.

[22] *Picturegoer Weekly*, 16 Jan. 1937. The title is revealing: 'The Film Star Nobody Knew'. Pagination not clear.

the star so appealing to readers/viewers. For this life was rather like those of the consumers of fan magazines and of films. Even more attractive was Robson's term as welfare worker in a shredded-wheat factory at Welwyn Garden City, a career incarnating working-class labour and the distinct suburban character of this particular neighbourhood. She too 'roughed it' in the mill. As a leading article in *Picturegoer Weekly* put it, the actress's honest, anonymous life, her thrift and hard work, made her a new model of stardom and celebrity.[23] It was precisely the lack of glamour in her life that made her ideal for the role of Elizabeth. Indeed Robson's unglamorous look and appearance and the fact that, unlike her Hollywood counterparts in monarchs' roles (Garbo, Dietrich, and Davis herself immediately spring to mind), she was never hyped as a sex symbol. And it was this very lack of sexual appeal that helped buttress the image of a forceful woman/queen of and for the people, an image welding together power and ordinariness. The image links some characteristics of the 'modern woman' which evolved after the First World War—notably economic independence, social mobility, and a working-class identity—with the images of the historical female monarch. Significantly, the sexuality of the 'modern woman', so central in contemporary literature and the press, is muted.[24] Intriguingly, the image of the working woman as popular queen lived on until Robson's death in 1987 and beyond it.[25] Her obituary in the *Sunday People* of this year labelled her a 'national character' who had never forgotten her 'working-class roots' and who in appropriate retirement in Brighton appropriately played Bingo in a church hall. A working woman, neither a beauty nor married, she was a democratic 'replica' of the historical Elizabeth whom she so wonderfully interpreted.[26]

HISTORY AS PROPAGANDA? DEFINING ANEW THE 'NATIONAL FILM'

It was Robson's invention and self-fashioning as a star of the people in the role of the people's monarch that made her persona as the queen a symbol of the 'right' kind of democratic patriotism and a maritime empire. *Fire Over England*, first released some time before the Munich crisis, nevertheless is literally swarming with transparent analogies between Elizabethan England and Britain and the other Western democracies of the late thirties, and between Habsburg Spain and modern Fascist and Nazi dictatorships. Indeed *Fire* is possibly the earliest exemplar of the pillaging of Tudor history on film for war-propaganda purposes.

[23] *Picturegoer Weekly*, 16 Jan. 1937.

[24] On the discourse on the 'Modern Woman' see Melman, *Women and the Popular Imagination in the Twenties.*

[25] *Daily Telegraph*, 1 June 1990; *The Guardian*, 9 July 1984.

[26] *Sunday People*, 8 July 1987.

It advocates military preparedness for war and a tough foreign policy (actually the very opposite of Elizabeth's tactics in regard to Spain). It may well be that this line, which certainly collided with official appeasement policy and popular anti-militarism, detracted from the film's appeal when it made its debut. After the outbreak of the Second World War, its outright nationalism and association between democracy and military power made it and Robson morale boosters. At the very beginning of the film viewers are treated to a text arranged on five cards (rather like schoolroom placards) explaining issues of national security at the time of the Spanish invasion and, implicitly, in 1937: 'In 1587 Spain powerful in the Old World is Master of the New'; 'Its King Philip Rules by Force and Fear'; 'But Spanish Tyranny is challenged by the Free People of Little Island England'; 'Everywhere English Traders Appear, English Seamen Threaten Spanish Supremacy'; 'A Woman Guides and Inspires them, Elizabeth the Queen'. Two or three years later, these allusions to the present were priceless. The entire scene of the Tilbury speech was incorporated in the *Lion Has Wings*, Korda's sophisticated docudrama on the RAF, the first British propaganda film parading as a feature, and possibly the first film done after the outbreak of the war. That Korda and Robson were entrusted with popular morale says a great deal about their status. The entire script of *The Lion* abounds with comparisons between Elizabethan and wartime England. Elizabeth's sea dogs are likened to RAF aces, 'captains of the clouds'. The fire ships are like Spitfires, 'the battle-ships of the sky'. RAF's enacting of the attack on the Keel Canal is presented as a version of a naval 'epic of the sky'. This conflation, through montage, of modern technological warfare in a highly industrialized society and war in a pre-modern community rendered history as sequence and stressed causation. It was by dint of its historic role as a democratic and imperial power that Britain became destined to fight and win a modern global war against the dictators.

The connection between war, industry, and empire was capitalized upon even before the outbreak of the war when *Fire* was shown and publicized at the British Industries Fair on 27 March 1937. The Nazi leadership appreciated the film's propaganda value and it was banned throughout the Reich (but viewed in private showings by Goebbels). Robson/Elizabeth's reputation was such that Warner Bros. cast her in the swashbuckling 1940 melodrama *The Sea Hawk*, starring Errol Flynn as a sea dog and featuring Elizabethan expeditions to America. In the final scene she delivers a patriotic speech, which was not lost on contemporaries. C. A. Lejeune, the *Observer*'s eminent film critic, pointed out that the Nazis turned up in this Elizabethan romance, with the fleet standing between the German tyrant and his dream of world conquest. She appreciated Robson as 'a Munich-minded queen who eventually addresses her people'. Robson's Elizabeth war speech has a Churchillian ring: 'My loyal subjects, a grave duty confronts us all: to prepare our nation for a war none of us wants—least of all your queen. We have tried by all means within our power to avert this conflict... But when the ruthless ambition of a man threatens to engulf the world, it becomes the solemn obligation of free men, wherever they may be',[27] to stand up to him. The message of the speech, and that of the various film versions of the Tilbury speech, resonated well at a time when the new monarch George VI and his family showed a steadfastness which distinguished their behaviour as royals from that of Edward VIII during the Abdication crisis of 1936. When Warner contemplated cutting out the speech, they faced public outcry and had to include it in what became the final version of the *Sea Hawk*. Robson's interpretation long survived the Second World War and the time of national emergency. The Tilbury speech was a staple of her repertoire which she was called to perform as late as the late sixties. In 1968 she delivered it under Elizabeth I's Darnley portrait at the National Gallery to an audience which included some of Britain's leading experts on the Elizabethan era like the historian Frances Yates and the art historian Roy Strong.[28]

The biographies of the film and of Robson related here may well be located within an official popular culture with a conservative bent, bolstering monarchy, patriotism, and empire. And the history of both the star and the entire Tudor cycle may easily be interpreted as a conservative, perhaps even Tory, history, stressing the hegemony of a rule based upon popular acquiescence and ignoring social tension in a highly industrialized society in the throes of the deep economic depression of the 1930s, with its record-breaking unemployment. Such an interpretation would fit neatly with the Marxian interpretation of British nationalism and culture put forward by Tom Nairn. British elites, more than any other national bourgeois elite, needed to baptize the working masses in the nation and 'to invite the masses into history and the invitation card had to be written in a language they understood'.[29] What more fitting than the nationalist history film to inculcate the working classes in an official culture of history, thus achieving a desired democratization of the past to gain political acquiescence? But this important analysis, which bears notable allegiance to the Gramscian model of hegemony via cultural consent, may prove all too neat. In the first place, it omits the part consumers purchasing the ticket to history played in the new kind of culture and which was studied in the previous chapter. Secondly, the definition and description of the culture-producing elite solely as an agent of global capitalism is far too narrow to be usable by historians of this culture. And thirdly, the notion of British 'national culture' too is used rather generally and impracticably. Film production and distribution were one territory where the nation was defined and regulated and its borderlines contested.[30]

The Cinematograph Film Act of 1927, rather unsuccessfully meant to stem the American takeover of the market, set the famous quota for home-made

[27] C. A. Lejeune, 'The Sea Hawk', in *The C. A. Lejeune Film Reader*, ed. Anthony Lejeune (Manchester, 1991), 96.

[28] For perceptive report on the event see A. S. Byatt, *The Virgin in the Garden* (1978; Harmondsworth, 1986), 9 and 14.

[29] Nairn, *The Break-up of Britain*, 41.

[30] See Street, *British National Cinema* and Higson, *Waving the Flag*.

productions and for the distribution of British as against foreign (i.e. American) films and was superseded by an amending act in 1938. The legislation did not just attempt to boost national industry and labour; it sought to preserve an English culture in danger of Americanization. The fear of colonization by Hollywood was expressed in the *Daily Express*'s lament that several million Britons, most of them women, had become temporary American citizens.[31] Similar fears were shared by the cultural elites, which attributed the levelling down of audiences and consumers in the USA to films. Historical films made in Britain were seen as a check against American cultural colonization. But the quota and other regulatory means designed to control a national industry (such as various forms of censorship) in effect enhanced cooperation across nations, creating the giant American–British combines such as United Artists (cooperating with Korda) and Gaumont British, which took over distribution. Moreover, the production of home-made films, let alone Hollywood ones, was too multinational and global. The classic British historical film, inaugurated in the very first Tudor film, is an exemplar of the hybrid character of national history and culture through film. The new genre raised a set of questions about who were entitled to make features which shaped notions of the past (and present), and to whom this past belonged. What Andrew Higson termed the 'instability of the national' had to do primarily with the process of culture production and the identity of producers and cultural agents.[32]

Fire, like *Henry VIII* and another blockbuster, *Scarlet Pimpernel*, was produced by Alexander Korda, a Hungarian Jew strongly influenced by the German film industry and Freudian psychology who became a naturalized British subject and established the London Films studios, boosting the entire film industry in Britain. Throughout his career, Korda was quite close to the Conservative Party. While supervising his productions, he employed executive producers for specific films, most notably Eric Pommer, one of the stellar team of UFA (Germany's national film company) made refugee by the Nazi regime and hired to produce *Fire* with the aid of an American director (Howard), an Asian-American cameraman (James Wong Howe), not to mention a Scot in the role of Elizabeth. *Henry VIII* was financed by the Italian banker Leo Toeplitz, produced by him and Korda, directed by the Hungarian Lajos Biro, and starred the Eurasian Merle Oberon as Anne Boleyn. The Hollywood versions combined American finance and studio work and British casts, and their marketing and distribution necessitated transatlantic cooperation. Thus the very term 'national film', which was frequently used in public debate on the cinema and, more specifically, on cinema and history, was open-ended. The most openly nationalist films, having to do with the rise of the national monarchy and empire, were transnational

31 Cited in McKibbin, *Classes and Cultures*, 427.

32 Andrew Higson, 'The Instability of the National', in Justine Ashby and Andrew Higson (eds.), *British Cinema Past and Present* (London, 2000), 35–49.

commodities, manufactured by multinational elites different from the traditional British intellectual elites, and screened to British, American, and imperial audiences. Hence the complexity of the monarchy and the plurality of the nation that they offer, which will be discussed later. This multinationality incensed some observers like Graham Greene, who indulged in cultural xenophobia. It was precisely the non-existence of a 'pure' film culture and the contamination of the national history by foreign film-makers that made these observers phobic. Thus Greene in one notorious review of Korda's *The Marriage of Corbal* (1936) acerbically wonders:

an English film? . . . England, of course, has always been the home of the exiled; but one may at least express a wish that émigrés would set up trades in which their ignorance of our language and our culture was less of a handicap; it would not grieve me to see Mr Alexander Korda seated before a cottage in an Eastern county, following an older and better tradition. The Quota Act has played into foreign hands, and as far as I know, there is nothing to prevent an English film unit being completely staffed by technicians of foreign blood. We have saved the British film industry from American competition only to surrender it to a far more alien control.[33]

For 'alien' read 'Jewish'. It was at precisely this time that anti-Semitic propaganda targeted 'aliens' as a force which threatened British labour. 'Alien' also denoted 'Continental'—mainly central European, both contingents being quite prominent in Hollywood too.[34] Greene's readers would not have failed to notice his crude allusion to a 'cottage in an Eastern county', the traditional symbolic site of 'Merrie England' and the setting for parts of Korda's Tudor films, and that presented a decidedly rural society. Phobia of foreignness lingered long and in unexpected quarters and could be extended to whoever did not qualify as purely English. As late as 1984 *The Guardian*, in an article summing up Robson's career, noted a 'certain un-Englishness' in her demeanor, citing a fellow actress who claimed that 'she (Robson) was not Anglo-Saxon: she might have been a blazing Russian actress'.[35] These and other voices notwithstanding, Robson was anglicized and made a popular national icon. Her contemporary in historical productions, Leslie Howard, the son of émigrés and a Jew, would become the proverbial Englishman, the definer of what seemed quintessentially British and an enormous propaganda asset (see Ch. 8).

The scope and limits of the nation were contested not only in and by the economy of production and distribution and the composition of the elite of film creators, but also, and perhaps to a greater extent, in the production of texts and visual images, most notably in relation to the innovative ways in which the Tudor cycle was the juncture of gender and power, private lives and public histories. The cycle, as the remainder of the chapter demonstrates, contested and

33 Higson, 'The Instability of the National', 43.

34 Korda was referred to as 'rank foreigner'. Martin Stockham, *The Korda Collection: Alexander Korda's Film Classics* (London, 1992), 105.

35 *The Guardian*, 9 July 1984.

expanded the borderlines of femininity and masculinity, in tune with shifting notions about gender and modernity, at the same time as it extended and opened up notions about the monarchy and the nation.

THE QUEEN'S TWO BODIES: GENDER, NATION, AND POWER

The ten major films in the cycle and the two earlier silent movies are all set in moments of national crisis, typically in such moments of danger to the succession, hence to the very continuity of the monarchy, and of a military emergency that threatens the nation. *Les Amours de la Reine Elizabeth* and *Private Lives of Elizabeth and Essex* focus on the nadir of Elizabeth's long reign, during the crucial year of the Irish campaign and the Essex rebellion. *Virgin Queen* and the features on Mary Stuart are about the succession problem at different points of the reign. *Fire* of course is about the Catholic rebellions and the threat of invasion, and *Henry VIII*, *Tudor Rose*, and *Young Bess* all narrow in on the issue of the legitimacy and authority of the monarch as the basis of political and social stability. In each and every one of these examples, crisis is, in the most literal sense of the word, embodied in the monarch; literal, because her body, or rather bodies, which camera, props, and décor represent and reproduce, is the cycle's central image.

The history of the image of the plurality of the monarch's body is of course long and goes back to the Tudors themselves. As Ernst H. Kantorowicz has noted in his epochal *The King's Two Bodies* in 1957, this image, with the cluster of legal fictions appended to it, was invented by the Tudor lawyers, mostly Elizabeth's jurists, to help buttress royal authority and the idea of the continuity of the body politic.[36] This elaborate Tudor construction drew from and on the perception that the king was a 'corporate *sole*', that is one person, with two bodies: the body corporeal and natural and the body politic. The first was subjected to age, disease, and infirmity, the second supra-human and immortal and embodied in a continuous and unbroken royal line. During the reign of Elizabeth the legal fiction sprang to be a constitutive myth of royal power, bolstering the absolute monarchy. It was during the early twentieth century, at a time when the monarchy had long lost all substantive power, that historians rediscovered the myth. Kantorowicz's own work draws on that of the great legal historian F. W. Maitland, whose 1901 scathing attack on the legal fiction of any king as a multibodied corporation was reprinted in 1936 to some acclaim.[37]

[36] Ernst H. Kantorowicz, *The King's Two Bodies: A Study in Medieval Political Theology* (Princeton, 1957), Introduction.

[37] F. W. Maitland's study first appeared in *Law Quarterly Review*, 17 (1901), 131–46 and reappeared in *Selected Essays* (Cambridge, 1936), 104–27.

Maitland and Kantorowicz did not touch on the relation between royal authority, gender, and sexuality, which had been so crucial in the Tudor debates on the succession and royal authority. But J. E. Neale grasped and demonstrated the tension between Elizabeth's gender and her role as a monarch in a patriarchal political culture and society. It is significant that Neale paid the closest attention to the queen's identity as a woman ruler in his most popular text, the biography intended for a varied audience. Sixteenth-century government, he noted, was a 'male business'. The royal household was a 'male community' and the ritual of kingship had been primarily masculine. The queen was acutely aware of the need to operate as a woman, hence by definition one unfit to rule, in a male role.[38] His discovery and publicizing of what was taken to be the definitive version of the Tilbury speech, the most salient example of the queen's own use of the metaphor of the body and of gender, cemented his argument. As already noted, Robson put his discovery to use in her interpretation, which quickly became the model for all future cinematic ones.

The contrast between a royal body (female, or, in one case, *Henry VIII*, a male one) with private needs and public duty acquired a special resonance because of the growing cultural role of the monarchy within the inter-war democracy and the exposure of the Royal Family to the public eye. Royalty had long lost its traditional mystique and magic, but it was acquiring a modern aura which welded celebrity to a transparency that allowed the masses vicarious intimate knowledge about royals. This transparency, which accompanied the centring of the monarchy in the public consciousness through the mediation of the popular press, documentary films, and the wireless, had its complement and articulation in the historical film's dramatization of the conflict between personal good on the one hand and public duty and service on the other. The idea of royal service for the people's good was advanced and shrewdly practised by the Royal Family, most notably by George V, who astutely used the media to propagate it. Royal charities, studied by Frank Prochaska, were publicized together with the 'modernity' of royals, a modernity embodied in the figure of the Prince of Wales, later Edward VIII.[39] The dilemma of service versus domestic happiness became more pronounced in films created after the crisis following his abdication and which developed into the constitutional crisis of 1936. Edward VIII abdicated his public role for a private life, a choice that was the subject of a tumultuous debate. Since direct critique of the monarchy was silenced, the crisis was transported into history.

This relocation allowed freedoms that would have been unthinkable outside a historical genre. As will be shown in detail, the entire cycle represented royals who renounced private fulfilment for duty, as befitting democratic 'people's monarchs', a symmetric opposite to Edward's private (but highly visible) citizen. But the cycle went further than utilizing a historical myth and traditional scholarship to

38 Neale, *Queen Elizabeth*, 69.

39 Frank Prochaska, *Royal Bounty: The Making of a Welfare Monarchy* (New Haven, 1995).

comment on and reinterpret current politics and celebrity. By gendering the royal body and furthermore suggesting that the gender of Elizabeth and Henry was itself ambiguous, they anticipated much later expert interpretations of Tudor and, more broadly, early modern politics and culture. It may serve as a sobering lesson to professional historians, not least to cultural historians and feminist ones, as well as to students of literature, that the popular film of the thirties and forties explored Elizabethan gender ambiguities and self-fashioning decades before these topics were acknowledged and became respectable.[40]

Ambiguity does not characterize the early silent films. The 1912 Merckenton–Zukor version, distributed to English-speaking audiences as *Queen Elizabeth* (but henceforward referred to as *Les Amours*), features a domestic, almost homely and feminine queen. Domesticity is manifest in the cinematography, direction, and above all in Sarah Bernhardt's deportment and dialogue with the camera. *Les Amours* is photographed theatre rather than a film, and Bernhardt's interpretation of the queen a rather exaggerated version of her highly mannerist style of acting. Interestingly, she had a record in male roles of young royals, notably as Hamlet. In the film she is aging, she has lost her legendary svelte and serpentine figure, half female and half male, and is a hardly mobile older woman (with one leg amputated), using only her arms and face for gesture.[41] Her body is utterly covered in a hybrid dress, a cross between late Tudor and belle-epoque. Shooting the entire film indoors further enhances the sense of domesticity, lending the Essex affair a claustrophobic air. The 1924 version, starring Diana Manners as the queen, emphasizes traditional gender roles even further.

Fire Over England, thanks to Robson, discards the silent-film model. The film constructs a popular queen whose femininity, though it appears to maintain traditional images, blurs the definition of gender and of the body. Thus the Tilbury speech is located after a series of short and medium shots of the queen feeding and nursing the frail Sir William Cecil, Lord Burghley, her longest-serving Councillor and the staunchest supporter of her non-war policy. The same scene, it may be recalled, was used for tie-ups and advertisements (see Ch. 6). This indoor scene is then followed by shots of the more public parts of the palace and a gallop through the countryside to Tilbury, at the end of which Elizabeth, mounted on a charger, armoured and helmeted, speaks to her troops (see Fig. 15). In less than two minutes, she is transported from a classically domestic scene to the most public and military setting possible, the battlefield where, of course, the presence of the early modern monarch was vitally important. But women, who could not be soldiers, were—by definition—excluded from command, military or other. In Robson's interpretation the speech exploits the rich possibilities of the discourse on the monarch's bodies,

[40] For gender-focused interpretations of Elizabeth I see Levin, *The Heart and Stomach of a King*.

[41] On Bernhardt's body see Mary Louise Roberts, *Disruptive Acts: The New Woman in Fin-de-Siècle France* (Chicago, 2002), 165–221.

Fig. 15. Elizabeth addresses the troops at Tilbury, in *Fire Over England.* Tudor films suggested a blurring of gender roles and images of a democratic and patriotic monarchy

blending together images of the masculine and military Renaissance prince and that of women as frail vessels in a 'democratic' address:

My loving people . . . I have always so behaved myself that, under God, I have placed my chiefest strength and safe guard in the loyal hearts and good will of my subjects: and therefore I am come amongst you, as you see, at this time . . . being beloved at the midst and heat of battle, lay down for my God, my kingdom, and for my people, my honour and my blood, even to the dust. I know I have the body of a weak and feeble woman, but I have the heart and valour of a king, and a king of England too, and think foul scorn that Parma or Spain, or any prince of Europe should dare invade the borders of my realm; to which rather than my Dishonour shall grow by me, I myself will take up arms, I myself shall be your general.[42]

Attuned to contemporary jargon, Robson replaced the original 'heart and stomach of a king' with the more elevated and, since the outbreak of the First

[42] Transcribed from an original copy at BFI Collections.

World War, rather arcane 'valour'.[43] By the early twenties 'stomach' had completely lost its original meaning as 'courage' and was reserved to low diction and ridicule. Robson's fashioning of Elizabeth as king and queen, the people's sovereign who is both a soldier and a nurturer (the Burghley episode), drew significance from her status as star and previous career on stage, which included cross-dressed and cross-gender roles. In one of these, she played Mary Beard, a seventeenth-century female pirate in a play written especially for her. Her lack of glamour and the fact that, as she confided to the *Daily Mail*, she 'couldn't be sexy', served to further enhance the two-bodies image.[44] Female historical roles made it possible for character actresses to explore gender and carve new models of powerful and political women that would be quite impossible in films set in the present and make these roles (and the monarchy) appear relevant to modern times. Robson's declamatory style, the trademark of the so-called 'Flora Robson roles', rendered her impact on contemporaries even more effective.[45]

Davis did not lack glamour and modernity, certainly not during the middle stage of her career, when her sex appeal was vigorously marketed. But as Warner Bros.' leading female star with two Oscars and moreover one categorized as 'character actress', she too could exercise autonomies in constructing the role of the queen. Her two interpretations of Elizabeth in 1940 and 1955 too draw heavily on the image of the two bodies, the female and male, the one symbolizing authority and public duty, the other weakness and private needs and desires. But the conflict, recognizable by audiences, between the monarch's private and domestic life and public duty is played out not on the battlefield but in the queen's Council room, the palace's rooms of audience, and on her own bed. The Davis films evolve around the relationship between the old queen and the young Robert Devereux, Earl of Essex, presented as the queen's rival, almost a competing monarch in *Elizabeth and Essex*, and her friendship with Sir Walter Raleigh in *Virgin Queen*. The earlier film and, to a degree, the later one, were based on Lytton Strachey's 1928 biography *Elizabeth and Essex*, revealingly subtitled *A Historical Tragedy*, probably the supreme example of the inter-war experimental historical biography. Initially written in 1911 as a poem in blank verse, *Elizabeth and Essex* was reworked into a corrosive iconoclasm of accepted forms of historical writing, both academic history and Whig historiography, and was seen by G. M. Trevelyan as a suave example of a wider practice of denigrating the historical subject and the historian's art.[46] Lay readers were much less threatened than professional and 'public' Whig historians, the latter represented by Trevelyan. The book became a blockbuster, selling 110,000 copies in Britain and 150,000 in the USA (where it made publishing history) in less

[43] On 'courage' and 'valour' in 'high diction' language see Fussell, *The Great War and Modern Memory*, 21–2. On the choice of 'stomach' see Barrow, *Flora*, 101.

[44] *Daily Mail*, 23 Nov. 1961.

[45] *Daily Telegraph*, 1 June 1990.

[46] Victor Feske, *From Belloc to Churchill: Private Scholars, Public Culture, and the Crisis of British Liberalism, 1900–1939* (Chapel Hill, NC, 1996), 145–9.

than one year, and inspiring a Broadway adaptation. In 1933 the versatile Rowse, ever sensitive to the potential of the popular market, would try his hand at a play based on the Essex episode, tentatively entitling it *Essex and Elizabeth*, conspicuously unsuccessfully. Stretching sequence, causality, and narrative beyond limits that were acceptable to historians, *Elizabeth and Essex* focused on character and sexuality, creating both the Queen and Essex as androgynous characters, inhabiting androgynous bodies. Such crossing of the borderlines of gender was characteristic during the twenties not only of Strachey's own Bloomsbury milieu, but, as already noted, of popular representations of the 'modern man' and 'modern woman'. Strachey's interpretation of political and personal motives may be described as psychobiography, frankly using Freud's interpretation of sexuality and sexual potentials and tensions within the family (here the Tudor dynasty) to interpret the personalities of the queen and Essex, her political manoeuvering and conduct, and even imperial foreign policy. Freud's own response in a letter from Vienna dated Christmas Day 1928 is worth quoting:

> This time you have moved me deeply, for you yourself have reached great depths. You are aware of what other historians so easily overlooked—that it is impossible to understand the aspect with certainty, because we cannot divine men's motives and the essence of their minds and so cannot interpret their actions.

Nor were psychologists who, in regard to their interpretation of people in the past were 'in the same position as with dreams to which we have given no association'. Strachey's analysis of 'one of the most remarkable figures of your country's history . . . trace[d] back her character to the impression of her childhood . . . touched upon her most hidden motives with equal boldness and discretion, and it is possible that you have succeeded in making a correct reconstruction of what actually occurred'.[47]

In both the stage version of *Elizabeth and Essex* and the films, Strachey's psychobiography of character and his treatment of sexuality were necessarily diluted and the theme of androgyny toned down, and the relationship between the powerful old queen and a young and ambitious courtier was marketed as a romance. Fan magazines like *Picturegoer Weekly* carried stories on the supposed love affair, based on the script and using romance to educate readers on late Elizabethan foreign policy, the Essex plot, etc.[48] Viewers, as my discussion of the film biographies in Chapter 6 shows, greatly resented the stress on romance, which they judged excessive and implausible.[49]

But even in diluted form, the film remained subversive, due in great part to Davis's interpretation. Without public and military addresses to build from, Davis refashioned her own body to construct the queen's body and its symbolism—construct in the most literal sense of the word. In *Elizabeth and Essex* she insisted

[47] Quoted in Michael Holroyd, *Lytton Strachey: The New Biography* (London, 1994), 615.

[48] *Picturegoer Weekly*, 9 May 1940, pp. 15–16.

[49] See Ch. 6, pp. 209, 212.

upon shaving her head (her hair had been one of her trademarks) and eyebrows. In *Virgin Queen* she appeared in a bed scene (taken from Strachey) completely bald, allowing the young Raleigh and the audience to see her 'for real'.[50] This and the make-up masking her face made a total and stark contrast to Hollywood images of the female body, including the aging body. Put differently, Davis employed the contemporary icon of modern femaleness to bring forth the Tudor image of female sexuality and earthliness in its conflict with the very idea of monarchical power. To bring forth the body, she adopted in the 1939–40 production a 'masculine' walk, almost a swagger, a shrewd emulation of Charles Laughton's 'Henry's walk' in *Henry VIII*, which he copied from the National Gallery Holbein portrait of the king standing astride. In 1955 she developed the swagger to an exaggerated gait. Even more shrewdly, she and her directors drew on *Fire* for further comment on the opposites private/public, love/duty, and corporality/unearthliness by tying these opposites to the gaze at the female face, another central motif of classical cinema which, as already noted, had bordered on fetishism.[51]

In each and every one of the films featuring the mature Elizabeth, indeed in virtually all the classical screen biographies of the early female monarchs, there is at least one scene in which the queen gazes at her reflection in a mirror as she makes up her face. All the scenes involve her self-reflection upon her old age, infertility, fragility, and eventual mortality (see Fig. 16). This set-scene may be traced back to the Bernhardt's version, but is at its most elaborate in Davis's first interpretation in *Elizabeth and Essex*, in which the queen smashes the mirror (hence her own face) and indulges in an orgy of rage, destroying all mirrors around her. She in fact destroys the body private, her own frustration at having no private life and children. The mirror scenes contain a wealth of references not only to other films in the cycle, but to the literary motif of a woman gazing at a mirror, a motif characteristically associated with female anger. The best-known examples are the mirror scenes in *Jane Eyre* and Louisa May Alcott's *Little Women* and the queen's gaze in her mirror in *Snow White*. As Sandra Gilbert and Susan Gubar have noted, this motif, which was so ubiquitous in the novel and folk literature, served as a constituting frame for writers and readers for understanding and picturing subjects like female anger as a reaction to the limitations on women.[52] That the motif and the image of the mirror were familiar to audiences possessing various degrees of literacy is clear from the mention of small mirrors in the films' tie-ups advertising Tudor 'hand mirrors'.[53] Audiences that would not have recognized any of the literary references, or those used by Strachey, would have made cinematic connections of the angry gaze (with the film version of Jane Eyre and Disney's *Snow White*).

It is difficult to retrace viewers' response to the scene—and probably impossible. Even had we had appropriate documentation in the film-goers'

[50] Walker, *Bette Davis*, 107–8 for her construction of the queen.

[51] See above, p. 219.

[52] Gilbert and Gubar, *The Madwoman in the Attic*, 3–45.

[53] *Fire Over England*, tie-ups, BFI.

Fig. 16. The Queen contemplating her aging face, in *Fire Over England*. Tudor films harped on the notion of the private and fragile body of monarchs and offered a glimpse into their private lives

autobiographies which single it out, we probably would have to settle for much less than a complete recovery of audiences' gaze at stars and the perceptions such gazes activated in viewers. In this connection it is important frankly to note the limits to our ability. But the multilayered representation on screen of the royal female gaze certainly challenges the tendency to dehistoricize the female film star and to exclude women viewers from actually looking at cinematic images on their own terms. The camera, especially during the cinema's classical era of the 1930s and 1940s, Laura Mulvey has noted, transported the female body into a male object of desire, hence making possible only a gaze that is 'male'. This, of course, excludes the possibility of a women's look at the films. True, more recent scholarship has mitigated this notion about star-gazing and sought to historicize female viewing. But we have yet to map the possibilities of active usage of the images projected to historical female viewers, who made up the majority of film-goers.[54] Such evidence as we have does not allow us to deny them action as consumers who make do, in a selective manner, with the female images of the past available to them. Furthermore, even if we ignore viewers and speculate on and from representation only (which, as historians, we may not do), we must allow that the very usage of the theme of the queen's gaze intervenes to complicate assumptions about manipulation of the female body. For the queen's gazing at herself suggests an activity that questions the limits of gender. It is also quite certain that those who participated in producing the set-scenes were aware of Elizabethan attitudes to womanhood. Thus the mirror scene in *Elizabeth and Essex* is followed by a spectacle of gender reversal. The queen's ladies-in-waiting sing to her a ballad by Christopher Marlowe, titled 'The Passionate Shepherd to his Love', and Raleigh's retort to Marlowe. This reference to texts written by two of Elizabeth's chief propagandists and makers of the myth of Gloriana is quite shrewd, as is that to old age and youth. Even shrewder is the reference to Elizabethan gender play and reversal. The women sing the men's roles—the reverse of the practice in Elizabethan theatre.

In all the films of the Tudor cycle the conundrum of the two bodies is resolved by the queen's abdication of femininity and sexuality for power and for her people. As befits a people's, rather than aristocratic, monarch, she lives and rules for the former. This is a point that the working-class viewers cited earlier noted and responded to pragmatically. Mayer's interviewees, like the school essays commenting on the greatness of Elizabeth I cited earlier, totally rejected a sentimental notion of a romantic solution to the conflict between duty and domesticity.[55]

THE KING'S BODY: THE PRIVATE HISTORY OF HENRY

It is the king's body, rather than the queen's, that is prone to carnal desires and other weaknesses. The fragility and temporality of royals is apotheosized in *Henry VIII*, which is all about the body corporeal, in the most literal sense of the term. As the publicity material put it: 'Was he a tyrant, was he a monster, concerned with nothing but his own lascivious pleasures?'[56] Significantly, the film narrows in on pleasure described as private and the king's private life, and evolves around his position as man, husband, and father and only then as sovereign. Indeed he is more distinctly identified with the private and domestic than any of the queens in the Tudor cycle. As a number of film historians have pointed out, it was precisely the focus on the monarch in private and his sexualization that made the

[54] For Mulvey see n. 2. On desire and fantasy in the build-up of stars in historical films see Landy, *Cinematic Uses of the Past*, especially her analysis of *Scarlet Empress*, pp. 151–91.

[55] See Ch. 6, p. 209, p. 212.

[56] Harper, *Picturing the Past*, 21–2; Richards, *The Age of the Dream Palace*, 259.

film a sensational blockbuster, netting some £500,000 in its first world run and going into some 500 prints across the Atlantic, in Europe and Asia.[57] Its approach to history incensed guardians of public morals, professional historians, and government circles. Quite a few contemporary critics considered it disrespectful of the monarchy and constitution and not patriotic enough (this last a sterling quality of Korda's later historical films). Yet the apparently plebeian character of the early modern monarch, and the access to his private and intimate life—two aspects that became central to the image and celebrity of the inter-war monarchy—endeared the film to mass audiences.

Henry VIII deliberately shuns the political, social, and religious context of the Reformation, as well as the public aspects of authority and government. Henry the king is never measured according to his success on the battlefield or capabilities as administrator, but by his sexual performance and fertility. For his power and the stability of the kingdom, the very continuity of the Tudors, all depend on his ability to breed. Fertility and reproduction, typically seen as the role of the royal women, whether these are consorts or monarchs, are here relegated to the male head of the dynasty. The king's life is rendered episodically in a sequence composed of his serial marriages to women who dominate his desire and body. Characteristically, his marriage to Catherine of Aragon is dismissed because of her being a 'respectable woman', hence 'having no interest for a *modern* audience' (my emphasis). The film draws on the popularity of Henry as a Bluebeard figure of voracious appetite for women. But this myth is punctured because the king's sexual prowess and sometimes even sensuality fail him: he barely succeeds in producing a male heir and is cuckolded. He copulates to procreate and usually fails in his duty to family and country. Revealingly, his failures are recounted in a series of female voices and represented through female eyes. The key scene of the entire narrative, which is repeated three times and divides the film into five parts, is a bedchamber scene showing the making of the royal bed on the eve of the royal marriages to Jane Seymour, Anne of Cleves, Catherine Howard, and Catherine Parr. In each of the takes, the changing of monogrammed pillowcases and sheets precedes the change of wife, with the camera switching from monogram to new queen. The making of the bed is entirely controlled by women—court women and servants, who implicitly and in explicit gesture refer to the king's sexuality (see Fig. 17). In the script, and sequence of directions, the women's talk may be restrained, but on screen the dialogue and the exchange of looks become full of innuendo:

Camera shooting towards the bed-hangings, with embroidered corners 'H' and 'A' above the bed.

[57] On the film's distribution see Sarah Street, 'Stepping Westward: The Distribution of British films in America, and the Case of the *Private Life of Henry VIII*', in Ashby and Higson (eds.), *British Cinema*, 51–63.

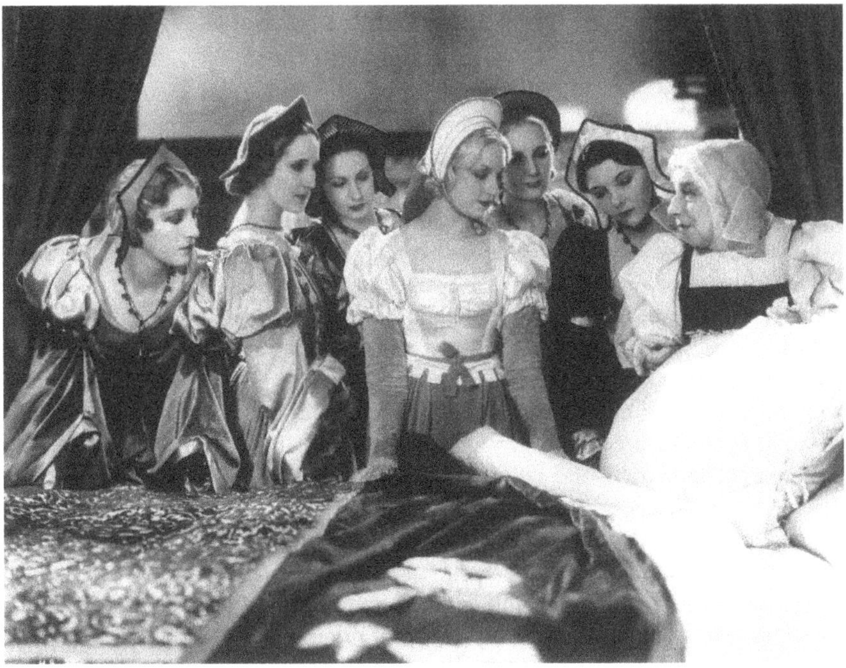

Fig. 17. Court women making Henry's bed, in *The Private Life of Henry VIII.* The intimate lives of monarchs became the stuff of a 'democratic' and modernized monarchy

Scene 2—medium shot

The old nurse peeps into the room. She enters and beckons to unseen people outside the door. Half a dozen ladies in waiting enter. They look round the room with great interest.

Scene 3—full shot

The young ladies approach the bed. The old nurse leading them. It is a very exciting adventure for the young ladies. When they get near the bed, the old nurse turns her head and indicates the bed, as if to say Here it is!

Scene 4—medium shot

Old nurse with a very spirited young lady. She follows the old nurse into the immediate proximity of the bed. The old nurse smiles at her encouragingly. She is all excitement, but speaks at last.

1st lady: So that's the King's bed. Nurse: Yes my dear. (Slips her hand down the bed). And he has not long left it—feel! The girl feels the warm sheets. Her eyes are creating a picture—there is a tiny pause before she speaks. Other girls now come into the picture.

1st lady: I wonder what he looks like in bed.

2nd lady: You'll never know.

1st lady: Well, there's no need to be spiteful, is there mistress nurse?

Nurse (consolingly): No, my dear, and you've as good a chance as another when the King's in one of his merry moods.[58]

Not only bedding, but the king's eating, bordering on gluttony—another primary need and activity of the body—is conspicuously displayed. Biro and Wimperis's script and Laughton's acting clearly and very explicitly associate excess in sex with excessive eating, and Henry's gargantuan appetite with his enslavement to and by women. Eating, like intercourse, although apparently private is also a public activity, which viewers are invited to watch. In this sense they fulfil a role which brings to mind that of sixteenth-century courtiers and more occasional observers of the royal courts who, of course, were spectators in a courtly theatre in which the royal body was constantly performing and watched at the dining table and in the bedchamber. At the same time film-viewers shared in the entirely contemporary role of the mass audience vis-à-vis the increasingly visible Royal Family. Laughton in particular was quick to grasp and utilize this aspect of the spectacle of monarchy and relished in making the king's body transparent and exposed to a merciless gaze. Like Robson and Davis after him, he literally transformed his own body into that of the sixteenth-century monarch. He grew a beard, studied Henry's deportment from the same Holbein portrait showing the king standing astride that Davis would emulate, and mastered the design of the king's clothing, which he researched from copies of original sketches preserved by three of London's oldest tailoring firms. His self-fashioning as Henry is apparent in his self-direction in what came to be the film's single most famous and most controversial scene: Henry's devouring a capon in front of a roomful of spectators, then burping (see Fig. 18). The analogue between disorderly and uncontrolled eating on the one hand, and breeding on the other, is transparent. The king is shown pushing his plate away disgustedly, punching a chicken:

Call this a capon? Look at that! All sauce and no substance—
He tears off a leg
Like one of Cromwell's speeches—and just as difficult to swallow
He tears it limb from limb
Too many cooks, that's the trouble . . .—
He throws a leg over his shoulder
Marry again—breed more sons! Coarse brutes!
He plunges his fingers inside the bird
There's no delicacy nowadays. No consideration of others. Refinement's a thing of the past
He throws the carcass over his shoulder
Manners are dead . . . Marry, Marry, Marry! Am I a king or a breeding bull?[59]

The sheer hilarity of the whole scene, with the sly reference to bad manners and lack of civility, anticipated the outcries of critics who bewailed the degradation of the monarchy and indeed of history. The royal burp was the most

[58] Ernest Betts (ed.), *The Private Life of Henry VIII Directed by Alexander Korda, Story and Dialogue by Lajos Biro and Arthur Wimperis* (London, 1934), 2.

[59] Ibid. 45–6.

Fig. 18. The King consuming a capon, in *The Private Life of Henry VIII.* The film's focus on eating and bedding made up the image of an earthy people's monarch

taxing. For his part Laughton insisted that 'the real Henry ate so dirtily that they had a cloth in front of his face. He was dirty mouthed, but a great statesman at that.'[60] His point is that 'dirt' makes history 'real' and true. It is also that the kitchen, dining room, and bedroom, rather than statesmanship and the battlefield, are the core of history, a point which audiences before the Munich crisis could sympathize with. Translated into professional historians' vocabulary, his perception stresses the importance of social history and everyday life over politics. His contaminating penchant for accuracy in detail changed the initial production policy, setting standards for historical feature films. The dinner scene was played by 150 participants at one dining table in a seventy-foot-long hall, with the walls hung with Holbein tapestries. But the effort to create verisimilitude concerned not only items of luxury but also material detail which had to do with the everyday, notably with food production (as in the kitchen scenes) and food consumption, in the great hall. The table was laden with hundreds of chickens and capons, meat pies three feet in diameter, and loaves of fresh bread

60 Kurt Singer, *The Charles Laughton Story: An Intimate Story of Charles Laughton* (Philadelphia and Toronto, 1954), 119–21 for his active part in the production. See also Charles Higham, *Charles Laughton, an Intimate Biography* (New York, 1976).

four feet long. Food and eating, so revolting to connoisseurs and moralists, appealed to audiences. Royals' eating appealed even more. We may relate this appeal both to the growing visibility and transparency of the monarchy, and to that same common-sense approach of viewers which they used to connect visual detail and fragments to parts of their own material world and to the everyday, thus fitting visual history into the social. Publicists were quick to realize the appeal of themes like eating and table manners, organizing Henry VIII eating contests and bone-throwing tournaments. Restaurants and American diners displayed posters advising customers on 'How to eat like Charles Laughton' beginning with: 'tear the bird to shreds with your hands' and ending with 'finish meal with a few choice burps'.[61]

In the same way that audiences connected with Henry's earthiness and accentuated plebeian conduct they responded to earthy and non-ceremonial aspects in Elizabeth's behaviour. The audience at a matinee of *Elizabeth and Essex* at Regal Theatre in Stretham, on 17 October 1940, good-humouredly watched 'one scene where Essex slaps her on the behind, and they indulge in horseplay on the floor'. Observed for MO by a surprised (and, one cannot help thinking, slightly disappointed) Len England, this audience did not protest, the scene 'simply caus[ing] loud laughter, no shocked comment at such treatment of an English Queen'.[62]

Yet Henry's private life was not wholly divorced from matters of state and nation. The uneasy coexistence, conflation even, of the private and public that had been such a saliency of the early modern court, and which the mass media made into a hallmark of the 'democratic' and modern monarchy, is acknowledged in the script and on screen, most effectively in the king's own body and sexuality. In one prize scene he ventures into the royal bed, murmuring 'the things that I do for England', a recognizable reversal of the adage directed at brides, 'close your eyes and think of England' (or in another version, 'the Empire'). This utterance too adds to his feminization. In almost symmetrical opposite to the queen in a masculine role, the king is stripped of most of the conventional signs of manhood. This interpretation of the historical Henry is bolstered by the gender of Laughton himself, who never played overtly 'manly' roles and who enjoyed stretching the borderlines of masculinity on and off stage (though it is very doubtful that his homosexuality was known to viewers during the inter-war period). His was one of two competing images of men in the historical film, the one rather effeminate, not physical, and asexual (notwithstanding Henry's philandering), the other muscular and oozing physical presence and even sex appeal, what popular discourse in the thirties would have termed a 'he man'. In the Tudor films this type of masculinity is distinctly imperial and military and played by action actors like Errol Flynn in the role of Geoffrey

61 Singer, *The Laughton Story*, 124.
62 MO archives, Topic Collections/Film Collections 7/g, LE.

Thorpe, the sea captain dedicated to war with Spain in the *Sea Hawk*, or that of Essex in *Elizabeth and Essex* and Olivier as Ingolby in *Fire*. Significantly, these interpretations of masculinity remained almost unchanged from their literary origins. The origin of Thorpe is Sir Oliver Tressilian in Rafael Sabatini's eponymous 1915 novel, an orientalist swashbuckling melodrama set in Algiers.[63] In an earlier film version, directed in 1924 by Frank Lloyd, the 'Orient' is a luscious country, brimming with sexuality and violence. The Tudor sea dog is renamed 'Sakr-el Bahr' (sea hawk) and his simpering heroine undergoes slavery and sexual exploitation prior to her rescue. This orientalizing of the Elizabethan corresponds to the twenties' cult of orientalist fiction and the early orientalist film, apotheosizing in *The Sheik*, which I studied elsewhere.[64] The two genres addressed female audiences and featured exotic male stars like Rudolph Valentino, whose gender was rather ambiguous.

By the late 1930s, the genre was past its vogue and the maritime and imperialist feature film became 'masculinized' in the sense that it featured 'manly' men in the roles of colonizers. *The Sea Hawk* was revamped, with a new and vigorous territory of the new world—the Americas—substituting for the 'older' and corrupt Mediterranean 'East', and a manly and patriotic pirate replacing the ambiguously located Tudor hero and renamed Geoffrey Thorpe. This transfer of the Tudor 'empire' to the Americas matched the cooperation between Hollywood and Britain, the Anglo-American composition of audiences, and the possible military cooperation in the face of Nazi danger. As already mentioned, the film continuously harps on patriotism and the need for preparedness for war. To 'seal off' the revamping of the Tudor swashbuckling melodrama, Warner cast Flynn, one of Hollywood's most physical (and, to critics and audiences alike, least sophisticated) actors in the title role.

Significantly, British audiences preferred the Laughton and Howard interpretation of Englishness and masculinity to that presented in the *Sea Hawk* and later in *Elizabeth and Essex*. Both stars topped the popularity polls of British male actors. The preference for them, especially among women viewers, parallels the contemporaneous popularity of female stars who crossed the borderlines of gender either in roles of the modern woman, or in parts which featured strong historical women in authority. The early modern monarchs are *the* case in point.

The Tudor cycle, the first sequence of historical films, was and remains a definable body within the mass-produced historical culture. Interpretable as ultra-patriotic and conservative, these films actually complicate definitions of the nation and of social and gender hierarchies. Their complexities owe as much to the multinational economy of their production and the globalization of the

63 On the novel and the film versions see Sidney Rosenzweig, *Casablanca and Other Major Films by Michael Curtiz* (Studies in Cinema, 14; Ann Arbor, 1982).

64 Melman, *Women and the Popular Imagination in the Twenties*, 89–107.

popular historical artefact as to the new brokers of history, particularly the stars participating in the interpretation and representations of the past and practically redefining the role of the popular historian. The films, especially those representing female monarchs, but also *Henry VIII*, pioneered new approaches to the past, pre-dating by several decades interest within the historical profession in such topics as sexuality and gender, and the study of everyday life. The insight these films offer into the representational character of the Tudor monarchy, indeed all early modern monarchy, was also ahead in time of that in mainstream histories. However, more important than locating the films in a history of Tudor history is placing them in the rich grid of historical writing and spectacle of their time on and off screen and, more broadly, in inter-war culture. The films recycled available images and modes of representations of majesty, the monarchy, and the Empire, filched from historical novels, the struggling history profession, and experimental anti-Whig biography, and adapted and processed through the agency of the stars. Processing involved not simply adaptation from 'traditional' history, the theatre, literature, painting, and fashion, but also change, achieved through novel and sometimes radical interpretations of gender and the body. Utilizing film's most iconic, apparently ahistorical, and most objectified and fetishized 'commodity'—the star's body—the stars-cum-historians circulated a variety of novel images. They thus complicated both definitions of gender and the nation. As the following repartee on board the queen's flagship *Albatross* in the *Sea Hawk* makes plain:

Third Sailor: 'I hear her Majesty's the only woman he could talk to without his knees buckling.'
Fourth Sailor: 'That's different. Man to Man I calls it.'[65]

The original use of 'buckling', the term describing the genre of war heroism and masculinity, to describe the pirate's fear (buckling knees) was not to be lost on contemporaries. The 'historical' allure of such high-seas melodrama, or of the domestic plots of the film, was not only in their distinctiveness and remoteness but also in the timeliness of their appearance and the multiple possibilities they offered to relate the exoticism of time and place to the present. Most important, the films lent the monarchy a historical role, endowing it, rather than the parliamentary system or constitutional freedoms, with agency and power while at the same time depicting the monarchs as private and domestic persons. The films, to paraphrase Laughton, popularized and democratized the monarchy at the same time that they diffused its traditional aura, modernizing, as it were, its magic and appeal and making it seem relevant in and for a mass culture. Like the other mass media, the celluloid histories added enchantment to the age of modernity, an enchantment that could be reconciled with urbanism, democratization, and mass consumption. The transparent body of the early modern

[65] Transcribed from the original version.

monarch embodied in that of the modern and iconic star celebrity may be seen as the equivalent of the exposed life of his or her twentieth-century analogues: royals and their families. In this sense the vision of history complemented—rather than reflected—the centring of the monarchy in British popular culture of the inter-war era, both re-creating a monarchy fit for mass democracy.

PART IV

HISTORY AND GLAMOUR: THE FRENCH REVOLUTION AND MODERN LIVING, 1900–1940

8

The Revolution, Aristocrats, and the People: The Returns of the Scarlet Pimpernel, 1900–1935

REVERSALS

The development of popular histories of the monarchy as histories for a mass democracy corresponds to a class shift in the subject matter of the culture of history. The decades which saw the making of Elizabeth and the Elizabethans into modernized icons of imperial power, popular consent, and freedoms also witnessed the construction, in mass-produced histories, of the traditional landed elite as an agent of change and modernity. This shift of class emphasis and agency is typical of the third revival of interest in the French Revolution, which occurred a little after, but roughly coincided with, the discovery of the Elizabethans in the late nineteenth century and the early twentieth century.

By its centenary in 1889 the Revolution no longer represented a political and social threat. It had ceased to generate the mixture of awe and horror that it had had during the first half of the nineteenth century, or the urban anxiety about disorder and anarchy that had thrived during the century's middle decades. Late nineteenth-century histories of the Revolution had nothing of Carlyle's awe of the volcanic force of revolutionary crowds or of Dickens's agoraphobia and horror of the guillotine.[1] By the end of the century the Revolution also ceased to be an organizing metaphor for contemporary politics. One illustration of the change in the Revolution's impact is Lady Bracknell's indignant mention of it in Oscar Wilde's *The Importance of Being Earnest* (1895): 'To be born, at any rate bred, in a handbag, whether it had handles on or not, seems to me to display a contempt for the ordinary decencies of family life that reminds me of the French Revolution. And I presume you know what that unfortunate movement led to?'[2] To reduce the grand, world-historical event to a size that may fit in a handbag is to make this event the object of ridicule and also relate it to style. Significantly

[1] I thank David Trotter for letting me read unpublished material on agoraphobia in Dickens's work.

[2] Oscar Wilde, 'The Importance of Being Earnest', *Complete Works* (London; repr. 1969), 334.

and in a manner that overshadows most of this chapter, Lady Bracknell's sizing down of the Revolution takes place in a lashing comedy about Society, elites, glamour, manners, and morals.

The depoliticization of popular imaginings of the Revolution, the shift in their class emphasis, and the turn from history as the generator of horror (discussed in Chs. 1–5) to history as a lifestyle, all these coincided with the shifts in attitudes to the Tudors, and to royals, mapped in the previous two chapters. Like these shifts, the change discussed here corresponds to the particular juncture of changes in Britain's position in the world and vis-à-vis its rivals on the Continent and to the democratization of politics and of access to culture. I have noted these changes earlier.[3] Here it suffices to relate the renewed popular interest in France to the broader, slow, and consistent rapprochement between Britain and the Third Republic, which was initially propelled by the unification of Germany and its rise to a world power. This rapprochement matured during the 1880s and 1890s with the relatively successful defusing of Anglo–French colonial rivalries and came of age in 1904 with the signing of the Entente Cordiale. In the 1900s Republican and democratic France, heir to the First, Jacobin, Republic and the Revolution, could not comfortably be configured as England's 'other', or even as an adversary, certainly not before and during the Great War and the perturbed period of reconstruction that was to follow it. The French Republic graduated to Britain's chief political and ideological ally and at the same time France itself became more easily reachable to a widening cross-class public, owing to cheap travel and the rise of mass tourism. The Paris Exposition Universelle, celebrating the Revolution's centenary, and the following world exhibitions between 1900 and 1925 attracted large British audiences, and these events, like French politics, were consistently covered by the popular British press. The Great War created a different sort of travel, bringing at least five million soldiers and several hundred thousands members of the auxiliary forces and civilians across the Channel, acquainting them with fragments of French life and landscapes. The transfer, during the war, of the wax figures of Jacobin leaders from Madame Tussaud's Chamber of Horrors to the Great Hall registers the growing familiarity with contemporary France and the broader shift in views about and attitudes to the Revolution and republicanism.

But political and cultural rapprochement and the concomitant depoliticization of the Revolution by no means diminished its continuing wide appeal to diverse groups and classes of consumers. 1889 witnessed a phenomenal revival of the popular industry of Revolution histories, far surpassing in quantity and scope the earlier revivals, and coinciding with a flourishing of professional research. The latter, starting in a trickle of publications before the centenary, culminated in 1904 in the *Cambridge History of the French Revolution*. The Revolution came into its own as the subject of professional academic study, which, at the same

[3] See Ch. 6, pp. 187–8.

time, benefited an understanding of aspects of modernity and democracy. As Lord Acton, that doyen of modern history as an academic field and a chief instigator of professional study of the Revolution, put it: '[it was] an immense onward step in the march of mankind, a thing to which we are today indebted for some of the political benefits of history'.[4] The crop of professional histories literally drowned in a cascade of popular biographies churned out by 'public historians' such as Hilaire Belloc, translations of autobiographies and memoirs of revolutionaries, and, most astounding in volume, historical novels exploring every imaginable angle of the revolutionary period between 1789 and Napoleon's downfall and the subsequent convening of the Congress of Vienna in 1815.[5] This literary explosion coincided with the popularity of fiction featuring the Regency era, which had hitherto generated limited interest.

The explosion, which peaked between 1900 and the late 1930s, was not simply one of volume, but, as noted above, registered the shift in the class emphasis manifest in the move away from the 'people' towards elites (and royals) as the subjects of popular historical curiosity and the historical imagination. Reproductions of the Revolution turned away from the lower urban classes and the middle classes as the carriers of historical action and agency towards the landed interest and what David Cannadine has usefully called 'the landed establishment'.[6] Whereas Carlyle's agents of change were the sans-culottes (and, by implication, their British counterparts), and Dickens's London's plebeian crowds, and Paris's revolutionaries were emblazoned in the *tricoteuses*, and the middle and lower-middle classes, the third revival of the Revolution turned on the resurrection and rehabilitation of the traditional landed aristocracy. The best-selling, most popular, and most enduring historical image of the last decade of the nineteenth century and the early twentieth century was the aristocratic Englishman, avenging a 'true' aristocratic lifestyle identified with the *ancien régime*'s traditional elites by rescuing its most emblematic representatives: the old, hierarchic French aristocracy.

The invention of this apparently anachronistic and even atavistic image and a host of popular stereotypes attached to it may be confidently attributed to one cultural broker, the exiled Hungarian aristocrat who became a naturalized Briton, Baroness Emmuska Orczy, and traced from her play *The Scarlet Pimpernel*, premiered in 1903 and published as a novel in 1905. The Pimpernel was to become the prototypical 'masked avenger', an aristocratic swashbuckling hero, capable of taking on multiple social identities. His apparent cultural

[4] Cited in *The Nation*, 92 (30 Mar. 1911), 318. See also his *Lectures on the French Revolution*, published posthumously (London, 1910).

[5] Belloc published *Danton* in 1899, *Robespierre: A Study* in 1901, *Marie Antoinette* in 1909, and *The French Revolution* in 1911. For a consideration of his attitudes to the Revolution see Feske, *From Belloc to Churchill*, 40–5.

[6] David Cannadine, *The Decline and Fall of the British Aristocracy* (New Haven, 1990), Preface, p. xii.

atavism and the seemingly uncomplicated anachronistic and conservative character of the vision of the past he represents actually stood for and were relatable to modern lifestyles and pace. For the Pimpernel became the model for the twentieth-century Superman: some of the most successful archetypes of this figure in inter-war mass culture were emulations of him. These included Scaramouche, avenger of the victims of Napoleon, created in 1921 by another naturalized Briton, Rafael Sabatini; the Pimpernel's Latin-American version Zorro, created in the USA in 1919 by Johnston McCulley in his serial *The Curse of Capistrano*, later to appear in book form as *The Mask of Zorro* (1920), and Superman himself. Put succinctly, between the turn of the century and the 1930s, the French Revolution provided a background and an arsenal of mass-consumed images which welded together notions of the past adapted to modern notions of glamorous high-speed adventure, style, and concepts of nationalism and gender. The prototypical superman was an Englishman, embodying style and glamour, traditional leadership, nationalism, a newly defined masculinity, and a cult of physical adventure and risk.

The rise of the popular image of the superhero, and the array of images of modernity attached to it, corresponds with the wide spread, in political and social thought, of elitist notions of the superman, a physically or spiritually 'higher type', destined for leadership in a mass democracy. As Lucy Delap and Dan Stone have recently noted, the Edwardian era and inter-war period saw the spreading of a preoccupation, an obsession even, with such 'supermen' (and superwomen), not only within the political margins of the Right representing 'extreme Englishness' (Stone's term) or diehard Toryism, but across politics. Superheroes tantalized social democratic progressives, feminists, and aesthetes of all political hues.[7] The immanent individual possessed of social privilege and exceptional talent or an impressive physique became a liberal emblem of national leadership, or he (for, notwithstanding female superheroes, this was an emblem of masculinity) was seen as a vehicle for social change or a more general process of human evolution.[8] Put differently, the superhero, at the centre of the early twentieth-century culture of history, was part and parcel of the culture of democracy.

The centring of the traditional aristocracy in a historical genre, indeed in a popular culture of history, where it had previously played a marginal and generally negative role, is significant because it took place at precisely the time of the democratization of the electorate and of politics, the emergence of socialism and trade unionism, and the boom of the mass media. More significant even, the rise of the 'historic' aristocrat to a cult figure corresponds to a major change in modern British history, the 'decline and fall' of the aristocracy as an economic,

[7] Dan Stone, *Breeding Superman: Nietzsche, Race and Eugenics in Edwardian and Interwar Britain* (Liverpool, 2002), and Lucy Delap, 'The Superwoman: Theories of Gender and Genius in Edwardian Britain', *Historical Journal*, 47, no. 1 (March 2004), 101–26.

[8] On the female version and suffragist feminism see Delap.

political, and, later, social class, and the transformation in its role as carrier of culture and a way of life.[9] We cannot overstate this fascinating reversal in popular lore and images. The aristocracy did not merely figure, or figure prominently, in mass-produced historical narratives in print and on stage and, from the 1920s, on screen; it became essential for defining the past, at a time when this aristocracy was moving in an almost symmetrically opposite direction in 'real' life and politics. As is well known, from the 1880s until the outbreak of the Second World War, the landed interest was becoming economically vulnerable (due to the globalization of the economy and the assault of government on land), its political power was inexorably being eroded, and with it, the traditional social weight, social confidence, and social spaciousness once possessed by the landed establishment diminished. *The Scarlet Pimpernel* appeared five years before the demolition of the power of the House of Lords and six years before the 'People's Budget', which hit landed income. And the palmiest years of the genre in literature and on film coincided with the continuing reduction of this income by accelerating death duties and super tax, and increased exactions on 'old' traditional wealth and confidence.[10]

How and why did the new cult of the aristocratic superman come about at this junction? How and why did the culture of history come to present an apparent reversal of the politics and culture of class during the beginning of the twentieth century, and what does it tell us about culture at large? How indeed do we approach what may seem to be an inverse relation between images and representation and currents in a culture and society? Finally, how did popular history become the site of glamour and adventure and a source about and for style? These are the inextricable issues which this chapter addresses. But first we must measure the new phenomenon and draw the map of the new genre, sizing up its novelties alongside continuities in narratives and images of the Revolution.

REVOLUTION AND THE ARISTOCRACY: A MAP

The thriving new genre and the wider bonanza of Revolution narratives have been contemptuously denigrated by students of popular literature and virtually ignored by historians. There is not a single monograph on it and the few references that we do have are mainly taxonomic. Yet contemporaries, most notably lexicographers and bibliographers of popular historical fiction, were quick to note the phenomenal popularity of all forms of fiction to do with the Revolution. The wealth of Revolution fiction is recorded in the first two English bibliographies of historical fiction by Jonathan Nield (1902, 1911, and 1927)

[9] Delap, 'The Superwoman'; Cannadine, *Aspects of Aristocracy: Grandeur and Decline in Modern Britain* (New Haven, 1994); McKibbin, *Classes and Cultures*, 1–44.

[10] Cannadine, *Decline and Fall*, 88–138.

and Ernest A. Baker (1914), probably the first bibliographies of a popular genre. Their appearance itself testifies to the renewed and unprecedented popularity of the historical novel at the turn of the century.[11] The sheer quantity of novels in English and of translations from French and German necessitated not only listing and citation of prices, but also classification, according to subgenres, periods, settings, and the geography of the events described. Of the 254 novels Baker lists in the 1914 edition, some 141 are on the extended era of the Revolution (1789–1814) in France, and 113 on its impact on Britain and Ireland (there is an entire section on the 1798 rebellion of the United Irishmen), and these figures do not include many more novels on Spain and Portugal, mainly during the period of the Peninsular Wars, or novels set in central Europe.[12]

Certain themes were not novel and present continuities with the older, mid-century Revolution novel and, more broadly, with the sensationalist, cross-culture Revolution lore, with the Terror and guillotine as its central subjects and metaphors (see Chs. 1–3). Additionally, there is a great curiosity about the military aspects of the Revolutionary Wars, most notably about maritime battles, which proved a gold mine for authors specializing in juvenile fiction. Examples abound and include Gordon Stables's tale of the Battle of the Nile, *As We Sweep through the Deep* (1893), G. A. Henty, *At Aboukir and Acre* (1899), H. G. Hutchinson, *A Friend of Nelson* (1902), and Poynter H. May, *Scarlet Town: A Conceit*, published in 1894 by the Society for the Propagation of Christian Knowledge (SPCK). Of course, the maritime revolutionary tale had a precursor in early nineteenth-century panoramic spectacle, genre painting, and drawing, but came into its own after the 1870s with the rise of popular interest in the new Empire. The plethora of narratives of a threatened French invasion, hindered by a combined British naval and civilian effort, also reflects the periodic invasion scares which punctuated the period directly leading to the outbreak of the First World War and responding to the international (and mainly British–German) naval competition. Examples include R. D. Blackmore (known for his regional historical novel *Lorna Doon*), *Springhaven: A Tale of the Great War* (1887), and Avery Harold, *In Days of Danger: A Tale of the Threatened French Invasion* (1909).

Novels featuring aristocrats, the dispersed court at Versailles, and émigrés are legion and form an easily definable category of romance cum adventure. Molly Elliot Seawell, *The Last Duchess of Belgrade* (1908) is a lugubrious tale of imprisonment in the Temple Prison and the noble death of the scions of an

[11] Jonathan Nield, *A Guide to Historical Novels and Tales* (New York, 1902; repr. 1929); Ernest A. Baker, *History in Fiction*, 2 vols. (London and New York, 1907); and *A Guide to Historical Fiction* (New York, 1914; repr. 1969). For a more recent classification see Peter Keating, *The Haunted Study: A Social History of the English Novel 1875–1914* (London, repr. 1991), 351–66. Keating, however, does not include Revolution novels.

[12] Baker, *A Guide to Historical Fiction*. I use the 1969 edition and also rely on Nield's 1929 edition, pp. 179–221, 369–87.

aristocratic house. Stanley Weyman, *The Red Cockade* (1895) narrates the misfortunes and downfall of a Republican aristocrat, and P. A. Sheehan, *The Queen's Fillet* (1911) represents the Thermidorian backlash following the fall of Robespierre and the Jacobin Republic. A. H. Biggs, *The Marquis' Heir*; Mary C. Rowsell, *Monsieur de Paris*; and Mrs E. M. Field, *Little Count Paul: A Story of Troublesome Times* (1895), all featuring the doom of aristocrats, catered for the expanding juvenile market. Quite a few novelists tapped into the theme of Royalist landed revolts against the centralist Jacobin Republic to portray an aristocratic–plebeian alliance targeting the metropolitan middle and lower classes. Such an alliance could be taken to have duplicated the Tory ideal of a bond between the landed classes and the rural and urban lower classes. The war at the Vendée in Brittany in 1793 came to be seen as the epitome of such an alliance. Discovered in 1850 by Anthony Trollope in his failed novel *La Vendée*, dropped and taken up again by the novelists of the 1890s, the *petite guerre* of the Vendée and its aristocratic leadership were embraced by writers for adolescent readers, notably G. A. Henty (*No Surrender! A Tale of the Rising in La Vendée*, 1899); Hubert Rendel (*The King's Cockade*, 1903), D. K. Broster and G. W. Taylor, *Chantemerle: A Romance of the Vendean War* (1911); H. C. Bailey, *Storm and Treasure* (1910); and F. S. Brereton, *Foes of the Red Cockade* (1903). Victor Hugo's 1872 account of the rebellion, *Quatrevingt-treize*, inspired a number of translations and adaptations, and translations of French and German novels on the court and nobility during the *ancien régime* (by Alexandre Dumas and the popular German historical novelist specializing in fiction on aristocracies, Louise Mulbach) had a good run. The royalist rebellion's status as a domestically consumable story, easy to digest by both adults and juveniles and thus constituting 'family reading', was affirmed when the SPCK began to bring out novels on it like *Duchenier, or The Revolt of La Vendée* by J. M. Neale (1905).

To be sure, the Revolution's assault on privilege, the downfall of the monarchy, and the plight of the aristocracy had all been amply covered before the end of the nineteenth century in the historical novel, in historiography, and in painting, not to mention theatrical realizations, panoramas, and popular shows like the Tussaud collection. But characteristically in the earlier fiction and spectacle, the French aristocracy of the *ancien régime* and its British counterpart had been constantly vilified. One has only to recall Dickens's account of the Marquis St Évremonde in *A Tale of Two Cities*. To middle-class early and mid-Victorian novelists and their readers, these aristocrats and their English analogues were as corrupt and pernicious as their plebeian persecutors. Recall Dickens's and Thackeray's popular depiction of aristocratic renegades and louts. Mainstream historians too regarded the French nobility and the world of privilege as a major cause for the outbreak of the Revolution. Where the French royal family and aristocracy had been favourably depicted in hagiographies and in Madame Tussaud's shrine to the *ancien régime*, they had been cast as victims.[13] And either as victims or as villains, the nobility had been marginalized. One important innovation of the new popular histories was their removal to the centre of action and the plot: aristocrats 'move' the narrative, that is history. Another innovation is the introduction of the English aristocrat as, on the one hand, a mediator of style and the good life and, on the other, as a superhero whose adventures are the main feature of historical romance. The battle to preserve a kind of leadership based on privilege, hierarchy, and a distinct lifestyle is presented as a defence of English liberties. Put differently, the defence of liberty is pitted against the excesses of popular democracy. No less important than his agenda and deeds is the formulaic hero's masked identity: his swift change from a man of fashion, a Georgian or Regency 'beau' and dandy, to a redeemer of lives, limbs, and good causes.

The formula was hit upon in 1900 by Emma Magdalena Rosalia Maria Josefa Barbara Orczy, known to her millions-strong audience as Baroness Orczy, and slowly worked by her into *The Scarlet Pimpernel.* Rejected by a dozen publishers (including Macmillan, Murray, and Hutchinson), she adapted the novel to the stage, with the collaboration of her husband Montague Barstow, a fairly well-known illustrator and watercolourist. It was first staged by Fred Terry and Julia Neilson, one of the theatre's leading romantic couples (on stage and off it), in Nottingham; it toured the provinces, then, revamped, finally made its way to a London West End debut almost two years later, together with the novel, which was finally published by Greening, owners of *Picture Play* and with an interest in theatrical materials. Killed by the critics, the play was nevertheless a smash hit. It had a run of over 2,000 performances by the mid-thirties and was constantly revived. The novel instantaneously became a publishing phenomenon.[14] Standard six-shilling editions and cheap editions were followed by American editions and translations into twelve languages (including one into Russian made after the outbreak of the October Revolution) and a number of Indian dialects. French, Italian, Spanish, and German adaptations for the stage followed rapidly, with the French version bowdlerizing the original and substituting a bourgeois hero for the aristocrat. Stage versions were marketed to the Empire and enjoyed a good run in South Africa, before and after the First World War, and in the Far East. Matheson Lang's version, performed by him in all major South African towns (the rights for which had been bought from Orczy) and by subcontractors in small towns, proved a steady success.[15] The baroness, with remarkable business acumen, responded to popular demand and produced a sequel of ten

[13] See my detailed discussion in Ch. 1.

[14] The history of the publishing and dramatization of the *Pimpernel* is detailed in Orczy's autobiography, Baroness Orczy, *The Links in the Chain of Life* (London, 1941), 101–7, and in *The Bookman, A Magazine of Literature and Life*, October 1913, pp. 102–4.

[15] On the South African and other Imperial rights see the correspondence of Baroness Orczy and Matheson Lang via the Society of Authors, British Library, Add. MS 56767, fos. 134–57. See especially Matheson Lang to Thring, 29 Sept. 1917, fos. 147–8.

Pimpernel novels and two collections of short stories, appearing in three sequences. *I Will Repay* and *The Elusive Pimpernel* appeared in 1906 and 1908 respectively and *Eldorado* saw publication in 1913. After an interim of about a decade appeared *The League of the Scarlet Pimpernel* (1919), *The First Sir Percy* (1920), *Pimpernel and Rosemary* (1924), and *Sir Percy Hits Back: An Adventure of the Scarlet Pimpernel* (1927). The third crop of Pimpernel adventures overlaps the 1930s vogue for films on high society and the aristocracy with the film adaptation of Orczy's own original, an overlap that presents an accretion of production of historical genres and artefacts and their chain consumption, which were such staples of the culture of history. *A Child of the Revolution, The Way of the Scarlet Pimpernel*, and *A Spy of Napoleon* saw publication in 1932, 1933, and 1934, and a related, fictive, biography of the Duchess de Barry, *The Turbulent Duchess*, followed in 1935. *Mam'zelle Guillotine* brought up the rear in 1940.

The Pimpernel sequel offered readers an endless variety of the formula crystallized between 1903 and 1905. Sir Percy Blakeney Bt., a super-rich and useless fop, the husband of an ardent French Republican with Jacobin leanings (she is, it transpires in the 1922 sequence, *Triumph of the Scarlet Pimpernel*, the cousin of St Just, the Jacobin leader with a near Communist agenda and Robespierre's right hand), leads a double life as the 'Scarlet Pimpernel'. In this life, which becomes the stuff of nationalist legend in his home country and a rabid Anglophobe myth in France, he leads the clandestine 'League of the Scarlet Pimpernel', an organization of young aristocrats set on rescuing the lives of their counterparts during the reign of Terror. By 1922, the Pimpernel and his acolytes had become such familiar characters that *Punch*, which stated that Orczy no longer invented 'any very thrilling new situations or introduced us to any very lifelike new acquaintances', acknowledged readers' comfort at finding out that these 'old friends are there' for them.[16] The phenomenal appeal of the aristocrat adventurer-trickster is demonstrated by the success of the two subgenres of historical novels featuring an aristocrat posing as a useless fop to conceal his 'real' life as a masked avenger: the Scaramouche and Zorro tales. In the former, inaugurated in Sabatini's eponymous novel (1922), Andre-Louis Moreau is not an aristocrat by birth, but he is (metaphorically) 'fathered' by an aristocrat, the Marquis de Gravillac. An espouser of some revolutionary ideas and at one time a deputy of the People at the National Assembly, he is in fact an avenger of 'real' aristocratic and chivalric values under his disguise as Scaramouche, the master manipulator of commedia dell'arte, played by Moreau as a popular actor. Pimpernel's other successor, Zorro, constituting another deviation from Orczy's historical model, is an Americanized and republican version of the aristocratic hero. Transferred by McCulley from France and England to Spanish California, Zorro made an American Pimpernel, more suited to a republican

[16] *Punch*, 4 Oct. 1922, p. 336.

US readership: by day a phlegmatic and useless Latin dandy, Don Diego Vegas, by night the black-masked 'Zorro', the Fox, a social anarchist, righter of wrongs.[17]

Orczy's blueprint and its emulations were given new lease of life by film. Even more than the writers of Tudor and Elizabethan best-sellers, whose fiction was adapted to the screen, the three churners of aristocratic romance were aware of the new medium and produced high-velocity action adapted to modern readers/spectators and the generic modern form of telling about the past. Orczy especially, with her knowledge of the stage, appreciated the power of film as a mediator of history. Since non-fiction rights on the original were held by Terry, early film adaptations drew on sequels. *The Elusive Pimpernel*, a Stoll Pictures production directed by Maurice Elvey, who also played Sir Percy, was released in 1919, and *I Will Repay*—produced by Henry Kolker—in 1923. The best of this early batch, *The Triumph of the Scarlet Pimpernel*, starring Matheson Lang and directed by T. Hayes Hunter, was released in 1928. But undoubtedly the definitive, most popular, and most enduring film version was London Films' Alexander Korda's production, with Leslie Howard as its millions of spectators' ultimate Sir Percy. Follow-ups included BFP's *The Return of the Scarlet Pimpernel*, produced in 1938 with Barry K. Barnes in the title role. A colour version of the original, directed in 1950 by Michael Powell and starring David Niven in the title role, proved a disaster. Both the 1905 novel and its sequel are still 'steady sellers', inspiring film, television, and theatre productions (lately music-hall productions).

URBAN ARISTOCRATS

We should be wary of bracketing the emerging of the new kind of hero and Revolution narrative simply as traditionalist and backward looking: both complicate and expand notions about the landed elite and aristocratic living and action by detaching (though not dissociating) the former from land and the countryside. The Pimpernel sequence does not resurrect a bygone rural and agricultural world and nostalgia for the countryside as the resort of 'true' life. Unlike its contemporary novels on the *Vendée*, the sequence and its hero are located mainly in urban settings and move between Paris and London, thus apparently conforming to the mid-nineteenth-century structure of *A Tale of Two Cities*. But whereas in the older narrative and its broader contemporary lore on the Revolution the two capitals are monster metropolises ruled by the gallows or the guillotine and by crowds, the London evoked by Orczy in her books, and even more forcefully in their film adaptations, is an aristocratic city, a capital of style and urbanity. And urbanity stands for the refinement and achievements of

[17] The American and Latin American imitations are discussed by Jeffrey Richards, *Swordsmen of the Screen from Douglas Fairbanks to Michael York* (London, 1977), 2–5; 162–84.

a ruling elite. The aristocratic characters are 'urbanized' in another sense: it is cities and urban centres which they inhabit and whose rhythm they embody, not the countryside.

True, the word 'pimpernel' itself, designating an uncultivated, unattended flower, found 'on waysides' and used both as the hero's sobriquet and his trademark, evokes a countryside which is 'natural' as well as native and simple. Shrewdly, the little flower is constantly referred to in the novel, by the English and the French characters. And this evocation was constantly played upon in the advertisements for the play, the novel, and the film. Early cloth editions had a drawing of the flower on their front cover. Souvenirs of theatre performances, such as that for the 100th London performance of 3 April 1905, featured four pimpernels, three in full bloom, against a pink background of a field with a hint of a sunset. And the play's star, Julia Neilson, in the role of Marguerite, Sir Percy's wife, donned embroidered frocks with scarlet pimpernels for pattern, and had this rural image mass produced on postcards. Occasionally too there are references to country cottages (Blakeney's hideout near Dover, complete with a creeper and a cottage garden with daffodils) and road inns and pubs. But these references to the countryside and rural landscapes are consciously non-specified, perfunctorily described, and lack details that would give the 'heart of England' atmosphere credence. As Orczy herself plainly admits in her autobiography, the blankness of rural England served as a shield against topographical errors and historical inaccuracy, to avoid the criticism of an astute and informed readership.[18]

These rural references notwithstanding, the novel and the early film versions are strangely devoid of any detailed description of the country and symbolic depictions of the traditional ancestral country house, which had played such a prominent role in literary and visual materials throughout the nineteenth and early twentieth centuries. In this sense *Pimpernel*, like *A Tale of Two Cities* and its many realizations, is an *urban* narrative, representing an urban interpretation of the Revolution.[19] Detail and attention are limited to sites and abodes of Society in the centre of the metropolis or near it, the latter completely suburbanized by the 1900s (Richmond, which accommodates Blakeney's abode, for example), or to urban centres of fashion and high life such as Bath. Indeed some of the novels have a distinct air of, and must have been read as, a Georgian revival. Thus *The Scarlet Pimpernel* includes tableaux of Covent Garden where late eighteenth-century Society meets, hobnobs, gossips, and negotiates during a performance of Gluck's *Orphée*—a distinctly *ancien régime* Frenchified *opera seria* (and Gluck had been Marie-Antoinette's protégé) on a classical subject of the kind favoured by eighteenth-century classicists and academicians. Next, readers are treated to

18 Baroness Orczy, *The Links in the Chain of Life*, ch. 14, '1918'.

19 For detailed studies of *fin de siècle* and early 20th-c. depictions of 'green England' or 'deep country' see Mandler, *The Fall and Rise of the Stately Home*; Matless, *Landscape and Englishness*; and Colls, *Identity of England*, Introduction, n. 10.

four chapters which take place at a ball in the town house of the Foreign Secretary, Sir William Grenville. In both settings, the Prince of Wales, politicians of the period, and men and women of fashion make constant appearances. In *Lord Tony's Wife*, the Assembly Rooms in Bath figure as a meeting place, dancing hall, and venue for the Prince's coterie, a bevy of social climbers, émigrés, and French spies. Most important, the identity of the masked hero himself is urban. Sir Percy Blakeney is 'the richest man in England' and it is implied that his wealth welds together land and industry (he owns coal mines, among other things). Wealth, combined with breeding, shines in London and Bath, where he is 'so prominent a figure in fashionable English society'. He is the highest authority on fashion, etiquette, style, and gambling. Wearing his 'Society' mask, he cuts a burlesque figure of a fop, whose inanity and apparent emptiness, highlighted by an exaggerated and ritualized elegance, successfully camouflage his sterling character, audacity, and natural leadership. His first and fullest description is to be found in the chapter in the *Scarlet Pimpernel* emblematically titled 'an exquisite of 1792' and is worth quoting:

> Physically, Sir Percy Blakeney was undeniably handsome—always excepting the lazy, bored look which was habitual to him. He was always irreproachably dressed, and wore the exaggerated 'Incroyable' fashions, which had just crept from Paris to England, with the perfect good taste innate in an English gentleman. On this special day in September, in spite of the long journey by coach, in spite of rain and mud, his coat set irreproachably across his fine shoulders, his hands looked almost effeminately white, as they emerged through the billowy frills of his Mechlin lace: the extravagantly short-waisted satin coat, wide-lapelled waistcoat, and tightfitting [*sic*] striped breeches, set off his massive figure to perfection, and in repose one might have admired so fine a specimen of English manhood, until the foppish ways, the affected movements, the perpetual inane laugh, brought one's admiration of Sir Percy Blakeney's to an abrupt end.[20]

Sir Percy's sartorial extravagances define him as a later Georgian dandy, or beau, an urban icon. And of course dandyism itself, which reached its heyday between the late 1780s and the 1820s, was a distinctly metropolitan cult, characterizing Regency London. Orczy herself was interested in dandyism, researched its history, and in 1929–30 would embark on a series of public lectures on seventeenth- and eighteenth-century beaux and dandies (delivered quite appropriately in Monte Carlo). She ostensibly denied having modelled Sir Percy on a specific historical figure and his apparent fictitiousness made possible a rather promiscuous pastiche she employed for the part of the aristocratic fop, mixing the traits and tags of different sorts of dandies: the Regency Beau, the sporty urban rambling 'Corinthian' (immortalized by Pierce Egan), the Buck, and the foppish and effeminate 'macaroni', imitating extravagant French fashions. This mix served its purpose because it allowed Orczy and her readers to treat aristocratic style humorously and even with ridicule,

[20] Baroness Orczy, *The Scarlet Pimpernel* (London, 1905; repr. 1974), 42.

yet at the same time positively and appreciatively. Early readers of the novels with even rudimentary knowledge on the Regency era could find in it abundant reference to George Bryan (Beau) Brummell, the icon of Regency society, for about fifteen years London's ruler in matters of style, an idol of the Prince of Wales, a wit, and an urban spectacle. Numerous remarks on Sir Percy's cravat and his mode of tying it, his eyeglass and repartees directly refer to Brummell's elaborate toilette and his methods of tying cravats—a daily spectacle at which court members and members of the 'ton' in London had been present:[21] 'All done in the tying of a cravat', Sir Percy had declared to his clique of admirers.[22] And in *Lord Tony's Wife*: "t'was the fault of my cravat'. 'Your cravat'? 'Aye indeed! I spent the whole of the day in perfecting my new method of tying a butterfly bow, so as to give the neck an appearance of utmost elegance with a minimum of discomfort.'[23]

Additional information on the 'new fashions of this memorable year of 1793' is imparted to readers.[24] Brummell's penchant for repartee, double meanings, and innuendo, captured in the dialogues on cravats (prefiguring the other, ominous 'tying' of neck, on the guillotine) is writ large in phrases and doggerel which became the first novel's (and later the 1935 film's) trademark and best-loved lines:

> We seek him here, we seek him there,
> Those Frenchies seek him everywhere.
> Is he in heaven? – is he in hell?
> That demmed, elusive Pimpernel

> Sir Percy's *bon mot* had gone the round of the brilliant reception-rooms. The Prince was enchanted. He vowed that life without Blakeney would be a dreary desert. Then, taking him by his arm, had led him to the card-room, and engaged him in a long game of hazard.[25]

The introduction of a wide readership, and later film spectators, to an aristocratic Georgian England, conceived and represented as urban, exclusive, and cultured, certainly differs from evocations of eighteenth-century England in previous popular historical novels. Ainsworth, as demonstrated in Chapter 5, invoked Georgian low life, both on the highway and in the metropolis's labyrinth. Polite society and the Georgian world of 'ton' touches on the narrative and image of the past in *Jack Sheppard* only marginally, regarding topics such as high-class prostitution, gambling, and a corrupt legal system. The world of the Pimpernel is completely cut off from low life in England. Crime is associated

[21] Brummell and dandyism as an urban, metropolitan phenomenon are discussed in Venetia Murray, *High Society: A Social History in the Regency Period, 1788–1830* (London, 1999), 24–47.

[22] Baroness Orczy, *Scarlet Pimpernel*, 92.

[23] Baroness Orczy, *Lord Tony's Wife: An Adventure of the Scarlet Pimpernel* (1917; Thirsk, 2002), 72.

[24] Ibid. 62–3.

[25] *Scarlet Pimpernel*, 92–3.

with the Revolution 'over there', in democratic, Jacobin France, not 'here' in a friendly and amusing London, or Bath.

Georgianism, as well as the eminence of the aristocratic type, is all the more notable because it probably emanated from popular, mass-produced culture. And the timing of the appearance of the aristocratic beau/avenger is as crucial as the origin of this Georgianism, with its myth of the aristocracy. Cultural historians (notably Peter Mandler), historians of urbanism (Donald Olsen), and students of the film (Sue Harper and Pam Cook) have noted the discovery and rehabilitation of the Georgian era, especially the Regency, during the first half of the twentieth century and located this discovery in the inter-war period (Mandler), or immediately after the Second World War (Cook).[26] 'After the Victorians', admiration of Georgian styles grew apace.[27] Georgianism is conventionally attributed to an elite of specialists, connoisseurs, and aesthetes in the literary world, the world of the arts, architecture, and town planning. The rise of a version of the English past with room in it for positive images of the eighteenth century has been examined in relation to the vogue (dated from the late 1920s) of eighteenth-century furniture, the rehabilitation of Georgian urban architecture, culminating in the publication of John Summerson's *Georgian London* in 1945, efforts to preserve the Georgian countryside and landscape, and finally in the attempt to salvage Georgian country houses. Elite hankering after the eighteenth century was described as either elegiac and backward-looking (in the work of novelists such as Evelyn Waugh) or forward-looking and seeking to weld the preservation of the achievements of this period to a modern lifestyle (as in the writing of Christopher Hussey, from 1933 editor of *Country Life*).[28]

Collecting Regency furniture and bric-a-brac and displaying them were embraced during the inter-war era by 'moderns', most notably by members of the glamorous high-class metropolitan coterie of 'Bright Young People'. Collectors, amateur historians, and other cognoscenti were increasingly attracted to Regency things and fashions. The social worker and amateur historian Maurice Birley, that pillager of historical texts and drawings, devoted an extended part of the twenty-fourth volume of his manuscript 'Illustrations of British History' to Regency fashions, focusing on 'Ladies' dress under the Regency'. His year-by-year survey of changes in 'les modes' adopted in elegant London elaborates on productions of paintings (like Adam Buck's 'skating lovers'; see Fig. 19) and fashion caricatures he pilfered from catalogues and books. In his version the

[26] Mandler, *The Fall and Rise*, 265–310, esp. 278–84; Harper, *Picturing the Past*, 25–8; Cook, *Fashioning the Nation*, 80–119, on the resurrection of late Rococo style and the late 18th c.

[27] A paraphrase on Susan Pedersen and Peter Mandler (eds.), *After the Victorians: Private Conscience and Public Duty in Modern Britain* (London, 1994). On Victorian non-acceptance of Georgian architecture and town planning see Donald Olsen, *The Growth of Victorian London* (Harmondsworth; repr. 1979).

[28] Mandler, *The Fall and Rise*; John Summerson, *Georgian London* (New Haven, repr. 2003); Olsen, *The Growth of Victorian London*, 1–52.

Fig. 19. Regency fashions: 'Skating Couple', by Adam Buck. Birley, 'Illustrations of British History'

post-revolutionary changes in dress marked the move of political power from the French absolutist monarchy to a British elite comprising aristocrats, glamorous personages of the theatre, and fashionable upper-class people: 'Paris continued to be the centre of fashion . . . But no longer were these fashions set by the royal ladies.' Style and elegance became English and their locale London. Thus the adoption, by upper-class women during the Thermidor era and the Consulate, of classical Greek style, diaphanous garments, and elegant 'undress' was not a French fad for the classical era but an English invention, evolving from home-grown fashions and native forms of consumption. Birley's lingering description of elegance more than hints at the open but controlled sensuality of the new aristocratic style which appealed to admirers of the Regency:

> The classic line of Ancient Greece of the fashionable one-piece garment worn at this time was actually evolved from the English chemise. It was naturally longer & wider than the chemise, but it had a . . . draw-string all around the neck and another draw-string . . . by which it would be gathered in to suit the woman's fancy. This was the first costume for several centuries in any way pronunciating the natural feminine form. In course of time the neck-line grew lower while the draw-string under the breast was brought up.[29]

Georgianism, with its accompanying favourable image of an aristocratic eighteenth century, far from being a fad of a coterie of intellectuals, travelled across audiences and appeared quite early in mass-produced fiction, to be later popularized in the film. Indeed this early fiction, avowedly written for unsophisticated readers with no special knowledge of history, or about style, anticipated the

[29] Toynbee Hall Library and Archive, BRC/MBI/IBH, vol. 24, pp. 67–8.

'higher' culture. For every Pimpernel novel, there were several Regency tales, focusing on late Georgian Society, without paying much attention to the French Revolution. Cyrus Brady, *The Adventures of Lady Susan*, with appearances of the Prince of Wales; Eliza Pollard, *A Girl of the Eighteenth Century*; and Emma Marshall, *Up and Down the Pantiles*, featuring Hampstead and Royal Tunbridge Wells and including star entries of personalities like Mrs Piozzi, all exemplify the new trend. Revealingly, all three novels were classified as juvenile literature, a sign that the Georgians became 'safe' and domestic. Regency films circulated the set of images of an urban and modern late eighteenth century, and etched on the popular imagination the notion of history itself as a place of style. Regency films, noted the lowbrow *Picturegoer* on 27 October 1934, served as a 'History Class'. Commenting on the production of *The Iron Duke* and the *Pimpernel*, it informed readers that:

> Practically all the genuine Regency period furniture and bric-a-brac in London seems to have been brought to the studios in plain vans and immense care has been taken to have the various details right. Quite a lot of furniture has also journeyed to Elstree for the *Scarlet Pimpernel*, which also concerns the Regency period. Earnest students of history, one pace forward please! Very good. Now you shall have the special treat of observing the difference in costume, furnishing, manners, and so forth that took place in twenty years of British history when these two films come to the screen.

We now recognize the direction of the circulation of images of a historical period, historical themes, and representations from 'low' culture to 'high'. We saw it in the spreading of horror histories from plebeian sensationalism to genteel and middle-class prison and gallows literature, and the innovative 'social histories' of gender and power constructed in the Tudor films decades before these histories entered historiography narrowly defined. The same dynamics of this 'upward' and sideways movement of images is traceable in the emergence of the aristocrat as both a popular historical hero and the centre of a cult of action and adventure. But such tracing of general modalities in the culture of history is not enough. It is the specificities of the double appeal of the beau and superhero, of history as style and action, as well as what these specificities could have meant and did mean to readers and spectators, that we must clarify.

HISTORY AND THE HISTORICAL HERO AS SIGNIFICATIONS OF MODERNITY: MAKING SENSE OF THE EIGHTEENTH CENTURY

The Regency and Revolution were relatable to a compound of developments largely assumed to make up modernity: the gradual democratization of politics and society, rapid urbanization, and the spread of technologies, not necessarily technologies of production (for the genre barely hints at industrialization), but such technologies as influenced transport and individuals' movement. An urban, densely paced narrative, featuring a dynamic and enterprising aristocrat, suited the fledging urban democracy and the evolving mass culture. The Revolution itself, once it ceased to present a direct threat, could be accommodated within a narrative of political modernity and the modernization of everyday life. This is evident in the work of sympathetic historians like Acton cited earlier. Baroness Orczy's attitude to the Revolution has nothing of this sympathy and is quite innocent of Acton's historicism. However, she was very conscious of the 'modernity' of the time and society described in her apparently totally escapist romance. What her works impart is a sense of a past that is not anachronistic and bygone but is strange and colourful, yet familiar and modern enough to be recognizable and even identified with. Put another way, her Pimpernel modernizes the past. The touch of modernity in this version of history may be juxtaposed with the sense of a venerable 'Olden Time', so often attached to the extended sixteenth century, and obviously out of place in regards the eighteenth, with its Industrial Revolution, the democratic revolutions, nationalism, and the beginning of rapid urbanization. This last trait could be especially useful in the presentations of the Georgians and the French revolutionaries as urban heroes and villains. Urban aristocrats and plebeians across the Channel, their lives and deeds, were connectable to the texture and feel of life in the present in the mega-city in a rapidly democratizing society and even offered readers a solace.

Orczy herself cultivated the idea of urban historical romance for an urban mass readership. History alone, she insisted, can distract the millions living out their drab lives in crowded, congested, and drab cities. History alone could take millions 'Out of the drabness of their surroundings', of its daily duties, or even of its amusement, out of the daily round of 'buses and trains, or swagger Rolls-Royces, of lunches at Claridge's or the A.B.C. tea-shops. Rich and Poor, life was all of the same . . . '.[30] Significantly, she suggests transferring components of the modern experience like a new sense of place and time, apparent in new registers of speed and velocity and in the intensity of urban life, onto the revolutionary decades. She conceived and 'saw' her superhero within this modern context. As she puts it in the much publicized paragraph which describes the 'invention' of the Pimpernel:

I first saw him standing before me . . . on the platform of an underground station, the Temple . . . I was waiting for my Inner Circle train for Kensington . . . as I was sitting there on the Inner Circle platform . . . It was foggy too and smelly and cold. But I give you my word that as I was sitting there, I saw—yes, I saw—Sir Percy Blakeney just as you know him. I saw him in his exquisite clothes, his slender hands holding up his spy

[30] Baroness Orczy, *Links in the Chain of Life*, ch. 13, on the Pimpernel.

glass: I heard his lazy drawling speech, his quaint laugh . . . it was the whole life-story of the Pimpernel.[31]

The scene of the birth of the Pimpernel on an underground platform, circulated in numerous publications, from trade magazines and the dailies to film-fan magazines, may well have been a concoction, or a reworking of an established convention. By the 1900s transport, above and under ground, became a clichéd metaphor for both the modernity of the metropolis and its malaises. Movement and transport in the mega-city had of course been a major preoccupation of the mid-Victorian urban writers discussed in Chapter 3, not least of Dickens in his urban histories. But the mid-Victorians had been concerned with (and about) congestion and free circulation and about the danger in the movement of crowds. The Edwardians considered the impact of speed, noise, and the very pace of city life on a unique experience of urban disconnectedness, a deprivation of the senses, and the ennui of the masses of dwellers of the city, notably Londoners. About the same time, urban sociologists like Georg Simmel diagnosed the ominous pressure of modern life and technologies on the modern soul of town-dwellers as a threat to physical existence.[32] The modern metropolis dangerously exposed its dwellers to unceasing stimulation. The new city type became passive and inert and, in the view of Simmel and other social commentators, experienced what Richard Sennett has called 'de-sensitization'.[33]

It is, of course, not the veracity of the Circle Line episode that is significant but Orczy's capitalizing on widely available symbols of urban modernity to convey the relevance of historical adventure as a romance. Similarly, she connects the idea for a novel on the Revolution to the Exposition Universelle in Paris in 1900, which marked the beginning of the modern century and was a paean to modern Western civilization, technologies, and lifestyles. The connection of the revolutionary events to a recognizable modern urban topography and signposts of modernity (the Inner Circle Line, cars and trains, the Tour Eiffel) is revealing and self-conscious. In *The Scarlet Pimpernel Looks at the World*, her rumination on the 'modern world' seen 'through the eyes of the Pimpernel', Orczy has him advise readers, and particularly youth, to live dangerously and adventurously and take advantage of the 'velocity' and rhythm of contemporary life. Like the familiar urban setting, the Pimpernel's audacity and his taste for risk and adventure are associated with elements which her contemporaries considered to be the essence of modern urban experience, like speed, intensity, and excitability. At the same time the advice book, like the novels, perorates on the weaknesses

[31] Ibid. 97.

[32] Georg Simmel, 'Die Grosstädte und das Geistesleben', in *Die Grosstadt*, ed. Theodor Petermann (Dresden, 1903), 187–206. See also Robert Park, E. W. Burgess, and R. D. McKenzie (eds.), *The City* (Chicago, 1967), especially Parks's inter-war diagnosis, pp. 1–46.

[33] Richard Sennett, *Flesh and Stone: The Body and the City in Western Civilisation* (New York, 1994).

and malaise of modern life.[34] The modernity and appeal of her histories lie in their motion and fast pace. And these characteristics made the histories ideally suited to the most modern genre, which captured the essence of the modern dynamics: the film. 'Introspective' rather than 'active' historical writing, or, for that matter, any writing, failed the ultimate test of modernity, the screen, whereas the *Scarlet Pimpernel* was easily transferable 'from print to celluloid'. As Orczy told fans of the film version: 'I wanted the picture to have action. I wanted it to be a motion picture in the proper sense of the term . . . The art of camera is motion.'[35]

The association between the tags of modern life and aristocratic lifestyle and leadership corresponded to some crucial changes, widely noted at the time, which the elites and Society underwent from about the 1880s and which registered in society at large. These changes present the reversed relationship between a decline of political power on the one hand and a symbolic role and cultural capital—noted earlier in relation to the monarchy—on the other. Political and social leadership was gradually but inexorably shifting from the landed interests towards the new plutocracy and elites, which were becoming considerably less cohesive religiously and nationally as well as economically, and comprised American plutocrats, Jews (this last change much decried by contemporaries), and a mixture of socialites, comprising the rich, the glamorous, and the Bohemian. Already during the 1890s and 1900s, the lifestyle and exploits of this changing stratum aroused a curiosity tapped by the popular press, whose extensive coverage of Society fuelled interest in it. Like royals, Society was a construct of the media, the stuff of glamour which was becoming highly visible to all. The high visibility and exposure of Society, especially of sections within it which were deemed the avant-garde of modernity, reached its zenith during the inter-war period, when the pranks and antics of the metropolitan golden modern youth made news material and was chronicled by mass-circulation dailies such as the *Daily Mail* and *Daily Express*.[36] Historical fiction and films, featuring the style, high adventure, and dangerous lives of an aristocratic leadership, fit well with the new kind of fast modern living depicted in popular journalism, advertising, and in the inter-war best-selling Society novel chronicling the deeds of contemporary coteries (Michael Arlen's *The Green Hat* (1924) comes to mind).[37] The constant movement of members of 'The League of the Scarlet Pimpernel' between London and Paris, Dover and Boulogne, no longer

34 Baroness Orczy, *The Scarlet Pimpernel Looks at the World* (London, 1933); *Times Literary Supplement*, 29 June 1933.

35 'Baroness Orczy Talks about the Filming of her Best Selling Novel', *Film Weekly* 12 Oct. 1934.

36 Cannadine, *The Decline and Fall*, 341–87. Ross McKibbin and Billie Melman each discuss the coverage of glamour and the mixed elites, and the media–society nexus during the inter-war period. McKibbin, *Classes and Cultures*, 22–44; Melman, *Women and the Popular Imagination in the Twenties*, 65–76.

37 See Melman, ibid.

presented the dark danger of travel across the Channel in *A Tale of Two Cities*. Rather, crossing the Channel could easily be taken to represent the annual migration of modern aristocrats and socialites to France (where, of course, life was cheaper), addictively chronicled in the large-circulation dailies.

What gave the urban, modernized aristocratic prototype credence was Baroness Orczy's own biography, lifestyle, and image. Unlike some other cultural entrepreneurs discussed in this book, her reputation and the popularity of her novels did not derive from an expertise—real, or assumed—that had drawn on historical research. In this way she differed not only from professional and amateur historians but also from contemporary film stars like Robson and Laughton and producers like Korda. Orczy's reputation as popular chronicler and *raconteur* is closest to Madame Tussaud's in that both depended heavily on a constructed and expertly marketed personal experience: Tussaud's record as an eyewitness and passive participant in the French Revolution and Orczy's as a dispossessed late nineteenth-century aristocrat-entrepreneur, willing to accommodate to democracy and modernity. To date, virtually all references to Orczy emphasize her background as the only daughter (and heiress) of an aristocratic Hungarian family, the family's financial collapse which forced her out of her ancestral land, subsequent exile in London, constant travel, a typical Catholic upper-class girl's convent education on the Continent, and a less typical subsequent study at the West London School of Art, and a short career as a painter.[38]

During her lifetime this colourful background had great publicity value. Certain details in her life story, like the uprising of peasants on Orczy's family estate, which ended in burning buildings and crops ready to harvest in protest against mechanization and the introduction of modern technology and 'progress', were a special asset. The uprising not only formed her avowed suspicion of revolts and revolutions, but also made her experience and life credibly similar to (and almost interchangeable with) those of both the dispossessed eighteenth-century émigrés and some of the English adventurers she described. Baroness Orczy could be a character in one of her historical novels; her characters could have lived her own life. Her foreignness was a bonus, not a flaw. It made her nationalist version of the past all the more convincing, and in this too her role as broker of popular histories is comparable to that of Madame Tussaud, Rafael Sabatini, and the Korda brothers. Travel and life abroad, in the French Riviera, Monte Carlo, and the Italian Riviera, favoured destinations of English upper-class men and women, also contributed to her status as an expert on Society, not to mention on French life and history. It is notable that the biography of Rafael Sabatini, her most important emulator and one of Britain's top-selling historical novelists with an expertise in the Napoleonic empire, had similar

[38] The best summary is by Lucy Sloan in Janet Todd (ed.), *Dictionary of British Women Writers* (London, 1989), 516–19.

ingredients: birth and life abroad (though he had plebeian origins), impressive linguistic talents, acquired 'aristocratic' manners and style and cosmopolitanism, a penchant for the eighteenth century, and an enthusiasm for his adopted home country.

Above all, Orczy's biography and lifestyle endowed her popular histories with an authority which readers and filmgoers recognized. Patricia Beer, growing up in the 1920s in a working-class home, and feeding on a diet of edifying literature, including Hesba Streton, Mrs Walton, and Baroness Orczy, was exhilarated by the Baroness's novels. What she would later recognize to be anti-revolutionary and conservative initially appealed to her because: 'For one thing it was by a Baroness, and so both begetter and begotten were of noble blood. We all identified absolutely with the persecuted aristocrats of the story.'[39] This identification of a working-class reader with aristocratic characters may appear, and indeed was judged by Beer, to counter her own class. As she noted: 'It seemed not to occur to us that had we lived then we should by reason of our social status have been *sans-culotte*... rather than *vicomtes*.'[40] What caused this deviation from class disposition was Orczy's authority and reputation. Her authority was sanctioned by the educational system when abridged editions of the novel were integrated in schools' curricula featuring the French Revolution and Georgian England. A University of London Press edition, one of many, lending the novel a desired academic aura, praised the Baroness's insight into English history and the novel's value as historical aid and stated: 'To read the story is to gain an unforgettable picture of the French Revolution.'[41] The incorporation of the novel in school curricula, like the schools' adoption of historical films examined in Chapter 6, registers their respective legitimation as respectable histories. By the mid-thirties schools routinely performed both the original play version and independent (and piratical) versions of the novel. One such version, staged at the Doncaster Central School for Girls in December 1934 and performed several times to aid school funds, demonstrates the ways in which readers adapted the popular historical text to the modern and everyday, 'dramatis[ing] it in their own fashion... The story opens at the Fisherman's Rest, Dover, and after rapid action in London and the surrounding districts, moves over to the Calais.' The fact that the play was an all-female production with cross-dressed girls and young adolescents in masculine roles, indeed that the Pimpernel himself was a young and modern woman, produced an extra thrill, not least because the performers enthusiastically flogged the French Jacobin agent Chauvelin: 'All parts were taken by the girls of the school, and the play... abounds in thrilling and hairbreadth adventures, and there are sufficient realistic screams and "noises off" (especially when Chauvelin receives a flogging) to keep the audience in a state of excitement.'[42]

[39] Quoted in Rose, *The Intellectual Life of the British Working Class*, 388. [40] Ibid.

[41] Baroness Orczy, *The Scarlet Pimpernel, Edited and Abridged for Class Use* (London, 1937), Preface. [42] British Library, Add MS 56767, fo. 196. See also fos. 197–200.

Cross-dressing and cross-gender performance and roles could doubly appeal to the provincial school audience because they too 'modernized' history and connected it to contemporary debates about the modern man and modern woman and the blurring of their gender and sexual identities—all topics obsessively covered by the press and film.

ENGLISHNESS AND ARISTOCRACIES

Orczy and Sabatini and their works not only redefined and, in a sense, reversed the traditional role of the aristocracy in earlier cross-class repertoires, they redefined it vis-à-vis national identity. Sir Percy's appeal was double: in his (reversed) class role, and the embodying of the nation in him and his league, rather than in middle-class characters. Both in his role as foppish society leader and as the Pimpernel, he became the quintessential Englishman, 'a perfect representation of an English gentleman', as Orczy herself boasted.[43] His status as a paragon of English qualities was enhanced by each sequence and soared in the 1935 film edition, in Leslie Howard's interpretation of him. This star's role in defining the nationalist version of the Revolution and indeed of the English past will be dealt with separately. Here it is necessary to emphasize Orczy's own role as articulator of this national identity, a role which again challenges notions of the 'nation'. For as many of her contemporaries noted, the most overtly celebratory history of the English gentleman was invented by a foreigner, albeit one who became a naturalized Briton. A 'Hungarian born', with 'nothing English about [her]', 'a pure blooded Hungarian', possessed of a 'wonderful understanding of the English character and [who had created] such a perfect representation of an English gentleman'. What better testimony to her success than the adulating remark of Joynson-Hicks, Lord Brentford, that 'he [the Pimpernel] is so English' and that Orczy put her finger 'on the best and truest in English character'?[44]

'The best and truest in English character' predictably compounds class, birth, and lifestyle. Sir Percy's own pedigree is traceable to Bosworth Field and the Tudors and careless later support of the Jacobite cause. Character is also about physical traits and a certain form of masculinity. Members of the League of the Scarlet Pimpernel may first appear as eugenic specimens, rather reminiscent in fact of representations of a 'higher' national 'type'. They are indeed described as a 'specimen' of English upper-class manhood: 'tall, broad of shoulders' sportsmen. Their unparalleled bravery, chivalry (towards women, children, and the weak, usually of their own class), and willingness to sacrifice themselves to rescue the persecuted are accomplished without violence. The most significant trait of the Pimpernel is that he does not carry a sword—or any other weapon. His being

[43] *Links in the Chain of Life*, 7. [44] Ibid. 98–9.

without arms distinguishes him (and his followers) not only from the French revolutionaries, especially of the lower classes, but also from the succession of literary and celluloid swashbuckling heroes, including later twentieth-century supermen modelled after him. Scaramouche is a master of fencing and Zorro a gifted swordsman. Sir Percy lacks this class tag and, by implication, eschews the aristocrat's traditional occupation: fighting. His weapon in his defence of native liberties and of the refugees of the *ancien régime* is disguise and the ability to change identities with dress. He appears as a priest and a soldier (French), a sans-culotte woman, and a Jew, a giant asthmatic veteran of the French army, a crippled pauper, and many other characters.

It is precisely his astounding ability to change masks, the very ruse that makes him a hero with brains, not brawn, that stretches the very definition of 'English' and distinguishes his image from elitist, biologist, and other renditions of the super, or higher national, class or racial type.[45] In addition to his doubling as fop and avenger, his very body is changeable. His mutability and constant role-playing effectively blur differences of gender, nationality, and ethnicity. Readers first 'see' him as an old *tricoteuse*, the fanatic sans-culotte woman knitting at the guillotine, undoubtedly a reference to Dickens's manic knitters in *A Tale of Two Cities*. In this disguise he smuggles three aristocrats out of the gates of Paris, waving a whip adorned with samples of hair, torn for a keepsake from the skulls of beheaded 'aristos'. In *The Triumphs of the Scarlet Pimpernel* he appears as a giant asthmatic, limping through the Rue St Honoré, to burn in effigy a family of royalists. Again in *Scarlet Pimpernel* he makes an appearance as Benjamin Rosenbaum, a Polish Jew, filthy, grovelling, and crafty. The Rosenbaum character is one of the most blatant examples of crude anti-Semitism in early twentieth-century English fiction and proved too strong for many a contemporary. He appeared in the last scene in the original Nottingham stage version, but was completely cut out in the West End one. Apparently metropolitan theatre audiences were deemed more sensitive to such explicit anti-Semitism.[46]

This constant masquerading is far more than just a device aimed at entertainment through featuring heroes and their 'doubles'. If the Pimpernel is a man of many masks and identities, some of them embodying the very reverse of the ultimate Englishman, if he is as comfortable in his role of a sans-culotte woman or a Jew as in that of a fop, then who really is he? The tension between a sure nationalism, sometimes turning into vulgar chauvinism and xenophobia, and the challenging of the terms of Englishness was crucial to the making of Orczy herself as a broker of the culture of history in a mass democracy. The foreign, eastern European exotic aristocrat/bohemian constructed herself, and was seen by her contemporaries, as an authoritative mediator of historical notions of

[45] On such renditions see Stone, *Breeding Superman* and Delap, 'The Superwoman'.
[46] *Links in the Chain of Life*, 104.

English patriotism. Her cosmopolitan lifestyle sat comfortably with a patriotism which bordered on intolerance and Jingoism and was frankly anti-Semitic. During the First World War she was active handing white feathers to men in civilian clothes, who, it seemed, 'shirked' the front. She was also active in voluntary work for women and as a member of authors' patriotic associations. During the inter-war period she was a rabid anti-Communist. Yet life in France and Italy made her denounce Fascism early on, as well as high-class British Fascist sympathies.[47] And this and the variability of her principal hero detach her—and certainly him—from contemporary and overlapping conservative or extreme notions of Englishness and fads for the superhero.

THE MAKING OF A NATIONAL IDOL: THE PIMPERNEL ON SCREEN

The tension between Orczy's chauvinism and the potential for a challenge to the terms of Englishness was brought to the fore in the screen versions of the *Pimpernel*, whose production overlapped with and influenced the later sequences of the novel. The definitive 1935 version did not 'replace' the novel as the most popular interpretation of the Revolution but enhanced the novel's original status. The film, especially through its star Leslie Howard in the title role, came to be regarded as the most English celluloid history, even more patriotic than Robson's interpretations of Elizabeth I. Like her interpretations, it expanded notions of identity and history, not least concerning the role of class and gender in both.

Like the most significant films in the Tudor cycle, the *Scarlet Pimpernel* was produced by a team with allegiances to Continental film-making traditions and to Hollywood. The production was run and controlled by Alexander Korda, with Vincent Korda as Art Director, Lajos Biro and Arthur Wimperis as scriptwriters, the American Harold Young as Director, and a South African Jew, Arthur Benjamin, as composer. Howard came from a family of Hungarian Jewish immigrants and Merle Oberon, his co-star, was Eurasian. Orczy herself praised Korda's acumen for collecting 'Hungarian talent', grudgingly acknowledging that it represented a constructive Jewish acumen.[48] The international product was immediately embraced as a national and native success, a booster to the British film industry and an achievement in a continuous struggle against Americanization and cultural colonization by Hollywood. The *Sunday Times* noted that 'in every respect it constitutes a triumph for the British film world'. Even the *New York Times* had to grudgingly concede that the gorgeous

[47] *Links in the Chain of Life*, 104. [48] Ibid. 165–7.

product carved 'from the pages of the Baroness Orczy's novel permits the English to recover some of their recent losses in cinema prestige'.[49] It grossed £420,000 (costing £81,000), of which £270,000 came from foreign earnings in the USA and on the Continent. Its success with audiences was signalled by an outstanding attendance at the Leicester Square Theatre, Korda's special 'shop window', where he aired all his historical films.[50] It ranked third among the top 126 films showed in Britain in 1935 and a respectable seventh in Bolton ('Worktown' of Mass Observation surveys), faring well in Lancashire as well as in southern towns and resorts like Brighton and Hove, ranking third in these last two.[51] It certainly did better than most historical films, beating *Henry VIII* and scoring a second in *Film Weekly*'s popularity survey of British films on 2 May 1936. Notwithstanding its anti-republicanism (and some hostility to Orczy's defence of the *ancien régime)* it did well with American audiences, though, again like the original, it encountered considerable antagonism in France, where dubbing effectively bowdlerized all 'anti-French' dialogues. Even the Board of Film Censors and the Foreign Office deemed it uncontroversial enough to be included in film programmes of British embassies during Coronation Week in 1935, together with *Rhodes of Africa*.[52]

In contradistinction to Korda's *Henry VIII*, the *Pimpernel* was deemed a worthy history, serious, and authoritative. The latter, noted C. A. Lejeune, was not only entertainment but a 'reasonable film' which 'introduced you to a London, a Paris, in which people lived, and died, and worked, and paid visits to their tailors; it presented a problem of contemporary history, of one nation's doings as seen and reported by the people of another'. The mention of visits to tailors, of course, refers to the many vignettes of dialogue on sartorial etiquette and elegance, introducing Sir Percy as the Georgian fop. The film's 'all round craftsmanship', Lejeune summarized, merited 'a considerable amount of national pride'.[53] She, like other critics, could appreciate Korda's adaptation far more than the original, which had lacked the impact of reliable history. The screen version had 'background authority, and a certain expression that the original never knew'.[54]

Leslie Howard's authority as popular historian and culture broker was analogous to Orczy's. Contemporaries cast him in the role of the ultimate interpreter both of a desirable form of aristocratic life, customs, and manners, and of Englishness. But his status and influence with critics and audiences did not

[49] *New York Times*, 13 Feb. 1935.

[50] See Paul Tabori, *Alexander Korda* (London, 1959), 152.

[51] I rely on Sedgwick's tables of popularity, based on his Popstat index and ranking. See Sedgwick, *Popular Filmgoing in 1930s Britain*, 121; 134.

[52] Harper, *Picturing the Past*, 18; 11.

[53] Lejeune, 'Scarlet Pimpernel, Film of the Week', 23 Dec. 1934 in *The C. A. Lejeune Film Reader*, ed. Lejeune, 95–6.

[54] Ibid. And see also *Punch*, 9 Jan. 1935, p. 38.

emanate from birth and rank but from the man himself, 'naturally' and effortlessly. The star, the historical role he 'was' rather than 'made', and the kind of Englishness he stood for all overlapped. As with the historical-national icons discussed in Chapter 7, so with Howard, stardom and authority were carefully constructed to fit with a model of a much advertised private life and a set of qualities. Although by 1935 Howard had already acquired a reputation both in Britain and in Hollywood, his image as a national icon truly took off with the *Pimpernel*. By his death in an aircraft crash in June 1943 he would be universally identified as the ultimate Briton and his Englishness would be practically equated with the compound of qualities of the late eighteenth-century aristocratic leader which had made him so famous. Intriguingly, in popular renditions of his life and work some compromising elements were sifted out. Leslie Howard Stainer, born László Horvath, had been a first-generation Londoner in a family of Jewish-Hungarian emigrants. Graduating from Dulwich College, he briefly worked in the City, then went on stage. His career was cut short by the First World War; he suffered severe shell shock and was discharged from service. His shortened service and central-European/Jewish origins were somewhat dimmed by advertisers—both could have compromised his aura as an all-English type and consummate patriot. As actor, director, producer, and essayist, Howard helped cultivate the idea that on screen and in life he was one and the same man: an upright, sometimes idealistic, tender yet irreverent Englishman, naturally so. Ironically, the naturalization of his identity had to do with style and artifice: Howard developed a 'natural' approach to acting which was tailor-made for the screen and endowed even his historical roles with a credibility and realness. During the Second World War this credibility proved a propaganda asset, in war films, on Howard's missions abroad, and in his service on the BBC brain trust.

Howard, his contemporaries agreed, did not act the historical figure: he *was* the aristocratic patriot and leader. 'Leslie Howard', noted *Punch*, 'may not have quite the bulk of *Sir Percy Blakeney*, but he is tall, he has fair hair, he is English and he knows how to look elegant. Whether his eyes too, like *Sir Percy*'s, are a lazy blue is a point well known no doubt to his feminine fans but of no importance on the screen. What does matter is that his acting is very good indeed.'[55] 'Mr. Howard', critics were unanimous, 'is the Pimpernel himself.'[56] Audiences did more than identify the star with the historical figure; they literally cast Howard in the role, thus intervening in the early stages of production. Korda's initial choice for the Pimpernel was Charles Laughton, but he was deluged with letters of protest canvassing for Howard and submitted to consumers' pressure, thereafter publicizing the role of 'public opinion' in the making of Howard/the Pimpernel.[57]

55 *Punch*, 9 Jan. 1935, p. 38. 56 *New York Times*, 13 Feb. 1935.
57 *Film Weekly*, 12 Oct. 1934.

During the late 1930s, both the actor/figure and the rescue narrative at the basis of Orczy's plot and the film rapidly acquired political meanings, evolving around unlikely analogues between the Jacobin Revolution and the fascist dictatorships. Such analogues reworked the allusions from historical emergencies and scares in the light of the international crisis of the 1930s and, of course, the Second World War. In this manner, Howard and the film fulfilled a function that was rather similar to Flora Robson's and the Armada story in *Fire Over England.* His role as a Georgian aristocrat redeeming his confreres from the horrors of the guillotine was transplanted into Nazi Germany in *Pimpernel Smith*, in which he played the apparently dim-witted professor of archaeology leading an underground to smuggle the victims of the Gestapo out of the Third Reich. Indeed quite a few of his late films replayed the patriotic and aristocratic model set out in the *Scarlet Pimpernel*, culminating in the wartime roles and in his propaganda work. It is no wonder that his violent death on a British Airways aircraft, shot down by the Luftwaffe on the way from Lisbon to London, brought on an avalanche of obituaries celebrating the very qualities he 'acted' as the Pimpernel. 'As the Pimpernel concealed a strength and tenacity of purpose behind flippant air, so did Howard disguise an art conceived in terms of hard work and perfect timing behind the casual understatement, the off-hand approach, the quietly humorous habit of self-depreciation.'[58] He had, lamented *Manchester Guardian*, '[a] frank, intensely English quality in his voice, face, bearing. It was this same intensely English quality which made him popular everywhere in intensely English film parts like Sir Percy Blakeney.'[59]

The image of the aristocratic leader and patriot was considerably gentler and more open-ended than those of the contemporary images of the patriotic early modern female monarchs. The former was less declamatory and formal and, most important, exuded elegance and style. The strength of Korda's interpretation of the book and Howard's acting, as some sharp contemporaries noted, was precisely in the emphasis on the making of a stylish past. The elegant and enlightened aristocratic world which Orczy sought to create in her novels was admirably captured by the camera, in elaborate decor, mainly interior decor, Georgian and Regency props, and meticulously designed men's costumes (the costumes of the female lead are less accurate and actually follow 1930s fashions). Elegance is limited to the parts of the film which are set in London, almost all of them indoors; outdoor scenes are mostly Parisian, noisy, crowded, and chaotic. The comparison between the cities, a staple of the urban history of the Revolution since *A Tale of Two Cities*, here takes on an added dimension. Paris is represented as Gothic and even medieval, in long shots of its roofs and churches with a surreal air, and in medium shots featuring crowded and congested streets and alleys, cellars and prisons, walls, gates, and narrow passages. The Palladian and late Georgian London interiors are spacious and tasteful and are recovered

[58] *The Times*, 4 June 1943. [59] Quoted in Richards, *The Age of the Dream Palace*, 234.

for spectators with painstaking care. The Regent's apartments in St James's Palace and Black's Club (a shrewd reference to White's, the leading Regency club), the staircase, hall, and library of a town house (Lord Grenville's) and Blakeney's Richmond mansion are all 'restored' in a way that could be appreciated by fashionable audiences in the know about the returning vogue of the Regency and initiate those audiences not familiar with period architecture, decoration, and aristocratic tastes. As the *Picturegoer* noted, the film offered a 'history class' on styles and fashions.[60] The camera lingers on pieces of furniture, decorative objects, and period paintings, including portraits. In one key scene Lady Blakeney's portrait is being painted by Romney to an audience of female connoisseurs which is joined by the gullible but stylish Sir Percy. Period textiles in upholstery and women's and men's clothes are lavishly photographed. And there are added touches of style in the choreography, score, and photography of a minuet, as the dancers are seen passing briefly through an arch and their shadows are projected on the wall behind, creating an artistic effect that refers to the nineteenth-century magic lantern.

In the film, the eighteenth century exudes kinds of glamour equivalent and relatable to contemporary notions of glamorous urban life. Older notions of the magnitude of the Revolution and its horrors lingered. And they lived on in reproductions of the older, mid-Victorian urban lore. *A Tale of Two Cities*, which as *The Only Way* held sway on the stage since 1899, had a number of film versions between 1922 and 1958. And the novel's definitive film version was released in exactly the same year as the *Scarlet Pimpernel*.[61] However, in the *Pimpernel* itself, and in the popular imagination, the mixture of spiritualism and sacrifice and older notions of Revolution horror was often and easily outweighed by an appreciation of style, role-playing, and adventure, identified with the male lead. The competing notions of glamour and modernity on the one hand and horror on the other are apparent in the advertisements and posters which display the heads of Howard and Oberon on two circles with thick diameter. The heads face each other across a guillotine and the circles represent both a film reel and a revolving knife, but are also made to look like portrait miniatures or commemorative coins (see Fig. 20).

Viewers responded to the lead star's glamour, which they considered absolutely essential to the feel of veracity and authenticity. Children's and juveniles' essays collected by the sociologist J. P. Mayer and his team for his *Sociology of Film* (1945) express just this. One especially articulate 15-year-old North London girl chose to devote an essay on the book or film she liked most to *The Scarlet Pimpernel*, 'an unknown Englishman who saved members of the French aristocracy from the horrible deaths of either torture, or the Guillotine, during

[60] *Picturegoer*, 27 Oct. 1934, p. 30.
[61] Pointer (ed.), *Charles Dickens on the Screen*, 128–36.

Fig. 20. *The Scarlet Pimpernel*, advertisement in *Kine Weekly* (1935). The stars' heads, facing each other across the guillotine, are mounted on reels which resemble coins or period miniature portraits. The advertisement exudes a mixture of glamour, stylishness, and horror

the French revolution'. She enjoyed both book and film since the former gave the reader more historical detail, while the latter 'brought the scenery and costumes more vividly to the watcher's eye'. What made this history so real for her was Howard, who 'played the role of the dreamy pleasure-loving baronet who made himself a butterfly of society to hide his courage and sympathy for

Fig. 21. Leslie Howard and Merle Oberon as the Pimpernel and Marguerite, *Kine Weekly* (1935)

the illtreated [*sic*] French aristocrats'.[62] A younger respondent, whose favourite films were 'historical ones', thought the *Pimpernel* 'the best of these'. She too was attracted to the mixture of the guillotine horror and the 'awful pleasure of the French People to go and watch people guillotined with such joy on their faces' and the hero/star's quality and style.[63] Even juveniles who 'detested films' and thought them unreal and 'glamorous in an unpleasant way' warmed to the glamour in the *Pimpernel* and its star, which they regarded as an exception.[64] (See Fig. 21.)

Orczy's formula and its emulations across different genres and media changed the subject of the century-old popular discourse on the Revolution. The new formula substituted the aristocrat-patriot for the plebeian revolutionary (or his/her English counterpart, the responsible middle-class citizen) and juxtaposed

[62] Mayer, *Sociology of Film*, 69–70. [63] Ibid. 103. [64] Ibid. 102.

a new urban image of opulence, order, and style and the older image of political and social disorder, violence, and crime. It is quite possible to interpret this change as an example of popular conservatism, manufactured by a vested international capitalist elite of producers of mass culture, buttressing British inter-war Conservatism, elitism, and forms of elite sociability, and feeding both to mass consumers. But such an interpretation is all too simple. To begin with, the formula did not just offer a vision of the past fit for an urban mass democracy; it made available consumers' use of history as a repository of style and high life and of a taste for a dense material world of objects and designs. Together with these aesthetic pleasures the formula and the lives of some of its chief brokers, most notably Orczy herself, Leslie Howard, and his female lead Merle Oberon, offered readers/viewers a set of sensations relatable to modern urban living and its rhythm and perceptions, chiefly of action, movement, and speed. Modernity was also relatable to the open-ended interpretations of gender and sexuality in both the novel and film, chiefly in the Pimpernel/Howard's interpretation of masculinity. His foppishness, penchant for dress and fashion, and avoidance of violence, all apparently 'feminine' qualities, made his popularity. In this sense he is the equivalent of Charles Laughton in *Henry VIII*: both actors presented an open-ended interpretation of masculinity, resonant with notions of and about the modern man which emerged during the inter-war period. Finally, as examples like the campaign for Howard's casting show, audiences were not passive consumers of the new formula and representations but actively participated in their circulation, which they sometimes redirected.

The change of the class emphasis and shift towards history as site of glamour are simultaneous with the centring of the monarchy in popular history outlined in Chapters 6 and 7. This simultaneity is not just one of chronologies, with the movement beginning in the late nineteenth century and peaking during the inter-war period, but indicates a broader synchronic relationship between the culture of history and culture at large. In both, the democratization of access to the past and to commercial culture 'modernized' history's subject matter and historical characters. Aristocratic heroes and superheroes were transplanted onto an urban and modern experience and temper in a way similar to the transformation of the early modern monarch to a popular icon (and the inter-war monarchy's own modernization and self-fashioning as a 'democratic' institution), welding new kinds of fame and celebrity fit for modernity and the early twentieth-century version of political democracy. We now have to examine the shifts within the popular historical imagination that would occur with the move towards a different kind of democracy.

PART V

NEW ELIZABETHANS? POST-WAR CULTURE AND FAILED HISTORIES

9

Gloriana 1953: Failed Evocations of the Past

1953: CONTINUITIES AND CHANGE IN THE PRODUCTION OF THE CULTURE OF HISTORY

The sixteen months between 6 February 1952 and 8 June 1953 were especially opportune for a collective binge of revivals of and spending on the Elizabethans. What better moment for resurrecting the first Elizabeth than the accession and coronation of her namesake? Viewed in comparison with the inter-war preoccupation with the Elizabethans, the moment of the Coronation may be regarded as a phase in a continuous shift in the popular historical imagination towards the monarchy and aristocracies as the agents and carriers of change. This long-term view, stressing continuities in the subject matter of the culture of history, corresponds with the move of the monarchy to the centre of popular culture, discussed earlier in the book. Sebastian Haffner, puzzling over the 'unexplained' and 'unstudied' stability of the British monarchy and 'monarchy conscious[ness]' in Britain, noted in June 1953 that the monarchy's unmatched prestige was acquired after the First World War at the time of a universal eclipse of monarchies as institutions and symbolic sites of collective emotions and beliefs and soared after the Second World War.[1] British Royals gradually strengthened their hold on peoples' imaginary and their social life, until in 1953 their presence in everyday life and talk was 'probably shared only by their most intimate relations and friends'.[2] This new form of intimacy, between 'a sovereign whose contact with the people is at once so vast in its extent' and 'ordinary' people, was entirely modern and democratic and drew on the media revolutions. The 'intimate character' of the bond between people and monarch, observed historian C. V. Wedgwood at the time of the Coronation, explained the longevity of the popularity of the monarchy within modernity.[3] Like Haffner she locates the beginning of the modern cult of the monarchy at the beginning of the twentieth century: the Coronation and the national and international frenzy surrounding it were the culmination of an already established collective mood and attitudes.

1 Sebastian Haffner, 'The Renascence of Monarchy', *Twentieth Century*, 153, no. 916 (June 1953), 415–24 at 415–16.

2 Ibid. 416.

3 C. V. Wedgwood, 'Our Queen, Crown and Monarchy', *News Chronicle*, Background to the News Series, no. 11 (London, 1953), 5–41 at 7.

In this chapter, which focuses on the dynamics of the culture of history between the 'two festivals', the 1951 Festival of Britain and the Coronation, I am attuned to the continuities between the post-war revival of the Elizabethans and earlier resurrections, as well as to the long-term view, exemplified by Haffner and Wedgwood, and stressing contiguities in the culture of history; at the same time I am attentive to changes. 1953 saw not only continuity in themes but also the resurrection of literary, visual, and vocal forms of commemoration of the past, ranging from forms and artefacts regarded as modern, such as the experimental historical psycho-biography and the film, to considerably older musical forms—notably vocal music, reviving Elizabethan themes, and historical opera, resuscitated in the early 1950s. Opera, apparently an old and traditional form of historical spectacle, one that conserved traditional hierarchies and forms of art patronage, serves to anchor my discussion of post-war culture. It particularly serves to highlight discontinuities and fissures in images of the Elizabethans, forms of their celebrations, and in the structures of cultural production and brokerage of the past. It may be worth our while briefly to outline these discontinuities and locate them in the broader transitions in post-war culture at large, before fixing on the dynamics of the last Elizabethan revival and the role it played in the collective ritual of the Coronation and the monarchy.

Change may be summarized under three headings. First and most significant is the new role of the post-war state as culture broker, a role evolving in relation to the shift, described by Ross McKibbin, from an individualistic definition of democracy to a social definition, including the working classes.[4] The post-war settlement, originating during the 'people's war' and constituting a capitalist welfare state, premissed not only a distribution of material 'goods' and benefits like full employment, protection from dearth, and decent housing, but also that of cultural goods, including education and the universal availability of the kind of 'quality' culture formerly accessible to minorities and denied to majorities. The extension of the idea of welfare from the economy and society to culture involved not merely diffusion but the necessary transformation of the relationship between the state and cultural production. This transformation took shape during the war and its immediate aftermath, with the emergence of state apparatuses for the distribution of high culture, including CEMA (Council for the Encouragement of Music and the Arts, 1942), predecessor of the Arts Council of Great Britain (1945) and the BBC Third Programme (1946). Commitment to a democratization of 'quality', minority culture resonated in a post-war culture rhetoric which stressed the state's responsibility 'in particular to increase the accessibility of the fine arts to the public throughout Our Realm' and to develop 'greater knowledge, understanding and practices of the fine arts', yet at the same time preserved notions of cultural paternalism, apparent in the

[4] McKibbin, *Classes and Cultures*, 535.

wording of the Council's Charter of 9 August 1946.[5] This kind of paternalism and a minoritarian sense about the right contents and values of culture carried on pre-war and even earlier liberal ideas, transmitted through the new state apparatus and its advocates. John Maynard Keynes, the pioneering theorist of the new macro-economic (and liberal) policies, was founder of the Council and first chair of its flagship, the Royal Opera House at Covent Garden.

The contradictory pulls within the vision of diffusion are also apparent in the new trend towards the nationalization of culture and its mechanisms. State patronage, its architects repeatedly stressed, did not mean the collectivization of culture, standardization, or limits to the freedoms of the creators and mediators of arts and tastes. Such intrusions smacked of the dictatorial Bolshevization of culture (and indeed of the Communist threat to the post-war settlement), or of vulgar, American-style cultural capitalism. Significantly, Keynes described the new mixed system of patronage and brokerage in a phrase drawing on the popular historical imagination: 'Let every part of Merry England be merry in its own way. Death to Hollywood.'[6] State interventionism in the production of versions of history, under the auspices of the new apparatus embodied in the Arts Council, by no means precluded commercial private patronage and the private entrepreneurship of brokers of the past like popular historians, writers, and artists and the popular media, all of whom drew on traditional patronage. Far from it, as we shall see: the Elizabethan revival and the 'consciousness of monarchy' feeding it and fed by it were the outcome of cooperation and compromises between private capital and interests and the state. Moreover, as Robert Hewison has argued, the concept of welfare culture was 'translated' into policies in quite a selective manner, supporting privileged initiatives while marginalizing culture in general.[7]

The second change, coinciding with the realignment of the structure of the brokerage of culture, was the appearance of a new medium, presenting an entirely new mode of visual consumption and new forms of spectatorship, creating possibilities for mass participation in great public events, ceremonies, and rituals of the state and transforming them into world events. Television, inaugurated during and by the Coronation, held possibilities for transforming the consumption of the monarchy and its history into global subjects, attracting, in addition to some twenty million spectators in the UK—almost half of the population—millions of viewers in Western Europe and North America. Radio broadcasts of the ceremony at Westminster Abbey were 'listened in' by many more millions throughout the Commonwealth, the two media together catering for an estimated 150 millions. As the ever perceptive Haffner noted, never was the sentiment for the monarchy so popular and global.[8]

[5] Brandon Taylor, *Art for the Nation: Exhibitions and the London Public 1747–2001* (Manchester, 1999), 175; Alan Sinfield, *Literature, Politics and Culture in Postwar Britain* (Oxford and Berkeley, 1989), 47–59.

[6] Taylor, *Art for the Nation*, 175.

[7] Robert Hewison, *Culture and Consensus: England, Art and Politics since 1945* (London, 1995).

[8] Haffner, 'The Renascence of Monarchy'.

A third change is the reworking of ideas about the purpose and function of a revival of the Elizabethan era and its adaptation to post-war society and its visions of modernity. Interest in the Elizabethans, and indeed in history, now came to signify not only an effort of recovery and rehabilitation of a slice of the past, nor simply its revival in the sense of bringing it back into popular consciousness and uses, or into vogue, but also renewal and regeneration. Renewal spelt out rejuvenation and was constantly attached to images of youth. The epithet 'New Elizabethan Age', coined by Rowse during the war, probably in 1942, was recycled by the popular dailies and aired after the accession, coming into common usage by 1953. By the time of the Coronation 'New Elizabethans' and 'Young Elizabethans' became exchangeable notions, standing for attachments to 'worthy' cultural values and expectations on the one hand, and modern lifestyles and consumption on the other. *Collins Magazine* for boys and girls, liked chiefly for its cover illustrations by John Verney, was rechristened *Collins Young Elizabethan* two months before the Coronation. At two shillings it promised a link to the past and the possibilities for a modern lifestyle. 'Not really about history... despite the gesture in the title', and in articles about the monarchy, heraldry, and historical novels, *Young Elizabethan* offered 'worthy' contents, including information on pets and horses, a smattering of information on new technologies and new literature, but also a way of living advertised in the subtitle: *The Magazine to Grow Up With*.[9] Youth, growth, and contemporary life were embodied in the Queen herself. She became a glamorous symbol and icon of post-war modernity. Rowse himself, churning out for the Coronation rewrites of older journalistic writings titled 'A New Elizabethan Age?', which appropriately concluded a slim volume of essays titled *An Elizabethan Garland*, stressed her youth and connected it to that of her namesake:

> With the accession of a young Queen, at just the same age as that of the first Elizabeth when she came to the throne; at her side, at the head of our affairs, a man who is directly in his own time a historical figure; the wars, we hope, over: what more natural than that people should wonder whether another age may not be opening to us like that which has proved itself unforgettable in the memory of the English people?[10]

The aura of youth was described to have radiated throughout the Empire; indeed it fitted with Britain's changing role as an imperial and world power. While older imperial motifs were kept alive in evocations of the adventurous and masculine spirit of the early Elizabethan colonizers, the contemporary empire was being modernized. It was a 'new', 'people's', rather than a 'subjects', empire symbolized in 'A Young Queen for a Young Commonwealth'.[11] The conquest of Mount Everest, by two colonials, a white, ordinary New Zealander

[9] Janet L. Nelson, correspondence with author, 22 July 2002; Michael Wolfers, correspondence with author, 18 July 2002.

[10] Rowse, *An Elizabethan Garland*, 144.

[11] *Daily Mail*, 2 Apr. 1953. On the Coronation visions of the Empire see Wendy Webster, *Englishness and Empire, 1939–1965* (Oxford, 2005), 92–119.

and a Sherpa from Nepal, reported on Coronation day, further enhanced the image of regeneration and an egalitarian adventure celebrated across the globe.

Youth also connected the Queen to the generation coming of age during the war and after it. Thus Philip Gibbs in his 1953 survey of post-war youth in Britain, appropriately titled *The New Elizabethans*:

> When she had been proclaimed Queen, I like most others, had had a jog at heart, and my mind was invaded by the ghosts of history. We are now Elizabethans again. Could we hope for a new Elizabethan era with its flowering of genius, its high spirit of adventure, its golden share in the renaissance of learning and arts?[12]

Gibbs, novelist, veteran military correspondence (who had made a name in reportage on the Great War), a Tory, and member of the British Legion, shrewdly exploited the historical analogues between the Spanish threat to Elizabethan England and the Nazi and Communist threat to wartime and post-war Britain respectively, attaching these to the imagery of youth and rejuvenation. British youth were literally Britain's conduit to a grasp on the past and a path to a better future. 'So now that we have the new Queen', Gibbs rhapsodized,

> we may well believe that it is the beginning of a new era as well as of a new reign. A new mood, a new spirit, a change in the *tempo* of life, a call to a new form of adventure in the minds and heart of the people, may, and indeed certainly will, come with the younger generation now pressing forward.

For the queen herself, who Gibbs, in avuncular tones (rather reminiscent of Churchill's) liked to call 'the young queen', was a prototype for the new generation and a renewing post-war country: 'Already she has called out a romantic loyalty and affection by her charm—so young, so gay, so exquisite—as all her pictures show her on every screen, every cinema, in television, by flashlight and sunlight.'[13]

Such affection and intense popularity were compared by Wedgwood to those of the first Elizabeth at the time of her accession and during the Armada crisis. Wedgwood's pamphlet for the 'Background to the News' series of the left-oriented *News Chronicle*, on the origins of the monarchy and the Crown, concluded with the Coronation (1953) speech and the Tilbury address, placed next to each other.[14] The acknowledgement of the global role of the modern media in the renaissance of youth is strangely at odds with Gibbs's (and Rowse's) attack on aspects of modern mass culture, which they condemned for its shallowness, mediocrity, and democratic and socialist antagonism to excellence. Their vision of a new Elizabethan Age expresses a critique and a deep mistrust of the post-war settlement and the new role of the state in culture. Yet both, like the 'Whiggish' Wedgwood, are well aware of the indispensability of the media—old

[12] Philip Gibbs, *The New Elizabethans* (London, 1953), 22. [13] Ibid. 213–14.
[14] Wedgwood, 'Our Queen, Crown and Monarchy', 10.

and new—for the new renaissance; and both are aware (like her) of the limited possibilities for a revival of Britain's position as a world power and its survival as a cohesive society.

My focus in the following on the short term is not the only departure from the method of the book, which throughout has considered processes within the culture of history rather than select events like festivals and coronations. My choice of grand opera, a form of telling about the past that is specifically aimed at elite consumption, with origins in traditional upper-class rather than in democratic mass culture, may court more criticism. At the centre of my discussion is not just opera but Benjamin Britten's *Gloriana*, produced for the Coronation, commemorating the first Elizabeth. Though not the first English opera on a historical subject, *Gloriana* was the first English Coronation opera and at the time probably the single most expensive state-sponsored historical spectacle ever staged in the UK. It was allotted unprecedented financial support, was the most expensive Arts Council Coronation production, and apparently exemplified the workings of the new kind of state support of culture. But *Gloriana* did not become the English *Aida*, a national opera reverberating across class, as some of its producers had hoped. It crashed to a cacophony of public disapproval. Its staging, failure, and short life may seem of little interest to the historian of popular and cross-class culture: why pick on them?

In a book on successful histories, there is room for a discussion of failed versions of the past: these would highlight common themes in the culture of history and the dynamics of acceptance and rejection within it. *Gloriana*'s crash started a public debate, conducted on various platforms, on the control over history in a democratic, culture-sponsoring state, on what should, and should not, be included in productions of the past, and on who should pay for them. Moreover, the making of the opera demonstrates the interplay of select state support and private initiative apparent in the working of post-war 'welfare culture'. Furthermore, the opera and its social biography also expose the coeval albeit contradictory images of the pasts discussed throughout the book, as places of insecurity and as the source of glamour and power. Apparently celebrating the might and power of the monarchy and the state, *Gloriana* dramatized images of insecurity and decay. Set in a mass ritual celebrating youth, the opera represented death and aging, thus contrasting with the New Elizabethanism. These contradictions are located in urban settings, but the settings are distinctly different from the post-war landscape of wreckage and debris still highly visible in the early 1950s. The opera thus complicates the image of an Elizabethan Golden Age, indeed the very notion of a Golden Age and the organic and rural concepts adopted in conservative interpretations of the Elizabethans. Before constructing the history of *Gloriana* and setting it within the larger story of the Coronation, I owe it both to the form and to my readers briefly to sketch the particularly British development of opera and the special relationship of this development to long-standing debates on national history and music.

NO NATIVE OPERA: THE BELATED EMERGENCE OF ENGLISH HISTORICAL OPERA

Of all the forms of historical spectacle discussed in this book, opera probably is the oldest. Drama set to music and drawing on a reservoir of mythologies and histories may be dated back to the early seventeenth century. In Britain, however, native opera on a historical English subject, written and performed in the vernacular, was a wholly new artefact in the late seventeenth century. From Purcell's death in 1691, opera remained foreign and was imported from Italy and then from Germany and France. The so-called 'English musical Renaissance', conventionally dated from the 1870s, skipped opera, leaving Britain behind these two younger nations and behind older ones like France.[15] The lack of a native operatic tradition and of an appropriate apparatus for cultivating it (until 1946 there was no national opera house) was decried as a loss of national prestige and an international humiliation. Francis Hueffer's exhortation to England in 1879, to 'occupy her proper place amongst musical nations', would be repeated, again and again, well into the 1940s.[16] In 1921, the Carnegie Trust's 'Report upon the History and Present Prospects of Music in the United Kingdom' described this history as a state of foreign occupation: 'England was handed over to the shackling conventions of the Italian stage.' And as late as 1946, J. A. Fuller Maitland echoed Hueffer's complaint: 'Why is it that London, the wealthiest capital city in the world, has never maintained a Royal National Opera comparable to those of Paris, Vienna, Rome, Berlin, or even those of Copenhagen and Stockholm?'[17]

Virtually all advocates of national opera, from Frederick Crowest in the 1880s and 1890s to Ralph Vaughan Williams in the 1910s and 1920s, regarded it as a vehicle for the transmission of the nation's history to 'the people' by inculcating notions of its origins and identity.[18] Ideas about 'musical citizenship', cultivated through an apprenticeship in history and via an exposure to forms of music which represented native traditions and history, were in essence democratic. But before the aftermath of the Second World War they had little or no relation to actual

[15] There are numerous works on the English musical renaissance. Most useful are Frank Howes, *The English Musical Renaissance* (New York, 1966) and Meirion Hughes and Robert Stradling, *The English Musical Renaissance 1860–1940: Construction and Deconstruction* (London, 1993). They neglect, however, to look at the plurality of opera and its revival in Wales, Scotland, and Ireland. Jean Marie Hoover's 'Constructions of National Identities: Opera and Nationalism in the British Isles' (Ph.D. diss., Indiana University, 1999), fills in this gap.

[16] Francis Hueffer, 'The Chances of English Opera', *Macmillan Magazine*, 40 (May 1879), 57–65 at 57.

[17] Quoted in Edward J. Dent, 'The Future of English Opera', in Eric Crozier (ed.), *Opera in English, Sadler's Wells Opera Books* (London, 1946), 26–41.

[18] Their views on national opera formed a part of a continuous debate on the subject of musical nationalism. Frederick Crowest's *The Story of British Music: From the Earliest Times to the Tudor Period* (London, 1896) was followed by Cecil Forsyth, *Music and Nationalism: A Study of English Opera* (London, 1911). Vaughan Williams's *National Music and Other Essays* appeared in 1931.

developments: opera certainly did not belong to the people. Indeed it probably was the least democratic and most exclusive form of spectacle and history. And its exclusivity preserved social and cultural distinction. Opera in Britain, noted its critics in the late nineteenth century, was the province of a 'fraction of society', royalty and the rich. In the sharp words of George Bernard Shaw, a music critic from 1876, Covent Garden was the refuge of the 'exceedingly rich for the purpose of maintaining a postprandial resort for themselves', a veritable 'class mumbo jumbo'.[19] Royal patronage and the support of the aristocratic and wealthy, noted detractors, cultivated foreignness and caused a grievous neglect of home-grown efforts to create native opera. Covent Garden itself, initially called the 'Italian Opera', was the venue for imported art. Although operas in the vernacular on 'national' topics had been composed since 1833, the Garden did not stage an opera in English during its regular season before 1895 (Frederic Hymen Cowen's *Harold, or the Norman Conquest*) and this was highly exceptional. To be sure, various private commercial opera groups performed in London and in the provinces, in Cardiff (in Welsh), Edinburgh, and Dublin, but the metropolitan repertoire remained 'foreign', and from the late nineteenth century German and distinctly Wagnerian.

The apparatus for and of a central, state-supported English national opera developed piecemeal during the Second World War and emerged after it. This belated emergence, which quickly evolved to a surge of creative composing, production, and performance, in small groups and in grand operas, is partly attributable to the Arts Council's selective support of the arts and definite preference for opera—above all other forms of music and indeed most other arts—as an instrument for the spreading of quality culture. The Council, not least because of Keynes's own preferences, generated, commissioned, subsidized, and attempted to control the production of music in general, while granting degrees of autonomy to a substantial number of musicians. The introduction of state patronage of opera and music has been recently surveyed and it should suffice here to repeat its chronology. Indirect support of opera groups, including the Royal Opera Co. Ltd (one of a number of private syndicates and companies), was granted from 1934 in the form of tax relief. Shortly after the outbreak of the war, the Pilgrim Trust (one of the first agencies to support preservation of heritage and historical monuments as well) began offering direct subvention for the arts; it was succeeded by CEMA, to be succeeded in 1945 by a permanent institution of national arts funding, chartered as the Arts Council.[20] The favouring of opera may be understood as an example of a cultural politics of distinction ingrained in the post-war policy of the diffusion of culture, as well as a perpetuation of the longer-term cultural elitism of the inter-war liberal state.

[19] *Shaw's Music: The Complete Musical Criticism of Bernard Shaw*, ed. Dan E. Lawrence (London, 1981), 713–14.

[20] Eric Walter White, *A History of English Opera* (London, 1983), 405–10 and Taylor, *Art for the Nation*, 176–7.

Such a view is well presented by Alan Sinfield.[21] But, as I show later, a number of agents involved in opera production after the war, not least the composers themselves, came from a long tradition stressing the social and even a political role of music 'for the people', Britten himself being one example of this tradition.

As Paul Kildea has convincingly demonstrated, the Council sought to establish an English tradition of the spectacular grand opera, the definitive nationalist form of historical musical spectacle, so conspicuously absent in Britain.[22] In 1946 the Council reopened the Royal Opera House at Covent Garden with its first resident state company and began sponsoring operas in the vernacular by 'native' composers and performers. From the start, the definition of national historical opera and the national institutions supporting it was intertwined with the policy of reviving a past deemed national. The juncture of concepts of national culture and history on the one hand, and state intervention on the other, is easily noticeable before and during the Festival of Britain in 1951. As Becky E. Conekin has recently shown, the Festival was considerably more than just a 'tonic for the nation' and a 'pat on its back', celebrating Britain's survival of the destruction and deprivations of the war and the prolonged ensuing period of austerity. The Festival's planners imagined a 'New' and modern 'Britain' that was consensual and united across classes, a social democratic community with universal access to an educative culture.[23] This was a vision of a 'people's Britain', symbolizing the post-war agenda of the Labour Party. The vision of Britain's modernity in the sciences and the arts, as well as in a preserved 'British way of life', drew on and utilized representations of the past as timeless, emphasizing the ancient traditions of 'deep England' and its people rather than sequences of events and periods, and celebrated British character. 'The Land and the People' in their organic and symbiotic relationship were celebrated. These were ordinary people rather than exceptional heroes, and the very ordinariness of their lives and struggles made up the fabric of their and the nation's survival. At the same time, the very notion of Britishness excluded coloured people, Jews, and, to a great extent, women, as Conekin, Wendy Webster, and Sonya Rose have demonstrated.[24]

Whereas representations of history on the South Bank and in the Festival's official publications were traditional, sometimes Whiggish, and occasionally organic in their emphasis on the land and on a quintessentially English instinct for liberty (with landmarks such as the Constitution, the judicial system, Roman Catholic Emancipation, and, of course, the freedom to unionize), some of the music created for the Festival, especially operas, presented a more complex approach to history. The Arts Council Music Panel initiated a number of

21 Sinfield, *Literature, Politics and Culture*, 50–3.

22 Paul Kildea, *Selling Britten : Music and the Market Place* (Oxford, 2002).

23 Conekin, *'The Autobiography of a Nation'*, 7–18.

24 Ibid. 80–116; Webster, *Englishness and Empire*; Sonya O. Rose, *Which People's War? National Identity and Citizenship in Wartime Britain 1939–45* (Oxford, 2003), 71–151.

operatic projects with no parallel in Britain, encouraging small companies to mount revivals of operas, and sponsoring an open competition for British operas, to be submitted anonymously. The competition itself, the subjects chosen to celebrate the past, and the very identity of some competitors, punctured definitions of a homogenous national history and could not easily be accommodated within the guiding plan and vision of the Festival. Of the four winners three were immigrant Jews, one of them, Arthur Benjamin, a 'colonial' from South Africa, and two, Karl Rankl (Covent Garden's manager) and Berthold Goldschmidt, musical refugees from National Socialism. The one truly 'English' winner transpired to be a Communist: Alan Bush.

The four historical operas they produced did not fit comfortably with the official notions of 'Land' and 'People', intriguingly stretching both. Indeed with one exception, these operas flouted the Festival's definition of English character and tradition. Benjamin picked Dickens's *A Tale of Two Cities*, which, as shown in Chapter 3, became a part of the popular repertoire of histories of the French Revolution, notably popular theatre and Revolution films. But what the popular stage and the film accommodated proved problematic for a festival of unity. Goldschmidt's *Beatrice Cenci*, based upon Shelly's torrid *The Cenci* and set in a turbulent late sixteenth-century Rome, was a far cry from the consensual notions of an English Renaissance. The opera was not only 'foreign', but countered every sanctified notion about the family and a congenial domestic environment as a conservatory for the nation which the Festival so carefully cultivated. *Beatrice Cenci* was about abuse, torture, and patricide within one household. Small wonder that it was rejected by Covent Garden as 'too foreign'. Rankl's adaptation of a classic of the Irish cultural revival of the 1900s, John Millington Synge's *Deirdre of the Sorrows* (1909), drawing on Gaelic mythologies and lore, could hardly be deemed fit for performance in a festival of British unity. Notwithstanding Rankl's position as Director of Covent Garden, the opera would never be performed. More surprisingly, Bush's *Wat Tyler*, celebrating the 1381 peasants' rebellion and evoking recycled and apparently safe notions of liberty and the 'Englishman's rights', also proved indigestible to the Council, probably because Bush's commitment to Communism, membership in the Communist Party, and biography as a 'revolutionary' artist creating 'for the people' was not agreeable to mainstream cultural impresarios. During the 1930s Bush was involved in the organization of working men's choral societies in London (a consensual enough venture), and in 1934, during Britain's worst period of unemployment, he mounted in the Crystal Palace the first Workingmen's Pageant to celebrate the centenary of the trial of the Tolpuddle Martyrs. The Saints, whose construction as TUC icons was completed in the Festival itself, were 'safe history'. Bush apparently was not deemed a 'safe' creator of the past, being a dissident from consensual Labour. Three of the prize-winning operas took decades to be performed in Britain; one (Rankl's) was never staged. Of the four, Bush's oeuvre fared best, being staged periodically in the

DDR, where the very first performance of *Wat Tyler* during the very year of the Festival got him a twenty-five-minute standing ovation.

The fate of the winning operas discloses a narrow definition of Englishness on the part of the music establishment. And there is additional evidence to the excluding definition of native music and musicians. Hostility to German artists lingered after the war and, ironically, hit refugees from Nazism, typically Jews. A Memorandum to the Music Panel of the Arts Council by Stuart Wilson, the Panel's director, dated 29 January 1946, was critical of CEMA's stated policy not to employ foreigners and objected to outright discrimination that would create a 'Ghetto' unfavourable to musical standards. Proposing not to exclude 'resident foreigners' in practice, he advocated avoidance of an official commitment against discrimination and distinguished between German men and women of middle age entering Britain before 1936 and not applying for naturalization before the war (to be excluded), and 20-year-olds educated in Britain.[25] To be sure, later the Council did not prevent the employment of former German or Austrian immigrants, Rankl himself being an example. But prejudice on account of nationality and ethnicity lingered. Exclusion from the emerging English musical 'canon' that was also regarded as 'modern' sometimes had to do with competing notions of modernism and the modern in opera and in music generally. As I demonstrate in my analysis of the dynamics of the rejection of the Coronation opera, 'modern' was defined in terms that were both historical and national. The foreign (and dominant) influence on English music was rejected by sizeable sectors within the world of British music. During and after the Second World War, German influences in particular proved problematic, both the Wagnerian school, which swept musicians before the war, and 'modernist' German schools, represented by composers like Arnold Schoenberg (Goldschmidt's mentor, whose reception in Britain had been problematic). Bush adhered to musical schools and traditions of modernity outside the mainstream English musical renaissance (notably to Shostakovich). To be sure, these affiliations did not intervene in the competition itself; they did contribute to the suppression of the operas and their marginalization.

NO ENGLISH *AIDA*: NATIONAL HISTORICAL OPERAS, 1951–1953

Yet the Arts Council's policies may not be interpreted as a case of simple 'exclusion' of motifs and creators on the margins of the consensus about Englishness and opera. True, the Festival staged safe and uncontroversial musical historical spectacles like Vaughan Williams's opera *The Pilgrim's Progress*, written between 1920 and 1949 and incorporating his 1906 incidental stage adaptation

[25] 'Arts Council of Great Britain: Fourth Meeting of the Council's Music Panel', Britten–Pears Library (henceforward BP), BP/1/348.

of Bunyan's text and his own 1921 *Shepherds of the Delectable Mountains.* The opera benefited from the aura of its revered source, which had long been a part of the culture and political language of the Labour movement. A 'tale of morality', it also contained many pastoral and folkish motifs, which had been the trademark of Vaughan Williams's native operas. But the other Festival opera, Benjamin Britten's *Billy Budd,* staged in Covent Garden on 1 December 1951, presented a considerably more complex rendering of historical periods, motifs, and native traditions. It focused not on a narrative of individualistic progress dressed up in the traditional garb of a Christian *Bildung,* but on collective disobedience, revolt, and arbitrary rule on board a ship during the revolutionary decades at the end of the eighteenth century. Notwithstanding explicit criticism of its subject matter and implied disapproval of its representation of male sexuality (it had an all-male cast), *Billy Budd* enjoyed great popularity, far surpassing Vaughan Williams's oeuvre and, high on the heels of the 1945 success of *Peter Grimes,* made Britten a 'national composer' and a modernist deemed a true representative of the 'English' way in music. His reputation would be further enhanced with the publication, early in 1952, of a collection of papers summarizing his work. The Royal Permission granted to *Gloriana* and subsequent honours seem to have firmly located him within the consensus about history and

Fig. 22. Benjamin Britten *c.*1953

the monarchy and to have put a seal on his status as 'court artist' and official interpreter of the past. (See Fig. 22.)

And yet both the composer and the opera puncture notions of centrality and marginality, consensus and disagreement, minority and diffusion in the national culture, as well as the brokerage of national history. Britten's very Englishness was far more complex and open-ended than that of the group of the 'nationalist' (and pastoralist) composers like Vaughan Williams himself and William Walton, not to mention Edward Elgar. To start with, Britten's politics and ideological affiliations could have compromised his identity as an Englishman in the eyes of custodians of national music, hence his mandate to be an interpreter of English history. Becoming an avowed pacifist in the mid-thirties, he upheld his anti-armament, anti-war positions throughout the Second World War, leaving Britain for the USA in 1939 and returning in 1942 to face a military tribunal. His cooperation with W. H. Auden (before the war and during his stay in the States) too cast him as a different Briton and, at times, as an 'other'. His homosexuality, never flaunted yet widely known, and his professional relationships with homosexual artists (E. M. Forster and William Plomer as librettists, Auden himself, not to mention his partner and the leading man in his operas, Peter Pears) were resented as an additional sign of sectarianism and separateness, often associated by critics and self-appointed guardians of modern national art with his music, and described as the tag of a 'clique' within the 'nation'.[26] Britten's position vis-à-vis the art establishment and the Council, a position manifest in the process of the commissioning and production of *Gloriana*, also complicates assumptions about patronage and control of the post-war work of art. For here, more than anywhere else, traditional aristocratic and direct royal patronage played a central role; Council support followed, and the combination of both made the opera itself and the whole notion and institution of national opera and national history an easy target for public criticism.

Gloriana was conceived and produced in the space between private artistic enterprise, court patronage, and the newer kind of state sponsorship. This had to do with Britten's own role as cultural entrepreneur and his abilities to make good use of changes in the apparatuses of art and music production. From his earliest career he had been able to work alongside the brokers of modern musical tastes such as academic and commercial publishers (Oxford Music and later Boosey & Hawkes), who also served as the distributors of music in London and the provinces, the BBC Third Programme, that arbiter of improving culture, and music critics and journals, not to mention his ability to appropriate popular media like the film, both for and in his work. He also strongly advocated a role for the artist in a changing society and the state, consistently urging the creation of art 'outside

[26] Britten's politics during the thirties and early forties are discussed in Paul Kildea, 'Britten, Auden and "Otherness"', in Mervyn Cooke (ed.), *The Cambridge Companion to Benjamin Britten* (Cambridge, 1999), 36–54 and Humphrey Carpenter, *Benjamin Britten* (London, 1992).

art' and 'for the people'. He summed up his views on social art in a speech given at Hull University in 1962, later published in a special 1963 issue of the *London Magazine*, dedicated to his fiftieth birthday: 'artists are not only artists, they are men, members of society, and must take their place in society . . . Artists cannot work in a vacuum—they need society and society needs them.' Moreover, artists should write and 'compose for particular performers or groups (even if they are young or inexperienced), write for special occasions even if they seem trivial'.[27] Even before the Coronation his reputation as a 'social' composer writing for the people had been well established. His interest in 'the people' had manifested itself in the histories of ordinary men and women who were the heroes and heroines of his two best-selling operas: sailors and fishermen, workers and publicans. Indeed his histories expressed interest 'in the people around him'. As *Young Elizabethan* pointed out in a feature devoted to Britten in the special Coronation number:

> He knows sea-faring people, the fishermen who are his neighbours in Aldeburgh. The hero in Billy Budd though he came from Bristol might just as well have been an Aldeburgh boy of the time of the Napoleonic war. It is Benjamin Britten's interest in the people around him, the men of the lifeboat, the fishermen who go out to the North Sea and come home . . . He is a keen observer of people's lives and activities.[28]

The death of George VI and the accession of Elizabeth in 1952 created both an opportunity and the 'special occasion' sought by Britten. The change of government in October 1951 effectively killed off the Festival idea of a demotic Labour culture, substituting it with a revivalist notion of the past. To be sure, despite the different agendas of Labour's 'Lord Festival' (Herbert Morrison and his team of experts) and those of Churchill's cabinet, there were continuities between the Festival's resurrections of the past and those emerging before and during the Coronation. Not least among these were the stress on unity, family values, and the sophisticated usages of modern technologies to promote both a vision of the future and the ideal of unity. Moreover, the imagery of the Young Elizabethans and the idiom of youth and rejuvenation, both originating during the war, cut across political divisions. There are, however, marked differences between the so-called 'two Festivals' in their treatment of history. The first Festival evolved around a mundane and everyday people's history. The second occasioned another revival of a heroic past of monarchs as the focus of people's collective emotions, and as the engine of change—much in tune with the early twentieth century and inter-war 'democratic' monarchism discussed in Chapters 6 and 7. Moreover, the obvious connection with the Elizabethan past called for the inclusion of the Empire and colonies, old and new, within the collective biography of people and monarch, thus 'modernizing' the notion of the Empire

[27] *The London Magazine*, 3, no. 7 (Oct. 1963), 90.
[28] 'Fanfare for Britten', *Young Elizabethan*, 6, no. 6 (June 1953), 20.

and substituting it with one of the young Commonwealth (the description of Elizabeth II as the young queen of a young Commonwealth immediately springs to mind). This was in stark contrast to the muting and, as Conekin has pointed out, deliberate neglect of the history of the Empire in the Festival's central venue on the South Bank in London. The post-war decline of the Empire, highlighted in the handing over of India and Burma, parts of the Middle East, and the colonial wars in Kenya and Malaya, as well as the change in the monarch's constitutional status into head of a divisible empire, made the revival of a past imperial England all the more appealing.[29]

Such changes in the political climate and in political priorities in themselves are not enough to explain the status accorded by the establishment and the state to a particular history. The promotion of *Gloriana* to state opera and the centrepiece of the Coronation celebrations was paved by the patronage of Lord George Harewood, the Queen's cousin, a modern music and literature enthusiast. From *Gloriana*'s very inception, both he and Britten represented and constructed it as a 'national opera'. The idea for a national English opera that would compete with the great European historical operas was aired after the King's death:

> What was 'national' expression in opera, we asked ourselves: what were the national operas of different countries? *The Bartered Bride* for the Czechs, said Ben, *Manon* for the French, *Boris* [*Godunov*] and all that for the Russians. We weren't happy about the Germans—had it to be Lortzing, whom we none of us liked, or must it be *Meistersinger*... For the Italians undoubtedly *Aida*, said Ben. 'It's the perfect expression of every kind of Italian nationalist feeling, national pride—but where's the English equivalent?' 'Well you'd better write one.'[30]

The image of Britten as the creator of the first English historical national opera flows from this story, with its unhidden snobbish tone and appeal; the discussion on the first English opera takes place on Austrian soil, in a high-class ski resort. The right past, 'a period' that would serve as the basis for the national epos, was vehemently discussed. 'The Merrie England of the Tudors or Elizabethan?—and a subject—Henry VIII? Too obvious, and an unattractive hero. Queen Elizabeth? Highly appropriate! What about a national opera in time for the next Coronation?'[31]

Harewood's mediation between Britten and the court was reinforced by the *gravitas* of another courtier, Sir Alan Lascelles, his cousin and, like him, a first cousin to the Queen, an influential Private Secretary to her father and herself, and a strong persona at court, as well as by the support of the Royal Family.[32] An

[29] P. C. Gordon Walker, 'Crown Divisible', *Twentieth Century*, 153, no. 916 (1953), 245–9.

[30] *Manon* by Jules Massenet, *The Bartered Bride* by Bedrich Smetana, *Boris Godunov* by Modeste Musorgsky. Albert Lortzing was a composer and librettist, and establisher of 19th-c. German light opera. George Harewood, *The Tongs and the Bones* (London, 1981), 134.

[31] Ibid. 135.

[32] Plomer to Britten, 2 Aug. 1952, BP (237/2) Plomer. Later correspondence with the Queen and Queen Elizabeth the Queen Mother reveals an easy-going and (on their part) informal relationship. BP/Elizabeth II, Queen of England, letters dating 25 June 1966 to May 1975.

eager Covent Garden and a compliant Arts Council granted the considerable finance necessary for the production of a national grand opera (mounting eventually to over £23,000) which fitted so well with the Council's notion of musical and artistic revival.[33]

HISTORY AT THE OPERA: COMPETING INTERPRETATIONS OF THE ELIZABETHANS

Gloriana's relatively padded way to Covent Garden, and its very subject, composition, décor, and staging may seem, and to many a contemporary did seem, to guarantee a fanfare to 'merrie England', a historical pageant on the lines of previous traditions of nineteenth- and early twentieth-century spectacles of the Tudors. Indeed most of the ingredients of the opera predisposed spectators to expect a traditionalist historical spectacle, reviving Elizabethan musical repertoires and even emulating great foreign historical operas.[34] Yet the spectacle, first performed in an ostentatiously decked Covent Garden on the night of 8 June 1953 and more modestly during the following months, blasted expectations for an easy reconciliation between past grandeur and a national present and future. This spectacle also frustrated the hopes of those who expected it to be simply the transmitter of political and artistic conservatism.

The tension between audiences' predispositions, based on familiar representations and images of Elizabeth I and the Elizabethans, and the rejection of some of these older images is already apparent in the title and the selection of subject matter and period within her reign. The title is, of course, the appellation invented by the courtiers and artists of the Tudor queen to celebrate her powerful public persona, and had had a majestic and mythical aura. The reference to Edmund Spenser's *Faerie Queene*, the prototypical allegory of Elizabeth-Gloriana, too was promising. Thus the 1953 spectacle, written and composed to be a part of the larger spectacle and media event of the Coronation, appeared to have been a court opera, paying direct homage to Spenser's allegory with the divine queen at its centre (and, of course, *Faerie Queene* in its entirety is constructed as a pageant). This homage seemed to be completely in tune with the broader musical revival generated by and for the Coronation and initiated by the Council. To celebrate the New Elizabethan Age the Council initially proposed a 'Coronation Festival' located in London and focusing on grand, spectacular revivals of early modern musical forms in the opera, ballet, and an Elizabethan 'masque' to be staged at Hampton Court, as well as low-cost commissions from composers and poets to make up a

[33] Robert Hewison, '"Happy Were He"': Benjamin Britten and the Gloriana Story', in Paul Banks (ed.), *Britten's Gloriana* (Aldeburgh Studies in Music, 1; Woodbridge, 1993), 1–16. On the Arts Council see p. 12.

[34] See pp. 302–4, 308.

collection of a cappella pieces.[35] The latter would later be substituted by madrigals.

The careful instructions to the artists composing the madrigals specified the kind of relationship between history and the present which the Council favoured. Aspects of contemporary Britain were to be treated 'in a spirit of acceptance, praise, loyalty or love'. Sardonic tones, brittleness, and satire were deemed 'out of place and damaging'. 'Contemporary Britain' contained the countryside and the city and city life, the public and private, tradition and innovation, a catholic inventory rather reminiscent of that of the Festival. Historical analogues and genealogies stretching from the first to the second Elizabethans were positively encouraged: 'A search for modern parallels with the age of the first "Oriana" may prove fruitful: the continuing spirit of discovery; the renascence of music or of the Arts as a whole, loyalty to the monarchy, and compliment to the first lady of the land.'[36] The word 'Oriana' itself is a supreme example of the language and practice of revival in the production of history, for it refers to Thomas Morley's *Triumphs of Oriana*, the collection of madrigals by twenty English composers published in 1601 in honour of Gloriana herself. The madrigal itself was considered a national, or naturalized, form (as it emanated from the original Italian form or an Italianate version). The outcome of the Council's initiative was the collection of 'modern' madrigals known as *Garland for the Queen*, or *Oriana*, premiering during Coronation week (and performed again in early 2003 for the Golden Jubilee). The composers themselves rose to the expectations of the Music Panel by utilizing various Tudor techniques as well as drawing on Tudor motifs, a very common practice of the English musical renaissance. The *Garland*, other musical projects and events initiated by the Council, and the myriad exhibitions and pageants with Elizabethan and other historical themes were seen as 'revivals'. The 'new' creative and well-orchestrated outburst was aimed at echoing the Elizabethan Renaissance, when 'English genius burst forth in glory', when 'England was a nest of singing birds. Poets flashed out like stars above the darkness of men's minds.'[37]

The idea of a second English Renaissance under the auspices of a democratic version of the monarchy supported by the Arts Council generated sceptical comment and witticism, as in the 'Elizabethan', a pastiche on court art and state-financed cultural revival, by Sagittarius:

> This Age hath genius too of high report,
> And now, conjoined with some artistic Earls, Arts Council gallants
> Do cheer them on to bow before the Court,
> As Shakespeare once, and Spenser, Tudor churls,
> Displayed their talents[38]

[35] Arts Council of Great Britain, EL5/85, Archive of Art and Design, V&A Museum, 'Operation Gloriana', document 1. No date.
[36] Quoted in Kildea, *Selling Britten*, 132.
[37] Gibbs, *The New Elizabethans*, 17.
[38] *New Statesman and the Nation*, 7 June 1952.

Sagittarius's allusion to Britten as an artist-courtier, much in the line of the Elizabethan propagandists of the monarchy, struck a chord. For *Gloriana*, more than any other Coronation project, was a spectacle about power and the state, a direct reference to the Elizabethan spectacle of the monarchy with the monarch at its centre. At the same time it related to the grander pageant staged in London and Westminster Abbey on 2 June 1953, a pageant that was traditional and modern at the same time, presenting continuity between the ancient and even timeless monarchy and the declining Empire of the present. Modern technologies, especially television, were harnessed to transmit the spectacle with its plethora of 'invented traditions' to over twenty million spectators in Britain and millions in Europe and North America, and broadcast it to over 100 millions the world over.[39] In the opera, the role of the queen in the drama of power is echoed in Gloriana's words in the second scene of Act III:

> Hearken, it is the prince who speaks
> A prince is set upon a stage
> Alone, in sight of all the world[40]

However, the operatic theatre of power was never conceived or represented by Britten and William Plomer, the librettist, as straightforward national symbols. The opera is set in 'The later years of her [Elizabeth's] reign' and the most troubled ones, witnessing inflation, social and political unrest in the home counties, and rebellion in Ulster, as well as recusant activity and a wider Roman Catholic opposition. The drama focuses on the two years between 1599 and 1601 and is entirely on the last phase of the torrid relationship between the Queen and Robert Devereux, Earl of Essex, from his appointment as Elizabeth's Lord Deputy of Ireland to his rebellion and subsequent execution. Topics and motifs etched on the collective memory, like the victory over the Armada, the maritime empire, and the triumph of the Reformation, are altogether excluded. Naval might is referred to only indirectly in scattered and sometimes unflattering mentions of the controversial Sack of Cadiz in 1596, in which Essex himself played a dubious part. Overseas rule is represented through the Ulster episode and Elizabeth's disastrous attempt to conquer Ireland, a rather sensitive topic. The selection of period and focus on the relationship between the old queen and her young courtier was determined by Britten's and Plomer's main source, Lytton Strachey's 1928 biography *Elizabeth and Essex*, introduced to Britten by the enthusiastic Earl of Harewood and immediately appealing to the composer. To tone down Strachey's version of the late Elizabethans, Plomer used Neale's work, but it is clear from the libretto and the correspondence

[39] The invention of traditions of the monarchy is thoroughly discussed by Cannadine, 'The Context, Performance and Meaning of Ritual'.

[40] Benjamin Britten, 'Gloriana: An Opera in Three Acts by William Plomer', in *The Operas of Benjamin Britten: The Complete Librettos Illustrated with Designs of the First Productions*, ed. David Herbert (London; repr. 1979), Act III, Scene iii, p. 229.

between the composer and librettist that the biography remained the opera's main written source.

Britten and Plomer discarded Strachey's radical approach to gender and sexuality apparent in his representation of the queen and Essex as androgynous characters. They also discarded much of his Freudian reading of Elizabeth's conduct and policies throughout the affair, which Strachey had interpreted as a wronged child's vindication of her murdered mother, to repay a powerful father/monarch. What they retained of Strachey's experiment in historical biography was his dramatic interpretation of the last years of the Elizabethan era as a 'tragedy' and his broader interpretation of the sixteenth century as both brutal and illustrious. Throughout, *Elizabeth and Essex* stresses the interdependence of these two faces of the Elizabethans, apparent in the power and majesty of the early English state and in its resort to violence and torture, which Strachey found appealing and occasionally sexually titillating (as is evident in his repeated reference to the slicing of young men's bejewelled ears): 'Thus it happened that the glory of her Age could never have existed without the spies of Walsingham, the damp cells of the Tower, and the notes of answers, calmly written down by cunning questioners, between screams of agony.'[41]

Like the biography, *Gloriana* moves between the spectacle of royal power that draws popular love and acclaim, and manifestations of the instability and arbitrariness of the monarchy. The opera also draws on the repertoire of the inter-war Tudor films (themselves based, as shown earlier, on Strachey's experimentalism), especially on juxtapositions of public pageantry and private anxiety. The opera's first scene takes place in the tilting ring (not actually seen by the audience). Dramatic action then moves to a private apartment at Nonesuch Palace, witnessing in rapid succession high politics in the form of a consultation between Cecil and the Queen, then a private audience between her and Essex, including the opera's most lyrical pieces, revivals of two of the Earl's own ballades, accompanied by the lute. The interruption, disruption even, of public spectacle and pageant by private tragedy and ambition recurs in the queen's 'progress' and masque at the Guildhall at Norwich, a reworking of the famous progresses, intended to 'show' Elizabeth I to her subjects and muster loyalty, with Essex's frustration worked out in the background. Later, the queen herself interrupts the sumptuous choral dances at Whitehall Palace with a grotesque entry, donning the splendid dress of Frances, Lady Essex, to signal displeasure at the latter's presumption to out-dress royalty. In the most private space, the queen's bedchamber, she is interrupted, in her informal dress, wigless, and without make-up, by the disobedient Essex, returned from Ireland, supplicating her to share her rule with him. The remainder of the story swiftly moves from the London streets during the Essex rebellion to the Queen's death scene.

[41] Lytton Strachey, *Elizabeth and Essex: A Tragic History* (London and New York, 1928).

As with the inter-war Tudor film, the shifting boundaries between public power and private tragedy, between the beloved Bess and Elizabeth the arbitrary ruler, are represented in gendered terms. The aging queen is an absolute ruler but also a woman; Essex obeys her in his role as courtier and subject, but as a young and ambitious man rejects her capricious supremacy, callously describing her decaying femininity and mortality. In the third scene of Act III, he and his aggrieved wife Frances, just slighted by the Queen, sing in unison:

Lady Essex
My friends take care:
Her sudden rage is over now.
Essex
Who last year struck me with her hand
Before the Council!
Who taunts my wife before her Court!
Lady Essex
She is the Queen!
Essex
No spiteful woman ever born
Shall with impunity do this!
Lady Essex
Robert, take care:
She is the Queen,
And as the Queen
Hath her conditions.
Essex
Conditions! Conditions!
Her conditions are as crooked as her carcass.[42]

The duality within the image of queenship and that of the monarchy, as both majestic and fragile and even decomposing, was fraught with unresolved tensions. And this duality contradicted both the images and metaphors of youth and renewal at the very centre of the young Elizabethans ethos, effectively destabilizing the idea of a historical revival as a form of repetition and optimism. Moreover, the introduction of old age and mortality into the ritual of the Coronation inaugurating a young 'modern' monarch with the glamour and aura of a media and film star could be far more disturbing than representations of the mature and even old Elizabeth I during the 1930s and 1940s (see Ch. 7). For the glamour of the new Elizabeth and the New Elizabethans countered Britain's post-war gradual abdication from the Empire and the reality of its decline as a world power. The forceful and uncomfortable duality of power and decline becomes almost threatening in the opera's last scene, just before the final curtain,

[42] *Gloriana*, Act III, Scene iii, p. 223.

Fig. 23. 'Dead, dead, but not buried': Joan Cross as the Queen in *Gloriana* (1953)

when the dying Gloriana delivers her final words in a speaking voice rather than in arioso (see Fig. 23):

> *Queen*
> Mortua, mortua, sed non sepulta! . . .
> I see no weighty reason that I should be fond to live or fear to die[43]

As I show later, there is abundant evidence that the contrast to Elizabeth Windsor and the very complexity of the image of royal power taxed spectators present at Covent Garden and radio listeners who listened to its BBC recording.

Plomer and Britten were aware of these tensions and contradictions and exploited them, yet took care to counter the harsh images of death and tragedy with textual references allegorizing the queen's freshness and beauty. Thus the anonymous Elizabethan ballad, attributed to a schoolboy, on green leaves and a red rose, appears as a refrain throughout the text, representing adoration of the queen by her subjects:

> Green Leaves are we,
> Red Rose our golden Queen
> O crowned rose among the leaves so green[44]

[43] Ibid. 230. [44] Ibid., Act I, Scene i, p. 210.

The red rose had figured prominently in Elizabethan iconography; here it figures as a symbol of the loyalty of subjects to their queen, but is also transformed into an emblem of old age and mortality. Essex's burst into the royal bedroom, which exposes the bald and wrinkled queen's frailty and temporality, elicits from her the lines:

> And the rose must feel the frost
> And nothing renew us can
> When the flame in the rose is lost[45]

This explicit denial of the possibility for a renewal, like the preoccupation with decay and death, and the constant references to arbitrariness and instability all exemplify a rather complex attitude towards revival. A revival of the first Elizabethan age was not and could not be its 'duplication'. Nor was a national opera a pastiche of popular recollections of the past, or a mere pageant. To Britten a history in music and drama was a construction of a complex past that could be retrieved only critically and with attention paid to contexts of modernity. This approach did not exclude pageantry. *Gloriana* was, after all, a state opera. But as Plomer noted, 'it seemed advisable to shun everything that might smack of Wardour Street, Merrie England, Good Queen Bess, or the half-baked, half-timbering of debased twentieth-century "Tudor" styling', no doubt referring to inter-war suburban architecture and Tudor films (Wardour Street was the centre of the British film industry).[46]

MUSIC AS HISTORY: TRADITION AND MODERNITY

The challenge to the idiom and imagery of a New, Young Elizabethan era, indeed to nostalgic comparisons between post-war and Elizabethan England, as an appropriate feeling and an approach towards the past, is manifest in Britten's usage of available historical musical material. As much as *Gloriana* is a version of the history of the first Elizabethans, it is a history of their *music*; but it is one by a composer attuned, and seeking to create, modern musical forms. Practically all historians of music from 1953 onwards noted Britten's use of Tudor musical genres and instruments. Indeed the opera seems to be a condensed glossary as well as a history of sixteenth-century music. Two scenes of three in Act II, described by him as diversions, refer to original Tudor as well as Stuart music. The Choral Dances are a restitution of the allegorical masque, a generic Elizabethan form. The Court Dances in Act III, Scene ii include a dazzling succession of a pavan, a galliard, a lavolta, and a coranto. And to top the bill of historical 'types', there is a Morris dance, performed by a boy with a blackened face, a reference to the sixteenth-century *morisca*. In the less spectacular parts of

[45] *Gloriana*, Act III, Scene iii, p. 233.

[46] *Tempo*, no. 28 (Summer 1953).

the opera there is constant reference to ballads (notably a direct citation of Essex's own, in the Second Lute Song in Act I, Scene ii), madrigals, and popular Tudor motifs like 'Green Leaves', this last serving as a leitmotif throughout the entire drama. The combination of pieces of pageant, ballet, and music echoed the older, seventeenth- and eighteenth-century opera composed of 'numbers', or separable units, apparently without dramatic sequel and span. The serial and apparently disjointed structure of the opera was 'English' in yet another sense. 'Numbers opera' was favoured by nationalist composers because it was the opposite of the 'foreign' Wagnerian dramatic structure, with its narrative and compositional unity, a structure which British musicians had fought hard to resist. Though some music critics resented the apparent lack of structure, some of the numbers, especially adaptations of Tudor motifs, appealed even to the most hostile audiences, and were later broadcast and recorded separately.

The apparent historical accuracy of the music, and the richness of period forms, themes, and pageantry were hardly avoidable in an *opéra d'occasion*, as many a contemporary music critic noted, especially when the occasion was a Coronation. But the musical evocation of the Elizabethans is and was much more than 'Tudor pastiche'. It exemplifies and highlights the central characteristic of what may be seen as a modernist attitude to revival and the past: the creation of audience dispositions through a pastiche of familiar reference to the deliberately archaic and 'historic', which are then distorted, turned, and twisted to acquire new form and meaning.

In 1953, not only an audience of connoisseurs but wide and mixed publics had degrees of knowledge of and familiarity with Tudor and Merrie England music. For the Tudors and especially the Elizabethans had had a privileged place in the history of modern music in Britain since the late nineteenth century. The decades of the 1870s and 1880s, which had witnessed the Elizabethan revival in the popular culture of history studied in Chapter 6, also saw the budding of the English musical renaissance, that explosion of musical activity after over a century and a half of lethargy. It was during these decades that an institutional infrastructure of a musical establishment, including academies, schools and colleges of music in London and in provincial centres, was founded, a specialist music press and musical columns in the national press were started, and a 'native' national music on vernacular topics, using vernacular themes, appeared. From its very start this creativity was described as a national renaissance and referred to and characterized in historical terms. Most relevant here, the modern revival of music was directly connected to the Tudor era, the second renaissance to the first, Elizabethan, Renaissance.

The association between modernity and modern nationalism on the one hand, and the Tudor era as an authentically English age on the other, was firmly made in the very first usage of the term 'English Musical Renaissance' in Morton Latham's lecture in Cambridge in 1888 on this subject, followed by his 1890 book *The Renaissance of Music*. Of course, the very term 'renaissance' was borrowed by musicologists, music journalists, and composers from historians: the term comes from Jacob Burckhardt's *The Civilization of the Renaissance in Italy*, published in 1860 and translated into English in 1878, and was applied to the concept of cultural rebirth. This appropriation, indeed the resort to history to place 'modern' art and music, also enhanced the status of nineteenth- and twentieth-century music. The modern revival, it seemed, duplicated the Tudor rebirth. There was a linear development, a musical tradition, beginning in the long sixteenth century and ending with the Stuarts and the death of Purcell, then resuming in 'modern' times. This version of the history of English music not only elevated the Tudors to an iconic status, but also excluded parts of the seventeenth century, the entire eighteenth century, and most of the nineteenth from national history. Thus Handel, whose oratorios (as distinct from his Italian *opere serie*) had from the mid-eighteenth-century been 'anglicized' and regarded as a part of a national repertoire, was deemed 'foreign' (and, worse, 'German') in the new national version of music history, and disparaged as uncreative and even decadent.[47]

The growing contingent of adherents to the national school advocated not only emancipation from foreign tyranny, but also the recovery and development of genuinely English forms of music. Of these forms two, the pre-modern and specifically Tudor folk song (and folk dancing) and polyphonic Tudor music, enjoyed a widespread revival and were practised in both local and nationwide networks of choral societies, choral festivals, and folk music and dancing organizations, spreading at the beginning of the twentieth century and mushrooming during the inter-war period. As Mark Pattison, music critic of *Scrutiny*, noted in 1934, the vast use that numerous composers, headed by Ralph Vaughan Williams, made of Tudor modal polyphony and of folk music rescued the national repertoire from degeneration and atrophy. Composers and librettists extensively borrowed popular musical themes and tended towards the modality characteristic of the English folk song, consistently using the Dorian mode, common in folk songs (and identifiable in 'Greensleeves'). The wish to imitate 'true' historical English styles of the people also explains the preference for diatonic scales characteristic of folk music (contrasting with the Continental modernists' preference for chromatic scales).[48]

Most relevant here, the new renaissance was distinctly ruralist and pastoralist in outlook. It was, as Meirion Hughes and Robert Stradling have noted, a 'historical pastoral', celebrating the countryside, a non-industrial 'deep England', organically tying together people and land and occasionally (and disturbingly during the mid- and late 1930s), frankly folkish. Vaughan Williams's opera *Hugh the Drover* (1910–14) strove to achieve just this feel of the countryside and

[47] On Handel's status see T. C. W. Blanning, *The Culture of Power and the Power of Culture: Old Regime Europe 1660–1789* (Oxford, 2002), 266–79.

[48] Hoover, 'Constructions of National Identities', 516–36.

a typically English village, the everyday life of the common people and their pastimes. The opera was set in the eighteenth century, not in the sixteenth, but it did celebrate customs and manners of the Olden Time, resurrecting a thriving 'heart of England' community with direct references to the composer's own Gloucestershire. Miniature pastoral pieces by him (*The Lark Ascending*, set in 1914 to a poem of the same title by Meredith, is the best-known example) and Frederick Delius (*On Hearing the First Cuckoo in Spring*, 1912) articulated the same organicist feel for land, people, and history so prominent in some of the ruralist writing of the decades between the First and Second World Wars. Vaughan Williams's series of lectures on national music, delivered in the USA, then published in book form (and still widely in print), offered a list of worthy English composers with an appropriate approach to national history and folk music and included a who's who in twentieth-century modern music from Edward Elgar to Arnold Bax and Gustav Holst and from William Walton to Constant Lambert. He did not deign to mention by name those whose own country was not good enough for them and who 'went off to become little Germans or little Frenchmen'.[49] Britten, at the beginning of his career, was too young to have entered the inventory of doyens of pastoralist music. Given his development and Vaughn Williams's grudging regard for him, he would never have been included in it.

The debate on national music and history and its increasing politicization from the thirties on predisposed prospective audiences towards looking for and getting from *Gloriana* another exemplar of a worthy national history in the form of a Tudor and perhaps pastoralist revival. The abundance of precisely the most esteemed and widespread Tudor forms like the madrigal and dance music, not to mention the lavish use of choruses, promised a restitution of the Old Elizabethan Age for the New Elizabethans. However, such expectations were systematically dashed by an array of inventive uses of keys, pitches, orchestration, and composition. The anonymous Tudor ballad 'Green Leaves', recurring throughout the opera, is sounded in the orchestral prelude in a particular lyrical mode and rhythm (the Lydian) to express the people's loyalty to the queen. Later the ballad is obsessively repeated in different keys (D and E flat), the latter jarring the tonality and representing opposition to the queen. In Essex's lute songs and indeed in all of his appearances on stage, 'authentic' madrigal music and ballads are distorted by a profuse use of pedal to represent the Earl's complex personality and his private persona. And the grandiose and easily recognizable courtly dances are distorted by modern instruments and tempo.[50] The stately Pavan is repeated by trombones, accompanying the entry of the queen in the dress she stole from

[49] Quoted in Hughes and Stradling, 163.

[50] Detailed analysis of composition and orchestration is to be found in Donald Mitchell, 'The Paradox of *Gloriana*: Simple and Difficult' and Peter Evans, 'The Number Principle and Dramatic Momentum in *Gloriana*', in Banks (ed.), *Britten's Gloriana*, 67–77, 77–95.

Lady Essex, so that she becomes a clown who lampoons the courtly pageant and indeed the pomp and circumstance of her own court. Thus the dances, the opera's supreme representation of the opulence and brilliance of the monarch, subvert images of the glamour of the monarchy.

Gloriana also diverges from the pastoralist tradition. We may relate this diversion and its form to the changes in the urban scene wrought by the war. The unprecedented destruction of Britain's cities, notably London, a destruction surpassing all previous phases of man-made demolition (attached, as we saw earlier in the book, to modernization), made ruins and debris a part and parcel of post-war everyday urban experience. In conservative interpretations of the New Elizabethans, such as Gibbs's, the post-war ruined city and attempts to rebuild and replan it are condemned as disruptions of historical sequence and continuity.[51] He offers his readers escapes to a countryside that is apparently untouched by the post-war consensus and by the trend towards 'collectivism'. In some other interpretations, such as Rowse's, towns (not cities) figure alongside Country. The experience and sense of urban wreckage was by no means limited to conservatives and did not necessarily generate rural nostalgia. Thus Britten and Plomer evoked a vision of past cities by dramatic references to a rural and urban past which are far more complex than the pastoralists' nostalgia, using occasional and superficial citation of apparently rural themes and motifs only to distort them. *Gloriana* takes place in the bastions of royal power: in the court and in a succession of palaces, in towns and cities like Norwich and London, in guildhalls and on streets. The only countryside evoked in it is artificial and 'framed' in the masque. Reference to nature, not least in the leaves and rose motif, is highly stylized and artificial too. It is urban life, strife, and disorder—and its obverse, the urban populace's loyalty to the queen—which is invoked. Of course urban life is not and cannot be industrial life. And the opera may not be described as belonging to the tradition of post-war 'urban pastoralism' or romanticism, studied by Chris Waters. Act III includes London street-life scenes at the time of the Essex Rebellion and evokes plebeian forms of opera (such as Gay's eighteenth-century ballad opera). Significantly, the core of this scene is a ballad sung by a blind black man, interrupted by a gallery of common people: pedlars and hawkers, soldiers, housewives, and loafers.[52]

These many diversions from the historical pastoral and the so-called 'Tudor pastiche' do not in themselves fully account for *Gloriana*'s failure to become the definitive English historical opera. Moreover, discussion of the expectations addressed and distorted inside texts (or scores) may not explain the rejection of the opera and its exclusion from the repertoire of popular histories. Truly to comprehend the process of the reception and non-acceptance of such a history,

51 Gibbs, *The New Elizabethans*, 18.

52 For an urban 'pastoralism' with the industrial city at its centre see Chris Waters, 'Representations of Everyday Life: L. S. Lowry and the Landscape of Memory in Postwar Britain', *Representations*, 65 (Winter 1999), 121–50.

indeed of any version of the past, we have to recover the resonance it generated in and for different groups of consumers. Fortunately, the responses of spectators at Covent Garden, both cognoscenti with knowledge of opera and official audiences of courtiers, diplomats, and politicians, are well documented in the specialist music press, as well as in the music columns of the national one. There are even more traces of the varied responses of the considerably larger audience of radio listeners, tuning in to the two special opera broadcasts of BBC Third Programme, that vanguard and guardian of 'quality' culture. Their responses to the restitution of the 'First Elizabethans' and its relationship to the collective ritual of the Coronation they were experiencing stirred a heated debate on the nature of a historical revival, which occasionally bordered on scandal and touched upon political issues concerning public spending, citizen-consumers' rights, and history.

GALA: RITUAL AND SCANDAL AT COVENT GARDEN

Gloriana was bound to generate passions: it had been constructed as an 'event', both a cultural and a media event, and became one even before it premiered. Not only had it been popularly perceived as an *opéra d'occasion*, it had also been explicitly related to the bigger media event and spectacle of the monarchy at Westminster Abbey which had preceded it by six days. Like the ritual of the Coronation, the performance of a royal opera was, at one and the same time, seen as a novelty, a break from past traditions even, and as a repetition of an old and even atavistic practice. English operas for monarchs had been written before, by Thomas Arne in 1740 and even the great Purcell in 1691, but not on the occasion of a coronation and by Royal Permission.[53] A solemn Ralph Vaughan Williams (present at the gala, of course), wrote to the *The Times* that 'so far as I know, for the first time in history the Sovereign has commanded an opera by a composer from these islands for a great occasion. Those who cavil at the public expense involved should realize what such a gesture means to the prestige of our own music.' The acknowledgement by the emblem of national music of the historical importance of the event (he avoided comment on 'either the words or music of *Gloriana*')[54] was eagerly seized upon by many other commentators. Not only was English music well serviced on this historic occasion, Britain's place as musical superpower among the European nations was secured. In the words of Anthony Lewis, Chair of the Barber Institute of Fine Arts at Birmingham University, 'In the welter of indecision and frustration in which so

[53] Arne's masque *Alfred* was written to commemorate the ascension of George I and the birth of Princess Augusta and is known for 'Rule Britannia'. Purcell and Dryden brought out *King Arthur, or the British Worthy* in 1691, too late for the coronation of Charles II, and dedicated it to the Marquis of Halifax.

[54] Letter to the Editor, *The Times*, 18 June 1953.

much European music now finds itself, it is truly exhilarating to hear a score that unfolds with such originality'.[55] Britain was finally vindicated on the opera stage, a vindication that was gratifying to some expert listeners and critics precisely because *Gloriana* was up to date, breaking away from the isolationism of national music tastes, without being dangerously modern in a foreign way—'incomprehensible', or 'indecisive'. The reference to the British way in music, modern and up to date, yet not dangerously incomprehensible, is significant and may be related to the emphasis, after the war and throughout the late forties and early fifties, on a British way in politics, life, and culture. Novelty was also apparent in the production's explicit reference to the modern popular media, especially to films on the Elizabethans. The opera, noted the *Leiston Observer*, echoing the national press, was remarkably in tune with the cinema, as well as with other forms of spectacle.[56]

At the same time that the novelty and modernity of the occasion and the historical importance of the gala were remarked upon, there was much comment on its anachronism, on the fact that it actually was behind the times. An opera written for a special royal occasion was an old form of celebration, antiquated before it was even shown. Indeed *Gloriana* could be associated with the *festa teatrale*, the musical celebration of a special princely occasion during the seventeenth and eighteenth centuries. The bourgeois national grand opera of the nineteenth century, culminating in the great works celebrating nationalism like *Aida*, continued this older tradition. *Gloriana*, somewhat artificially, resurrected, or 'reinvented', a dying tradition: 'Verdi's work of 1871 would in fact have been the last of the kind in operatic history but for the reappearance of "Gloriana," the first two acts of which are the kind of *festa teatrale*.'[57]

The tension between the innovatory aspects of a Coronation opera and its setting on the one hand and the arcaneness of the occasion on the other, was especially apparent in Covent Garden, where the gala was 'an occasion of such splendour' off stage as well as on it, according to Frank Grenville Barker in *Opera News*, 'as the operatic world itself has not seen for many generations'.[58] A few days before the premiere, the *Daily Telegraph*, which had been carrying a special *Elizabethan Diary* for the Coronation, explicitly tied up the sumptuous decoration of Covent Garden to the setting of the Abbey for the sacred ceremony of the anointment and Coronation of the new monarch. The Royal Box at the Royal Opera House was 'transformed into a cloth-of-gold tent for the Queen and the Duke of Edinburgh', analogous to the golden cloth held above the person of the queen in the Abbey. And the entire house was decorated by designer Oliver Messel with a symbolic 3,000 red roses and oak leaves—

55 Letter to the Editor, *The Times*, 16 June 1953.
56 *The Leiston Observer and Aldeburgh, Saxmundham and Thorpeness News*, 15 June 1953.
57 Eric Bloom, 'Gloriana', *Observer*, 14 June 1953.
58 '*Gloriana*, the Coronation Opera', *Opera News*, 19 Oct. 1953, p. 10.

Fig. 24. Front and back covers of *Gloriana*'s programme, by Oliver Messel

matching the opera's theme of 'Rose and Leaves'. The roses were to be entwined around 'oak trees' forming supporting columns of the tent inside the Royal Box, with more roses used to garland it. The inevitable St George and Britannia were additional motifs.[59] The queen herself, decked in a white gown with a hint of gold (and accompanied by an almost identically dressed Queen Mother) became a part of the decor, as well as being a chief actress inside the opera house and outside it.[60] This splendour, Barker commented, 'surpassed even the wildest dreams of Ludwig of Bavaria', not least because Men of the Queen's Company of the Grenadier Guards lined the stairs 'resplendent in scarlet tunics and black bearskins'.[61] The reference to Ludwig of Bavaria, an extravagant and unstable (and ejected) ruler, famous opera patron, and supporter of Richard Wagner, is meaningful because it implicitly criticizes the expenditure of the gala. (See Fig. 24.)

Clearly the splendour and pomp of the gala, surpassing all other works of art and music performed for the Coronation, were such that they could seem jarring

[59] *Daily Telegraph*, 5 June 1953, p. 5.
[60] *Lowestoft Journal*, 12 June 1953.
[61] *Opera News*, 19 Oct. 1953, p. 10.

at a time when there were still remnants of wartime austerity. The British were 'still so unaccustomed' to such degrees of lavishness, the *Musical Times* noted. But the setting of the premiere matched that of the Coronation. Why then resent the gala? The answer probably is in their respective accessibility and the form of spectatorship they involved. The Abbey ceremony was watched by millions who were unfamiliar with the origins and significance of the ritual. The detailed 'historical' explanation in Richard Dimbleby's formal English (which many viewers found difficult to follow) and in the special Coronation Supplements of the newspapers served an educational purpose in addition to the ritualistic and ceremonial one. Furthermore, watching the service, or listening to it on the radio, was at one and the same time a collective communal experience that was also familial and domestic. As the contemporary sociologists Edward Shils and Michael Young famously noted, never before had so many participated (vicariously but undergoing the semblance of a first-hand visual experience) in a Coronation.[62]

At the gala of the Coronation opera, on the other hand, the audience was not only considerably smaller, it did not represent the modernized democratic nation (though ironically it did acknowledge the Commonwealth) and even excluded parts of the traditional elite with an access to and interest in 'high' music and the newer cadres of clients with an interest in modernist music. At least 80 per cent of Covent Garden's seating capacity of 2,026 were invited guests, making up a mixture of officialdom, the odd celebrity, and the musical establishment. And it was the composition of such an atypical opera audience that partly accounts for the gala's disaster and its rejection. It was an 'official' audience 'unworthy' of the music, the occasion, and the recovery of history. As the curtain fell over Joan Cross in her role as Gloriana, speaking her last words, there was a tense lull. Then the thirty-one members of the Royal family, seventy-five members of the Royal Household, 136 ambassadors and ministers, ninety-nine cabinet and shadow cabinet members, seventy-three delegates from the Commonwealth's Prime Ministers' Conference, thirty members of the Colonial Office, twelve Commonwealth Parliamentary Delegates (these last three cohorts invited as formal gesture to the new Empire), thirty people under the auspices of the Lord Chamberlain's Department for visiting Foreign Royalty, eighty guests of the Arts Council, not to mention several other hundreds of invited guests, dutifully clapped their gloved hands. Compulsory protocol white gloves muted the applause and signalled the scandal about to begin. The following twelve commercial performances fared considerably better and were warmly received. But with the exception of one performance on 13 June to a 93 per cent capacity (1,884 viewers), attendance was not impressive.[63] Altogether some 13,797 people saw *Gloriana* before it went down in history as a failure, not to be revived

[62] Edward Shils and Michael Young, 'The Making of the Coronation', *Sociological Review*, NS 1 (1953), 63–81.

[63] Kildea, *Selling Britten*, 136, 144.

in its original form before 1992. Two Third Programme broadcasts brought the opera to considerably larger audiences (though they should probably be estimated in hundreds of thousands), but did not redeem it. However, the fate of the opera and its special status immediately started a debate on history and art in the post-war democracy.

TAXPAYERS' HISTORY: THE DEBATE IN THE PRESS

The furore broke out after the gala and rapidly spilled from the musical press and the dailies' music columns to the correspondence columns. Three inextricable topics, pointing at broader public concerns, preoccupied correspondents: the relationship between official histories and state sponsorship of productions of the past through support for the arts; the liberty of artistic interpretation in a democracy; and the artist/historian status in the post-war democracy of taxpayers. The social make-up of the participants in the debate was more or less homogeneous. The class and to an extent the geographic profile of self-appointed cognoscenti and those radio listeners who have left records of their responses to the special broadcasts disposed them to take part in the debate on the opera with relative ease. They seem to have been middle class and predominantly metropolitan and 'home counties'—rather the profile of the Third Programme's early listeners (though a number of provincial comments may be cited too). What had been designed as a definitive national opera, it seems, failed to attract large cross-class sectors, even if it was accessible to them. And such failure hinted at the limits of the vision of a diffuse quality culture, available to majorities, a vision encouraged during and after the war. However, failure was not necessarily due to the genre itself: Britten's previous popular successes with *Billy Budd* and *Peter Grimes* are clear proofs that the failure was not generic and that opera could be democratized. Failure, as already implied, had to do with the gap between various audiences' expectations and the content and form of modern national music, with disagreement about the contents of and control over publicly financed versions of history and their relation to the present and to modernity, and with access to high culture.

Correspondents typically defined themselves as active and 'real' opera consumers and separated themselves from the official audience. The opera, they argued, was performed to a congregation of philistines, an uncultured public: 'ranging from Fiji Islanders and Mauritanians, to bewildered country clergymen loyally tuning to Covent Garden on what one presumes to be crystal receiving sets. Result consternation.'[64] The distinctly old-fashioned audience and representatives of the Empire (the condescension towards musically illiterate Fiji Islanders is transparent) expected a pastiche display of rabid patriotism

[64] *New Statesman*, 20 June 1953.

reminiscent of Victorian and Edwardian music-hall chauvinism, certainly not a sophisticated modern work. 'Did they perhaps expect some kind of loud and rumbustious amalgam of *Land of Hope and Glory* and *Merrie England*, and catchy tunes and deafening choruses to reproduce the blatant patriotism of the Boer War period?'[65] The active consumer of the modern historical opera, who knew better than that, had been excluded from the gala night, but was well represented in 'the opera-lovers general public' which saw the later performances, and by radio listeners.[66]

But the opera's 'general public' was deeply divided about the content and form of Britten and Plomer's version of history, especially about their selection of certain subjects and themes from the Tudor past and Tudor music and their rejection or subversion of others. Who were the old Elizabethans worth remembering by the Young Elizabethans? What segments of the first Renaissance were worthy of emulation in the age of modernity? Essex, or Drake? The Irish debacle or the defeat of the Armada? Rebellion and repression, or expansion and conquest? Clearly such questioning relates directly to the discussion on the decline and abandoning of the Empire and the attempt to modernize the imperial spirit during the Coronation celebrations and, more broadly, to the attempts, during the fifties, to revitalize images of Britain as a world power. Elizabeth Sellers of Pages Lane in North London commended the opera as a modern work 'which was not ashamed to look back at the past, partly showing distinct Elizabethan influences'.[67] And from the House of Commons, Woodrow Wyatt wrote that the opera was not 'a school book picture of the first Elizabeth and her age; instead we see an effective representation of a remarkable queen in her varying aspects of dignity, greatness, generosity, tragedy and human frailty against a background that is thoroughly English in conception and atmosphere'.[68] Yet it was precisely on what English background and atmosphere was meant to be that spectators and listeners disagreed. In Britten's own Aldeburgh, J. Thorburn felt that 'It is surely a great opportunity missed not to have chosen an episode more worthy of the great period in English history marked by the reign of Elizabeth I. It is on the score of belittling of an heroic reign and age that the public may be justly caviling at the expense.'[69] At 3 Cambridge Gate in North-West London, Caryl Brahms felt that 'English history has been slighted by the librettist choice of the petulant episode of Elizabeth and Essex from what was an age of vigour and adventure'.[70] And the righteously indignant Marie Stopes, that pioneer of birth control, protested from Norbury Park in Dorking, Surrey, in words resonant with 'deep England' and a surprising sense of propriety:

> Public resentment, intense and widespread, is not at the cost but that the opera was unworthy of the great occasion, uninspired, missing the glories of the times, its music

[65] William Plomer, 'Let's Crab an Opera', *London Magazine*, 3, no. 7 (Oct. 1963), 102.
[66] Elizabeth Sellers, Letter to the Editor, *The Times*, 19 June 1953. [67] Ibid.
[68] *The Times*, 20 June 1953. [69] *The Times*, 22 June 1953.
[70] *The Times*, 19 June 1953.

inharmonious and wearisome, and with at least two scenes profoundly affronting the glorious memory of Queen Elizabeth I, hence unsuitable for public performance before Elizabeth II.[71]

The sense of these listeners that *Gloriana* slighted the monarchy *and* history reverberates in the lashing criticism of conservative reviewers such as the *Evening Standard*'s music critic Beverley Baxter, who pompously accused Britten of 'putting a chill on the Merrie England Mood' and arbitrarily excluding from his version of the past a gallery of national characters, including Drake and Shakespeare.[72] Baxter himself would have written a different opera, using the Tilbury speech (with which newspapers readers and filmgoers had long been familiar) and 'translating' into music 'the storm which drove the beaten Armada to death upon our shores' and throwing in a dash of national sport in the form of an episode featuring Drake finishing a game of bowls before setting off to rescue the nation.[73] Significantly, Baxter ignores the inter-war popular representations of the Elizabethans and connects the offence to an acceptable history of the old Elizabethans ('Merrie England') and a sense of national harmony with an offence against English musical traditions. Britten's kind of modern music was 'as clamorous and ugly as hammers striking steel rails . . . I would rather sit in a boiler factory than listen again to the music of the last act.'[74] The analogy between disharmonious music and the cacophony and dissonance in boiler plants was not lost on the *Standard*'s correspondence editor and on numerous readers who entered the fray. In one letter evocatively entitled 'Britten's Boilers', William Blackwood of Harrow thanks Baxter for 'exploding the Benjamin Britten Myth'.[75] Others, however, disqualified Baxter for his lack of perception of what modernity meant, deeming him 'better employed in a boiler factory than smearing Gloriana'.[76] The connection made between a dissonance in the historical narrative and the music and the association of both to aspects of modern, urban, industrial life in the post-war city is telling and runs through the comments of detractors. The opera was full of 'dissonance' and 'discord' and instead of countering the characteristic of post-war city life, it represented just their characteristics: disharmony and speed.[77] Listening in, in High Wycombe, the Reverend John Sidferin was subjected to a three-hour 'painful cacophony' leaving 'lacerated nerves almost beyond endurance', manifesting the characteristics of the new age and offering little healing to the 'tensions of machine-ridden folk'.[78] His much-quoted letter, like other listeners' judgements aired in the daily and Sunday papers, was picked up by trade and specialist magazines for recirculation in a discussion about the opera and modern music.

[71] *The Times*, 20 June 1953. [72] *Evening Standard*, 9 June 1953.
[73] *Musical Opinion*, 910 (July 1953), 582. [74] Ibid. [75] Ibid., 10 June 1953.
[76] Ibid., 16 June 1953.
[77] C. A. Heron, Letter to the Editor, *Daily Express*, 15 June 1953; D. Swan, ibid.
[78] *Musical Opinion*, 910 (July 1953), 581.

Both detractors and enthusiasts felt themselves qualified to express their views on opera and history and their relevance to contemporary life, not so much because they were experts on these subjects, but because of their self-image as culture consumers in a democracy which, in theory at least, propagated the idea of the diffusion of 'worthy' culture. They expected the transfer of the support of the arts to the state (and, by implication, the state's role as patron of the production of history) to divert the power to control cultural products like history from old patrons and the minorities of culture producers to the new ones. As one listener put it: 'What the average taxpayer—as distinct from the musical taxpayer—thinks of the Coronation opera Gloriana, commissioned from Mr. Benjamin Britten at his expense, must surely depend on what he expects in his *piece d'occasion*.'[79] Taxation and the founding of state apparatus to stimulate the arts, correspondents felt, should have eliminated old systems of elite patronage of the arts. The Council ought to have exercised greater control over the taxpayer's paid-for history but failed, and 'the Arts Council should be made a whipping boy',[80] not least for its submission to Palace nepotism and protectionism. Over-control, however, would have been more dangerous. It would risk the liberty of expression and originality of the artist and, more importantly, his capacity to be innovative and even critical of his surroundings. This would subvert the very aim of the Council, which did not seek to subjugate culture producers to an ideology. Such control ran the risk of a bolshevization of the arts and of history, and smacked of a Soviet-style suppression of the arts.[81] Ironically, the opposition to over-control united both political conservatives, who during the fifties advocated de-control as a guarantee of individualism and freedom, and progressives, who valued both the opera's modernity and the critique implied in it of patriotic nostalgia.

CODA

The failure of *Gloriana* may be interpreted as a big non-event, atypical of the role of the post-war welfare state in culture and of productions of history. Big public investment in the arts was atypical, as already in the early fifties the idea of diffusion, at the centre of post-war cultural welfare, was abandoned. Support of culture was selective and ultimately marginalized, and Conservative governments sought to privatize 'quality culture' rather than diffuse it to majorities.

Yet failures and non-events may illuminate our assessment of successes in culture, and the social and cultural biography of *Gloriana* and its uses may serve as an appropriate coda to a discussion of the culture of history. The opera

[79] Caryl Brahms, Letter to the Editor, *The Times*, 19 June 1953.
[80] Susanne Cromer, Letter to the Editor, *Evening Standard*, 24 June 1953.
[81] Woodrow Wyatt, Letter to the Editor, *The Times*, 19 June 1953.

demonstrates differences and similarities between pre- and post-war visions about the diffusion of culture and history and their brokerage and between images of the past. As this book has stressed all along, the interplay of diffusion and distinction was a staple of the modern culture of history from its very beginning. Paradoxically, cultural distinction, apparent in the selectivity of investment in the celebrations of the Coronation, most notably in the production of *Gloriana*'s gala, climaxed at the same moment as the attempted universal social democracy of culture, a democracy which transferred the idea of welfare from material to cultural goods. The historical spectacle at Covent Garden, the keynote of the Coronation celebrations, was consumed by definable groups, the ceremony at the Abbey by tens of millions.

As for the images of the past which the opera presented, these too accommodated strands which were central to pre-war popular images that, themselves, contained avant-garde notions of the Elizabethans (Strachey's, for example) and commercial ones circulated through the mass media and film. Both the glamorous and uncosy images of the Elizabethans lingered after the war. In 1953 the latter were disturbing. On 11 March, Sir Kenneth Clark, opening an exhibition of Elizabethan portraits in Manchester, doubted whether 'merrie England' was at all 'merrie'. Traces of the Elizabethans in portraits and paintings, he sensed, did not convey to modern viewers a feel of security, comfort, or restfulness. Their subjects' mirthless and hopeless stares projected onto the viewer images of discomfort and insecurity—rather similar to his or her own.[82] Indeed 'spiritual discomfort' was common to old and new Elizabethans.[83] In *Gloriana*, the uncomfortable image of the Golden Age resonates in the theme of the fragility of the monarchy and the state, a theme manifest in the leitmotif of old age and death in a work apparently celebrating youth. The distance between the contents, messages, and even the narratives of the successful and rejected interpretation of the Elizabethans is not that great. The resemblances between the successes and the failure are proof of the repetitiousness within the culture of history. But why did the popular image of the fragile, earthly people's monarch and her old body appeal during the inter-war period and jar in 1953? The earlier representations could be accommodated with notions of power, modernity, and celebrity, as shown in Chapters 6 and 7. Associations of power with the old were not easily reconcilable with the wartime and post-war ethos of youth and the new version of modernity, of which the living queen was an icon.

There is also a lack of fit between the opera and party-line notions about the monarchy and Empire. *Gloriana* may have been a state opera sponsored by the court at the onset of a long Conservative rule, but it was not an expression of Tory celebration of ideas seeking to take the country 'back to the future', by employing a language of glory and renewal. Its idiom, imagery, and composition were not in unison with those of the central conservative propagators of the

[82] Tate Gallery Archives, 8812.2.2.276, Lord Clark's Collection. [83] Ibid.

ethos of the Young Elizabethans (Gibbs, or the owners and journalists of newspapers like *Evening Standard*, which promoted the Coronation as a true festival of unity, where they had vehemently criticized the Festival of Britain), ideological travellers like Rowse, and court officials. The opera's producers and performers, chiefly Britten himself, Plomer, Pears, and Cross, undermined the idea of renewal. In their pastiche of traditional forms of commemorations and dramatization of the notion of resurrection, they destabilized the idea of a possibility for a revival.

Conclusion

EPILOGUE: URBAN PATHS TO HISTORY

Jenny Paget (née Jane Pulcher), born in 1903, lived, worked, and moved in the same geographical orbit as the amateur historian, antiquary, and social worker Maurice Birley. She spent a lifetime in Poplar, West and East Ham, and Silvertown. Their paths, we may safely assume, never crossed. Class, gender, habitat, and family biographies made their respective accesses to history quite different. This was not simply and solely a matter of exclusion and denial: routes to the past were not determined by the constrictions of class or gender; rather these constrictions could dispose individuals towards different uses and modes of negotiation with histories. In Jenny's deprived and mean schooling there was an inadequate smattering of history, typically consisting of a chronology of the monarchy. And the cinema offered her for the taking glimpses on the past (though she probably did not make use of them). But she had never been to the Tower of London, so close to the three dismal houses she inhabited throughout her long life (she died at the age of 91), or to St Paul's Cathedral.[1]

Jack B. Rutstein, born in 1916 to Hyman Rutstein and Tilly Stander, Jewish refugees from Lithuania, moved along some of the routes and itineraries made by Birley and Pulcher. Living in relatively spacious Stepney Green, attending the Davenant Foundation School on Whitechapel Road, and regularly moving between the denser Commercial Street, Brick Lane, the meaner Old Montague Street (the abode of his maternal relatives), and the Assembly Hall and People's Palace down the Mile End Road, and sometimes venturing as far as the West End, he attached his city itineraries to histories.[2] As he would write in an unpublished history, he did not need to be taken on special trips to London's historical landmarks, certainly not to the Tower, as these 'were all within walking distance'. And the Tower especially 'was popular because we were also in sight of the waters of the Thames'. To him history, taught by a charismatic Marxist teacher, a Mr Lee, was not just a 'recitation of dates and names of kings and queens', but a useful way 'to give the events a social and maybe a political background'. And learning and understanding history was a key to 'gain a distinction' in the subject, but also and indirectly, in a future life.[3]

More than the West End of London lay between his itineraries and sites of history and those encountered by Cicely Veronica Wedgwood, a member of the

[1] Melanie McGrath, *Silvertown: An East End Family Memoir* (London, 2002), 233.

[2] Jack Rutstein, unpublished manuscript, described as 'extended commentary to family album'. I am most grateful to him and to Simon Rutstein for allowing me access to this record.

[3] Jack Rutstein, 'A Voice from the Past', unpublished manuscript.

great china-manufacturing family, a future student of A. L. Rowse and disciple of Trevelyan, a freelance historian of the Stuarts and seventeenth-century France, a broadcaster on history, for years a trustee of the National Gallery, and receiver of the CBE, DBE, and OM. The starting point of her path was 'a small room on the topmost floor of a majestic stuccoed house in Kensington', painted dark green and white, decorated with a picture of Wolfe scaling the Heights of Abraham, and dominated by a determined female teacher who unlocked the gates into a whole picture of 'an enormous history of England'.[4]

THE CULTURE OF HISTORY: REPETITIONS AND PATTERNS

The culture of history, explored and recovered in this book, lay in the space between these four very (albeit not entirely) different itineraries, the experiences they represent, the different idioms of their raconteurs, and between these itineraries and myriad previous and other contemporary paths to and uses of the past, uses which were made alongside, or under, constrictions and autonomies of choice of various degrees. Though easily confined chronologically between 1802 and 1953, this culture (indeed cultures) does not facilely yield to linearity. And to assess change, fissures, and breaks within the productions and consumptions of history along this continuum, we need first to bring together the modalities repeating themselves and reverberating throughout the long time-span followed in the book and presenting patterns. Most obvious and easiest to trace, of course, is the expansion of the new culture and the diffusion of its productions across audiences and across a variety of genres and modes, with a strong emphasis on the visual, even when these were literary genres. In a manner of speaking the culture of history was primarily about what people *saw* of the past and how they saw it. Consuming history was first (and literally) looking at its representations. Visuality, and an array of technologies for making history visible and procedures of looking, developed in a way that was inverse to the spread of literacy. The more literate the English became, the more visual their popular histories, and the greater the appeal of spectacle. This spread of 'visual production' and consumption is apparent in the development of the family of panoramas—the generic form of the first half of the nineteenth century, and the simultaneous growth of the panoramic literary history of the Revolution, discussed in Chapter 2, and in competing forms of spectacle and looking, which evolved in and were inspired by Madame Tussaud's and the urban spectacle of public

[4] C. V. Wedgwood, 'The Velvet Study', in *History and Hope: The Collected Essays of C. V. Wedgwood* (London, 1987), 12–19 at 16; Janet Todd, *Dictionary of British Women Writers* (London, 1991), 702–3; 'Veronica Wedgwood OM', Obituary, *Daily Telegraph*, 1997, www.geocities.com/Heartland/3202/Wedgwood.html.

execution, and resonated in serial fiction, the arrangement of monuments, theatrical realizations, and a melange of popular antiquarianism and a popular literature of tourism. Visual histories reached their apex in the generic form of the 'modern' twentieth century: film.

Diffusion and modernization did not take the form of a series of newly invented ways of production of history and of technologies and means of access to versions of the past, each following and substituting another. Rather the culture of history represents a process that may be best described as accretion, or a series of additions, in which newer layers of urban forms of representation and genres, evolving in relation to new technologies, practices of looking, and modes of multiple and chain consumption of historical texts and objects were grafted on to older forms and technologies which did not disappear. Again accretion is particularly apparent during the first six or seven decades of the nineteenth century, covered in Parts I–II. Following the French Revolution and in relation to it, there appeared new forms of looking and spectacle (the dungeon and the panorama), new genres and apparatuses for the distribution of histories. These were released into an older, mostly eighteenth-century, tradition and lore of sensationalism and spectacle, and modes of looking, which had developed around the culture of the gallows and public execution. And these were redirected through and into new forms and genres, ranging from wax objects and displays to historical urban novels, notably Revolution novels and the historical topographical novel set in the Tudor era, and to guidebooks to museums and monuments. At the same time, the application of new print and visual technologies 'modernized' the older lore. Similarly, the early and mid-nineteenth-century traditions of moving spectacles would later become the basis for historical films.

Accretion is also perceptible in the spread and survival of subjects and themes and of interpretations of the Revolution and the Tudors, circulating across genres and forms and cutting across audiences and, last but not least, extending to practices pursued by individuals to make use of the past. Most pervasive among these themes and the clusters of images attached to them are those of history as an unsafe and dangerous place, and of the city as the locus of change. Seeing and configuring the past as an uneasy city was by no means the only way of imagining it. The English, as numerous scholars have argued, nurtured a rural and often pastoral image of their pasts and located it in the Country.[5] And Country was the very heart of an imagined inward-looking, gentle 'Little England', almost apart from 'Greater Britain', let alone the Empire.[6] However, this book has sought to correct the neglect of the uneasy version of the past and its multiple uses by generations of consumers. It has attempted to recover the long-surviving appeal of history as a place of 'horrors', a term compounding

5 For an extended discussion of this interpretation see the Introduction.
6 Examples include Wiener, Colls, and Readman.

a sense of the horrible and awesome with that of the grotesque and thrilling, and generating a mixture of attraction and repulsion. The compound of sensations apparent in the lasting power of venues like the Chamber of Horrors and the Tower/dungeon, studied in Chapters 1, 4, and 5, as well as in urban histories and fiction, studied in Chapters 2 and 3, suggests not only the attraction of the dangerous in the past, but also the ways in which individuals and groups came to terms with the process of urbanization and modernization. Change and the sense of it, long recognized as central to the making of the experience of nineteenth-century people, were not necessarily imagined and represented in binary pairs, positing a rural and pastoral past against urban tempo, scale, and density. To come to grips with changes in the city, with its modernization and democratization, the English did not have to imagine the city's reverse, or simply 'escape' to the Country, or to visions of the constitution, or of freedom. Indeed it is possible to argue that change may be grasped not solely through an imagining of its reverse, but also via grappling with and making sense of its representation in the social world. The urban genres and urban forms of looking at the past were crystallized during the decades of massive changes in cities and especially in the metropolis, like the era of Georgian improvement before 1820, the period between 1850 and 1870, or that following the processes of massive suburbanization and the transport revolution from the 1900s, thence during the inter-war period. And the images of an insecure past lingered after the Second World War which wrought massive destruction and dislocation in urban areas, and was followed by visions of planning and modernity. This lingering of senses of urban insecurity and danger characterizes even the celebratory ethos and cult of the New Elizabethans revolving around the Coronation and studied in Chapter 9.

To be sure, the dungeon, gallows, and guillotine as metaphors for and configurations of history lost their intensity from the 1870s, when apprehensions about the repeatability of the Revolution and of the dangers of and in crowds slowly abated. This process is related to changes in urban space, governance, discipline, and control (like the abolition of public execution in 1868), and politics, the latter beginning in 1867, and to the rise of a new type of empire, based on direct rule and related to the rise of modern imperialist democracy, drawing on popular consent. However, the cluster of images of the uneasy past, even that of the past as a reservoir of 'horrors', was retained. Well into the inter-war period Madame Tussaud's Chamber of Horrors welded history to horror, attaching the repertoire of urban sensationalism and spectacles to the newest visual form and technology: film. This is apparent in the 1936 horror film *Midnight at Madame Tussaud*, shot in the Chamber, and inserting figures of the time of the *ancien régime* and the Revolution into a narrative of murder and torture, lumping together the guillotine and other instruments of torture with 'modern' murder. Even some of the state-sponsored spectacles produced for the Coronation, most notably the state opera *Gloriana*, projected images of insecurity onto the hopeful mood of anticipation of a New Elizabethan Age.

Democratization, which manifested itself in the growing affordability of the past and its accessibility to ever-growing audiences, was, as I have attempted to show throughout, a two-way process, in which consumers as well as the producers of culture took an active part. The culture of history had a varied social *and material* life, or rather lives, outside and beyond representation, in individuals' uses and in the relations between images and visions of the past, the lived experiences of readers, tourists, spectators, and viewers, especially in their movement through, and spatial experience in, the urban environment.

The spatial and material aspect of the relation to time, experienced through a sense of and movement in place, is noted by Wedgwood in her essay on Henry James's fragment 'the Sense of the Past', whose hero Ralph Penderl is engaged in writing *An Essay in Aid of the Reading of History*. The sense of the city, central to the three other itineraries described above, is also behind the 'Picture plan of the village of Clerkenwell' which G. P. Norman, a junior draughtsman, living on 6 Compton Street East, displayed in 1864 in the 'Working Class Exhibition' in Islington and in the model T. Mathew, a carpenter and joiner, built for the same exhibition. Places, as the sites of history, are also the subject of Thomas Aldred of Fetter Lane, Holborn's replica of Elizabeth's palace at Greenwich. Mrs Aldred had her miniature Funeral Car of Nelson displayed in the same exhibition. In the hands of artisans like the Aldreds, and of myriad other small producers, history was material. And it was made from recycled materials and sources during their leisure and usually at home or the workplace.[7] Enthusiastic fans of Jack Sheppard cherished and re-enacted his urban experience and protest in workhouses and in the streets where this experience, they felt, 'belonged'. And East Enders' protest against limits on access to the Tower rang with a territorial idiom stressing the links between participation in history, locality, and political rights.

The democratization of access to the past involved the inclusion of individuals and groups in culture, a process which first touched on majorities, then, with the media and film revolution of the inter-war period, became, at least in theory, universal. But one pattern, recurring throughout the long term discussed here, is exclusion by cultural distinction.[8] Indeed the book has shown that the limitation of access to history was embedded in the process of democratization itself, which always operated through systems of distinction. Class, locale, and education—that is *social* difference—were grafted onto, but never determined, a cultural one. Explicit distinction was pursued by commercial cultural entrepreneurs like Madame Tussaud. It was consistently pursued by the state and government and resented, campaigned against, and fought by consumers—sometimes successfully. The prime example here is policy regarding the Tower, where free access, free movement, and viewing without control were withheld and campaigned for during the 1830s to 1850s, the 1860s to 1880s, and during the inter-war period,

[7] *Memorial of the North London Working Classes' Industrial Exhibition*, ed. J. F. Wilson (London, 1864).

[8] Bourdieu, *Distinction*. The term is used critically in Chs. 1, 4, and 9.

a contestation exposing no small amount of class prejudice and phobia. The appearance of mass consumption via the media revolution decreased distinction, but did not abolish it. The film, that generic form of twentieth-century popular history, evolved as a 'universal' apparatus catering for all and specifically addressing groups of consumers subject to exclusion like working-class women and schoolchildren. Yet the film industry's global apparatus of distribution and advertising 'distinguished' groups of consumers and made distinctions among these groups according to gender and age. And habitat and class continued to perpetuate already existing cultural distinctions. The flow of writer's pads scribbled over with 'histories' by Wedgwood during her privileged childhood and the riches of her father's library at Holland Park exemplify just this. During the final phase of democratization, coinciding with post-war social democracy and the extension of welfare to culture and the changes in the role of the state, the notion of diffusing 'quality' culture and histories to all was fraught with distinction, as demonstrated in Chapter 9.

Notwithstanding the indissoluble paradox of social and cultural distinction within democracy, we should be wary of regarding the former as systemic, simply manipulative, and impassable. If there is any one theme clear from, and in, this book, it is that the culture of history does not yield itself to simple or modified narratives of manipulation, or of forms of control, which analyse histories and narratives of the past as simply instruments for kinds of rule, mobilization, and civilizing, whether exercised by the 'nation', the Liberal state, elites, or transnational capital, or through and in an all-embracing discourse (as in the Foucauldian interpretations) exercised and inscribed on individual bodies. The notions and images of the uncosy past, even when these did not run counter to notions of progress and amelioration inscribed in the confident interpretation of history, often sat uneasily with it. The powerful image of the dungeon, for example, was created outside elites and defined classes and was a cross-breed between plebeian and middle-class genres and practices.

Indeed the social profile of the groups of the producers of history discussed in this book, from the first decade of the nineteenth century until the Second World War, displays a dynamism and openness which frustrates any attempt to describe it as a 'cultural elite' and to affiliate it with traditional literary or cultural elites. The collective portrait of some of the most popular cultural entrepreneurs whom I have described as 'brokers of history' and as mediators of popular historical tastes and fashions displays a number of similarities, first noted in Chapter 1 in the study of Madame Tussaud and the Tussaud family as impresarios of history and followed throughout. One prominent feature of this portrait is the initially peripheral status of these entrepreneurs. Occasionally these include a large number of women (among wax modellers, popular novelists, and film stars) and 'foreigners' with Continental allegiances, or allegiances to US popular cultures, who carved niches within the relatively open and not strictly hierarchical entertainment and culture industries (wax modelling and film are two examples). Significantly, these brokers used already existing forms and interpretations of the past, but reshaped them and, at the same time, changed characteristics of their adopted culture, which claimed and in turn 'adopted' their innovations. This mutual process of naturalization and the introduction and acceptance of new elements into Englishness is apparent in the transformation of Madame Tussaud's redefinition of 'horrors' and her welding of it to historical consciousness. The process is also evident in her transformation in the eyes of various publics from an exotic female French refugee to the matron of 'the most English of all institutions'. Comparable twentieth-century examples are the transformation, in public opinion and in the opinion of self-appointed guardians of the 'nation', of Baroness Orczy and Rafael Sabatini from colourful cosmopolitans to inventors of historic forms of Englishness, and that of the film-mogul Alexander Korda and some of 'his' international stars, notably Leslie Howard, from immigrants (whose Jewishness incurred an amount of anti-Semitic comment) into the promulgators of a 'quintessential' historic nation, these last transformations studied in Chapter 8. This repetitious process, also apparent in the search for and address to both a home audience and the domestic culture market and global ones (notably the USA and imperial markets), no doubt has to do with shifts and changes within literary culture and popular entertainment, as well as in the trend towards the globalization of both. The 'foreign' and global aspects and contexts of popular culture, apparent in the background of producers, in the economies of production and distribution of artefacts, and in the prominence of some motifs (notably the French Revolution and the Elizabethan overseas empire) force us to rethink recent definitions of history and Englishness as predominantly local, 'native', 'Little Englander', as inward-looking and rather separate from Empire and the world.[9]

Even more significant than this lack of fit between producers and specific elites and classes, and between the confident and uncosy interpretations and representations of history, are the dynamics of consumption itself, the ways in which individuals made actual, material and imaginary, uses of the past in their social life and habitat, endowing histories with meanings for and in everyday life and sometimes in fantasy. These consumers' insinuation of their experience and imagination into histories manifests itself in many examples: in readers' uses of histories (especially men and women autodidact readers of Carlyle), in the uncomfortably and orally literates' responses to and uses of Ainsworth's topographic novels, in the 'realizations' of his Tudor and eighteenth-century novels and Dickens's Revolution novel, and in the responses of readers and filmgoers to the texts and moving images describing aristocracies and the monarchy during the inter-war period.

The book's interest and investment in individuals' making do with histories and changing them in accordance with expectations, needs, and habitat is not

[9] One recent example is Readman, 'The Place of the Past in English Culture'.

meant to produce a story of the uses of the past as a narrative of resistance, a plebeian subversion of elite Whig histories. Such a narrative and approach to popular histories, and indeed to popular culture, may create the obverse of the manipulation or indirect-control interpretation, discussed in the Introduction and above, and runs the peril of ignoring or bypassing the constrictions which limited choice in uses of history.

GENDER AND THE CULTURE OF HISTORY

The interplay between forms of distinction, structures and frameworks inherent in culture at large, and the ways in which these were interfered with and criss-crossed by individuals' paths to history and their processing and uses of it, has been demonstrated through looking at the central and indispensable role of gender in the culture of history. Gender has been useful precisely because it connects representations to people, allowing place for both individual experience and structure. To say that nineteenth- and early twentieth-century English people envisioned their past as a gendered country is not merely to claim a place for women as well as men in various historical representations. This project of recovery, across genres like historical fiction, biography, and academic histories, has been pursued by a number of historians including Bonnie L. Smith, Maxine Berg, Christina Crosby, and myself. Our work and that of others furthermore has demonstrated that history as a form of knowledge, a literary/amateur tradition, then, from the 1870s, an academic discipline, developed in relation to notions about masculinity and femininity.[10] To argue that the culture of history had gender is also more than to delineate the different and similar ways in which women and men gained (or lost) access to historical genres and forms as producers and readers, or viewers. This book has attempted to demonstrate not only the roles of both genders as the subjects of histories, and as producers and consumers, but also how notions about femininity and masculinity, and of difference between women and men, shaped the very imagining of history. Gender was a metaphor and a configuration for other hierarchies and differences in society and signified change, that difference between the past and the present.

First, roles. The culture of history was to a great extent public and social and evolved in a space and kinds of places which G. J. Barker-Benfield described as heterosocial spaces.[11] Unlike some gender-segregated polite and plebeian venues, which developed into same-sex urban enclaves (the club limited to men, or the department store developing as a safe female space), those venues which circulated and traded in histories were mixed. The wax and hands-on museum, the

[10] Christina Crosby, *The Ends of History: Victorians and 'the Woman Question'* (London, 1991); Smith, *The Gender of History*; Melman, 'Gender, History and Memory' and 'Changing the Subject'.

[11] Barker-Benfield, *The Culture of Sensibility*.

reconstructed dungeon and torture route, the panoramas and dioramas, the theatre and cultural sites like the illustrated magazine, the serial novel, and the guidebook all admitted women and family audiences. The new nineteenth-century impresarios of history catered for such mixed audiences, often courting women in order to 'rationalize' consumption and make it respectable. Forms of distinction, operating within this process of courting, reproduced class difference and prejudice rather than the difference between and among genders. The mixing of gender and age groups is all the more apparent in the twentieth-century's generic venue of entertainment: the cinema theatre.

Another consistency is the deployment of gender to represent and make comprehensible social and political inequalities and arbitrariness and to configure difference between the past and the present. During the 'short nineteenth century', that is between the 1800s and 1870s, gender came to represent inequality and oppression on the one hand, and social transgression on the other. As shown in Chapters 2–3, the sans-culotte women embody the suffering of the French people and the revolutionary drive; their political action, however, stands for political upheaval and turmoil and transgresses not solely the boundaries of gender, but also urban and social boundaries. Similarly, in narratives of the dungeon and gallows, both the 'rough' masculine narrative, apotheosized in the story of Jack Sheppard, and the feminine version, exemplified in the myth of Lady Jane Grey, oppression is configured in gender terms and images. In the earlier prison lore it is resisted actively and sometimes successfully. In the feminized story of Jane and its myriad visual reproductions studied in Chapter 6, resistance is passive and domestic. Contemporaries projected the theme of domesticity (of women) and political oppression (of the 'people') onto these prison histories. The move from an imprisoned child-queen to a powerful female monarch, Elizabeth I, as popular icon, around the 1870s, further demonstrates the shaping of histories by gender. The second resurrection of the Tudors, revolving around the popularization of Elizabeth, coincides with the era characterized by 'gender flux', or the blurring of borderlines apparent in the appearance of the 'new woman' in culture and society.[12] Elizabeth and the array of early modern female monarchs transgressed earlier Victorian perceptions of femininity; Elizabeth and the Elizabethans fit in the shifting of definitions of gender 'after the Victorians' and especially during the inter-war period.

The centrality of gender in and for the popular culture of history does not of course exclude actual women and men: they, indeed individual bodies, as the book has consistently sought to demonstrate, mattered. These individuals were both the producers of gendered histories and their consumers. The meanings given to notions of difference and gender by individuals were not only creative

12 Elaine Showalter, *Sexual Anarchy: Gender and Culture at the Fin de Siècle* (New York, 1990); Billie Melman (ed.), *Borderlines: Genders and Identities in War and Peace 1870–1930* (London, 1998).

and innovative but often ran counter to what gender (and class) disposed them to. These 'deviations' (in both senses of the term) may be tracked down to the actual physical uses and responses and to sensations. The instant of 'seeing' sans-culotte women described by Carlyle, the particular moment the reader's eye 'met' the text, was transformed in the imagination of working-class women readers to the start of their own biography and life of action. And as shown in Chapters 6 and 8, working-class readers of Baroness Orczy, or of Margaret Erwin, or the viewers of films based on their novels, endowed monarchical and aristocratic female heroes with meanings, including certain freedoms which they themselves were fully aware had run counter to the constrictions and disposition of their class and gender.

CHANGE

The stress on repetitions and persisting modalities may create the impression that the culture of history was autonomous and developed discretely. This book has made allowances for degrees of autonomies of the workings of culture. But it has also insisted throughout on the need to tie culture to 'big change' in political structures, Britain's position as an empire and world power, and urbanization and technologies of communication. The continuous, long-surviving patterns—traceable in repetition and consistencies and change—are not mutually exclusive. It was the tension between them which made the histories examined here circulate and appeal to masses.

As implied above, change, even dramatic change, in culture related to the emergence of new technologies and new ways of telling about the past (like film) may not be adequately described as an impassable divide, but is best referred to as a porous borderline, retaining residues or even segments of the older culture, evident in the newer developments. We may situate this borderline between the 1870s and 1900s, decades which saw shifts in the subject matter of popular histories of the Tudors and the Revolution, and in modes of the production and marketing of these histories. This changing of history's subject may be located in and attributed to the much broader movements which Parts III–V have followed: the rise of a mass culture for democracy, the expansion of the Empire and its vacating after the Second World War, and new forms of modernity. Throughout, 'democracy' has not been used to connote equal access to politics and power, or to culture. Indeed the 'borderline' decades witnessed neither universal political democracy ('individual democracy') nor a 'social' democracy—both would take long to arrive, the latter until the Second World War.[13] But the democratization of culture did mean diffusion and the potential equality in access to the past via new commercial forms and apparatuses of consumption.

[13] McKibbin, *Classes and Cultures*, 523–36.

Change in the contents and roles of history crystallized around the 1900s and became conspicuous during the crucial inter-war period. The single most significant manifestation of this change was a shift towards the monarchy as a central subject of histories and its representations as a positive agent, and as the mover and activator of historical action. The centring of the monarchy in mass-produced histories and in the popular historical imagination was accompanied by a class shift, detectable in a move from the popular classes to traditional landed elites. To be sure, the biography of the great had been conspicuous in amateur histories and historical spectacles well before the divide. Suffice it to mention here the voluminous biographies of female monarchs and princesses manufactured by such historians as the Strickland sisters and pouring from the presses during the middle decades of the nineteenth century, or Carlyle's own fascination with heroes, not to mention Madame Tussaud's trafficking in celebrity and fame, apotheosized in her pantheon of native and foreign royals, a line of trade pursued alongside the museum's manufacture of horrors. However, between the cusp of the eighteenth and nineteenth centuries and the 1860s (and even the 1870s), the monarchy, the state, authority, and all manifestations of power—the law, the prison, holders of privilege—are identified with arbitrariness, danger, and kinds of corruption or, alternatively, marginalized and represented as victims (Marie Antoinette and Jane Grey being two examples).

From about the 1870s and increasingly from the 1900s, the monarchy, in actuality divested of 'real' power, evolves to an accepted configuration of popular power. Put differently, power was 'democratized' and modernized. Elizabeth's belated transformation to an icon, earlier connected to gender, is a case in point here too. She was not just rehabilitated; by the 1930s, she was increasingly identified with popular freedoms, a popular empire, national independence, and, most significantly, with democracy itself, as demonstrated in Chapters 6 and 7. Aristocracies too, previously identified in popular culture with medieval or *ancien régime* sectarianism, or with corruption, and alternately vilified and caricatured, were resurrected as the carriers of national qualities, leadership, and style. In the early and mid-nineteenth century, the carriers of change are distinctly plebeian if not socially marginal and unacceptable figures: revolutionary crowds and sans-culottes, risen from deprivation and oppression to vulcanic action, peasants and town labourers, victimized women, and middle-class men, these last circling around the hubs of urban power, but not holding it and, most enduringly popular, the infringers of power and challengers of authority: highwaymen, thieves and felons, 'social' criminals, whether they be condemned criminals or political extremists moving in the shadow of the guillotine. Suffice it to mention here readers' and audiences' passionate admiration of Jack Sheppard and their intense reaction to revolutionary women. The obverse of this lineage of trespassers, protesters, and transgressors of urban spaces and hierarchies are the (mostly female) victims of the law, state prisoners and those oppressed by aristocratic and royal dynasties: powerless and wronged queens, imprisoned middle-class women, violated peasants, and the urban poor, and similar. During the first half of the twentieth century, the social profile and collective biography of heroes change dramatically. Aristocrats are transformed from paragons of the old and changeless to heralds of change and modernity. They are constructed, as demonstrated in Chapter 8, as the first supermen. The Scarlet Pimpernel, replacing the outlaw and revolutionary, develops into a transnational figure, adapted to different national cultures in France, the USA, and Latin America. And one major tag of this transformation is the new aristocrats' 'urbanizing' and their location in cities, rather than in their traditional abode, the countryside.

The modernization of the monarchy and aristocracy and their remaking as cohesive centres of popular democratic histories may be interpreted simply as reversals of the long-term decline of the landed elites and interest, the monarchy's abdication of 'real' power, and the expansion of political democracy. Similar reversals in popular culture were approached, derogatorily, in terms of escapism, directed by the mass media.[14] Or, the centring of the monarchy and Empire was explained as a regress from working-class or plebeian oppositional politics to culture—a culture of acquiescence, introspective and quintessentially conservative.[15] Yet another interpretation attributes popular monarchism to a broader popular conservatism which was not political, but expressed a world-view and temper relatable, it has been argued, to varieties of consensus and hegemony, or, alternately, to a 'politics of envy'.[16] From such (and similar) interpretations assumptions are spawned about the traditionalism and conservatism inherent in popular culture—and specifically in working-class culture and history's conserving role.

However, fixing on history's or culture's conservatism (or indeed gauging them in binary sets of terms like acquiescence and subversion, or progressivism and conservatism) sidesteps the question of the relationship between attitudes to the past and its uses, culture, modernity, and mass democracy. The history of the monarchy became a history for modern mass democracy. By this I mean that catchwords and notions about democracy were, during the twentieth century, attached to the image of the monarchy, that monarchs became the symbols of popular versions of the past and of democracy. Mass democracy went hand in hand with notions of the 'modern' in the sense that its images and representations kept pace with the temper of the times, with tags of modernity and modern lifestyles, and with the new tempos. 'Modern' also applied to new technologies of visual consumption of the past, notably the cinema, and new forms of celebrity. The swing to the monarchy peaked between the 1930s and 1950s when, as

[14] In its classic form in Q. D. Leavis, *Fiction and the Reading Public* (1932; Harmondsworth, 1979) and F. R. Leavis, *Mass Civilisation and Minority Culture* (London, 1930).

[15] See e.g. Gareth Stedman Jones, *Languages of Class: Studies in English Working-Class History 1832–1982* (Cambridge, 1983), 179–239.

[16] Light, *Forever England*. For histories and working-class politics of 'envy' see Carolyn K. Steedman, *Landscape for a Good Woman: A Story of Two Lives* (New York, 1992).

contemporaries put it, 'an intense and unrelenting mechanism of publicity exists in conjunction with an increasing classless and democratic attitude to society'.[17] At the centre of the Elizabethan inter-war resurrection in fiction and on screen is the powerful female people's monarch, guarantor of their well-being and freedoms. This image, and those projected by a line of monarchs on screen, and by the array of film stars re-enacting their deeds, also projected royals as earthly and very physical beings, visible in their everyday life and 'in private', thus extending and resonating with contemporary new images of the monarchy and stardom which the media and royals themselves astutely cultivated. The twentieth-century histories recovered here were remarkably contiguous with the increasing visibility and cultural role of the monarchy, self-styled and consciously created in the context of democracy, media exposure, and the changing relationship between the state and sectors within it, notably the civil sector. As Frank Prochaska has demonstrated, the monarchy, especially from the 1900s, actively represented itself as being close to and active for the people and their welfare. Its visibility—mediated by the media—as a benevolent agent, caring for the underprivileged, made it relevant for a democracy where civil society, its apparatuses and tools performed roles of the state. Royalty's close and visible involvement with the sick and apparent alertness to the suffering of the unemployed did not just make possible its survival, but also its modernizing.[18] At the same time, the visibility of modern forms of 'royal bounty', whose high symbolic value was amplified through media technologies, also made the monarchy the model for celebrity, representing longevity and durability on the one hand, and glamour on the other. In similar manner, the aristocrat as superhero, leader, and arbiter of style was contiguous with the new kinds of celebrity accorded in and by the media to the heterogeneous elites of the inter-war period. The association, examined in Chapter 8, between the Scarlet Pimpernel and fast and dynamic modern living immediately springs to mind.

To be sure, a chorus of disapproval accompanied this new modernized version of the past. One 13-year-old, whose comments were recorded by Kate Stevens in her 1899 report on a North London Board School article on 'Lessons from the standpoint of the Child', thought it 'very easy to mix up the kings of one period with the kings of another'.[19] And a few decades later, Cecil Rolph Hewitt, writing from 1924 under the pen-name C. H. Rolph, condemned histories of heroes (popular heroes, plebeian as well as high-class ones) as uninspiring and boring.[20] But other readers, sidestepping habitat, class, and politics, responded to extracurricular interpretations and representations of the historic monarchy positively and sometimes enthusiastically, inhabiting these representations with meanings through their uses of them, as Alison Light has demonstrated in her

[17] Wedgwood, 'Our Queen, Crown and Monarchy', 7.

[18] Frank Prochaska, *Royal Bounty*.

[19] *Child Life*, 1 (Oct. 1899), 4.

[20] C. H. Rolph, *London Particulars: Memories of an Edwardian Boyhood* (London, 1980), 29.

memoir of women's historical reading on Elizabeth I in a working-class part of Portsmouth.[21]

The itineraries to the past recovered throughout this book were by no means the only ones taken by individuals and groups during the nineteenth and early twentieth centuries. There were, as I have been well aware, other persisting versions and interpretations, elaborating the comfortable and confident version of history, which have been meticulously and widely covered by others.[22] My own incomplete study has sought to 'write into' our interpretations of the role of the past in modernity the narratives, spectacles, and usages which deviated from and evolved alongside the secure, comfortable, Country version of English history and sometimes contradicted it. This recovery may make our history of history's uses fuller, less homogeneous, and perhaps seem less 'natural' and obvious; it has also shown how individuals matter by looking at how the past percolated into their experiences and how they used and shaped it. This two-way travel from images and representations, unlocked from texts, to material lives and bodies, and backwards, has demonstrated the workings of culture. If this study has any future use, it will be as a small contribution to our understanding of this working, of how histories lived, and of modernity.

21 Alison Light, '"Young Bess"'.

22 Introduction, nn. 9, 10.

Bibliography

MANUSCRIPT SOURCES AND ARCHIVAL MATERIAL

British Film Institute, Library

Press 'tie-ups' and files:
- Fire Over England
- The Lion Has Wings
- A Tale of Two Cities
- Young Bess
- Scarlet Pimpernel

Scripts:
- Private Life of Henry VIII
- Scarlet Pimpernel

British Film Institute, Special Collections

London Film Production Collection.
Leslie Howard Collection.
Cinema Ephemera Collection.

British Library

Add. MSS 46560, 46650, 46676 A–B, 59626, Bentley Papers.
Add. MS 56767, Society of Authors, Emmuska Orczy's (Baroness Orczy) correspondence.

Britten–Pears Library, Aldeburgh

B/P/1/348.
B/P/Elizabeth II, Queen of England.
B/P/Plomer.

Guildhall Library, Manuscript Department

GL MSS 16310, 16348–9, Hodder and Stoughton Archives.

London Metropolitan Archives

CHR/LB/4.
COL/LB/3.
CUB/LB/2.
DAL/LB/5.
EO/DIV5/ALT/LB/1–3.
FI/LB/1.
RIC/LB/2.

Madame Tussaud's Archives

Lists of figures, 1830–40, 1850–70, 1878–90, 1914–30.
Press-cuttings collection.

MO-Mass Observation Archives, University of Sussex

Children and Education, 1932–52, 4/f, g, h.
File Reports, 176.
Topic Collections, Films, 3/f, 4/f, 7/g.

Oxford University Press Archives

Oxford English Dictionary, MS slips (1st edition, superfluous).

Public Record Office

WORK 14/1/7.
WORK 14/4/6.
WORK 14/226.
WORK 14/281.
WORK 14/952.
WORK 14/972.
WORK 14/1008.
WORK 14/2386–98.

WO 44/304.
WO 44/296.
WO 94/65/1.
WO 94/66/1–3.
WO 304.

Tate Gallery Archives, The Hyman Krietman Research Centre

Sir Kenneth Clark's Collection, 8812.1.2.–8812.2.2.

Toynbee Hall, Special Collections

BRC/MBI/IBH, vols. 1, 3–6, 9, 12, 14, 16, 18, 19, 22, 24, 26, Maurice Birley, 'Illustrations of British History' part of Barnett Research Centre 'Toynbee Hall Residents 1884–*c.*1940' database, compiled by Katherine Bradley, Barnett Research Centre.

Victoria and Albert Museum, Archive of Art and Design

Arts Council of Great Britain EL5/85, 'Operation Gloriana'.

Written memoirs and testimonies, author's collection

Brickman, Joyce, née Gildersleve, written on 10 May 2002.
Curtis, Sidney, 21 March 2002.
Davin, Anna, 18 July 2003.
Foot, Richard, 25 March 2002.
Hogarth, Denis, 2 April 2002.

Jaffa, Renee, née Purkis, 22 March 2002.
Nelson, Janet, 22 July 2003.
Rutstein, J. B., 'The Rutstein and Stander Families, a Memoir', date unknown, copy sent to author 28 March 2002.
——'A Voice from the Past by Jack Rutstein', ditto.
Scotchmer, W. G., 26 March 2002.
Shaw, Jennifer B., on Edna Lewis Shaw (née Lawrence), 25, 27 September 2004.
Smercovitch, Martin, 23 March 2002.
Wolfers, Michael, 18 July 2003.

FILMS

Catherine the Great (London Films, 1934).
Drake of England (Associated British Picture Cooperation, 1935).
Fire Over England (London Films, 1937).
Henry V (Two Cities Company, 1944).
Les Amours de la Reine Elizabeth (Famous Players, 1912).
The Lion Has Wings (London Films, 1941).
Mary of Scotland (RKO, 1936).
The Only Way (Herbert Wilcox, 1925).
The Private Life of Elizabeth and Essex (Warner Bros., 1939).
The Private Life of Henry VIII (London Films, 1933).
Queen Christina (Warner Bros., 1933).
Scarlet Empress (Universal, 1934).
The Scarlet Pimpernel (London Films, 1935).
The Sea Hawk (1924).
——(Warner Bros., 1940).
The Sword and the Rose (Walt Disney, 1953).
A Tale of Two Cities (Master Films, 1922).
——(MGM, 1935).
——(Rank, 1958).
The Tower of London (Universal, 1939).
Tudor Rose (Gainsborough, 1936).
Virgin Queen (Twentieth Century Fox, 1955).
Young Bess (MGM, 1953).

GOVERNMENT PUBLICATIONS

House of Commons Parliamentary Papers

'National Monuments and Works of Art: Report from the Select Committee on National Monuments, Minutes of Evidence (1841)', *British Parliamentary Papers, Education and Fine Arts*, vol. 2 (Shannon, Ireland).
49.325, 1845, vol. xix.
50.224, 1846, vol. v.
54.265, 1850, vol. xxxiii.
59.432, 1854–5, vol. liii.

PRINTED PRIMARY SOURCES

Literature

ACTON, JOHN, *Lectures on the French Revolution* (London, 1910).
ALISON, A., *History of Europe during the French Revolution*, 10 vols. (Edinburgh, 1833–42).
AINSWORTH, W. H., *Jack Sheppard* (London, 1839).
—— *Old St Paul* (London, 1841).
—— *The Tower of London: A Historical Romance* (London, 1840; 1854).
BAGEHOT, WALTER, 'Charles Dickens', *National Review*, 7 (Oct. 1858).
BAKER, ERNEST, *A Guide to Historical Fiction* (New York, 1914; repr. 1969).
—— *History in Fiction*, 2 vols. (London and New York, 1907).
BAYLEY, JOHN, *The History and Antiquities of the Tower of London with Biographical Anecdotes of Royal and Distinguished Persons* (London, 1821).
—— *The History and Antiquities of the Tower of London with Memoirs of Royal and Distinguished Persons* (London, 1825).
BELLOC, HILAIRE, *The French Revolution* (London, 1911).
—— *Marie Antoinette* (New York, 1909).
—— *Robespierre: A Study* (1901; repr. New York, 1928).
BERNSTEIN, SIDNEY, *The Bernstein Film Questionnaire Report* (London, repr. 1947).
BETTS, ERNEST (ed.), *The Private Life of Henry VIII Directed by Alexander Korda, Story and Dialogue by Lajos Biro and Arthur Wimperis* (London, 1934).
Biographical and Descriptive Sketches of the Distinguished Characters which Compose the Unrivalled Exhibition and Historical Gallery of Madame Tussaud and Sons (1869).
Biographical and Descriptive Sketches of the Distinguished Characters which Compose the Unrivalled Exhibition of Madame Tussaud and Sons (1847).
Biographical and Descriptive Sketches of the Whole Length Composition Figures and Other Works of Art Forming the Unrivalled Exhibition of Madame Tussaud (1826).
BRAND, J., 'Account of the Inscriptions Discovered on the Walls of the Tower of London', *Archaeologica*, 13 (1800), 68–99.
BRITTEN, BENJAMIN, 'Billy Budd', in *The Operas of Benjamin Britten: The Complete Librettos Illustrated with Designs of the First Productions*, ed. David Herbert (London, repr. 1979).
—— 'Gloriana', ibid.
BROSTER, D. K., *Chantmarle: A Romance of the Vendean War* (1910).
BRYSON, ELIZABETH, *Look Back in Wonder* (Dundee, 1966).
BULWER-LYTTON, EDWARD, *Lucretia or the Children of the Night* (London, 1846).
—— *Zanoni* (London, 1842).
BUSH, ALAN, *Wat Tyler: Opera in Two Acts with a Prologue, Libretto by Nancy Bush* (London; repr. 1957).
BYATT, A. S., *The Virgin in the Garden* (1978; Harmondsworth, 1986).
CARLYLE, THOMAS, *The French Revolution, a History* (London, 1837; New York, n.d., repr. Modern Library edn.).
The Chronicles of Queen Jane and the Two Years of Queen Mary . . . Written by a Resident of the Tower of London, ed. J. V. Nichols (London, 1850).
City of Manchester Art Gallery, Coronation Exhibition: *16th-Century Portraits of Famous Early Elizabethans* (May–June 1953).

COCKBURN, HENRY, *Memorials of his Time* (1856; Chicago, 1974).
CONSITT, FRANCES, *The Value of Films in History Teaching, Being the Report of the Enquiry Conducted Under the Auspices of the Historical Association* (London, 1931).
CROWEST, FREDERICK, *The Story of British Music: From the Earliest Times to the Tudor Period* (London, 1896).
Curiosities in the Tower of London, 2 vols. (London, 1741).
DE ROS, LORD, *Memorials of the Tower of London* (London, 1866).
DICKENS, CHARLES, *Barnaby Rudge; A Tale of the Riots of 'Eighty* (1841; Harmondsworth, 1997).
—— *Gone Astray and Other Papers from Household Words, 1851–59*, ed. Michael Slater (Dent Uniform Edition of Dickens Journalism, iii; Columbus, Ohio, 1999).
—— *Old Curiosity Shop* (1841; repr. Oxford, 1951).
—— *Sketches by Boz and Other Early Papers 1833–39* (Dent Uniform Edition of Dickens Journalism, i; Columbus, Ohio, 1994).
—— *A Tale of Two Cities* (1859; repr. London, 1994).
ENGELS, FRIEDRICH, *The Condition of the Working Class in England* (1844; repr. St Albans, 1982).
'Fanfare for Britten', *Young Elizabethan*, 6, no. 6 (June 1953), 20.
FORSYTH, CECIL, *Music and Nationalism: A Study of English Opera* (London, 1911).
FOX COOPER, FREDERICK, *see* Rivers, Henry J.
FULLER MAITLAND, J. A., *English Music of the Nineteenth Century* (London, 1902).
GIBBS, PHILIP, *The New Elizabethans* (London, 1953).
GOODMAN, WALTER, *The Keeleys on the Stage and Home* (London, 1895).
HAREWOOD, EARL OF, GEORGE LASCELLES, *The Tongs and the Bones* (London, 1981).
HARRIS, HAMILTON, *The Tower of London: An Address Delivered before the Young Men's Association, in the City of Albany, November 28, 1878* (Albany, NY, 1878).
HENTY, G. A., *No Surrender! A Tale of the Rising in La Vendée* (London, 1900).
HUEFFER, FRANCIS, 'The Chances of English Opera', *Macmillan Magazine*, May 1879, pp. 40–57.
An Historical Description of the Tower of London and its Curiosities (London, 1796).
An Historical Description of the Tower of London and its Curiosities (London, 1806).
HUGO, VICTOR, *Notre Dame de Paris: 1482* (1831; Paris, 1961).
—— *Quatrevingt-Treize* (1874; Paris 1987).
IRWIN, MARGARET, *Elizabeth and the Prince of Spain* (London, 1953).
—— *Elizabeth, Captive Princess* (London, 1948).
—— *Young Bess* (London, 1944).
KINGSLEY, CHARLES, *Alton Locke, Tailor and Poet* (London, 1850).
—— *Westward Ho! Or the Voyages and Adventures of Sir Amyas Leigh. Knight ... in the Reign of Queen Elizabeth* (London, 1855).
KNIGHT, CHARLES (ed.), *London*, 6 vols. (London, 1841–4).
LAVER, JAMES, 'Dates and Dresses', *Sight and Sound*, 8, no. 30 (Summer 1939), 50–1.
LEJEUNE, C. A., *The C. A. Lejeune Film Reader*, ed. Anthony Lejeune (Manchester, 1991).
MCGRATH, MELANIE, *Silvertown: An East End Family Memoir* (London, 2002).
Madame Tussaud's and Sons Catalogue (London, 1869).
—— (London, 1873).
—— (London, 1918).
—— (London, 1928).

MASON, A. E. W., *Fire over England* (London, 1936).
MAYER, J. P., *British Cinemas and their Audiences: Sociological Studies* (London, 1948).
—— *Sociology of Film: Studies and Documents* (2nd edn., London, 1948).
MAYHEW, HENRY, *London Labour and the London Poor* (1850–1; repr. New York, 1968).
Memorial of the North London Working Classes' Industrial Exhibition, ed. J. F. Wilson (London, 1864).
MOSS, LOUIS, and BOX, KATHLEEN, *The Cinema Audience: An Enquiry Made by the Wartime Social Survey for the Ministry of Information*, New series no. 37B (June–July 1943).
NEALE, J. E., *Queen Elizabeth I* (London, 1934; repr. Harmondsworth, 1961).
A New and Improved History and Description of the Tower of London, Including a Particular Detail of its Numerous and Interesting Curiosities (London, 1825).
A New and Improved History and Description of the Tower of London (London, 1837).
NIELD, JONATHAN, *A Guide to Historical Novels and Tales* (New York, 1902; repr. 1929).
O'NEILL, GILDA, *My East End: Memories of Life in Cockney London* (Harmondsworth, 2000).
ORCZY, EMMUSKA (BARONESS ORCZY), *Beau Brocade* (Philadelphia, 1907).
—— *Eldorado, a Story of the Scarlet Pimpernel* (London, 1913).
—— *The Elusive Pimpernel* (London, 1908).
—— *The First Sir Percy—An Adventure of the Laughing Cavalier* (London, 1920).
—— *The League of the Scarlet Pimpernel* (London, 1919).
—— *The Links in the Chains of Life* (London, 1941).
—— *Lord Tony's Wife: An Adventure of the Scarlet Pimpernel* (1917; Thirsk, 2002).
—— *Mam'zelle Guillotine: An Adventure of the Scarlet Pimpernel* (London, 1940).
—— *The Scarlet Pimpernel* (London, 1905; repr. 1974).
—— *The Scarlet Pimpernel, Edited and Abridged for Class Use* (London, 1937).
—— *The Scarlet Pimpernel Looks at the World* (London, 1933).
—— *The Triumph of the Scarlet Pimpernel* (London, 1922).
PETRIE, CHARLES, 'The Historical Film', Pamphlet reprinted from *The Nineteenth Century and After*, 117 (May 1935), 613–32.
RIVERS, HENRY J., *The Tale of Two Cities: A Drama in Three Acts and a Prologue Adapted from Mr. Charles Dickens's Story* (London, 1860).
ROLPH, C. H., *London Particulars: Memories of an Edwardian Boyhood* (London, 1980).
ROWSE, A. L., *An Elizabethan Garland* (London, 1953).
—— *The England of Elizabeth: The Structure of Society* (London, 1950).
SABATINI, RAFAEL, *Captain Blood* (1922, repr. Harmondsworth, 2003).
—— *Scaramouche, the Kingmaker* (1921, repr. London, 2001).
—— *The Sea Hawk* (New York, 1915).
SALA, GEORGE AUGUSTUS, *Madame Tussaud's Exhibition Guide* (London, 1905).
SHAW, GEORGE BERNARD, *Shaw's Music: The Complete Musical Criticism of Bernard Shaw*, ed. Dan E. Lawrence (London, 1981).
A Short History of the Tower of London Including a Particular Detail of its Interesting Curiosities (London, 1849).
SMITH, MARY, *The Autobiography of Mary Smith, Schoolmistress and Nonconformist* (London, 1892).

Society for Obtaining Free Admission to National Monuments and Public Edifices. Report to the Committee (London, 1839; 1841).
STONELAKE, EDMUND, *The Autobiography of Edmund Stonelake*, ed. Anthony Mor-O'Brien (Brigend, 1981).
STRACHEY, LYTTON, *Elizabeth and Essex: A Tragic History* (London and New York, 1928).
STRICKLAND, AGNES and ELIZABETH, *The Lives of the Queens of England*, 12 vols. (London, 1840–8).
—— *The Lives of the Tudor Princesses Including Lady Jane Grey and her Sisters* (London, 1868).
TAYLOR, TOM, *A Tale of Two Cities: A Drama in Two Acts and a Prologue, Adapted from the Story of that Name by Charles Dickens* (London, 1860).
THACKERAY, WILLIAM MAKEPEACE, 'Going to See a Man Hanged', *Fraser's Magazine*, 22 (Aug. 1840), 150–8.
TODD, JANET, *Dictionary of British Women Writers* (London, 1991).
TROLLOPE, ANTHONY, *Autobiography* (1883; Oxford, 1989).
—— *La Vendée* (London, 1850).
TUSSAUD, MARIE, *Memoirs and Reminiscences of France, Forming an Abridged History of the French Revolution*, ed. Francis Hervé (London, 1838).
Tussaud's Economical Guide to London, Paris and Brussels Specifying the Cheapest Mode by which these Capitals May Be Visited (London, 1852).
VAUGHAN WILLIAMS, RALPH, *Hugh the Drover: or Love in the Stocks, a Romantic Ballad Opera in Two Acts* (London, 1924).
—— *National Music and Other Essays* (1931; Oxford, 1963).
—— *The Pilgrim's Progress, a Morality in a Prologue, Four Acts and an Epilogue Founded on Bunyan's Allegory* (Oxford; repr. 1952).
A Visit to Madame Tussaud's (London, 1876).
WEDGWOOD, C. V., 'Our Queen, Crown and Monarchy', *News Chronicle*, Background to the News Series, no. 11 (London, 1953), 5–41.
—— 'The Sense of the Past' (1957), in *History and Hope: The Collected Essays of C. V. Wedgwood* (London, 1987), 416–34.
—— 'The Velvet Study' (1946), in *History and Hope*, 12–19.
WILDE, OSCAR, *The Importance of Being Earnest*, in *Complete Works* (London; repr. 1969).
WILLS, FREEMAN, and LANGBRIDGE, FREDERICK, *The Only Way: A Dramatic Version in a Prologue and Four Acts of Charles Dickens's A Tale of Two Cities* (1899; London, 1942).
[WRIGHT, THOMAS], *Some Habits and Customs of the Working Classes by a Journeyman Engineer* (1867; repr. New York, 1967).

Newspapers and Periodicals

Bookman
Child Life
Christian Examiner
Collins Young Elizabethan
Contemporary Review

Daily Express
Daily Mail
Daily Telegraph
East End News
East London Observer
Eastern Argus and Borough of Hackney Times
Eastern Post
Era
Evening Standard
Examiner
Film Monthly Magazine
Film Weekly
Fraser's Magazine
The Guardian
Hollywood Spectator
Household Words
Illustrated London News
Kine Weekly
Leiston Observer and Aldeburgh, Saxmundham and Thorpeness News
Listener
London Magazine
Lowestoft Journal
Macmillan Magazine
Monthly Film Bulletin
Monthly Review
Motion Picture Herald
Music & Letters
Music and Musicians
Musical Opinion
New Statesman
New York Times
Observer
Opera
Opera News
Penny Magazine
Pictorial World
Picturegoer (later *Picturegoer Weekly*)
Punch
Scrutiny
Sight and Sound
Tempo
The Times
To-Day's Cinema
Tower Hamlets Independent
Variety
Vocal Music

SECONDARY LITERATURE

Ackroyd, Peter, *London: The Biography* (London, 2000).

Aldgate, Anthony, and Richards, Jeffrey, *Britain Can Take it: The British Cinema in the Second World War* (Oxford, 1986).

Alexander, Lynn M., *Women, Work and Representation: Needlewomen in Victorian Art and Literature* (Athens, Ohio, 2003).

Altick, Richard, *The English Common Reader: A Social History of the Mass Reading Public 1800–1900* (Chicago, 1957).

—— *The Shows of London* (Cambridge, Mass., 1978).

Anderson, Benedict, *Imagined Communities: Reflections on the Origin and Spread of Nationalism* (London, 1983; repr. 1991).

Anderson, Patricia, *The Printed Image and the Transformation of Popular Culture 1790–1860* (Oxford, 1991).

Andrews, Malcolm, *The Search for the Picturesque: Landscape, Aesthetics and Tourism in Britain, 1760–1800* (Stanford, Calif., 1989).

Appadurai, Arjun (ed.), *The Social Life of Things: Commodities in Cultural Perspective* (Cambridge, 1988).

Ashby, Justine, and Higson, Andrew, *British Cinema Past and Present* (London, 2000).

Aurbach, Jeffrey A., *The Great Exhibition of 1851: A Nation on Display* (New Haven, 1999).

—— 'Exhibiting the Nation: British National Identity and the Great Exhibition of 1851' (Ph.D. diss., Yale University, 1995).

Bailey, Peter, *Leisure and Class in Victorian England: Rational Recreation and the Contest for Control, 1830–1885* (London, 1978).

—— *Popular Culture and Performance in the Victorian City* (Cambridge, 1998).

Banks, Paul (ed.), *Britten's Gloriana* (Aldeburgh Studies in Music, 1; Woodbridge, 1993).

Bann, Stephen, *The Clothing of Clio: A Study of the Representation of History in Nineteenth-Century Britain and France* (Cambridge, 1984).

—— *The Invention of History: Essays in the Representations of the Past* (Manchester, 1990).

—— *Paul Delaroche: History Painted* (London, 1997).

Barczewski, Stephanie, *Myth and National Identity in Nineteenth-Century Britain: The Legends of King Arthur and Robin Hood* (Oxford, 2000).

Barker-Benfield, G. J., *The Culture of Sensibility: Sex and Society in Eighteenth-Century Britain* (Chicago, 1992).

Barrow, Kenneth, *Flora: An Appreciation of the Life and Work of Dame Flora Robson* (London, 1981).

Barthes, Roland, *Mythologies*, trans. Annette Lavers (New York, 1972).

Baumgarten, Murray, 'Fictions of the City', in Jordan (ed.), *The Cambridge Companion to Charles Dickens*, 106–18.

Ben-Israel, Hedva, *English Historians on the French Revolution* (Cambridge, 1968; reissued 2002).

Benjamin, Walter, *Charles Baudelaire: A Lyric Poet in the Era of High Capitalism*, trans. Harry Zohn (London, 1983).

BENNETT, TONY, *The Birth of the Museum: History, Theory, Politics* (London, 1995; repr. 1999).
—— 'The Exhibitionary Complex', in David Boswell and Jessica Evans (eds.), *Representing the Nation: A Reader. Histories, Heritage and Museums* (London, 1999), 332–63.
BERG, MAXINE, 'The First Women Economic Historians', *Economic History Review*, 45 (1992), 308–29.
BERMINGHAM, ANN, *Landscape and Ideology: The English Rustic Tradition, 1740–1860* (Berkeley, 1986).
BERMINGHAM, ANN, and BREWER, JOHN (eds.), *The Consumption of Culture, 1600–1800: Image, Object, Text* (London, 1995).
BERNSTEIN, GEORGE L., *The Myth of Decline: The Rise of Britain since 1945* (London, 2004).
BHABHA, H. K. (ed.), *Nation and Narration* (London, 1990).
BINDMAN, DAVID, *The Shadow of the Guillotine: Britain and the French Revolution* (London, 1989).
BLACK, BARBARA J., *On Exhibit: Victorians and their Museums* (Charlottesville, Va., 2000).
—— 'A Sisterhood of Rage and Beauty: Dickens's Rosa Dartle, Miss Wade and Madame Defarge', *Dickens Studies Annual*, 26 (1998), 91–106.
BLANNING, T. C. W., *The Culture of Power and the Power of Culture: Old Regime Europe 1660–1789* (Oxford, 2002).
BLASS, P. B. M., *Continuity and Anachronism: Parliamentary and Constitutional Development in Anti-Whig Reaction between 1890–1939* (The Hague and Boston, Mass., 1978).
BOASE, T. S. R., *English Art 1800–1870* (Oxford, 1959).
BOLTON, PHILIP, *Dickens Dramatized* (Boston, 1978).
BOOS, FLORENCE S. (ed.), *History and Community: Essays in Victorian Medievalism* (New York, 1992).
BOSWELL, DAVID, and EVANS, JESSICA (eds.), *Representing the Nation: A Reader. Histories, Heritage and Museums* (London, 1999).
BOURDIEU, PIERRE, *Distinction: A Social Critique of the Judgment of Taste*, trans. Richard Nice (London; repr. 2000).
—— *The Field of Cultural Production: Essays on Art and Literature*, ed. Randal Johnson (Cambridge, 1999).
BOWLBY, RACHEL, *Just Looking: Consumer Culture in Dreiser, Gissing and Zola* (New York, 1985).
BRENNAN, THERESA, and JAY, MARTIN (eds.), *Vision in Context: Historical and Contemporary Perspectives on Sight* (London, 1996).
BRIGGS, ASA, *Saxons, Normans and Britons* (Hastings and Bexhill, 1966).
—— *Victorian Things* (Chicago, 1989).
BROOKS, PETER, *The Melodramatic Imagination: Balzac, Henry James, Melodrama and the Mode of Excess* (New Haven, 1976).
BUCK-MORSS, SUSAN, *The Dialectics of Seeing: Walter Benjamin and the Arcades Project* (Cambridge, Mass., 1989).
BULLOCK, NICHOLAS, *Building the Post-War World: Modern Architecture and Reconstruction in Britain* (London, 2002).

BURN, W. L., *The Age of Equipoise: A Study of the Mid-Victorian Generation* (New York, 1965).
BURROW, JOHN W., 'Images of Time: From Carlylean Vulcanism to Sedimentary Gradualism', in Stefan Collini, Richard Whatmore, and Brian Young (eds.), *History, Religion and Culture: British Intellectual History 1750–1950* (Cambridge, 2000), 198–224.
——*A Liberal Descent: Victorian Historians and the English Past* (Cambridge, 1981).
——' "The Village Community" and the Uses of History in Late Nineteenth-Century England', in Neil McKendrick (ed.), *Historical Perspectives: Studies in English Thought and Society in Honour of J. H. Plumb* (London, 1971), 255–84.
CALDER, ANGUS, *The Myth of the Blitz* (London; repr. 2000).
——*The People's War* (London, 1969; repr. 2002).
The Cambridge Social History of Britain, 1750–1950, ii: *People and their Environment*, ed. F. M. L. Thompson; iii: *Social Agencies and Institutions*, ed. F. M. L. Thompson (Cambridge, 1990).
The Cambridge Urban History of Britain: 1540–1840, ii: *1840–1950*, ed. Peter Clark (Cambridge, 2000); iii: *1840–1950*, ed. Martin Daunton (Cambridge, 2001).
CANNADINE, DAVID, *Aspects of Aristocracy: Grandeur and Decline in Modern Britain* (New Haven, 1994).
——'The Context, Performance and Meaning of Ritual: The British Monarchy and the "Invention of Tradition" c.1820–1977', in Eric Hobsbawm and Terence Ranger (eds.), *The Invention of Tradition* (Cambridge, 1983), 101–65.
——*The Decline and Fall of the British Aristocracy* (New Haven, 1990).
CANTOR, NORMAN F., *Inventing the Middle Ages* (Cambridge, 1991).
CARPENTER, HUMPHREY, *Benjamin Britten* (London, 1992).
CERTEAU, MICHEL DE, *The Practice of Everyday Life*, trans. Steven Rendall (Berkeley, 1988).
Chambers's Twentieth-Century Dictionary, ed. E. M. Kirkpatrick (Edinburgh, 1983).
CHANDLER, ALICE, *A Dream of Order: The Medieval Ideal in Nineteenth-Century English Literature* (London, 1970).
CHAPMAN, PAULINE, *The French Revolution as Seen by Madame Tussaud, Witness Extraordinary* (London, 1989).
——*Madame Tussaud in England: Career Woman Extraordinary* (London, 1992).
——*Madame Tussaud's Chamber of Horrors* (London, 1984).
CHARLTON, JOHN (ed.), *The Tower of London its History and Institutions* (London, 1978).
CHARTIER, ROGER, and CAVALLO, GUGLIELMO (eds.) *A History of Reading in the West* (Philadelphia, 1999).
CHERRY, DEBORAH, *Beyond the Frame: Feminism and Visual Culture in Britain, 1850–1900* (London, 2000).
CHRIST, CAROL, 'Victorian Masculinity and the Angel in the House', in Martha Vicinus (ed.), *A Widening Sphere: Changing Roles of Victorian Women* (London, 1980), 146–63.
CLARK, KENNETH, *The Gothic Revival: An Essay in the History of Taste* (3rd edn., London, 1963).
CLARKE, PETER, *Hope and Glory: Britain 1945–1990* (Harmondsworth, 1996).
CLUNAS, CRAIG, 'Modernity Global and Local: Consumption and the Rise of the West', *American Historical Review*, 104 (1999), 1497–1511.

COLLEY, LINDA, *Britons: Forging the Nation 1707–1837* (New Haven, 1992).
COLLINI, STEFAN, *English Pasts: Essays in History and Culture* (Oxford, 1999).
——*Public Moralists: Political Thought and Intellectual Life in Britain 1850–1930* (Oxford, 1991).
COLLINI, STEFAN, WHATMORE, RICHARD, and YOUNG, BRIAN (eds.), *History, Religion and Culture: British Intellectual History 1750–1950* (Cambridge, 2000).
COLLINS, PHILIP, *Dickens and Crime* (London, 1964).
——'A Tale of Two Novels: *A Tale of Two Cities* and *Great Expectations* in Dickens's Career', *Dickens Studies Annual*, 2 (1972), 336–51; 378–81.
COLLS, ROBERT, *Identity of England* (Oxford, 2002).
COMOLLI, JEAN-LOUIS, 'Machines of the Visible', in Teresa de Lauretis and Stephen Heath (eds.), *The Cinematic Apparatus* (Basingstoke, 1980), 121–41.
CONEKIN, BECKY E., *'The Autobiography of a Nation': The 1951 Festival of Britain* (Manchester, 2003).
——Mort, Frank, and Waters, Chris (eds.), *Moments of Modernity: Reconstructing Britain 1945–1964* (London, 1999).
COOK, PAM, *Fashioning the Nation: Costume and Identity in British Cinema* (London, 1996).
COOKE, MERVYN (ed.), *The Cambridge Companion to Benjamin Britten* (Cambridge, 1999).
CORBEY, RAYMOND, 'Ethnographic Showcases, 1870–1930', in Jan Nederveen Pieterse and Bhikhu Parekh (eds.), *The Decolonization of Imagination: Culture, Knowledge and Power* (London and Atlantic Heights, NJ, 1995), 57–81.
CRAFTON, LISA PLUMMER (ed.), *The French Revolution Debate in English Literature and Culture* (Westport, Conn., 1997).
CRARY, JONATHAN, *Suspensions of Perception: Attention, Spectacle, and Modern Culture* (Cambridge, Mass., 2000).
CROSBY, CHRISTINA, *The Ends of History: Victorians and 'the Woman Question'* (London, 1991).
CROSSLEY, CERI, and SMALL, IAN (eds.), *The French Revolution and British Culture* (Oxford, 1989).
CUMMING, MARK, *A Disimprisoned Epic: Form and Vision in Carlyle's French Revolution* (Philadelphia, 1988).
CUSTEN, GEORGE F., *Bio/Pics: How Hollywood Constructed Public History* (New Brunswick, NJ, 1996).
DAUNTON, MARTIN, 'Introduction', in *The Cambridge Urban History of Britain*, iii: *1840–1950*, ed. Martin Daunton (Cambridge, 2001), 1–59.
——'The Material Politics of Natural Monopoly: Consuming Gas in Victorian Britain', in id. and Matthew Hilton (eds.), *The Politics of Consumption: Material Culture and Citizenship in Europe and America* (Oxford, 2001), 69–89.
DAVIDOFF, LEONORE, and HALL, CATHERINE, *Family Fortunes: Men and Women of the English Middle Class, 1780–1850* (London, 1988).
DAVIN, ANNA, 'Historical Novels for Children', *HWJ* 1 (1976), 154–65.
——'History, the Nation and the Schools', *HWJ*, 29 (1990), 92–4.
DE GRAZIA, VICTORIA, *The Sex of Things: Gender and Consumption in Historical Perspective* (Berkeley, 1996).

DELAP, LUCY, 'The Superwoman: Theories of Gender and Genius in Edwardian Britain', *Historical Journal*, 47, no. 1 (Mar. 2004), 101–26.
DELLAMORA, RICHARD, and FISCHLIN, PAUL (eds.), *The Work of Opera: Genre, Nationhood, and Sexual Difference* (New York, 1997).
DELLHEIM, CHARLES, *The Face of the Past: The Preservation of the Medieval Inheritance in Victorian England* (Cambridge, 1982).
DENNIS, RICHARD, 'Modern London', in *The Cambridge Urban History of Britain*, iii: *1840–1950*, ed. Martin Daunton (Cambridge, 2001), 95–133.
DENT, EDWARD J., 'The Future of English Opera', in Eric Crozier (ed.), *Opera in English, Sadler's Wells Opera Books* (London, 1946), 26–41.
DOANE, MARY ANN, 'The Economy of Desire: The Commodity Form in/of the Cinema', *Quarterly Review of Film and Video*', 11 (1989), 22–33.
DURING, SIMON, *Modern Enchantments: The Cultural Power of Secular Magic* (Cambridge, Mass., 2002).
DUTTON, DAVID, *British Politics since 1945* (Oxford, 1991).
DYOS, H. J., and WOLFF, MICHAEL (eds.), *The Victorian City: Images and Realities*, i: *Past and Present*; ii: *Shapes on the Ground* (London, 1973).
EISENSTEIN, ELIZABETH, *The Printing Press as an Agent of Change: Communication and Cultural Transformation in Early Modern Europe* (Cambridge, 1980).
ELHANATI, MOSHE, 'Engineers and Gentlemen: The Engineering Press and Cultural Discourse—from Technological Optimism to Gentlemanly Capitalism, England 1840–70' (MA thesis, Tel Aviv University, 2001).
ELIAS, NORBERT, *The Civilizing Process: Sociogenetic and Psychogenetic Investigations*, rev. edn., ed. Eric Dunning, Johan Goudsblom, and Stephen Mennell (Oxford, 2000).
ELLIS, STEWART M., *William Harrison Ainsworth and his Friends* (London and New York, 1911).
EMSLEY, CLIVE, *British Society and the French Wars 1793–1815* (London, 1974, repr. 1996).
—— *Crime and Society in England, 1750–1900* (London, 1979; repr. Edinburgh, 1996).
EVANS, PETER, 'The Number Principle and Dramatic Momentum in *Gloriana*', in Banks (ed.), *Britten's Gloriana*, 77–95.
FELDMAN, DAVID, and JONES, GARETH STEDMAN (eds.), *Metropolis London: Histories and Representations* (London, 1989).
FESKE, VICTOR, *From Belloc to Churchill: Private Scholars, Public Culture, and the Crisis of British Liberalism, 1900–1939* (Chapel Hill, NC, 1996).
FINN, MARGOT C., *After Chartism: Class and Nation in English Radical Politics, 1848–1874* (Cambridge, 1993).
FLEISHMAN, AVROM, *The English Historical Novel: Walter Scott to Virginia Woolf* (Baltimore, 1971).
FLINT, KATE, *The Victorians and the Visual Imagination* (Cambridge, 2000).
FORD, CHARLES, 'Sarah Bernhardt, Notes on a Dying Legend', *Films in Review*, 5, no. 10 (Dec. 1954), 515–19.
FORSTER, JOHN, *The Life of Charles Dickens*, 2 vols. (London, 1927).
FOUCAULT, MICHEL, *Discipline and Punish: The Birth of the Prison*, trans. Alan Sheridan (London, 1977).
—— 'Governmentality', in Graham Bruchell, Colin Gordon, and Peter Miller (eds.), *The Foucault Effect: Studies in Governmentality* (Chicago, 1991).

FRANCIS, M., and ZWEINIGER-BARGIELOWSKA, INA (eds.), *The Conservatives and British Society, 1880–1990* (Cardiff, 1996).
FRY, LOWELL T., '"Great Burke", Thomas Carlyle and the French Revolution', in Lisa Plummer Crafton (ed.), *The French Revolution Debate in English Literature and Culture* (Westport, Conn., 1997), 83–106.
FUSSELL, PAUL, *The Great War and Modern Memory* (Oxford, 1975).
GASH, NORMAN (ed.), *Wellington: Studies in the Military and Political Career of the First Duke of Wellington* (Manchester, 1990).
GATRELL, V. A. C., *The Hanging Tree: Execution and the English People 1710–1868* (Oxford, 1994; repr. 1996).
GILBERT, SANDRA M., and GUBAR, SUSAN, *The Madwoman in the Attic: The Woman Writer and the Nineteenth-Century Literary Imagination* (New Haven, 1984).
GIROUARD, MARK, *Life in the English Country House: A Social and Architectural History* (New Haven, 1978).
—— *The Return to Camelot: Chivalry and the English Gentleman* (New Haven, 1981).
—— *Sweetness and Light: The Queen Anne Movement 1860–1900* (Oxford, 1977).
GODINEAU, DOMINIQUE, 'Masculine and Feminine Political Practice during the French Revolution, 1793—Year III', in Harriet B. Applewhite and Darline G. Levy (eds.), *Women and Politics in the Age of the Democratic Revolution* (Ann Arbor, 1993), 61–81.
—— *The Women of Paris and their Revolution*, trans. Katherine Streip (Berkeley, 1998).
GOLBY, J. M., and PURDUE, A. W., *The Civilisation of the Crowd: Popular Culture in England, 1750–1900* (Stroud, repr. 1999).
GOLDBERG, MICHAEL, *Carlyle and Dickens* (Athens, Ga., 1972).
GOOCH, G. P., *History and Historians in the Nineteenth Century* (1913; repr. Boston, 1959).
GOODMAN, WALTER, *The Keeleys on the Stage and at Home* (London, 1895).
GOODWAY, DAVID, *London Chartism 1838–1848* (Cambridge, 1982).
GREENBLATT, STEPHEN, *Renaissance Self-Fashioning from More to Shakespeare* (Chicago, 1980).
GREENHALGH, PAUL, *Ephemeral Vistas: The Expositions Universelles, Great Exhibition and World Fairs, 1851–1939* (Manchester, 1988).
HAFFNER, SEBASTIAN, 'The Renascence of Monarchy', *Twentieth Century*, 153, no. 916 (June 1953), 415–24.
HALL, CATHERINE, 'Competing Masculinities: Thomas Carlyle, John Stuart Mill and the Case of Governor Eyre', in *White, Male and Middle Class: Explorations in Feminism and History* (New York, 1992), 255–96.
HALLIDAY, STEPHEN, *The Great Stink of London: Sir Joseph Bazalgette and the Cleansing of the Victorian Metropolis* (London, 1999).
HAMMOND, PETER, '"Epitome of England's History": The Transformation of the Tower of London as Visitor Attraction in the Nineteenth Century', *Royal Armouries Yearbook*, 4 (1999), 144–74.
HARPER, SUE, 'Historical Pleasures: Gainsborough Costume Melodrama', in Christine Gledhill (ed.), *Home is Where the Heart Is: Studies in Melodrama and the Woman's Film* (London, 1987), 167–97.
—— *Picturing the Past: The Rise and Fall of the British Costume Film* (London, 1994).

HARRIS, JOSÉ, *Private Lives, Public Virtues: A Social History of Britain, 1870–1914* (Oxford, 1993).
HARVEY, PAUL, *The Oxford Companion to Classical Literature* (repr. Oxford, 1986).
HAYS, MICHAEL, and NIKOLOPOULOU, ANASTASIA (eds.), *Melodrama: The Cultural Emergence of a Genre* (Basingstoke, 1996).
HEFFER, SIMON, *Moral Desperado: A Life of Thomas Carlyle* (London, 1995).
HEWISON, ROBERT, *Culture and Consensus: England, Art and Politics since 1945* (London, 1995).
——Hewison, '"Happy Were He"': Benjamin Britten and the Gloriana Story', in Banks (ed.), *Britten's Gloriana*, 1–16.
HEWITT, MARTIN (ed.), *An Age of Equipoise? Reassessing Mid-Victorian Britain* (London, 2002).
HIBBERT, CHRISTOPHER, *The Road to Tyburn: The Story of Jack Sheppard and the Eighteenth-Century Underworld* (Harmondsworth, 2001).
HIGHAM, CHARLES, *Charles Laughton, an Intimate Biography* (New York, 1976).
HIGSON, ANDREW, 'The Instability of the National', in Justine Ashby and Andrew Higson (eds.), *British Cinema Past and Present* (London, 2000), 35–49.
—— *Waving the Flag: Constructing a National Cinema in Britain* (Oxford, 1995).
HOCHBERG, SHIFRA, 'Madame Defarge and a Possible Carlylean Source', *Dickensian*, 91 (1995), 99–101.
HOFFENBERG, PETER H., *An Empire on Display: English, Indian and Australian Exhibitions from the Crystal Palace to the Great War* (Berkeley, 2001).
HOLLINGSWORTH, KEITH, *The Newgate Novel 1830–47: Bulwer, Ainsworth, Dickens and Thackeray* (Detroit, 1963).
HOLROYD, MICHAEL, *Lytton Strachey: The New Biography* (London, 1994).
HOOVER, JEAN MARIE, 'Constructions of National Identities: Opera and Nationalism in the British Isles' (Ph.D. diss., Indiana University, 1999).
HOWES, FRANK, *The English Musical Renaissance* (New York, 1966).
HOWKINS, ALUN, *The Death of the Countryside: A Social History* (London, 2003).
——'The Discovery of Rural England', in Robert Colls and Philip Dodd (eds.), *Englishness: Politics and Culture 1880–1920* (Beckenham, 1987), 62–89.
HUGHES, ALBERT HILLIARD, 'Sarah Bernhardt on the Screen', *The Silent Picture*, 7, no. 26 (Summer 1970), 9–10.
HUGHES, MEIRION, and STRADLING, ROBERT, *The English Musical Renaissance 1860–1940: Construction and Deconstruction* (London, 1993).
HUNT, LYNN, *The Family Romance of the French Revolution* (Berkeley, 1992).
——(ed.), *The New Cultural History* (Berkeley, 1989).
——and Bonnell, Victoria E. (eds.), *Beyond the Cultural Turn: New Directions in the Study of Society and Culture* (Berkeley, 1999).
HYDE, RALPH, *Panoramania! The Art and Entertainment of the 'All–Embracing' View* (London, 1988).
INGRAM, PATRICIA, *Dickens, Women and Language* (Toronto, 1992).
JAMES, LOUIS, 'Cruikshank and Early Victorian Caricature', *HWJ* 6 (Aug. 1970), 107–20.
——*Fiction for the Working Man, 1830–1850* (Oxford, 1963).
JAY, MARTIN, *Downcast Eyes: The Denigration of Vision in Twentieth-Century French Thought* (Berkeley, 1993).

JENNINGS, HUMPHREY, *Pandaemonium 1660–1886: The Coming of the Machine as Seen by Contemporary Observers* (New York, 1985).

JOHN, JULIET, *Dickens's Villains: Melodrama, Character, Popular Culture* (Oxford, 2001).

JONES, EDWIN, *The English Nation: The Great Myth* (Stroud, repr. 2000).

JONES, GARETH STEDMAN, *Languages of Class: Studies in English Working-Class History 1832–1982* (Cambridge, 1983).

JORDAN, JOHN O. (ed.), *The Cambridge Companion to Charles Dickens* (Cambridge, 2001).

JOYCE, PATRICK, *The Rule of Freedom: Liberalism and the Modern City* (London, 2003).

—— *Visions of the People: Industrial England and the Question of Class* (Cambridge, 1991).

KADISH, ALON, *Historians, Economists and Economic History* (London, 1989).

KANTOROWICZ, ERNST H., *The King's Two Bodies: A Study in Medieval Political Theology* (Princeton, 1957).

KAPLAN, FRED, *Thomas Carlyle: A Biography* (Berkeley, repr. 1993).

KAYE, HARVEY J., *The British Marxist Historians: Introductory Analysis* (Cambridge, 1984).

KEATING, PETER, *The Haunted Study: A Social History of the English Novel 1875–1914* (London, 1991).

KENYON, J. P., *The History Men: The Historical Profession in Britain since the Renaissance* (London, 1983).

KILDEA, PAUL, 'Britten, Auden and "Otherness"', in Mervyn Cooke (ed.), *The Cambridge Companion to Benjamin Britten* (Cambridge, 1999), 36–54.

—— *Selling Britten: Music and the Market Place* (Oxford, 2002).

KLONK, CHARLOTTE, 'The National Gallery in London and its Public', in Berg and Clifford (eds.), *Consumers and Luxury*, 228–50.

KORNMEIER, UTA, 'Madame Tussaud's as a Popular Pantheon', in Matthew Craske and Richard Wrigley (eds.), *Pantheons: The Transformation of a Monumental Idea* (London, forthcoming).

KOSOFSKY, EVE SEDGWICK, *The Coherence of Gothic Conventions* (New York; repr. 1986).

KOVEN, SETH, *Slumming: Sexual and Social Politics in Victorian London* (Princeton, 2004).

KWINT, MARIUS, 'Introduction: *The Physical Past*', in id., Breward, and Aynsley (eds.), *Material Memories*.

—— Breward, Christopher, and Aynsley, Jeremy (eds.), *Material Memories* (Oxford, 1999).

LAMONT, MICHÈLE, review of Michel de Certeau, *The Practice of Everyday Life*, in *American Journal of Sociology*, 93 (1987), 721–2.

LANDES, JOAN, *Women and the Public Sphere in the Age of the French Revolution* (Ithaca, NY, 1993).

LANDY, MARCIA, *British Genres: Cinema and Society 1930–60* (Princeton, 1991).

—— *Cinematic Uses of the Past* (Minneapolis, 1996).

LANG, TIMOTHY, *The Victorians and the Stuart Heritage: Interpretation of a Discordant Past* (Cambridge, 1995).

LEAVIS, F. R., *Mass Civilisation and Minority Culture* (London, 1930).

LEAVIS, Q. D., *Fiction and the Reading Public* (1932; Harmondsworth, 1979).

LEMAHIEU, D. L., *A Culture for Democracy: Mass Communication and the Cultivated Mind in Britain between the Wars* (Oxford, 1988).
LEMIRE, MICHEL, *Artistes et mortels* (Paris, 1990).
LESLIE, ANITA, and CHAPMAN, PAULINE, *Madame Tussaud: Waxworker Extraordinary* (London, 1978).
LEVIN, CAROLE, *The Heart and Stomach of a King: Elizabeth I and the Politics of Sex and Power* (Philadelphia, 1994; repr. 1996).
LEVINE, PHILIPPA, *The Amateur and the Professional: Antiquarians, Historians and Archaeologists in Victorian England, 1838–1886* (Cambridge, 1986).
LEVY, DARLINE G., and APPELWHITE, HARRIET B., 'Women, Radicalization, and the Fall of the French Monarchy', in Applewhite and Levy, *Women and Politics*, 81–109.
LEWIS, GWYNNE, *The French Revolution: Rethinking the Debate* (London, 1993).
LEWIS, JAYNE ELIZABETH, *Mary Queen of Scots: Romance and the Nation* (London, 1998; repr. 2004).
LIGHT, ALISON, *Forever England: Femininity, Literature and Conservatism between the Wars* (London, 1991).
—— '"Young Bess": Historical Novels and Growing Up', *Feminist Review*, 33 (Autumn 1989), 57–71.
LINEBAUGH, PETER, *The London Hanged: Crime and Civil Society in the Eighteenth Century* (2nd edn., London, 2003).
LODGE, DAVID, 'The French Revolution and the Condition of England: Crowds and Power in the Early Victorian Novel', in Ceri Crossley and Ian Small (eds.), *The French Revolution and British Culture* (Oxford, 1989), 123–42.
LONGFORD, ELIZABETH, *Wellington: The Years of the Sword* (London, 1969).
LOWENTHAL, DAVID, *The Heritage Crusade and the Spoils of Modern History* (Cambridge, 1997).
—— *The Past is a Foreign Country* (Cambridge; repr. 1995).
LYONS, MARTIN, 'New Readers in the Nineteenth Century: Women, Children, Workers', in Roger Chartier and Guglielmo Cavallo (eds.), *A History of Reading in the West* (Philadelphia, 1999), 78–92.
MCCRACKEN, GRANT, *Culture and Consumption: New Approaches to the Symbolic Character of Consumer Goods and Activities* (Indianapolis, Ind., 1988).
MACKAY, CAROL HANBERY, '"Before the Curtain": Entrances to the Dickens Theatre', in ead. (ed.), *Dramatic Dickens* (Basingstoke and London, 1989), 1–10.
MAITLAND, F. W., *Selected Essays* (Cambridge, 1936).
MCKENDRICK, NEIL, BREWER, JOHN, and PLUMB, J. H. (eds.), *The Birth of Consumer Society: The Commercialization of Eighteenth-Century England* (Bloomington, Ind., 1985).
MCKIBBIN, ROSS, *Classes and Cultures: England, 1918–1951* (Oxford, 2000).
MCLEISH, KENNETH and VALERIE (eds.), *Long to Reign over Us* (London, 1992).
MAITZEN, ROHAN AMANDA, *Gender, Genre and Victorian Historical Writing* (New York, 1998).
MANDLER, PETER, *The Fall and Rise of the Stately Home* (New Haven, 1997).
—— *History and National Life* (London, 2002).
—— '"In the Olden Time": Romantic History and English National Identity, 1820–50', in Lawrence Brockliss and David Eastwood (eds.), *A Union of Multiple Identities: The British Isles, c.1750–1850* (Manchester, 1997), 78–92.

MANDLER, PETER, '"The Wand of Fancy": The Historical Imagination of the Victorian Tourist', in Kwint, Breward, and Aynsley (eds.), *Material Memories*, 125–43.
MARCUS, LEAH S., 'Erasing the Stigma of Daughterhood: Mary I, Elizabeth I and Henry VIII', in Lynda E. Boose and Betty S. Flowers (eds.), *Daughters and Fathers* (Baltimore, 1989), 384–400.
MATLESS, DAVID, *Landscape and Englishness* (London, 1998).
MEISEL, MARTIN, *Realizations: Narrative, Pictorial and Theatrical Arts in Nineteenth-Century England* (Princeton, 1983).
MELMAN, BILLIE, 'Changing the Subject', in Ina Zweiniger-Bargielowska (ed.), *Women in Twentieth-Century Britain* (London, 2001), 16–35.
—— 'Claiming the Nation's Past: The Invention of an Anglo-Saxon Tradition', *Journal of Contemporary History*, 26, nos. 3–4, Special Issue: *The Impact of Western Nationalisms*, ed. Jehuda Reinharz with George L. Mosse (1991), 575–97.
—— 'Gender, History and Memory: The Invention of Women's Past in the Nineteenth and Early Twentieth Centuries', *History and Memory*, 5 (1993), 5–41.
—— *Women and the Popular Imagination in the Twenties: Flappers and Nymphs* (London, 1988).
—— (ed.), *Borderlines: Genders and Identities in War and Peace 1870–1930* (London, 1998).
MITCHELL, DONALD, 'The Paradox of *Gloriana*: Simple and Difficult', in Banks (ed.), *Britten's Gloriana*, 67–77.
MITCHELL, ROSEMARY, *Picturing the Past: English History in Text and Image, 1830–1870* (Oxford, 2000).
MITCHELL, TIMOTHY, 'Orientalism and the Exhibitionary Order', in Nicholas Dirks (ed.), *Colonialism and Culture* (Ann Arbor, 1992), 289–319.
MODELSKI, TANIA, *Loving with Vengeance: Mass Produced Fantasies for Women* (London, 1982).
MORGAN, JAMES, 'Coronatiana U.S.A', *Sight and Sound* (1953), 43–7.
MORGAN, P., 'Early Victorian Wales and its Crisis of Identity', in Brockliss and Eastwood (eds.), *A Union of Multiple Identities*, 93–107.
MORLEY, MALCOLM, 'The Stage Story of *A Tale of Two Cities*', *The Dickensian*, 51 (1954), 34–40.
MORT, FRANK, 'Fantasies of Metropolitan Life: Planning London in the 1940s', *Journal of British Studies*, 43, no. 1 (Jan. 2004), 120–53.
MOSSE, GEORGE L., *Nationalism and Sexuality* (New York, 1985).
MULHERN, FRANCIS, *Culture/Metaculture* (London, 2000).
MULVEY, LAURA, 'Afterthoughts on "Visual Pleasure and Narrative Cinema" Inspired by *Duel in the Sun*', *Framework*, 6, nos. 15–17 (1981), 12–15.
—— *Visual and Other Pleasures* (Basingstoke and Bloomington, Ind., 1989).
—— 'Visual Pleasure and Narrative Cinema', *Screen*, 16, no. 3 (Autumn 1975), 6–18.
MURRAY, VENETIA, *High Society: A Social History in the Regency Period, 1788–1830* (London, 1999).
NAIRN, TOM, *The Break-up of Britain: Crisis and Neo-nationalism* (London, 1977).
—— *The Enchanted Glass: Britain and the Monarchy* (London, 1988).
NEAD, LYNDA, *Victorian Babylon: People, Streets and Images in Nineteenth-Century London* (London and New Haven, 2000).

NORD, DEBORAH EPSTEIN, *Walking the Victorian Streets: Women, Representation and the City* (Ithaca, NY, 1995).
NOVICK, PETER, *That Noble Dream: The 'Objectivity Question' and the American Historical Profession* (Cambridge, repr. 1993).
OLLARD, RICHARD, *A Man of Contradictions: A Life of A. L. Rowse* (Harmondsworth, 2000).
OLSEN, DONALD, *The City as a Work of Art: London, Paris, Vienna* (New Haven, 1986).
—— *The Growth of Victorian London* (Harmondsworth; repr. 1979).
—— *Town Planning in London: Eighteenth and Nineteenth Centuries* (New Haven, 1982).
OETTERMANN, STEPHAN, *The Panorama: History of a Mass Medium*, trans. Deborah Lucas Schneider (New York, 1997).
OWEN, DAVID (ed.), with MacLeod, Roy, *The Government of Victorian London, 1855–1899: The Metropolitan Board of Works, the Vestries and the City Corporation* (Cambridge, Mass., 1982).
The Oxford Dictionary of the Christian Church, ed. F. L. Cross and E. A. Livingstone (2nd edn., Oxford, 1988).
PAGET, VIOLET, 'Carlyle and the Present Tense' (Studies in Literary Psychology, iii) *Contemporary Review*, 85 (1904), 386–92.
PARK, ROBERT, BURGESS, E. W., and MCKENZIE, R. D. (eds.), *The City* (Chicago, 1967).
PARNELL, GEOFFREY, *English Heritage Book of the Tower of London* (London, 1993).
—— 'The Rise and Fall of the Tower of London', *History Today*, 42 (Mar. 1992), 13–20.
—— *The Tower of London, Past and Present* (London, 1999).
PARTRIDGE, ERIC, *Slang and Unconventional English: Colloquialisms and Catch Phrases, Fossilized Jokes and Puns* (8th edn., London, 1984).
PATTEN, ROBERT L., *Charles Dickens and his Publishers* (Oxford, 1978).
—— *George Cruikshank's Life, Time and Art*, 2 vols. (Cambridge, Mass., 1996).
PEARS, IAIN, 'The Gentleman and the Hero: Wellington and Napoleon in the Nineteenth Century', in Roy Porter (ed.), *Myths of the English* (London, 1992), 216–36.
PEDERSEN, SUSAN, and MANDLER, PETER (eds.), *After the Victorians: Private Conscience and Public Duty in Modern Britain* (London, 1994).
PILBEAM, PAMELA, *Madame Tussaud and the History of Waxworks* (London, 2002).
PIMLOTT, BEN, *The Queen: A Biography of Elizabeth II* (New York, 1997).
PIMLOTT, J. A. R., *Toynbee Hall: Fifty Years of Social Progress, 1884–1934* (London, 1934).
PINKNEY, DAVID H., *Napoleon III and the Rebuilding of Paris* (Princeton, 1958).
PLOMER, WILLIAM, 'Let's Crab an Opera', *London Magazine*, 3, no. 7 (Oct. 1963), 102.
POINTER, MICHAEL (ed.), with Slide, Anthony, *Charles Dickens on the Screen: The Film, Television and Video Adaptations* (London, 1996).
POMIAN, KRZYSZTOF, *Collectors and Curiosities: Paris and Venice 1500–1800* (Cambridge, 1990).
POOVEY, MARY, *Making a Social Body: British Cultural Formation 1830–1864* (Chicago, 1995).
—— *Uneven Developments: The Ideological Work of Gender in Mid-Victorian England* (Chicago, 1988).
PORTER, ROY, *London: A Social History* (Harmondsworth, 2000).

POTTS, ALEX, 'Picturing the Modern Metropolis: Images of London in the Nineteenth Century', *HWJ* 26 (Autumn 1988), 28–56.

POWICKE, F. M., *Modern Historians and the Study of History* (London, 1955).

PRATT, BRANWEN BAILEY, 'Carlyle and Dickens: Heroes and Hero Worshippers', *Dickens Annual Studies*, 13 (1983), 233–46.

PRIESTLEY, J. B., *English Journey* (London, 1933).

PROCHASKA, FRANK, *The Republic of Britain: 1760 to the Present* (Harmondsworth; repr. 2001).

—— *Royal Bounty: The Making of a Welfare Monarchy* (New Haven, 1995).

PYKE, E. J., *Bibliographical Dictionary of Wax Modellers* (Oxford, 1973: Supplement, London, 1981).

RAPPAPORT, ERIKA, *The West End and Women's Pleasures: Gender and Commercial Culture in London 1860–1940* (Princeton, 2001).

READMAN, PAUL, 'The Place of the Past in English Culture c.1890–1914', *Past and Present*, 186 (Feb. 2005), 147–201.

RICHARDS, JEFFREY, *The Age of the Dream Palace: Cinema and Society in Britain 1930–39* (London, 1984).

—— 'Dame Flora's Crowning Glory', *Daily Telegraph*, 1 June 1990, p. 14.

—— *Films and British National Identity: From Dickens to Dad's Army* (New York, 1997).

—— *Swordsmen of the Screen from Douglas Fairbanks to Michael York* (London, 1977).

RICHARDS, THOMAS, *The Commodity Culture of Victorian England: Advertising and Spectacle 1851–1914* (London, 1991).

ROBERTS, HELENE E., 'Marriage, Redundancy or Sin: The Painter's View of Women in the First Twenty-Five Years of Victoria's Reign', in Martha Vicinus (ed.), *Suffer and Be Still: Women in the Victorian Age* (Bloomington, Ind., 1972), 45–77.

ROBERTS, MARY LOUISE, *Disruptive Acts: The New Woman in Fin-de-Siècle France* (Chicago, 2002).

ROBERTS, ROBERT, *The Classic Slum: Salford Life in the First Quarter of the Century* (Manchester, 1971).

ROSE, JONATHAN, *The Intellectual Life of the British Working Classes* (New Haven, 2001).

ROSE, SONYA O., *Which People's War? National Identity and Citizenship in Wartime Britain 1939–45* (Oxford, 2003).

ROSEN, DAVID, '"A Tale of Two Cities": Theology of Revolution', *Dickens Studies Annual*, 27 (1998), 171–85.

ROSENBERG, JOHN D., *Carlyle and the Burden of History* (Cambridge, Mass., 1985).

ROSENZWEIG, SIDNEY, *Casablanca and Other Major Films of Michael Curtiz* (Studies in Cinema, 14; Ann Arbor, 1982).

ROSIE, GEORGE, *Curious Scotland: Tales from a Hidden History* (London, 2004).

ROWSE, A. L., *The Diaries of A. L. Rowse*, ed. Richard Ollard (Harmondsworth, 2003).

ST CLAIR, WILLIAM, *The Reading Nation in the Romantic Period* (Cambridge, 2004).

SALER, MICHAEL, '"Clap if You Believe in Sherlock Holmes": Mass Culture and the Re-Enchantment of Modernity, c.1890–c.1940', *Historical Journal*, 46 (2003), 599–623.

SAMUEL, RAPHAEL (ed.), *Patriotism: The Making and Unmaking of British National Identity*, 3 vols. (London, 1989).

—— *Theatres of Memory*, i: *Past and Present in Contemporary Culture* (London, 1994); ii: *Island Stories: Unravelling Britain* (London, 1999).

SANDERS, ANDREW, *The Victorian Historical Novel 1840–1880* (London, 1978).

SCHAMA, SIMON, *Citizens: Chronicles of the French Revolution* (New York, 1989).

SCHIVELBUSCH, WOLFGANG, *The Railway Journey: The Industrialisation of Space and Time* (Leamington Spa, 1986).

SCHNEER, JONATHAN, *London 1900: The Imperial Metropolis* (New Haven, 1999).

SCHWARTZ, VANESSA R., *Spectacular Realities: Early Mass Culture in Fin-de-Siècle Paris* (Berkeley, 1998).

SCHWARZ, LEONARD, 'London 1700–1840', in *The Cambridge Urban History of Britain*, ii: *1540–1840*, ed. Peter Clark (Cambridge, 2000), 641–71.

SCOTT, JOAN W., '"*L'Ouvrière! Mot impie, sordide*...": Women Workers and the Discourse of French Political Economy, 1840–1860', in ead., *Gender and the Politics of History* (New York, 1988), 139–67.

SEDGWICK, JOHN, 'Cinema Going Preferences in Britain in the 1930s', in Jeffrey Richards (ed.), *The Unknown Thirties*, 1–35.

—— *Popular Filmgoing in 1930s Britain: A Choice of Pleasures* (Exeter, 2000).

SEMMEL, STUART, *Napoleon and the British* (New Haven, 2004).

—— 'Reading the Tangible Past: British Tourism, Collecting and Memory after Waterloo', *Representations*, 69 (Winter 2000), 9–37.

SENNETT, RICHARD, *The Conscience of the Eye: The Design and Social Life of Cities* (New York, 1992).

—— *Flesh and Stone: The Body and the City in Western Civilisation* (London, 1994).

SEWARD, THEODORE J., NELSON, ALFRED L., and CROSS, GILBERT B. (eds.), *The Adelphi Calendar Project 1806–50: Sans Pareil Theatre 1806–19, Adelphi Theatre 1819–50* (Westport, Conn., 1990).

SEWELL, WILLIAM H., Jr., 'The Concept(s) of Culture', in Gabrielle M. Spiegel (ed.), *Practicing History: New Directions in Historical Writing after the Linguistic Turn* (New York, 2005), 76–97.

SHEPPARD, FRANCIS, *London 1808–1870: The Infernal Wen* (London, 1971).

SHERWOOD, CHARLES, *Farce and Fantasy: Popular Entertainment in Eighteenth-Century Paris* (Oxford, 1986).

SHILS, EDWARD, and YOUNG, MICHAEL, 'The Making of the Coronation', *Sociological Review*, NS 1 (1953), 63–81.

SHOHAT, ELLA, and STAM, ROBERT, *Unthinking Eurocentrism: Multiculturalism and the Media* (London, 1994).

SHOWALTER, ELAINE, *Sexual Anarchy: Gender and Culture at the Fin de Siècle* (New York, 1990).

SILLARS, STUART, *Visualisation in Popular Fiction 1860–1960: Graphic Narratives, Fictional Images* (London, 1995).

SIMMEL, GEORG, 'Die Grosstädte und das Geistesleben', in *Die Grosstadt*, ed. Theodor Petermann (Dresden, 1903), 187–206.

SIMMONS, J. C., *The Novelist as Historian: Essays on the Victorian Historical Novel* (The Hague and Paris, 1973).

SINFIELD, ALAN, *Literature, Politics and Culture in Postwar Britain* (Oxford and Berkeley, 1989).

SINGER, KURT, *The Charles Laughton Story: An Intimate Story of Charles Laughton* (Philadelphia and Toronto, 1954).
SMITH, BONNIE G., *The Gender of History: Men, Women and Historical Practice* (Cambridge, Mass., 1998).
SMITH, R. J., *The Gothic Bequest: Medieval Institutions in British Thought 1688–1863* (Cambridge, 1987).
SOFFER, REBA, 'British Conservative Historiography and the Second World War', in Benedikt Stuchtey and Peter Wende (eds.), *British and German Historiography 1750–1950* (Oxford, 2000), 373–99.
—— 'The Conservative Historical Imagination in the Twentieth Century', *Albion*, 27, no. 4 (Winter 1995), 1–17.
—— *Discipline and Power: The University, History and the Making of an English Elite, 1870–1930* (Stanford, Calif., 1994).
—— 'The Historian, Catholicism, Global History, and National Singularity', *Storia della storiografia*, 35 (1999), 113–27.
SRENSEN, DAVID, 'Carlyle's Method of History', *The Carlyle Society*, 9, sessions 1982–3 (Edinburgh).
SROKA, KENNETH M., 'A Tale of Two Gospels: Dickens and John', *Dickens Studies Annual*, 27 (1998), 145–69.
STACEY, JACKIE, *Star-Gazing: Hollywood Cinema and Female Spectatorship* (London, 1994; repr. 1998).
STANSKY, PETER, *Redesigning the World: William Morris, the 1880s and the Arts and Crafts* (Princeton, 1985; repr. 1996).
STEEDMAN, CAROLYN K., *Landscape for a Good Woman: A Story of Two Lives* (New York, 1992).
STOCKHAM, MARTIN, *The Korda Collection: Alexander Korda's Film Classics* (London, 1992).
STONE, DAN, *Breeding Superman: Nietzsche, Race and Eugenics in Edwardian and Interwar Britain* (Liverpool, 2002).
STOREY, JOHN, *Cultural Consumption and Everyday Life* (London, 1999).
STREET, SARAH, *British National Cinema* (London, 1997).
—— 'Stepping Westward: The Distribution of British Feature Films in America and the Case of the *Private Life of Henry VIII*', in Ashby and Higson (eds.), *British Cinema*, 51–63.
STRONG, ROY, *And When Did You Last See Your Father? The Victorian Painter and British History* (London, 1978).
SUMMERSON, JOHN, *Georgian London* (New Haven; repr. 2003).
SUTHERLAND, JOHN A., *The Longman Companion to Victorian Fiction* (London, 1988).
—— *Victorian Fiction: Writers, Publishers, Readers* (London, 1995).
—— *Victorian Novelists and Publishers* (London, 1976).
TABORI, PAUL, *Alexander Korda* (London, 1959).
TAMBLING, JEREMY, *Dickens, Violence and the Modern State: Dreams of the Scaffold* (London, 1995).
TAYLOR, BRANDON, *Art for the Nation: Exhibitions and the London Public, 1747–2001* (Manchester, 2001).
TESTER, KEITH (ed.), *The Flaneur* (New York, 1994).

THOMAS, PHILLIP DRENNON, 'The Tower of London's Royal Menagerie', *History Today*, 46 (Aug. 1996), 29–36.
THURLEY, SIMON, *Hampton Court: A Social and Architectural History* (New Haven, 2003).
TIMKO, MICHAEL, 'Dickens, Carlyle and the Chaos of Being', *Dickens Studies Annual*, 16 (1987), 1–15.
TODD, JANET (ed.), *Dictionary of British Women Writers* (London, 1989).
TOMLINSON, HOWARD, 'Ordnance Building at the Tower of London', *History Today*, 32 (Apr. 1982), 43–8.
TRELA, D. J., and TARR, ROGER L. (eds.), *The Critical Response to Thomas Carlyle's Major Works* (Westport, Conn., 1997).
TROTTER, DAVID, *Circulation: Defoe, Dickens and the Economies of the Novel* (London, 1988).
—— *The English Novel in History, 1895–1920* (London, 1993).
—— and Kempe, Sandra (eds.), *Edwardian Fiction: An Oxford Companion* (Oxford, 1997).
TUSSAUD, JOHN THEODORE, *The Romance of Madame Tussaud* (London, 1920).
TWYMAN, MICHAEL, *Printing 1770–1970* (London, 1970).
URRY, JOHN, *Consuming Places* (London, 1995).
—— *The Tourist Gaze: Leisure and Travel in Contemporary Societies* (London, 1990).
VAUGHN, WILL, 'London Topographers and Urban Change', in Ira Bruce Nadel and F. S. Schwarzbach (eds.), *Victorian Artists and the City: A Collection of Critical Essays* (New York, 1980), 106–25.
VICINUS, MARTHA (ed.), *Suffer and Be Still: Women in the Victorian Age* (London, 1972; repr. 1980).
VINCENT, DAVID, *Bread, Knowledge and Freedom: A Study of Nineteenth-Century Working-Class Autobiography* (Cambridge, 1982).
—— *The Culture of Secrecy: Britain, 1832–1998* (Oxford, 1998).
VLOCK, DEBORAH, *Dickens, Novel Reading, and the Victorian Popular Theatre* (Cambridge, 1998).
WAHRMAN, DROR, *Imagining the Middle Class: The Political Representation of Class in Britain c.1780–1840* (Cambridge, 1995).
—— *The Making of the Modern Self: Identity and Culture in Eighteenth-Century England* (New Haven, 2004).
WALKER, ALEXANDER, *Bette Davis* (London, 1986).
WALKER, P. C. GORDON, 'Crown Divisible', *Twentieth Century*, 153, no. 916 (1953), 245–9.
WALKOWITZ, JUDITH, *City of Dreadful Delight: Narratives of Sexual Danger in Late Victorian London* (Chicago, 1992).
WARDEN, BLAIRE, 'The Victorians and Oliver Cromwell', in Collini, Whatmore, and Young (eds.), *History, Religion and Culture*, 112–36.
WATERS, CHRIS, 'Representations of Everyday Life: L. S. Lowry and the Landscape of Memory in Postwar Britain', *Representations*, 65 (Winter 1999), 121–50.
WEBB, JEN, SCHIRATO, TONY, and DANAHER, GEOFF, *Understanding Bourdieu* (London, 2002).

WEBSTER, WENDY, *Englishness and Empire 1939–1965* (Oxford, 2005).
WHITE, ERIC WALTER, *A History of English Opera* (London, 1983).
WHITTALL, ARNOLD, *The Music of Britten and Tippett: Studies in Themes and Techniques* (Cambridge, 1982).
WIENER, MARTIN, *English Culture and the Decline of the Industrial Spirit, 1850–1980* (Cambridge, 1981; repr. Harmondsworth, 1985).
WILLIAMS, RAYMOND, *The Country and the City* (London, 1973).
—— *Culture and Society 1780–1950* (Harmondsworth, 1961).
—— *The Long Revolution* (Harmondsworth, 1965).
WOLF, JANET, 'The Invisible Flaneuse: Women and the Literature of Modernity', *Theory Literature and Society*, 2, no. 3 (1985), 37–76.
WORTH, GEORGE J., *William Harrison Ainsworth* (New York, 1972).

Index

Ingram Content Group UK Ltd.
Milton Keynes UK
UKHW020428160323
418662UK00003B/140

9 780199 296880